Collins

Edexcel GCSE
Maths

Higher Teacher Pack

Rob Ellis
Kath Hipkiss
Colin Stobart

Contents (Higher tier only material appears **bold**)

Introduction

Welcome to Collins *Edexcel GCSE Maths Higher Teacher Pack*, which has been written for the 2015 Edexcel GCSE (9–1) Mathematics Specification (1MA1). This Teacher Pack accompanies Collins *Edexcel GCSE Maths Higher Student Book 4th edition*, which contains the material needed to complete the Edexcel course.

The new GCSE contains some types of questions that have not appeared in GCSE Mathematics exams before. This guide and its lesson plans will help you prepare students to tackle the new aspects with confidence.

Aims and Learning outcomes

In Mathematics, topics are taught in progressively greater depth over the secondary phase. GCSE outcomes may reflect or build on subject content knowledge that is typically taught at KS3. There is no expectation that such content be repeated during the GCSE course, where it has already been taught effectively at an earlier stage. This allows for some increase in content, with the Government recommendation that Mathematics is taught for a minimum of seven hours per fortnight.

This GCSE course is designed to provide a broad and coherent course of study that encourages students to develop confidence in, and a positive attitude towards Mathematics. It enables students to recognise the importance of Mathematics in their own lives and to society.

The aims and objectives of this GCSE course in Mathematics are to enable students to:
- develop fluent knowledge, skills and understanding of mathematical methods and concepts
- acquire, select and apply mathematical techniques to solve problems
- reason mathematically, make deductions and inferences, and draw conclusions
- comprehend, interpret and communicate mathematical information in a variety of forms, appropriate to the information and context.

The new GCSE will have more focus on making sure that every student masters the fundamentals of Mathematics. These have been defined by the DfE as areas such as calculation, ratio and proportion.

Key changes to GCSE Mathematics:
- new content in both Foundation and Higher tiers
- longer assessment time (four hours)
- additional content in the Foundation tier
- more formulae need to be known (only cone, sphere and kinematics are given)
- seven hours of study per fortnight is recommended.

Modified content

Some content:
- is a result of more knowledge assumed from earlier key stages, for example, knowledge of up to the 12 times table from Key Stage 2
- is more explicitly stated but may or may not have been implied previously, for example, 'expansion of more than two binomials' and 'unique factorisation theorem'.

Content added to Foundation and Higher

Some content is completely new to both tiers, for example:
- systematic listing strategies
- Fibonacci-type sequences
- quadratic sequences
- simple geometrical progression
- pressure
- functions
- frequency trees
- Venn diagrams.

Examples of content added to Higher:
- inverse functions
- composite functions
- graph of $y = \tan x$
- velocity–time graphs
- areas under graphs
- equation of a circle/tangent
- quadratic inequalities
- other sequences
- nth term of a quadratic sequence
- rates of change
- iterative processes
- invariance.

Examples of content no longer in specification:
- stem-and-leaf diagrams[1]
- questionnaires and surveys
- 'chance' words.

New Assessment Objectives

Assessment Objectives (AOs) are those skills that are related to subject content, but not specifically. In Mathematics there were, and still are, three AOs. There are significant changes in the focus of the AOs to bring a new challenge to the examination papers.

The Department for Education (DfE) summarises these changes as:

'The assessment objectives place more emphasis on reasoning and problem solving.'

First, the language of the AOs has changed:

AO1 *'Recall and use their knowledge'* has become *'use and apply'* – and the move from AO2 *'Select, apply methods …'* is now *'reason, interpret and communicate'*. Both changes suggest a stronger emphasis on application rather than recall.

Secondly, the revised version provides more guidance as to what they mean in practice. For example, the old AO3 stated that students needed to *'interpret and analyse problems'*; the new AO3 states that they need to *'solve problems within Mathematics and other contexts'*. This includes making connections between different areas of Mathematics.

Finally, the weighting has changed with more marks for AO3 than before, with a new separation of Foundation and Higher weighting.

---

[1] Note that coverage of stem-and-leaf diagrams can still be found on this course and is therefore optional content.

- AO1 still includes recall and standard procedures, but has been extended to include multi-step solutions and questions set in context.
- AO2 is all about interpreting information and communicating solutions and arguments, giving these areas much more emphasis than previously.
- AO3 is still about solving problems, but the emphasis is on translating problems into mathematical processes, linking different areas of Mathematics and evaluating solutions.

	Assessment Objectives	Weightings	
		Higher	Foundation
AO1	**Use and apply standard techniques** Students should be able to: • Accurately recall facts, terminology and definitions. • Use and interpret notation correctly. • Accurately carry out routine procedures of set tasks requiring multi-step solutions.	40%	50%
AO2	**Reason, interpret and communicate mathematically** Student should be able to: • Make deductions, inferences and draw conclusion from mathematical information. • Construct chains of reasoning to achieve a given result. • Interpret and communicate information accurately. • Present arguments and proofs. • Assess the validity of an argument and critically evaluate a given way of presenting information. Where problems require candidates to 'use and apply standard techniques' or to independently 'solve problems', attribute a proportion of those marks to the corresponding Assessment Objective.	30%	25%
AO3	**Solve problems within Mathematics and in other contexts** Students should be able to: • Translate problems in mathematical or non-mathematical contexts into a process or a series of mathematical processes. • Make and use connections between different parts of Mathematics. • Interpret results in the context of a given problem. • Evaluate methods used and results obtained. • Evaluate solutions to identify how they may have been affected by assumptions made. Where problems require candidates to 'use and apply standard techniques' or to 'reason, interpret and communicate mathematically', attribute a proportion of those marks to the corresponding Assessment Objective.	30%	25%

The new GCSE is now split across five content areas:

Number	Algebra	Ratio and proportion	Geometry and measure	Probability and statistics
15%	30%	20%	20%	15%

There is ± 3% flexibility with these weightings.

Grading[2]

New grading structure									
9	8	7	6	5	4	3	2	1	U
Broadly the same proportion of students will achieve a Grade 7 and above as will achieve an A and above.				C ≈ 4		Broadly the same proportion of students will achieve a Grade 4 and above as currently achieve a Grade C and above. The bottom of Grade 1 will be aligned with the bottom of grade G.			
A*		A	B	C	D	E	F	G	U
Current grading structure									

Foundation Tier: grades 1–5
Higher Tier: grades 4–9

The structure of the Edexcel Mathematics papers

Paper 1 : non- calculator	Paper 2 : calculator	Paper 3 : calculator
Content from any part of the specification may be assessed	**Content** from any part of the specification may be assessed	**Content** from any part of the specification may be assessed
Assessment • 1 hour 30 minutes • Written exam • 80 marks • 33% of GCSE • Four multiple-choice questions at the start • First 50% to focus on grades 4, 5, 6 • Second 50% to focus on grades 7, 8, 9 • 'Allowed' formulae integrated into question • No formula sheet	**Assessment** • 1 hour 30 minutes • Written exam • 80 marks • 33% of GCSE • Four multiple-choice questions at the start • First 50% to focus on grades 4, 5, 6 • Second 50% to focus on grades 7, 8, 9 • 'Allowed' formulae integrated into question • No formula sheet	**Assessment** • 1 hour 30 minutes • Written exam • 80 marks • 33% of GCSE • Four multiple-choice questions at the start • First 50% to focus on grades 4, 5, 6 • Second 50% to focus on grades 7, 8, 9 • 'Allowed' formulae integrated into question • No formula sheet

---

[2] Note that this is based on the information from the Department of Education publicly available at the time of going to print.

How to use this book

Chapter overview

Each chapter starts with an outline of the content covered in the entire chapter, to help you plan ahead with ease.

- **Overview** shows the topic in each lesson at a glance.
- **Prior learning** indicates the mathematical ideas with which students will need to be secure, to enable them to access the topic content.
- **Learning objectives** list what students will learn.
- **Extension** suggests ways to broaden and deepen mathematical understanding with appropriate challenge for higher-attaining students.
- **Curriculum references** show how the material meets the requirements of the new GCSE curriculum with references to the KS3 and KS4 Programmes of Study.
- **Route mapping chart** for all exercises indicates, at a glance, the level of work students will meet. Key questions are referenced. These require a step-up in understanding or application and/or provide opportunities for students to demonstrate mastery of a concept.
- **About this chapter** explains how the content in the chapter links mathematical ideas and **makes connections**. The **relevance** to everyday life is highlighted, with references to core skills and possible career foci. Some ideas for probing questions are included to encourage students to **work mathematically** and suggestions are made for **assessment**. In addition, there are suggestions on how to use the **worked exemplars from the Student Book**.

Lesson plans

Every section in the Student Book is supported by a sequence of lesson plans. Each lesson plan follows the same format, making it easy to use as an aid in preparing lessons.

- Resources and homework **provide the corresponding Student Book** and **Practice Book page numbers.**
- **Learning objectives** indicate clearly what the lesson is about and the level of the content, providing a useful tool for measuring the success of a lesson.
- **Making mathematical connections** identifies areas of Mathematics that require similar skills.
- **Making cross-curricular connections** identifies how the skills and knowledge are used in other areas of the curriculum.
- **Prior learning** identifies the skills and knowledge that students will need in order to access the lesson.
- **Working mathematically** highlights and develops core skills that enable students to work independently and explain and apply their Mathematics.
- **Common misconceptions and remediation** explores common errors that students may make, with suggested approaches for identifying or avoiding the errors. It also highlights possible areas of misunderstanding.
- **Probing questions** offer some possible questions for teachers to ask of students to encourage mathematical thinking and explanations and to broaden and deepen their understanding of the core ideas.
- **Literacy focus** identifies the key terms and vocabulary. It also suggests written or spoken activities, where appropriate.

- **A three-part lesson plan for each section of the chapter**
  Part 1, Part 2 and **Part 3** structure the route through the lesson with references to Student Book exercises. This enables teachers to identify the core ideas to be taught before students attempt the relevant exercises and activities. Part 1 is intended to be an introductory activity; Part 2 is the main, application, part of the lesson; and Part 3 is the plenary or assessment opportunity.

Answers to questions
- Answers to the exercises and questions that appear in the **Student Book** are available online at **www.collins.co.uk/gcsemaths4eanswers** or on the CD-ROM that accompanies this Teacher Pack.
- Answers to the Practice Book questions can be found online at **www.collins.co.uk/gcsemaths4eanswers**

Schemes of Work
A flexible 5-Year Scheme of Work is available at the back of this Teacher Pack and also on the CD-ROM. This is based on the Collins *Maths Frameworking 3rd edition Pupil Books* 1.3, 2.3 and 3.3 plus the *AQA GCSE Maths Higher Student Book, 4th edition.* Flexible 2-year and 3-year Schemes of Work are provided in Word on the Teacher Pack CD-ROM.

CD-ROM
The CD-ROM contains the entire Teacher's Pack material in Word, to enable you to customise lessons.

It also includes:
- Activities (quick starter activities and extension activities)
- Literacy activities
- 2-, 3- and 5-year Schemes of Work
- Answers to the Student Book questions

5-year Scheme of Work

This 5-Year Higher Scheme of Work offers a flexible approach for Year 7 to Year 11. It is based on a minimum of seven one hour Maths lessons per fortnight (assuming a two week timetable of three lessons in one week and four in the second). This accounts for an average of 140 teaching hours per academic year, with the exception of Year 11, which has 115 due to GCSE examinations in summer (2). In addition to this, there are assessment and review sessions built in.

		Week	Book / Chapter: Topic	Topic break-down (sub-topics)	Total no. of teaching hours	Learning Objectives
Year 7	Term 1			Maths Frameworking Pupil Book 1.1		
		1/2	1: Using numbers	1.1 Charts and financial mathematics	7	• To carry out calculations from information given in charts and tables • To know and use financial vocabulary
				1.2 Positive and negative numbers		• To order positive and negative numbers using a number line • To use and apply comparison symbols such as > (greater than) and < (less than)
				1.3 Simple arithmetics with negative numbers 1.4 Subtracting negative numbers 1.5 Multiplying negative numbers		• To calculate addition, subtraction and multiplication problems involving directed numbers
				Travelling in Asia and Eastern Europe		• To use and apply directed number calculations in a real-life situation
		3/4	2: Sequences	2.1 Function machines	5	• To use function machines to generate inputs and outputs • To use given inputs and outputs to work out a function
				2.2 Sequences and rules		• To recognise, describe and generate linear sequences
				2.3 Finding missing terms		• To identify missing terms in a sequence
				2.4 Working out the nth term		• To identify the nth term of a linear sequence • To use the nth term to work out any term in a sequence
		3/4	2: Problem solving and reasoning	2.5 Other sequences	2	• To explore square and triangular numbers as sequences • To know and generate the Fibonacci sequence and Pascal's triangle
				Valencia Planetarium		• To apply knowledge of sequences in a context
		5	3: Perimeter, area and volume	3.1 Perimeter and area of rectangles	4	• To use a simple formula to work out the perimeter of a rectangle • To use a simple formula to work out the area of a rectangle
				3.2 Perimeter and area		• To work out the perimeter and area

			of compound shapes		of compound rectilinear shapes by using simple formulae
			3.3 Area of common 2D shapes		• To calculate the area of a triangle. • To calculate the area of a parallelogram • To calculate the area of a trapezium
	6	3: Perimeter, area and volume	3.4 Surface area and volume of cubes and cuboids	3	• To calculate the surface area of cubes and cuboids • To calculate the volume of cubes and cuboids
	6	3: Problem solving	Design a bedroom	1	• To calculate perimeters and areas in a real-life context
		Half term assessment		1	
		HALF TERM			
	7	4: Decimal numbers	4.1 Multiplying and dividing by 10,100,1000 and 10 000	7	• To multiply and divide decimal numbers by powers of 10
			4.3 Esimates		• To use rounding to estimate answers to calcuations, to spot possible errors
			4.2 Ordering decimals		• To order decimals, including numbers with different decimal places
			4.4 Adding and subtracting decimals 4.5 Multiplying decimals 4.6 Dividing decimals		• To add and subtract decimal numbers • To multiply and divide decimal numbers
			Financial skills – Shopping for leisure		• To solve multi-step problems involving decimals in a familiar context
	8/9/10	5: Working with numbers	5.1 Square numbers and square roots	10	• To recognise and use square numbers up to 225 (15^2) and corresponding square roots
			5.2 Rounding		• To round numbers to more than one decimal place • To round numbers to one or two significant figures
			5.3 Order of operations		• To use the conventions of BIDMAS to carry out calculations
			5.4 multiplications problems without a calculator		• To use an efficient written method of multiplication without a calculator
			5.5 Division problems without a calculator		• To use an efficient written method of division without a calculator
			5.6 Calculations with measurements		• To convert between common metric units • To use measurements in calculations • To recognise and use appropriate metric units
	10	5: Problem solving and reasoning	What is your carbon footprint?	2	• To apply number skills in real life contexts

		11/12	6: Statistics	6.1 Mode, median and range	7	• To calculate and use the mode, median and range of a set of data
				6.2 The mean		• To calculate and use the mean average of a set of data
				6.3 Statistical diagrams		• To be able to read and interpret different statistical diagrams
				6.4 Collecting and using discrete data		• To create and use a tally chart
				6.5 Collecting and using continuous data		• To understand continuous data and use grouped frequency
				6.6 Data collection		• To develop a greater understanding of data collection
				Challenge – School sports day		• To apply data handling skills to a real-life situation
		13		End of term assessment	1	
		13		*Assessment review*	1	
				CHRISTMAS HOLIDAY		
		1/2	7: Using algebra	7.1 Expressions and substitution	6	• To use algebra to write simple expressions and recognise equivalent expressions
						• To substitute numbers into expressions to work out their value
				7.2 Simplifying expressions		• To apply arithmetic rules to algebraic expressions
				7.3 Using formulae		• To use substitution in the context of formulae
				7.4 Writing formulae		• To construct formulae from contextual situations
		2	7: Problem solving and reasoning	Winter sports	1	• To use a formula to calculate costs
		3/4	8: Fractions	8.1 Equivalent fractions	7	• To find common equivalent fractions
						• To write fractions in their simplest form
				8.2 Comparing fractions		• To compare and order two fractions
				8.3 Adding and subtracting fractions		• To add and subtract fractions with different denominators
				8.4 Mixed numbers and improper fractions		• To convert between mixed numbers and improper fractions
				8.5 Calculations with mixed numbers		• To add and subtract simple mixed numbers with different denominators
		4	8: Challenge	Fractional dissection	1	• To explore fractions in the context of the part-whole relationship
		5/6	9: Angles	9.1 Measuring and drawing angles	5	• To use a protractor to measure an angle
						• To use a protractor to draw an angle
				9.2 Calculating angles		• To know the properties of parallel and perpendicular lines
						• To calculate angles on a line
						• To calculate angles at a point
						• To identify opposite equal angles
				9.3 Corresponding and alternate angles		• To calculate angles in parallel lines

(left margin: Term 2)

			9.4 Angles in a triangle		• To know that the angle sum in a triangle is 180°
			9.5 Angles in a quadrilateral		• To know that the angle sum in a quadrilateral is 360°
			9.6 Properties of triangles and quadrilaterals		• To know and use the properties of triangles
					• To know and use the properties of quadrilaterals
	6	9: Activity	Constructing triangles	1	• To use angles construction and measuring skills with confidence, fluency and accuracy
		Half term assessment		1	
		HALF TERM			
	7/8	10: Coordinates and graphs	10.1 Coordinates in four quadrants	7	• To use coordinates to identify and locate position points in all four quadrants
			10.2 Graphs from relationships		• To draw a graph using a simple linear rule
			10.3 Predicting graphs from relationships		• To know the connection between pairs of coordinates and the relationship shown in an equation and a graph
			10.4 Graphs of fixed values of x and y, $y = x$ and $y = -x$		• To recognise and draw linear graphs with values of x and y
					• To recognise and draw the graphs of
					• $y = x$ and $y = -x$
			10.5 Graphs of the form $x + y = a$		• To recognise and draw graphs of the form $x + y = a$
			10.6 Graphs from the real world		• To draw and use real-life graphs
					• To know how graphs can be used in real-life situations
	8	10: Challenge	Global Warming	1	• To apply graphing skills in a real-life situation
	9/10	11: Percentages	11.1 Fractions, decimals and percentages	5	• To know equivalences between common fractions, decimals and percentages
					• To understand and use percentages greater than 100%
			11.2 Fractions of a quantity		• To calculate a fraction of a quantity without a calculator
			11.3 Calculating simple percentages		• To calculate a percentage of a quantity without a calculator
			11.4 Percentages with a calculator		• To calculate a percentage of a quantity with a calculator
					• To know when it is appropriate to use a calculator
			11.5 Percentage increase and decrease		• To calculate the result of a percentage change
			Financial skills – Income tax		• To work out the result of a simple percentage change
					• To apply percentage skills in a real-life context
	11/12	12: Probability	12.1 Probability scales	3	• To know the vocabulary of

					• To know and use the 0–1 probability scale
			12.2 Combined events		• To use sample space diagrams to work out the probability of a combined event
			12.3 Experimental probability		• To know the difference between theoretical and experimental probability
					• To calculate and use experimental probability
			Financial skills – Easter Fayre		• To use experimental and theoretical probability in a real-life context
	12		*Revision*	1	
			End of term assessment	1	
			EASTER HOLIDAY		
Term 3	1/2	13: Symmetry	13.1 Line symmetry and rotational symmetry	4	• To recognise shapes that have reflective symmetry
					• To draw lines of symmetry on a shape
					• To recognise shapes that have rotational symmetry
					• To find the order of rotational symmetry for a shape
			13.2 Reflections		• To be able to reflect a shape in vertical and horizontal mirror lines
					• To use a coordinate grid to reflect shapes in lines, including $y = x$
			13.3 Rotations		• To be able to rotate a shape
			13.4 Tessellations		• To be able to tessellate shapes
	2	13: Activity	Landmark spotting	1	• To apply aspects of symmetry in real-life contexts
	2/3	14: Equations	14.1 Finding unknown numbers	6	• To find missing numbers in simple calculations
			14.2 Solving equations		• To solve equations involving one operation
			14.3 Solving more complex equations		• To solve equations involving two operations
			14.4 Setting up and solving equations		• To use algebra to set up and solve equations
			Challenge – number puzzles		• To identify and solve multi-step linear equations
	4/5	15: Interpreting data	15.1 Pie charts	6	• To read and interpret data from pie charts
					• To use a scaling method to draw a pie chart
			15.2 Comparing data using averages and the range		• To use the averages and range to compare and interpret data sets
			15.3 Statistical surveys		• To carry out a statistical survey
					• To use charts and diagrams to interpret data and write a report
			Challenge – Dancing		• To apply data interpretation skills in

				competition		everyday situations
				Half term assessment	1	
				HALF TERM		
		6/7	16: 3D shapes	16.1 Naming and drawing 3D shapes	5	• To know the names and properties of common 3D shapes • To use isometric paper to represent shapes made from cubes
				16.2 Using nets to construct 3D shapes		• To draw nets for 3D shapes • To construct 3D shapes from nets, including more complex shapes
				16.3 3D investigations		• To establish the rule connecting faces, edges and vertices in 3D shapes (Euler)
		7	16: Problem solving and reasoning	Delivering packages	1	• To solve 3D shape problems in everyday situations
		8/9	17: Ratio	17.1 Introduction to ratios	5	• To know ratio notation • To use ratios to compare quantities
				17.2 Simplifying ratios		• To write a ratio in its simplest terms • To write ratios in the form $1 : x$
				17.3 Ratios and sharing		• To use ratios to find totals and missing quantities • To write ratios to compare more than two items
				17.4 Ratios and fractions		• To use and apply the connection between ratios and fractions as a proportionality relationship
		9	17: Problem solving and reasoning	Smoothie bar	1	• To use ratios in a real-life context.
		10		End of term assessment	2	
		11		Assessment review	2	
				END OF YEAR 7 / SUMMER HOLIDAY		
Year 8	Term 1			Maths Frameworking Pupil Book 1.2		
		1/2	1: Working with numbers	1.1 Multiplying and dividing directed numbers	7	• To carry out multiplications and divisions involving negative numbers
				1.2 Factors and HCF		• To know and use highest common factors
				1.3 Multiples and LCM		• To know and use lowest common multiples
				1.4 Powers and roots		• To know and use powers and roots
				1.5 Prime factors		• To be able to identify the prime factors of any integer
				Challenge – Blackpool Tower		• To be able to use and apply number skills in a real-life situation
		3/4	2: Geometry	2.1 Parallel lines	7	• To calculate angles in parallel lines
				2.2 Geometric properties of quadrilaterals		• To know the geometric properties of quadrilaterals

			2.3 Translations		•	To be able to translate a shape
			2.4 Enlargements		•	To enlarge a 2D shape by a scale factor
			2.5 Constructions		•	To construct the mid-point and perpendicular bisector of a line
					•	To construct a perpendicular to a line from or at a given point
			Challenge – Constructions		•	To complete more complex constructions and produce a set of instructions
	5/6	3: Probability	3.1 Mutually exclusive outcomes and exhaustive outcomes	7	•	To recognise mutually exclusive outcomes and exhaustive outcomes
					•	To represent a chance on a probability scale
			3.2 Using a sample space to calculate probabilities		•	To use a sample space to calculate probabilities
			3.3 Estimates of probability		•	To use relative frequency to estimate probabilities
			Financial skills – Fun in the Fairground		•	To apply probability to a real-lifee situation
		Half term assessment		1		
		HALF TERM				
	7/8	4: Percentages	4.1 Calculating percentages	7	•	To write one quantity as a percentage of another
			4.2 Calculating percentage increase and decrease		•	To use a multiplier to calculate a percentage change
			4.3 Calculating a percentage change		•	To work out a change in value as a percentage increase or decrease
			Challenge – Changes in population		•	To apply percentages when analysing a real-life situation
	9/10	5: Congruent Shapes	5.1 Congruent shapes	7	•	To recognise congruent shapes
			5.2 Congruent triangles		•	To know the conditions for recognising congruent triangles
			5.3 Using congruent triangles to solve problems		•	To solve geometric problems using the rules of congruency
			Problem solving – Using scale diagrams to work out distances		•	Applying scale factors in real-life situations.
	11/12	6: Surface area and volume of prisms	6.1 Metric units for area and volume	6	•	To convert between metric units for area and for volume
			6.2 Surface area of prisms		•	To calculate the surface area of a prism
			6.3 Volume of prisms		•	To calculate the volume of a prism
			Investigation – A cube investigation		•	To apply knowledge of area and work systematically to solve a problem
		End of term assessment		1		
		Assessment review		1		

			CHRISTMAS HOLIDAY		
	1/2	7: Graphs	7.1 Graphs from linear equations	6	• To develop graphical fluency with a range of linear representations
			7.2 Gradient of a line		• To know the gradient of a line from its linear equation
					• To establish the equation of a line in the form $y = mx + c$ from its graph
			7.3 Graphs from quadratic equations		• To recognise and draw the graph from a quadratic equation
					• To solve a quadratic equation from a graph
			7.4 Real-life graphs		• To draw graphs from real-life situations to show the relationship between two variables
			Challenge – The M25		• To solve problems involving more than one variable in a real-life context
Term 2	3/4	8: Number	8.1 Powers of 10	7	• To multiply and divide by negative powers of 10
			8.2 Significant figures		• To round to a specific number of significant figures
			8.3 Standard form with large numbers		• To write a large number in standard form
			8.4 Multiplying with numbers in standard form		• To multiply with numbers in standard form
			Challenge – Space – to see where no-one has seen before		• To apply standard form to solve a problem in a real-life context
	5/6	9: Interpreting data	9.1 Interpreting graphs and diagrams	7	• To interpret different charts seen in the media
			9.2 Relative sized pie charts		• To draw pie charts relative to data size
			9.3 Scatter graphs and correlation		• To read scatter graphs
					• To interpret correlation
			9.4 Creating scatter graphs		• To construct scatter graphs and use a line of best fit to describe data trends
			Challenge – Football attendances		• To use and apply data handling skills in a real-life context
		Half term assessment		1	
		HALF TERM			
	7/8/9	10: Algebra	10.1 Algebraic notation	10	• To simplify algebraic expressions involving the four operations of arithmetic
			10.2 Like terms		• To simplify expressions by collecting up like terms
			10.3 Expanding brackets		• To multiply out brackets in an expression
			10.4 Using algebraic expressions		• To identify and manipulate algebraic expressions
			10.5 Using index notation		• To write algebraic expressions involving powers

			Mathematical reasoning – Writing in algebra		• To use and apply algebraic manipulation skills in a range of contexts
	10/11	11: Shape and Ratio	11.1 Ratio of lengths, areas and volumes	8	• To use ratio to compare lengths, areas and volumes of 2D and 3D shapes
			11.2 Fractional enlargement		• To enlarge a 2D shape by a fractional scale factor
			11.3 Map scales		• To be able to read and use map scales efficiently
			Activity – Map reading		• To use and apply skills and knowledge of area, ratio and data handling in a real-life context.
		Revision		1	
		End of term assessment		1	
		Assessment review		1	
		EASTER HOLIDAY			
	1/2/3	12: Fractions and Decimals	12.1 Adding and subtracting fractions	10	• To add and subtract fractions and mixed numbers
			12.2 Multiplying fractions and integers		• To multiply a fraction or a mixed number and an integer
			12.3 Dividing with fractions and integers		• To divide a fraction or a mixed number by an integer
					• To divide an integer or a mixed number by a fraction
			12.4 Multiplication with large and small numbers		• To multiply with combinations of large and small numbers mentally
			12.5 Division with large and small numbers		• To divide combinations of large and small numbers mentally
			Challenge – Guesstimates		• To use mental calculation strategies and estimation in real-life situations
Term 3	4	13: Proportion	13.1 Direct proportion	4	• To know what is meant by direct proportion
					• To find missing values in problems involving proportion
			13.2 Graphs and direct proportion		• To represent direct proportion graphically and algebraically
			13.3 Inverse proportion		• To know what is meant by inverse proportion
					• To use graphical and algebraic representations of inverse proportion
			13.4 Comparing direct proportion and inverse proportion		• To recognise direct and inverse proportion and work out missing values
			Challenge – Planning a trip		• To apply knowledge of proportion to a real-life situation
	5/6	14: Circles	14.1 The circumference of a circle	5	• To know the definition of a circle and be able to name the parts of a circle
					• To establish the relationship between the circumference and diameter of a circle (π)
			14.2 Formula for the circumference of a circle		• To calculate the circumference of a circle

			14.3 Formula for the area of a circle		• To calculate the area of a circle
			Financial skills – Athletics stadium		• To use and apply knowledge of number and circles to solve multi-step problems in real-life contexts
		Half term assessment		1	
		HALF TERM			
	7/8	15: Equations and formulae	15.1 Equations with brackets	7	• To solve equations involving brackets • To solve equations where the answers are fractions or negative numbers
			15.2 Equations with the variable on both sides		• To solve equations with the variable on both sides
			15.3 More complex equations		• To solve equations with fractions and fractional coefficients • To solve simple equations involving squares
			15.4 Rearranging formulae		• To change the subject of a formula, including formulae involving squares
			Mathematical reasoning – Using graphs to solve equations		• Be able to make links between graphical and algebraic representations to solve equations
	9/10	16: Comparing Data	16.1 Grouped frequency tables	7	• To create a grouped frequency table from raw data
			16.2 Drawing frequency diagrams		• To interpret frequency diagrams • To draw a frequency diagram from a grouped frequency table
			16.3 Comparing sets of data		• To be able to compare data from two sources
			16.4 Misleading charts		• To recognise when a statistical chart may be misleading
			Problem solving – Why do we use so many devices to watch TV?		• Be able to interpret and present data in order to make valid comparisons
	11	End of term assessment		1	
	11	*Assessment review*		1	
		END OF YEAR 8 / SUMMER HOLIDAY			
		Maths Frameworking Pupil Book 1.3			
Year 9 Term 1	1/2	1: Percentages	1.1 Simple interest	7	• To know what is meant by simple interest • To solve problems involving simple interest
			1.2 Percentage increase and decrease		• To use the multiplier method to calculate the result of a percentage increase or decrease • To calculate the percentage change in a value
			1.3 Calculating the original value		• To calculate the original value, given a percentage change
			1.4 Repeated percentage changes		• To calculate the result of repeated percentage changes

			Challenge – Exponential growth		•	Be able to use and apply prior knowledge to extend learning and make links with other areas of mathematics
3/4/5	2: Equations and formulae	2.1 Multiplying out brackets	10	•	To expand brackets and simplify more complex expressions
		2.2 Factorising algebraic expressions		•	To factorise more complex expressions
		2.3 Expressions with several variables		•	To expand and factorise expressions with more than one variable
		2.4 Equations with fractions		•	To solve equations where the variable is in the denminator of a fraction
		Investigation – Body mass index		•	To use and apply skills to solve problems in a real-life context
5/6	3: Polygons	3.1 Properties of polygons	5	•	To work out the sum of the interior angles of a polygon
				•	To work out the exterior angles of polygons
		3.2 Interior and exterior angles of regular polygons		•	To calculate the interior and exterior angles of regular polygons
		3.3 Tessellations and regular polygons		•	To establish which regular polygons tessellate
		Mathematical reasoning – Semi-regular tessellations		•	To use geometric reasoning and apply prior knowledge to extend learning

Half term assessment	1

HALF TERM

7/8	4: Using data	4.1 Scatter graphs and correlation	7	•	To infer a correlation from two related scatter graphs
				•	To draw a line of best fit to show a correlation
		4.2 Two-way tables		•	To interpret a variety of two-way tables
		4.3 Estimation of a mean from grouped data		•	To estimate a mean from grouped data
		4.4 Cumulative frequency diagrams		•	To draw a cumulative frequency diagram
				•	To find the interquartile range
		4.5 Statistical investigations		•	To plan a statistical investigation
		Challenge – Census		•	Use and apply statistical skills and analysis to a real-life situation
9/10	5: Applications of graphs	5.1 Step graphs	7	•	To interpret step graphs
		5.2 Time graphs		•	To interpret and draw time graphs
		5.3 Exponential growth graphs		•	To draw exponential growth graphs
		Problem solving – Mobile phone tariffs		•	To use and apply knowledge of graphs to solve best buy problems in real-life contexts

		11/12	6: Pythagoras' Theorem	6.1 Introducing Pythagoras	7	• To use Pythagoras' theorem to calculate missing sides in right-angled triangles
				6.2 Using Pythagoras' theorem to solve problems		• To use Pythagoras' theorem to solve problems in context
				6.3 The converse of Pythagoras' theorem		• To use the converse of Pythagoras' theorem to establish whether or not a triangle is a right-angled triangle
				Activity – Practical Pythagoras		• To apply Pythagoras' theorem in a practical context
		End of term assessment			1	
		Assessment review			1	
		CHRISTMAS HOLIDAY				
		1/2	7: Fractions	7.1 Adding and subtracting fractions	5	• To choose an appropriate method to add or subtract mixed numbers
				7.2 Multiplying fractions and mixed numbers		• To multiply two fractions or mixed numbers
				7.3 Dividing fractions and mixed numbers		• To divide one fraction or mixed number by another fraction or mixed number
				7.4 Algebraic fractions		• To add, subtract, multiply or divide fractions containing a variable
				Investigations – Fractions from one to six		• To apply knowledge of fractions to a more complex problem • To work systematically
		2/3	8: Algebra	8.1 Expanding the product of two brackets	6	• To multiply out (or expand) two brackets
				8.2 Expanding expressions with more than two brackets		• To multiply out three or more brackets
				8.3 Factorising quadratic expressions with positive coefficients		• To factorise quadratic expressions with positive coefficients
Term 2				8.4 Factorising quadratic expressions with negative coefficients		• To factorise quadratic expressions with negative coefficients
				8.5 The difference of two squares		• To recognise and use the difference of two squares to solve an equation
				Challenge – Graphs from expressions		• To use and apply knowledge of factorising and expansion in a practical context
		4/5	9: Decimal numbers	9.1 Powers of 10	7	• To calculate with positive and negative powers of 10
				9.2 Standard form		• To calculate using standard form for positive and negative powers of 10
				9.3 Multiplying numbers in standard form		• To multiply numbers in standard form
				9.4 Dividing with numbers in standard form		• To divide numbers in standard form
				9.5 Upper and lower bounds		• To use limits of accuracy when rounding data

			Mathematical reasoning – To the stars and back		•	To use and apply skills and knowledge of standard form in a real-life context
		Half term assessment		1		
		HALF TERM				
	6/7	10: Surface area and volume of cylinders	10.1 Volume of a cylinder	7	•	To calculate the volume of a cylinder
			10.2 Surface area of a cylinder		•	To calculate the curved surface area of a cylinder
					•	To calculate the total surface area of a closed cylinder
			10.3 Composite shapes		•	To calculate the volumes and surface areas of composite shapes
			Problem solving – Packaging soup		•	To use and apply knowledge of volume and surface area to solve a practical problem
	8/9/10	11: Solving equations graphically	11.1 Graphs from equations of the form $ay \pm bx = c$	10	•	To draw any linear graph from its equation
					•	To solve a linear equation graphically
			11.2 Solving simultaneous equations by drawing graphs		•	To solve a pair of simultaneous equations graphically
			11.3 Solving quadratic equations by drawing graphs		•	To solve quadratic equations graphically
			11.4 Solving cubic equations by drawing graphs		•	To solve cubic equations graphically
			Challenge – Maximum packages		•	To use and apply knowledge of functions to solve a real-life problem graphically
	10	End of term assessment		1		
	10	*Assessment review*		1		
		EASTER HOLIDAY				
Term 3	1/2	12: Compound units	12.1 Speed	7	•	To solve distance/time/speed problems
			12.2 More compound units		•	To solve problems involving density/mass/volume
			12.3 Unit costs		•	To apply the unit cost method to solve problems such as best value
			Challenge – Population density		•	To use and apply knowledge of compound measure strategies to a problem in a practical context
	3/4	13: Right-angled triangles	13.1 Introduction to trigonometric ratios	7	•	To know what trigonometric ratios are
			13.2 How to find trigonometric ratios of angles		•	To know how to find the trigonometric ratios of sine, cosine and tangent in a right-angled triangle
			13.3 Using trigonometric ratios to find angles		•	To find the angle identified from a trigonometric ratio
			13.4 Using trigonometric ratios to find lengths		•	To find an unknown length of a right-angled triangle given one side and an angle

				Investigation – Barnes Wallis and the bouncing bomb		• To use and apply trigonometry in a practical context

				Investigation – Barnes Wallis and the bouncing bomb		• To use and apply trigonometry in a practical context
			Note: the final references for Year 9 are intended as introductions only for those students who are ready for it.			
			Edexcel GCSE Higher Student Book			
		5/6	4: Introduction to algebraic proof	4.1 Reasoning about number patterns	7	• Make and test conjectures about patterns and relationships • Look for proofs and counter-examples
			Half term assessment		1	
			HALF TERM			
		7	12: Introduction to geometric proof	12.1 Properties and relationships	3	• Use known geometric results to obtain simple proofs
		8	13: Probability	13.2 Independent and combined events	4	• To calculate the probability of independent and combined events using a tree diagram
		9	4: Introduction to geometric Sequences	4.4 Generating non-linear sequences	3	• To generate and identify non-linear sequences from either a term-to term or a postion-to-term rule
		10	*Revision*		6	
			End of term assessment		1	
			Assessment review		1	
Year 10			**END OF YEAR 9 / SUMMER HOLIDAY**			
			Edexcel GCSE Higher Student Book			
	Term 1	1/2	1 Number: Basic number	1.1 Solving real-life problems	7	• To solve number problems in a real-life context
				1.2 Multiplication and division of decimals		• To multiply a decimal number by another decimal number • To divide by decimals by adjusting the calculation to division by an integer
				1.3 Approximation of calculations		• To round to a given number of significant figures in order to approximate a result before calculating • To round a calculation at the end of the problem to give a reasonable answer
				1.4 Multiples, factors, prime numbers, powers and roots		• To generate factors and multiples for any given integer • To identify prime numbers to 100 • To identify square and cube numbers and their roots to 100 • To identify and generate triangular numbers
				1.5 Prime factors, LCM and HCF		• To identify prime factors for any given integer • To identify the LCM of two integers • To identify the HCF of two integers

			1.6 Negative numbers		•	To multiply and divide by directed numbers
	3/4	2 Number: Fractions, ratio and proportion	2.1 One quantity as a fraction of another	7	•	To find one fraction as a quantity of another
			2.2 Adding, subtracting and calculating with fractions		•	To add and subtract fractions with different denominators
			2.3 Multiplying and dividing fractions		•	To multiply by proper and improper fractions
					•	To divide by a fraction
			2.4 Fractions on a calculator		•	To use the fraction button on a calculator to carry out calculations
			2.5 Increasing and decreasing quantities by a percentage		•	To increase and decrease quantities by a percentage
			2.6 Expressing one quantity as a percentage of another		•	To express one quantity as a percentage of another
					•	To work out percentage change
	5/6	3 Statistics: Statistical diagrams and averages	3.1 Statistical representation	7	•	To present, analyse and interpret discrete and continuous sets of data
			3.2 Statistical measures		•	To calculate the mean, median and mode of a set of data
					•	To choose the most appropriate average to use
					•	To calculate and interpret the range of a set of data
			3.3 Scatter diagrams		•	To draw, interpret and use scatter diagrams
					•	To identify correlation and draw a line of best fit
					•	To estimate missing values in a scatter diagram
		End of term assessment		1		
		HALF TERM				
	7/8	4 Algebra: Number and sequences	4.1 Patterns in number	7	•	To extend and identify number patterns
			4.2 Number sequences		•	To identify simple linear rules
					•	To generate sequences, given the rule
			4.3 Finding the nth term of a linear sequence		•	To generalise and find the nth term of a linear sequence
			4.4 Special sequences		•	To recognise and continue some special number sequences such as square numbers or a simple geometric progression
			4.5 General rules from given patterns		•	To find the nth term from a sequence of patterns
			4.6 The nth term of a quadratic sequence		•	To continue a quadratic sequence, given the rule
			4.7 Finding the nth term for quadratic sequences		•	To find the nth term of a quadratic sequence from second differences

		9/10	5 Ratio, proportion and rates of change: Ratio and proportion	5.1 Ratio	7	• To simplfy a given ratio
						• To express a ratio as a fraction
						• To divide amounts into given ratios
						• To complete calculations from a given ratio and partial information
				5.2 Direct proportion problems		• To recognise and solve problems using direct proportion
				5.3 Best buys		• To find the cost per unit weight and the weight per unit cost
						• To use the unitary method to identify the cheapest option
				5.4 Compound measures		• To solve problems involving speed/distance/time and density/mass/volume
				5.5 Compound interest and repeated percentage change		• To calculate simple and compound interest
						• To solve problems involving repeated percentage change
				5.6 Reverse percentages (working out the original quantity)		• To find percentage increases and reductions
						• To solve prolems that require the removal of a percentage interest by reducing the price by a different amount (reverse percentages)
		11/12	6 Geometry and measures: Angles	6.1 Angle facts	5	• To know the sum of the angles on a straight line, around a point, in a triangle and in a quadrilateral
				6.2 Triangles		• To solve missing angle problems in triangles
				6.3 Angles in a polygon		• To work out the sum of the interior angles in a polygon
				6.4 Regular polygons		• To be able to calculate the size of the interior and exterior angles of any regular polygon
				6.5 Parallel lines		• To solve problems involving alternate, corresponding, allied and opposite angles
				6.6 Special quadrilaterals		• To be able to calculate the size of angles in special quadrilaterals using their geometric properties
				6.7 Scale drawings and bearings		• To be able to make a scale drawing to a given scale
						• To be able to convert measurements to calculate actual distances
						• To be able to read, interpret and draw bearings diagrams
						• To use the geometrical properties of a diagram to calculate a bearing
		12	End of term assessment		1	
		12	Assessment review		1	
		CHRISTMAS HOLIDAY				

		1	7 Geometry and measures: Transformations, constructions and loci	7.1 Congruent triangles	4	• To identify two congruent triangles • To justify why two triangles are congruent
				7.2 Rotational symmetry		• To identify and describe the rotational symmetry of a shape
				7.3 Transformations		• To translate a 2D shape, using vectors to describe the transformation • To draw and describe the image of one or more reflections • To draw and describe a rotation that will take an object onto its image • To enlarge a 2D shape by a positive or negative integer or fraction scale factor and describe the transformation
				7.4 Combinations of transformations		• To combine transformations • To describe a sequence of transformations to map an object onto its image
				7.5 Bisectors		• To construct the bisectors of lines and angles
				7.6 Defining a locus		• To draw a locus for a given rule
				7.7 Loci problems		• To solve loci problems in practical contexts
				7.8 Plans and elevations		• To draw 2D representations of 3D objects from different views
Term 2		2/3	1:8 Algebra: Algebraic manipulation	8.1 Basic algebra	7	• To recognise expressions, equations, formulae and indentities • To substitute into, manipulate and simplify algebraic expressions
				8.2 Factorisation		• To factorise an algebraic expression
				8.3 Quadratic expansion		• To multiply out a pair of algebraic brackets such as $(x + a)(x - b)$
				8.4 Expanding squares		• To multiply out a pair of identical brackets such as • $(x + a)(x + a) = (x + a)^2$
				8.5 More than two binomials		• To multiply out a string of algebraic brackets such as • $(x + a)(x - b)(x + c)$
				8.6 Quadratic factorisation		• To factorise quadratic expressions with the coefficient of x^2 equal to 1
				8.7 Factorising $ax^2 + bx + c$		• To factorise quadratic expressions with the coefficient of x^2 not equal to 1
				8.8 Changing the subject of a formula		• Be able to rearrange formulae
		4/5	9 Geometry and measures: Length, area and volume	9.1 Circumference and area of a circle	7	• To calculate the circumference and area of a circle
				9.2 Area of a parallelogram		• To find the area of a parallelogram and a trapezium
				9.3 Area of a trapezium		

			9.4 Sectors		• To calculate the length of an arc and the area of a sector
			9.5 Volume of a prism		• To calculate the volume of a prism
			9.6 Cylinders		• To calculate the volume and surface area of a cylinder
			9.7 Volume of a pyramid		• To calculate the volume of a pyramid
			9.8 Cones		• To calculate the volume and surface area of a cone
			9.9 Spheres		• To calculate the volume and surface area of a sphere
		Half term assessment		1	
		HALF TERM			
	6/7	10 Algebra: Linear Graphs	10.1 Drawing linear graphs from points	7	• To draw a line graphs using three points (x, y)
			10.2 Gradient of a line		• To work out the gradient of a straight line
					• To know that the gradient of a line is the coefficient of x (m) in
					• $y = mx + c$, the general equation for a straight line.
			10.3 Drawing graphs by gradient-intercept and cover-up methods		• To draw graphs using the gradient / intercept method
			10.4 Finding the equation of a line from its graph		• To find the equation of a line, given its gradient and y-axis intercept
			10.5 Real-life uses of graphs		• To solve problems in practical contexts using graphs
			10.6 Solving simultaneous equations using graphs		• To use the graphical intercept method of solving simultaneous equations
			10.7 Parallel and perpendicular lines		• To know that parallel lines have the same gradient
					• To know that the product of the gradients of perpendicular lines is always -1
	8/9/10	11 Geometry and measures: Right-angled triangles	11.1 Pythagoras' theorem	9	• To calulate the length of the hypotenuse in a right-angled triangle
			11.2 Finding the length of a shorter side		• To calculate the length of a shorter side in a right-angled triangle
			11.3 Applying Pythagoras' theorem in real-life situations		• To solve real-life problems involving Pythagoras' theorem
			11.4 Pythagoras' theorem and isosceles triangles		• To use the geometry of isosceles triangles and Pythagoras' theorem to solve angle problems
			11.5 Pythagoras' theorem in three dimensions		• To use Pythagoras' theorem in problems involving three dimensions
			11.6 Trigonometric ratios		• To use the three trigonometric ratios
			11.7 Calculating angles		• To use the trigonometric ratios to calculate an angle

			11.8 Using the sine and cosine functions		•	To find the lengths of sides and sizes of angles in right-angled triangles using the sine and cosine functions
			11.9 Using the tangent function		•	To find the lengths of sides and sizes of angles in right-angled triangles using the tangent function
			11.10 Which ratio to use		•	To use 'SOHCAHTOA' to decide which ratio to use
			11.11 Solving problems using trigonometry		•	To solve practical problems involving trigonometry, including those with angles of elevation and depression
			11.12 Trigonometry and bearings		•	To solve bearings problems using trigonometry
			11.13 Trigonometry and isosceles triangles		•	To use trigonometry to solve problems involving isosceles triangles
	10	12 Geometry and measures: Similarity	12.1 Similar triangles	3	•	To show that two triangles are similar
					•	To work out the scale factor between similar triangles
			12.2 Areas and volumes of similar shapes		•	To solve problems involving the area and volume of similar shapes
			End of term assessment	1		
			Assessment review	1		
			EASTER HOLIDAY			
Term 3	1/2	13 Probability: Exploring and applying probability	13.1 Experimental probability	7	•	To calculate experimental probabilities and relative frequencies
					•	To estimate probabilities from experiments
					•	To use different methods to estimate probabilities
			13.2 Mutually exclusive and exhaustive events		•	To recognise mutually exclusive, complementary and exhaustive events
			13.3 Expectation		•	To predict the likely number of successful events, given the number of trials and the probability of any one event
			13.4 Probability and two-way tables		•	To read two-way tables and use them to work out probabilities and interpret data
			13.5 Probability and Venn diagrams		•	To construct and read Venn diagrams to represent probability
	3	14 Number: Powers and standard form	14.1 Powers (indices)	4	•	To use powers of numbers to describe large and small numbers and generate number patterns
			14.2 Rules for multiplying and dividing powers		•	To use the laws of indices to calculate or simplify algebraic expressions
			14.3 Standard form		•	To convert an ordinary number into standard form and vice versa
					•	To calculate using numbers in standard form, applying the laws of indices

		4/5/6	15 Algebra: Equations and inequalities	15.1 Linear equations	11	• To solve linear equations
				15.2 Elimination method for simultaneous equations		• To use the elimination method to solve simultaneous equations
				15.3 Substitution method for simultaneous equations		• To use the substitution method to solve simultaneous equations
				15.4 Balancing coefficients to solve simultaneous equations		• To use the method of balancing coefficients to solve simultaneous equations
				15.5 Using simultaneous equations to solve problems		• To solve problems, using simultaneous linear equations with two variables
						• To solve problems using linear and non-linear simultaneous equations
				15.6 Linear inequalities		• To solve a simple linear inequality
				15.7 Graphical inequalities		• To show a graphical inequality
						• To know how to find regions that satisfy more than one graphical inequality
				15.8 Trial and improvement		• To estimate the solution to an equation that does not have an exact solution, using the method of trial and improvement
Half term assessment					1	
HALF TERM						
		7/8	16 Number: Counting, accuracy, powers and surds	16.2 Estimating powers and roots	7	• To use known facts and trial and improvement to estimate the value of powers and roots
				16.3 Negative and fractional powers		• To represent roots and decimal numbers as indices
				16.1 Rational numbers, reciprocals, terminating and recurring decimals		• To recognise rational numbers, reciprocals, terminating and recurring decimals
						• To convert terminal decimals to fractions
						• To convert fractions to recurring decimals
						• To find reciprocals of integers or fractions
				16.4 Surds		• To simplify surds
						• To calculate with and manipulate surds, including rationalising a denominator
				16.5 Limits of accuracy		• To find the limits of accuracy of numbers that have been rounded to different degrees of accuracy
						• To identify the upper and lower bounds of an estimation
				16.6 Problems involving limits of accuracy		• Combine limits of two or more variables together to solve problems
				16.7 Choices and outcomes		• To work out the number of choices, arrangements or outcomes when choosing from lists or sets

		9/10	17 Algebra: Quadratic equations	17.1 Plotting quadratic graphs	7	• To plot quadratic graphs using a table of values
				17.2 Solving quadratic equations by factorisation		• To solve a quadratic equation by factorisation (by sight)
				17.3 Solving a quadratic equation by using the quadratic formula		• To use the quadratic formula to solve a quadratic equation where factorisation is not possible • To derive the quadratic formula by completing the square for • $ax^2 + bx + c = 0$ (extension)
				17.4 Solving quadratic equations by completing the square		• To solve quadratic equations by completing the square
				17.5 The significant points of a quadratic curve		• To identify and interpret roots, intercepts and turning points of quadratic functions graphically • To deduce roots algebraically and turning points by completing the square • To use this information to sketch the curve
				17.6 Solving equations, one linear and one non-linear usinggraphs		• To solve a pair of simultaneous equations where one is linear and one is non-linear, using graphs and where they intersect
				17.7 Solving quadratic equations by the method of intersection		• To solve quadratic equations using intersection points between graphs or at axes
				17.8 Solving linear and non-linear simultaneous equations algebraically		• To use algebraic techniques, including substitution and rearranging, to solve a pair of equations
				17.9 Quadratic inequalities		• To solve a quadratic inequality algebraically • To show a graphical quadratic inequality • To know how to find regions that satisfy more than one graphical inequality
		11/12	18 Statistics: Sampling and more complex diagrams	18.1 Sampling data	7	• To know the range of methods of sampling and decide which method is best when collecting reliable, unbiased data
				18.2 Frequency polygons		• To draw frequency polygons for discrete and continuous data • To draw histograms for continuous data with equal intervals • To construct pie charts
				18.3 Cumulative frequency graphs		• To find a measure of dispersion (the interquartile range) and a measure of location (the median) using a graph
				18.4 Box plots		• To draw and read box plots
				18.5 Histograms		• To draw and read histograms where the bars are of unequal width

						• To find the median, quartiles and interquartile range from a histogram
			End of term assessment		1	
			Assessment review		1	
			END OF YEAR 10 / SUMMER HOLIDAY			
Year 11	Term 1	1/2	19 Probability: Combined events	19.1 Addition rules for outcomes of events	7	• To work out the probability of two events such as $P(A)$ or $P(B)$
				19.2 Combined events		• To work out the probability of two events occurring at the same time
				19.3 Tree diagrams		• To use and construct sample space diagrams and tree diagrams to work out the probability of combined events
				19.4 Independent events		• To calculate using the 'and' and the 'or' rule to find the probality of combined events
				19.5 Conditional probability		• To work out the probability of combined events when the probabilities change after each event
		3/4	20 Geometry and measures: Properties of circles	20.1 Circle theorems	7	• To use circle theorems to find the size of angles in circles
				20.2 Cyclic quadrilaterals		• To find the size of angles in cyclic quadrilaterals
				20.3 Tangents and chords		• To use tangents and chords to find the size of angles in circles
				20.4 Alternate segment theorem		• To use the alternate segment theorem to find the size of angles in circles
		5/6	21 Ratio, proportion and rates of change: Variation	21.1 Direct proportion	7	• To solve problems where two variables have a directly proportional relationship (direct variation)
						• To work out the constant and equation of proportionality
				21.2 Inverse proportion		• To solve problems where two variables have an inversely proportional relationship (inverse variation)
						• To work out the constant and equation of proportionality
			Half term assessment		1	
			HALF TERM			
		7/8	22 Geometry and measures: Triangles	22.1 Further 2D problems	7	• To use Pythagoras' theorem and trigonometric ratios to solve more complex two-dimensional problems
				22.2 Further 3D problems		• To use Pythagoras' theorem and trigonometric ratios to solve more complex three-dimensional problems
				22.3 Trigonometric ratios of angles between 0° and 360°		• To find the sine, cosine and tangent of any angle between 0° and 360°
						• To use the symmetry of the circular function graphs to find trigonmetric values
				22.3 Solving any triangle		• To use the sine rule and the cosine rule to find sides and angles in non-right-angled triangles

			22.4 Using sine to calculate the area of a triangle		•	To use the sine rule to work out the area of any triangle, given two sides and the included angle
	9/10	23 Algebra: Graphs	23.1 Distance–time graphs	7	•	To draw and interpret distance–time graphs
					•	To know that the gradient represents the speed of the object
			23.2 Velocity–time graphs		•	To draw and interpret velocity–time graphs
					•	To know that the gradient represents the acceleration of the object
					•	To know that the area under the graph represents the distance travelled
			23.3 Estimating the area under a curve		•	To estimate the area under a curve by using rectangular strips
			23.4 Rates of change		•	To interpret the gradient at a point on a curve as the instantaneous rate of change
					•	To apply the concept of rates of change in numerical, algebraic and graphical contexts
			23.5 Equation of a circle		•	To recognise and plot the equation of a circle
					•	To use this equation to identify the centre and radius of the circle
					•	To find the equation of a tangent to a circle at a given point
			23.6 Other graphs		•	To recognise and plot cubic, exponential and reciprocal graphs
			23.7 Transformations of the graph $y = \mathrm{f}(x)$		•	To sketch translations and reflections of the graph of a given function
					•	To be able to transform graphs and identify the effect of transformations on functions such as $y = 2f(x)$; $y = f(2x)$;
					•	$y = f(x) + 2$ and $y = f(x + 2)$
	11	Revision for Mock Exam		4		
	12	MOCK EXAM		2		
	12	Mock exam review		1		
	12	Algebra recap – graphs		1		
	CHRISTMAS HOLIDAY					
Term 2	1/2	24 Algebra: Algebraic fractions and functions	24.1 Algebraic fractions	7	•	To simplify algebraic fractions
					•	To solve equations containing algebraic fractions
			24.2 Changing the subject of a formula		•	To change the subject of a formula where the subject occurs more than once

			24.3 Functions		•	To interpret simple expressions as functions with inputs and outputs
					•	To interpret the reverse process as the inverse function
					•	To use function notation to draw graphs and identify values by substitution
			24.4 Composite functions		•	To interpret the succession of two functions as a composite function and be able to find output values from given input values
			24.5 Iteration		•	To find approximate solutions to equations numerically using iteration
					•	To set up, solve and interpret the answers in growth and decay problems, including compound interest, working with general iterative processes
	3	25 Geometry and measures: Vector geometry	25.1 Properties of vectors	4	•	To add and subtract vectors
					•	To multiply vectors by a scalar
					•	To represent a vector in diagrammatic and column form
			25.2 Vectors in geometry		•	To use vectors to solve geometric problems
					•	To use vectors to construct geometric arguments and proofs
		The following topics are revisited to allow the most able to explore in greater depth				
	4/5	22 Trigonometry	22.4 Sine rule	7	•	Know and apply the sine rule to find unknown lengths and angles
			22.4 Cosine rule		•	Know and apply the cosine rule to find unknown lengths and angles
			22.5 Area of a triangle using sine		•	Know and apply area $= 1/2ab\sin C$ to calculate the area, sides or angles of any triangle
		Half term review/ assessment		1		
		HALF TERM				
	6	23 Rates of change	23.4 Gradients	4	•	Interpret the gradient at a point on a curve as the instantaneous rate of change
					•	Interpret the gradients of tangents and chords in numerical, algebraic and graphical contexts
	7/8	20 Geometric proof and reasoning	20.1 Circle theorems	7	•	Apply and prove the standard circle theorems concerning angles, radii, tangents and chords, and use them to prove related results
			25.2 Vectors		•	Use vectors to construct geometric arguments and proofs
			7.4 Transformations		•	Describe the changes and invariance achieved by combinations of rotations, reflections and transformations

		9/10	8 Algebraic proof and reasoning	8.1 Identities	7	• Know the difference between an equation and an identity • Argue mathematically to show algebraic expressions are equivalent • Use algebra to support and construct arguments and proofs
			EASTER HOLIDAY			
		1/2	Number recap		7	
		3/4	Algebra recap		7	
		5/6	Geometry recap		7	
			HALF TERM			
		7/8	Statistics and probability recap		7	
		9/10	Revision and exam preparation		7	
			GCSE MATHEMATICS EXAM (TBC)			

Chapter 1 Number: Basic number

Overview

1.1 Solving real-life problems	**1.4** Multiples, factors, prime numbers, powers and roots
1.2 Multiplication and division with decimals	**1.5** Prime factors, LCM and HCF
1.3 Approximation of calculations	**1.6** Negative numbers

Prior learning

Know how to add, subtract, multiply and divide with integers.
Know what multiples, factors, square numbers and prime numbers are.
Know the BIDMAS/BODMAS rule and how to substitute values into simple algebraic expressions.

Learning objectives

Ensure that students can: calculate with integers and decimals; round numbers to a given number of significant figures; work out and recognise multiples, factors, prime numbers and squares, cubes and their roots; find the prime factors of a number; work out lowest common multiples (LCM) and highest common factors (HCF); calculate with negative numbers.

In the examination, students will be expected to:
- solve problems set in a real-life context
- multiply a decimal number by another decimal number
- divide by a decimal by changing the calculation to division by an integer
- round to a given number of significant figures
- approximate the result before multiplying two numbers together
- approximate the result before dividing two numbers
- round a calculation, at the end of a problem, to give what is considered to be a sensible answer
- find multiples and factors
- identify prime numbers
- identify square numbers and triangular numbers
- find square roots
- identify cubes and cube roots
- identify prime factors
- identify the lowest common multiple (LCM) of two numbers
- identify the highest common factor (HCF) of two numbers
- multiply and divide positive and negative numbers.

Extension

Explore more complex roots, for example, square roots or cube roots of fractions made from two square or cube numbers. Discuss roots expressed as fractions if appropriate.

Curriculum references

Section	GCSE specification		Section	GCSE specification
1.1	N 2		1.4	N 4, 6
1.2	N 2		1.5	N 4
1.3	N 14, 15		1.6	N 2, 3

Route mapping

Exercise	Accessible	Intermediate	Challenging	AO1	AO2 MR CM	AO3 PS EV	Key questions
1A	1–7	8–11		1–3, 5–7, 9	4, 10	8, 11	7, 8, 11
1B	1–9	10, 11		1–5, 8	6, 9	7, 10, 11	6, 9
1C	1–8	9		1–5	7, 8	6, 9	4, 5
1D	1–6	7, 8		1–3, 5	4, 6	7, 8	4
1E	1–15	16–20		1–12, 15	13, 17, 18, 20	14, 16, 19	10, 16, 17
1F	1–14			1, 3–9, 13, 14	2, 11	10,12	13, 14
1G	1–8	9		1–4, 7	8, 9	5, 6	1
1H	1–8	9, 10		1, 3, 5–7	2, 8	4, 9, 10	1, 5, 8
1I	1–10	11, 12		1–6, 9, 10, 12	7, 8	11	3
1J	1–8	9, 10		1, 2, 4, 5, 7	3, 8	6, 9, 10	3, 5

Key questions are those that demonstrate mastery of the concept, or which require a step-up in understanding or application. Key questions could be used to identify the questions that students must tackle, to support differentiation, or to identify the questions that should be teacher-marked rather than student-marked.

About this chapter

Making connections: Explain an easy way to do this multiplication/division mentally. Why would knowledge of factors help with this?

Relevance: Linking into real-life problems involving estimation, the use of negative numbers will help students to see the relevance of this chapter.

Working mathematically: What do you look for when deciding if you can do a calculation mentally? Explain the steps of the calculation. Write the steps in order.

Assessment: In each section of this chapter, ensure that students have a good grasp of the key questions in each exercise before moving on. (Refer to the 'Route mapping' table above.) Encourage students to read and think about the 'Ready to progress?' statements on page 36 of the Student Book. Check students' understanding at the end of the chapter, formatively, using peer assessment. Students could do a mini test in the form of the 'Review questions' on pages 36–37 of the Student Book. Follow up the test with an individual target-getting session based on any areas for development that a student may have.

Worked exemplars from the Student Book – suggestions for use
- Use these as examples to show students how to attain maximum marks in examinations.
- Give students different numbers and encourage them to follow the correct steps.
- Copy and cut the working into cards but split the label/description from the working. Ask students to put the working in order, and then match them with the descriptions.

Answers to the Student Book questions are available on the CD-ROM provided.

Section 1.1 Solving real-life problems

Learning objectives
- Solve problems set in a real-life context

Resources and homework
- Student Book 1.1: pages 9–11
- Practice Book 1.1: pages 5–6

Making mathematical connections
- Calculations with different units with and without a calculator

Making cross-curricular connections
- **Food Technology** – calculating the cost of ingredients
- **Relevance** – developing mathematical fluency in calculating day-to-day problems

Prior learning
- Students should know the multiplication tables and be confident and accurate completing simple mental calculations.
- They should be able to multiply numbers such as 24 × 36, 162 × 78 and £24.50 × 15, and divide numbers such as 1035 ÷ 55 without using a calculator.
- Students should also be familiar with short division methods and know how to work out simple percentages of a quantity, for example, 10% or 5%.

Working mathematically
- Encourage students to practise their preferred methods for multiplying and dividing in order to minimise careless errors in calculations.
- Structure tasks so students can work out the methods for themselves, either by increasing the difficulty incrementally or through one straightforward and one complex example.

Common misconceptions and remediation
- Students might not round answers logically, e.g. rather than 18.81 coaches, it should be 19. Other common errors are generally based on careless errors in arithmetic.
- Students with a weak grasp of multiplication tables may make basic errors. Address this by regular testing of students' multiplication table skills.

Probing questions
- Describe the advantages and disadvantages of various methods of multiplying and dividing.

Literacy focus
- Key terms: column method (or traditional method), grid method (or box method), long division, long multiplication
- Ask students to write a step-by-step guide explaining their method of choice.

Part 1
- Ask some mental multiplications, e.g. 20 × 5 (100), 7 × 400 (2800) and 30 × 500 (15 000).
- Combine two similar multiplications, e.g. 30 × 8 (240); 2 × 8 (16); 32 × 8 (240 + 16 = 256). Repeat for other numbers, increasing the difficulty according to ability.
- Now ask some mental divisions using the multiplication tables up to 10 × 10. Include examples that have a remainder, for example, 40 ÷ 6 = 6, remainder 4.

Part 2

- In this section, focus on ensuring that students have methods of multiplying and dividing that they are comfortable using and can explain. **Less able** groups should, at least in this section, concentrate on using just one method of multiplying and one method of dividing.

Multiplication

- Demonstrate the grid (or box) method, e.g. with 213 × 54. Add each answer to find the total (11 502). Now demonstrate the same calculation using the column method.

  213
  × 54
  ─────
  852
  10650
  ─────
  11502

×	200	10	3
50	10 000	500	150
4	800	40	12

- Ask students which method they prefer. Students should stick to their preferred method.
- Repeat with other calculations for **less able** groups.
- Then work through Example 1, pointing out both methods.

Division

- Display and ask students to work out 430 ÷ 2 (215). Ask them to explain how they worked it out. Students are likely to say that they did a mental calculation.
- Increase the level of difficulty, e.g. ask: How would your work out 275 ÷ 25? Expect some to say that there are four 25s in 100, so 4 (100) + 4 (100) + 3 (75) = 11.
- Point out that this is a chunking method and write out the calculation as shown on the right.

  $4 \times 25 = 100$
  $4 \times 25 = 100$
  $3 \times 25 = 75$
  ─────────────
  $11 \times 25 = 275,$
  so $275 \div 25 = 11$

- Now demonstrate short division that gives an answer with a remainder, e.g. 100 ÷ 7 (14, remainder 2) or 300 ÷ 21 (14, remainder 6). Explain that some calculations will have remainders as the numbers do not divide exactly and that in some real-life or problem-solving (PS) questions, the remainder will need interpreting.
- Repeat the same question using long division. Explain that long division is similar to short division but requires them to show more working, which can help to reduce errors.
- Ask: There are 30 students in the dinner queue. They sit at tables with 4 seats. How many tables do they need? (8). Why do they need 8 tables? Discuss the 2 spare seats.
- Work through Example 2. Demonstrate the solution using their method, e.g. for chunking 10 × 53 = 530 leaves 672 − 530 = 142, 2 × 53 = 106 leaves 142 − 106 = 36 as the remainder, so 672 ÷ 53 = 12, remainder 36. Therefore, 13 coaches are needed.
- Encourage students to continue to use any successful method, to be precise with their calculations and to check that their answers seem sensible.
- **Students can now do Exercise 1A from the Student Book.**

N 1–3, 5–7, 9	Calculator n/a	CM n/a	MR 4, 10	PS 8	EV 11

Part 3

- Ask for the answer to 400 ÷ 24 (16). Ask students to write this as a question. (E.g. In total, 400 people are on a train; 24 people in each carriage except for the last one. How many people are in the last carriage?)
- **Less able** groups may find it easier to use questions involving money or smaller numbers. (E.g. My bus fare is £3 for day. I have £20. How many days' bus fare do I have? (6 days with £2 over)) Repeat for other numbers.
- Work these out using a non-calculator method: 318 × 46; 976 ÷ 61.

Section 1.2 Multiplication and division with decimals

Learning objectives

- Multiply a decimal number by another decimal number
- Divide by a decimal by changing the calculation to division by an integer

Resources and homework

- Student Book 1.2: pages 12–15
- Practice Book 1.2: pages 6–7

Making mathematical connections

- Place value manipulation
- Standard form

Making cross-curricular connections

- **Science** – calculating with decimal numbers
- **Relevance** – basic mathematical fluency with decimals

Prior learning

- Students must be able to multiply three-digit integers by two-digit integers. They should also be able to multiply decimal numbers by 10, 100, 1000 and so on.
- Students should be able to use pencil and paper methods for division of integers.

Working mathematically

- Encourage students to estimate the answer before calculating in order to check that their answers are sensible.
- Structure tasks so students can work out the methods for themselves, either by increasing the difficulty incrementally or through one straightforward and one complex example.

Common misconceptions and remediation

- **Multiplication:** Students may forget to insert the decimal point or put it in the wrong position.
- **Division:** Students may change both numbers into integers, and then have the decimal point in the wrong place.
- Students should be able to reduce these errors with repeated emphasis on the rules for multiplying and dividing with decimals.

Probing questions

- Use this calculation to write down more questions with the same answer: $108.8 \div 3.4 = 32$.

Literacy focus

- Key terms: decimal place (dp), decimal point
- Ask students to describe their method for multiplying and dividing with decimals.

Part 1

- Ask students quickfire, linked, mental multiplication questions, gradually increasing the level of difficulty, e.g. 6×7 (42) followed by 12×7 (84). Ask how they obtained the second answer. Students may know the 12 times table, or realise it is double the previous answer.
- Now use other numbers, e.g. 9×8 (72), then 90×80 (7200). Again ask how they obtained the second answer.
- Next give several division questions with integer values and answers, e.g. $342 \div 3$ (114), $8561 \div 7$ (1223), $2784 \div 12$ (232). Discuss the methods used: chunking, short division and long division.

Part 2

Decimal places; Multiplying two decimal numbers together

- Ask students to give the answer to 11 × 7 (77). Then ask for the answer to 1.1 × 7 (7.7). Show students the effect of the decimal point by setting out the calculations as shown on the right.

$$\begin{array}{r} 11 \\ \times\ 7 \\ \hline 77 \end{array} \qquad \begin{array}{r} 1.1 \\ \times\ 7 \\ \hline 7.7 \end{array}$$

- Now show students a more complex multiplication, e.g. 3.56 × 27.

$$\begin{array}{r} 3.56 \\ \times\quad 27 \\ \hline 2492 \\ 7120 \\ \hline 96.12 \end{array}$$

- Explain that the calculations now consist of multiplying two decimals together.
- Use the example above again but change 27 to 2.7. Explain that 3.56 × 2.7 is 10 times smaller than 3.56 × 27. So 3.56 × 2.7 = 9.612.
  Explain that 3.56 has two decimal places and that 2.7 has one decimal place, so the answer has 2 + 1 = 3 dp.

$$\begin{array}{r} 3.56 \\ \times\quad 2.7 \\ \hline 2492 \\ 7120 \\ \hline 9.612 \end{array}$$

- Work through Examples 3 and 4.

Dividing by a decimal

- Write 36 ÷ 2, 3.6 ÷ 2, 3.6 ÷ 0.2 and 36 ÷ 0.2.
- Then write the same calculations as fractions: $\dfrac{36}{2}, \dfrac{3.6}{2}, \dfrac{3.6}{0.2}, \dfrac{36}{0.2}$
- Ask for the answers (18, 1.8, 18, 180). Explain that dividing by 2 is easier than dividing by 0.2. Show that dividing 36 by 2 is the same as dividing 3.6 by 0.2 because multiplying by 10/10 is multiplying by a whole one, so the answer is unchanged:
$$\frac{3.6}{0.2} \times \frac{10}{10} = \frac{36}{2} = 18$$
- Show an example using division by a two-decimal place number: 3.4 ÷ 0.05.
- Write it as a fraction: $\dfrac{3.4}{0.05}$
- Explain that to change the format this time they must multiply by 100:
$$\frac{3.4}{0.05} \times \frac{100}{100} = \frac{340}{5} = 68$$
- Work through Example 5.
- **Students can now do Exercise 1B from the Student Book.**

N 1–5, 8	Calculator n/a	CM n/a	MR 6, 9	PS 10	EV 7, 11

Part 3

- Use this as a lead-in to Section 1.3 on approximation.
- Ask students to estimate answers using Exercise 1A or make up your own, e.g.
  67.2 × 35 = 2352 ≈ 70 × 40 = 2800 (less, as both numbers are rounded),
  so answers between 2000 and 3000 seem reasonable.
- Repeat for more calculations; then let students work out the reasonable estimations.
- Ask: Given that 56 × 254 = 14 224, find the answers to:
  5.6 × 254   56 × 2.54   560 × 25.4   14 224 ÷ 0.56

Section 1.3 Approximation of calculations

Learning objectives

- Round to a given number of significant figures
- Approximate the result before multiplying two numbers together
- Approximate the result before dividing two numbers
- Round a calculation, at the end of a problem, to give what is considered to be a sensible answer

Resources and homework

- Student Book 1.3: pages 15–22
- Practice Book 1.3: pages 7–9

Making mathematical connections

- Standard form

Making cross-curricular connections

- **Science** – approximating calculations from experiments to give sensible answers
- **PE** – approximating times and distances in athletics
- **Relevance** – day-to-day approximations, for example, in shops

Prior learning

- Students should be able to round to a given number of decimal places.

Working mathematically

- Explain how you would go about rounding a number to one significant figure (sf).
- Structure tasks so students can work out the methods for themselves, either by increasing the difficulty incrementally or through one straightforward and one complex example.

Common misconceptions and remediation

- These are best shown with two examples, both rounded to two significant figures (2 sf): 275 986 = 28, rather than 280 000 (the zeros are forgotten), 0.000 371 04 = 0.00 or 37, rather than 0.000 37 (2 dp instead or 2 sf, or zeros forgotten).
- Students often have difficulty with the power of 10 in the answer.
- Students may try to be too accurate when approximating calculations. They round to more than 1 sf, or do not round at all when using a calculator, assuming that a correct answer is better than an approximation. (Sometimes answers are better as 'roughly' or 'nearly'.)

Probing questions

- True or false?
  - 4.599 rounds to 4.510 to 2 dp
  - –8 is less than –6
  - 4.5 is closer to 5 than it is to 4
  - –46 is greater than –44
  - 9.5999 rounds to 9.6 to 1 dp

Literacy focus

- Key terms: approximate, significant figure
- Ask students to explain the difference between decimal places and significant figures in words.

Part 1

- Display: 0.04, 0.4, 4, 40, 400. Ask students what they have in common (4). What else? (0)
- Write: 0.065, 0.65, 6.5, 65, 650. Ask how these differ from the first set. (two non-zero digits)
- Ask for numbers with three non-zero digits, e.g. 0.0123, 0.123, 1.23, 12.3, 123, 1230.
- Ask quickfire questions involving multiplying integers by 10, 100 and 1000.
- Display the table of numbers on the right.
  Start with 31 and ask questions, e.g.
  'What is 31 × 10? What is 31 × 1000? What is 31 ÷ 10?'
  Continue, using a different starting number.

3.1	310
3100	0.031
31	0.31
0.0031	31 000

Part 2

Rounding to significant figures

- Look back at the numbers in Part 1. The first set had one non-zero digit (4), the second set two (65) and the third set three (123). Say that the non-zero digits are significant figures (sf). Explain that zeros before or after these digits maintain the value of the number but are not sf. Writing a number to 1 sf requires the nearest number with only one non-zero digit.
- Highlight the number 0.003 01 (Student Book page 15, table 1). Explain that this has 3 sf, since the middle 0 is holding a place.
- Ask students to explain why 45 281 (table 2) is 50 000 to 1 sf. (Only one non-zero digit, but place value must be correct.) Ask quickfire questions to reinforce the method.
- Work backwards. 'A number is 80 to 1 sf. What might the original number be?' (75–84.999...)
- **Students can now do Exercise 1C from the Student Book.**

N 1–5	Calculator n/a	CM 7, 8	MR n/a	PS 6	EV 9

Multiplying and dividing by multiples of 10

- Work through the Student Book examples (page 17) for practice. Ask students to multiply, e.g. 3 × 4, 3 × 40, 30 × 40, and to state any rules they notice. Tell them to be careful with zeros, e.g. 40 × 50 = 2000.
- Demonstrate how to set out divisions in fraction form and cancel zeros.
- **Students can now do Exercise 1D from the Student Book.**

N 1–3, 5	Calculator n/a	CM 6	MR 4	PS 7, 8	EV n/a

Approximation of calculations

- Introduce rounding numbers to 1 sf as a method of estimating calculations. Start with some straightforward examples, e.g. $19.8 \times 3.01 \approx 20 \times 3 = 60$, $491 \div 9.6 \approx 500 \div 10 = 50$.
- Now work on more complex examples involving division by a decimal between 0 and 1. Write $86 \div 0.21$ on the board. Explain that divisions are often better written as fractions and that multiplying a fraction by 1 leaves it unchanged:

$$\frac{86}{0.21} \approx \frac{90}{0.2} \quad \text{Since } \frac{10}{10} = 1, \ \frac{90}{0.2} = \frac{90 \times 10}{0.2 \times 10} = \frac{900}{2} = 450 \quad \text{So } \frac{86}{0.21} \approx 450$$

- **Students can now do Exercise 1E from the Student Book.**

N 1, 3–5, 7–10, 12	Calculator 2, 6, 11, 15, 16c, 17	CM 17, 18, 20	MR 13	PS 19	EV 14, 16

Part 3

- Write on the board: 571.8 to 1 sf = 6; 0.003 276 to 2 sf = 0.00; 25.37 to 1sf = 30.00
  Ask students to explain why these answers are incorrect; then to write the correct answers.
- Ask students to round the following (use whiteboards): 3.75 (1 dp); 186.04 (1 dp); 28.03 (1 sf); 44.992 (2 sf).

Section 1.4 Multiples, factors, prime numbers, powers and roots

Learning objectives

- Find multiples and factors
- Identify prime numbers
- Identify square numbers and triangular numbers
- Find square roots
- Identify cubes and cube roots

Resources and homework

- Student Book 1.4: pages 22–24
- Practice Book 1.4: page 10

Making mathematical connections

- Indices and fractional indices
- Prime factor form
- Factorising quadratics
- HCF, LCM

Making cross-curricular connections

- **Science** – using powers and roots in formulae
- **Relevance** – links to HCF and LCM

Prior learning

- Most of the learning objectives have been covered previously. This section is a reminder of the skills that students should already have or will need to acquire.

Working mathematically

- Ensure that students understand the concept of what makes a number prime, and the connection between powers and roots.

Common misconceptions and remediation

- Students often forget that 1 and the number itself are factors, so they may omit them from the full list of factors.
- Some students will think that 1 is a prime number or forget that it is a square number and a cube number.
- These topics crop up regularly, e.g. in patterns and sequences. Reminding and revising at every opportunity will help eliminate these errors.

Probing questions

- How do you write down all the factors of a number?
- Why is 1 not a prime number?
- How do you identify the factors of a number greater than 100?

Literacy focus

- There are no new key terms in this section, but students should know: multiple, factor, prime number, square, triangular numbers, square root, cube, cube root, powers.
- Revise the words on pages 22–23 of the Student Book. Check that students know what each word means and the etymology behind them. Ask students give an example or two of each.

Part 1

- Ask students to pick out, from the whole numbers 1 to 20:
  - all the multiples of 3 (3, 6, 9, 12, 15 and 18)
  - the factors of 20 (1, 2, 4, 5, 10 and 20)
  - the prime numbers (2, 3, 5, 7, 11, 13, 17 and 19)
  - the square numbers (1, 4, 9 and 16)
  - the triangular numbers (1, 3, 6, 10 and 15)
  - the cube numbers (1 and 8).
- Check that students know:
  - the square root of 9 (3 or –3)
  - the cube root of 8 (2) and –8 (–2).

Part 2

- Write the words 'Prime number', 'Square' and 'Cube' as column headings on the board.
- Under the appropriate headings, list the numbers 1 to 20 from Part 1.
- Ask students to complete the lists for all numbers up to 100 to find out how many of each type of number there are. (Prime numbers 25; Squares 10; Cubes 4)
- Extend the lists to 200 for **more able** students. (Prime numbers 46; Squares 14; Cubes 5)
- Highlight numbers that are in two or more columns. (1 and 64 are both squares and cubes.)
- Point out that square numbers and cube numbers can never be prime numbers.
- Explain that to show that a number is not prime, all that is needed is a factor other than the number itself or 1, e.g. 432 is not prime as it is even; the only even prime number is 2.
- **Students can now do Exercise 1F from the Student Book.**

N 1, 3–9, 13, 14	Calculator 12b	CM 11	MR 2	PS n/a	EV 10, 12

Part 3

- Finish by having a counting game using any of the words: prime, square, cube, none.
- The first student says '1' and 'square' (or 'cube').
- The second student says '2' and 'prime'.
- The third student says '3' and 'prime'.
- The fourth student says '4' and 'square', and so on.
- When someone makes a mistake, that person is out and the game starts again from 1.
- **More able** students can include answers such as '5' and 'square root of 25' or '6' and 'cube root' of 216.
- Find:
  - a prime number greater than 100
  - the largest cube number less than 1000
  - two prime numbers that add up to 66.
- Why are the following not prime numbers? 6184, 1785, 4251
- Write down all the factors of 24.

Section 1.5 Prime factors, LCM and HCF

Learning objectives

- Identify prime factors
- Identify the lowest common multiple (LCM) of two numbers
- Identify the highest common factor (HCF) of two numbers

Resources and homework

- Student Book 1.5: pages 25–29
- Practice Book 1.5: pages 10–11

Making mathematical connections

- Factorising

Making cross-curricular connections

- **Science** – using formulae
- **Relevance** – solving equations

Prior learning

- Students should understand what a factor is and be able to identify prime numbers.

Working mathematically

- Make sure that students can efficiently find the HCF and LCM of numbers using their preferred method.

Common misconceptions and remediation

- A common mistake, when students are using the division method to find prime factors, is to leave out the last factor when rewriting the answer in index notation. Encourage students to check their answers by multiplying the factors and checking that the answer is the original number.
- When finding prime factors, a common error is not using prime factors, e.g. $36 = 2 \times 2 \times 9$. Stress to students, the importance of checking that they have answered the question.

Probing questions

- Explain how to find the LCM of two numbers.
- Explain how to find the HCF of two numbers.

Literacy focus

- Key terms: highest common factor (HCF), index notation, lowest common multiple (LCM)
- Ask students to write a step-by-step method for working out both the LCM and HCF.

Part 1

- Give each pair of students a number.
- On one mini whiteboard, each pair must write all the factors of the number.
- On another mini whiteboard, pairs should write 'prime'.
- For every prime number they must hold up both boards. If it is not a prime number, they should simply hold up the board with the factors written on it. For example, if they are given the number 5, then they would write 1, 5 on one board and hold that up alongside the 'prime' board. If they are given the number 6, they should hold up one board with 1, 2, 3 and 6 on it.

Part 2

- Remind students that prime factors are factors that are also prime numbers.
- **Students can now begin Exercise 1G from the Student Book.**

N 1–4, 7	Calculator n/a	CM n/a	MR 8, 9	PS 5, 6	EM n/a

Lowest common multiple

- Ask students to give multiples of 2. (2, 4, 6, 8, 10, 12 ...)
- Now ask for multiples of 5. (5, 10, 15, 20 ...)
- Now ask for multiples that are common to both lists. (10, 20, 30 ...)
- Ask students to say which common multiple is the smallest (10). Explain that this is called the lowest common multiple (LCM). So 10 is the LCM of 2 and 5.

Highest common factor

- Ask students to work in pairs, writing factors of numbers on their whiteboards.
- Give one student the number 12 and ask for the factors. (1, 2, 3, 4, 6, 12)
- Give the second student the number 15 and ask for the factors. (1, 3, 5, 15)
- Now ask them for the highest number they have in common on their whiteboards. (3)
- Explain that this is called the highest common factor. Repeat for other numbers.
- **Students can now do Exercise 1H from the Student Book.**

N 1, 3, 5–7	Calculator n/a	CM n/a	MR 2, 8	PS 9, 10	EV 4

Part 3

- Show students how to find the LCM and HCF using a Venn diagram.
  For example, draw this Venn diagram for the numbers 42 and 63.

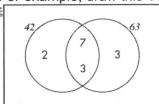

- To find the LCM, multiply the numbers from all the different regions in the diagram:
  $2 \times 3 \times 3 \times 7 = 126$
- The HCF of the two numbers is the biggest factor shared by both of them. From the diagram, this is the product of all the numbers in the intersection of the sets. ($3 \times 7 = 21$)
- Let students use this method to find the LCM and HCF of 28 and 40. (LCM = 280, HCF = 4)
- Give students a variety of questions involving HCF and LCM calculations.

Section 1.6 Negative numbers

Learning objectives

- Multiply and divide positive and negative numbers

Making mathematical connections

- Equations involving negative numbers
- Coordinates in four quadrants

Resources and homework

- Student Book 1.6: pages 30–33
- Practice Book 1.6: page 12

Making cross-curricular connections

- **Geography** – temperatures
- **Business studies** – profit and loss
- **Relevance** – temperature scales

Prior learning

- Students must be confident with adding and subtracting negative numbers.

Working mathematically

- Make sure that students can apply BODMAS/BIDMAS to calculations confidently.

Common misconceptions and remediation

- A common error is that students use these rules when they are set addition or subtraction questions. For example, −3 − 5 will be given as +8, as students interpret the rule that two negatives make a positive incorrectly. To avoid this, it is important to stress that the rule is: two negative numbers multiplied or divided make a positive number.

Probing questions

- The answer to a calculation is −8. Make up some questions that give this answer.

Literacy focus

- There are no new key terms in this section.

Part 1

- Ask students to copy the multiplication grid on the right. Explain that you have already filled in the zeros, as any number multiplied by zero is zero.
- Ask students to fill in the top left-hand corner, as shown in the table, below left.
- Now ask students to read the top row from left to right and continue the pattern: 9, 6, 3, 0, −3, −6, −9. Ask them to use the pattern to complete the top row.
- Repeat for the second and third rows.
- It should now appear as shown below, on the right.

×	−3	−2	−1	0	+1	+2	+3
−3				0			
−2				0			
−1				0			
0	0	0	0	0	0	0	0
+1				0			
+2				0			
+3				0			

×	−3	−2	−1	0	+1	+2	+3
−3	9	6	3	0			
−2	6	4	2	0			
−1	3	2	1	0			
0	0	0	0	0	0	0	0
+1				0			
+2				0			
+3				0			

×	−3	−2	−1	0	+1	+2	+3
−3	9	6	3	0	−3	−6	−9
−2	6	4	2	0	−2	−4	−6
−1	3	2	1	0	−1	−2	−3
0	0	0	0	0	0	0	0
+1				0			
+2				0			
+3				0			

Part 2

The number line

- Go through this section on page 30 of the Student Book.

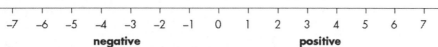

Adding and subtracting negative numbers

- Read through the rules and examples as stated in the Student Book.
- Check understanding by asking questions, e.g. –2 + 4 (2), –2 + –4 (–6), –6 – –1 (–5).

Multiplying and dividing negative numbers

- Read through the rules and examples as stated in the Student Book and summarise as:

× or ÷	+	–
+	+	–
–	–	+

- Stress that these results apply for multiplication and division only. Encourage students to learn this fact: *Two negative numbers multiplied or divided make a positive number.*

Negative numbers on a calculator

- Go through this section of the Student Book.
- **Students can now do Exercise 1I from the Student Book.**

N 2–6, 9, 10, 12	Calculator 1	CM 7, 8	MR n/a	PS 11	EV n/a

Hierarchy of operations

- Remind students of the order in which they must do mathematical operations, according to the **BIDMAS/BODMAS rule**:

B	Brackets
I/O	Indices (pOwers)
D	Division
M	Multiplication
A	Addition
S	Subtraction

- Go through Example 15 on the board, reminding students of what they learned from the previous exercise, along with the process of applying BIDMAS/BODMAS to the question.
- **Students can now do Exercise 1J from the Student Book.**

N 1–2, 4, 5, 7	Calculator n/a	CM 8	MR 3	PS 6, 9, 10	EV n/a

Part 3

- Ask each student a simple mental question (no writing allowed), e.g. 4 × –3 (–12), 8 ÷ –2 (–4); –5 × –9 (45).
- Now ask some additions or subtractions to check that students are not making the common error explained above. If they are, say: 'You are in a lift; you go down 3 floors, then you go down 5 more floors. How many have you gone down altogether?' Relate this to –3 – 5 = –8. Repeat for other numbers.
- Ask students to solve the following calculations on mini whiteboards:

–3 × 5   –2 × –3   –12 ÷ –6   –16 ÷ 8   24 ÷ –3

Chapter 2 Number: Fractions, ratio and proportion

Overview

2.1 One quantity as a fraction of another	**2.4** Fractions on a calculator
2.2 Adding, subtracting and calculating with fractions	**2.5** Increasing and decreasing quantities by a percentage
2.3 Multiplying and dividing fractions	**2.6** Expressing one quantity as a fraction of another

Prior learning

Know how to cancel fractions to their simplest form.
Know how to find equivalent fractions, decimals and percentages.
Know how to add and subtract fractions with the same denominator.
Know how to work out simple percentages, such as 10%, of quantities.
Know how to convert a mixed number to an improper fraction and vice versa.

Learning objectives

Ensure that students can: work out one quantity as a fraction of another; add, subtract, multiply and divide fractions with and without a calculator; use a percentage multiplier; work out percentage increase and decrease; work out one quantity as a percentage of another.

In the examination, students will be expected to:
- work out one quantity as a fraction of another
- add and subtract fractions with different denominators
- multiply proper fractions
- multiply mixed numbers
- divide by fractions
- use a calculator to add and subtract fractions
- use a calculator to multiply and divide fractions
- increase and decrease quantities by a percentage
- express one quantity as a percentage of another
- work out percentage change.

Extension

Give students questions involving the four operations with three fractions. **More able** students could design their own questions.

Curriculum references

Section	GCSE specification
2.1	N 2, 8, 12; R 3
2.2	N 2, 8, 12
2.3	N 2, 8, 12
2.4	N 2, 8, 12
2.5	N 2, 8, 12; R 9
2.6	N 2, 8, 12; R 3

Route mapping

Exercise	Accessible	Intermediate	Challenging	AO1	AO2 MR CM	AO3 PS EV	Key questions
2A	1–8	9, 10		1, 2, 4	3, 5–7	8–10	1, 4
2B	1–9	10, 11		1, 3, 4a, 9	2, 10, 11a	4b, 5, 8, 11b	1, 3, 8
2C	1–9	10–13		1–8, 10	9, 11, 13a	12, 13b	1, 2, 10
2D	1–10	11–13	14, 15	1–4a, 5, 7–9	4b, 11, 14	6, 10, 12, 13, 15	3, 5, 7, 8
2E	1–9	10–13	14, 15	1–5, 8a, 9, 12	6, 7, 10, 11, 13	8b, 8c, 14, 15	3, 4, 8, 12
2F	1–9	10–13		1–8	9–11	12, 13	3, 6

Key questions are those that demonstrate mastery of the concept, or which require a step-up in understanding or application. Key questions could be used to identify the questions that students must tackle, to support differentiation, or to identify the questions that should be teacher-marked rather than student-marked.

About this chapter

Making connections: This chapter builds on students' understanding of fractions and percentages, making connections with real-world problems such as questions on loan interest rates or bonus payments in the workplace.

Relevance: The ability to work fluently with fractions and percentages is part of everyday life. Students will need these skills in order to function effectively within the workplace.

Working mathematically: Make up two percentage increase questions with the answer 70 g: one easy, one hard. Give students some examples of the four operations involving fractions with some common errors in them. Ask students to explain the errors and how they would correct them.

Assessment: In each section of this chapter, ensure that students have a good grasp of the key questions in each exercise before moving on. (Refer to the 'Route mapping' table above.) Encourage students to read and think about the 'Ready to progress?' statements on page 56 of the Student Book. Check students' understanding at the end of the chapter, formatively, using peer assessment. Students could do a mini test in the form of the 'Review questions' on pages 56–57 of the Student Book. Follow up the test with an individual target-getting session based on any areas for development that a student may have.

Worked exemplars from the Student Book – suggestions for use
- Present students with the same question using different numbers. Encourage them to follow the steps in the exemplar to mirror the working, in full or just using the notes.
- Copy and cut the exemplar into cards. Students match the working with the notes. (You may need to remove the words 'first, second', and so on.)
- Ask students to write their own exemplar questions based on the questions in the Student Book.

Answers to the Student Book questions are available on the CD-ROM provided.

Section 2.1 One quantity as a fraction of another

Learning objectives
- Find one quantity as a fraction of another

Resources and homework
- Student Book 2.1: pages 39–40
- Practice Book 2.1: page 13

Making mathematical connections
- Equivalent fractions

Making cross-curricular connections
- **Science** – calculating with fractions and decimals in experiments, e.g. mixing chemicals
- **Food Technology** – comparing quantities in different packaging to evaluate different offers. For example: buy one get one free.
- **Relevance** – everyday use of fractions and fractional quantities

Prior learning
- Students will often have had to describe one quantity as a fraction of another. For example: 'about half' of the students at school are boys; 'a third' of their time is spent in bed; bus fares cost 'about a fifth' of their pocket money each week.
- Students should also know basic conversions, including kilograms to grams and simple facts such as the number of days in March (31).

Working mathematically
- Encourage students to check that the units are the same before they write the fraction.
- Structure tasks so students can work out the methods for themselves, either by increasing the difficulty incrementally or through one straightforward and one complex example.

Common misconceptions and remediation
- The most common error students make is that they do not match the units before comparing. For example, students may give 25p as a fraction of £2 as $\frac{25}{2}$ instead of $\frac{25}{200}$. Pointing out this error regularly should help students to avoid making it.

Probing questions
- What clues do you look for when cancelling fractions to their simplest form?
- How do you know when you have the simplest form of a fraction?
- How do you know which part is the numerator and which is the denominator?

Literacy focus
- Key terms: fraction, quantity
- Make sure students understand the meaning of a quantity and ask them to describe their methods by writing them down or saying them aloud.

Part 1
NB: This section may take more than 1 hour.

- Use a metre ruler or draw a metre ruler on the board. Show 20 cm on the ruler and ask: What fraction is this of the whole ruler? Can this be simplified?
- Repeat for other measures.

- Now ask, for example: What fraction is 20 cm of 2 m? and so on.
- Look at other measures such as money or time.
- For **more able** students, use mixed numbers. Ask what $12\frac{1}{2}$ cm is as a fraction of the whole ruler $\left(\frac{1}{8}\right)$, or what $22\frac{1}{2}$ minutes is as a fraction of an hour $\left(\frac{3}{8}\right)$.
- Ask students how they worked out these answers. Explain that 25 cm is $\frac{1}{4}$ of the whole ruler and $12\frac{1}{2}$ cm is half of that. Similarly for time, $7\frac{1}{2}$ minutes is half of 15 minutes, and $22\frac{1}{2}$ minutes is 15 minutes plus $7\frac{1}{2}$ minutes.

Part 2

- Give students three sets of jumbled cards, prepared and cut from a grid as shown.

Set 1	Set 2	Set 3	Set 1	Set 2	Set 3
30 cm	1 m	$\frac{3}{10}$	4 grams	1 kg	$\frac{1}{250}$
25p	£1	$\frac{1}{4}$	5 cl	$\frac{3}{4}$ litre	$\frac{1}{15}$
3 hours	1 day	$\frac{1}{8}$	6 cm^2	9 cm^2	$\frac{2}{3}$
2 days	3 weeks	$\frac{2}{21}$			

- Ask students to organise the cards so that:
  a card from set 1 as a fraction of a card from set 2 = a card from set 3.
  E.g. 30 cm as a fraction of 1m = $\frac{3}{10}$
- Students may spot the correct answers but ultimately, they need to learn the conversions.
- Show the class a formal method, e.g. 30 cm as a fraction of 1 m is the same as 30 cm as a fraction of 100 cm.
  So 30 as a fraction of 100 is $\frac{30}{100} = \frac{3}{10}$
- Work through Examples 1 and 2 on page 39 of the Student Book.
- **Students can now do Exercise 2A from the Student Book.**

N 1, 2, 4	Calculator n/a	CM 5, 6	MR 3, 7	PS 8–10	EV n/a

Part 3

- Explain that later in the course students will need to know fractions of 360° for drawing pie charts.
- Use a circle and ask questions about angles of sectors, such as, 'What fraction of a whole circle is 36°?' $\left(\frac{1}{10}\right)$
- What fraction of:
  - 1 m is 45 cm?
  - 1 kg is 84 g?
  - 1 hour is 34 minutes?

Section 2.2 Adding, subtracting and calculating with fractions

Learning objectives
* Add and subtract fractions with different denominators

Resources and homework
* Student Book 2.2: pages 40–42
* Practice Book 2.2: pages 13–14

Making mathematical connections
* Rearranging simple formulae including fractions
* Solving equations including fractions

Making cross-curricular connections
* **Food Technology** – fractions of ingredients
* **Economics and Business Studies** – VAT, unemployment figures
* **Relevance** – everyday use of fractions and fractional quantities

Prior learning
* Students should be able to find the lowest common multiple (LCM) of two or three numbers, and be able to convert mixed numbers into improper fractions and vice versa.
* Students should also know how to add and subtract fractions with the same denominator.

Working mathematically
* How do you find a common denominator when adding or subtracting fractions?
* Is there more than one possible common denominator you could use? What would happen if you used a different common denominator?
* Ask students to try to solve a question using different common denominators.

Common misconceptions and remediation
* Students often fail to convert to equivalent fractions to make the denominators the same; they simply add or subtract the numerators and the denominators.
* Students may change the denominators, but forget to change the numerators.
* Point out these mistakes each time they occur to help reduce errors.

Probing questions
* Give students some addition and subtraction of fractions questions with errors in them. Ask students to explain the mistakes and how they would correct them.

Literacy focus
* There are no new key terms in this section, but students should know the meaning of: numerator, denominator.
* Ask students to write a bullet point list summarising their method for answering this type of question.

Part 1
* Write the numbers 2, 3, 4, 5, 6, 7, 8, 9 and 10 on the board. Ask students for the LCM of 2 and 3 (6), 2 and 4 (4), 2 and 5 (10). For **more able** students, use more challenging numbers, such as 6 and 8 (24).
* Point out that when fractions are added, the lowest common denominator is the LCM of the denominators.

Part 2

- Write $\frac{2}{3} + \frac{1}{5}$ on the board. Ask students to change each fraction into fifteenths $\left(\frac{10}{15} + \frac{3}{15}\right)$.

- Draw a 3 by 5 rectangle. Shade 10 squares and then 3 more squares to show that $\frac{10}{15} + \frac{3}{15} = \frac{13}{15}$

- Work through Example 3. Write $\frac{5}{6} - \frac{3}{4}$ on the board and ask students to change the fractions into twelfths. $\left(\frac{10}{12} - \frac{9}{12}\right)$

- Now draw a 3 by 4 rectangle. Shade 10 squares and then shade out 9 of these squares to show that $\frac{10}{12} - \frac{9}{12} = \frac{1}{12}$.

- Now write $2\frac{3}{4} - 1\frac{5}{6}$ on the board and ask students to change the fractions into twelfths $\left(2\frac{9}{12} - 1\frac{10}{12} \text{ or } \frac{33}{12} - \frac{22}{12}\right)$.

- Draw three 4 by 3 rectangles and shade $2\frac{3}{4}$ (33 small squares shaded $=\frac{33}{12}$) and draw two 4 by 3 rectangles and shade $1\frac{5}{6}$ (22 small squares shaded $= \frac{22}{12}$).

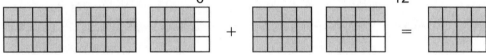

- Taking 22 small squares away from 33 small squares leaves 11 small squares $= \frac{11}{12}$, so $2\frac{3}{4} - 1\frac{5}{6} = \frac{11}{12}$.

- Show how they can do these without using diagrams.

$$2\frac{3}{4} - 1\frac{5}{6} = 2 + \frac{3}{4} - 1 - \frac{5}{6}$$
$$= 1 + \frac{3}{4} - \frac{5}{6}$$
$$= 1 + \frac{9}{12} - \frac{10}{12}$$
$$= 1 - \frac{1}{12}$$
$$= \frac{11}{12}$$

- Work through Examples 4 and 5 on pages 40–41 of the Student Book.
- **Students can now do Exercise 2B from the Student Book.**

N 1, 3, 4a, 9	Calculator n/a	CM 6, 7, 10a, 11a	MR 2, 10b	PS 5, 8	EV 4b, 11b

Part 3

- Write this calculation on the board: $\frac{1}{2} + \frac{1}{3} - \frac{1}{4} - \frac{1}{6}$

- Discuss strategies and how to make sure students find the answer most efficiently. $\left(\frac{6}{12} + \frac{4}{12} - \frac{3}{12} - \frac{2}{12} = \frac{5}{12}\right)$

- Ask students to use the fraction button on their calculators to check their answers and correct any errors.
- **Less able** students who have not completed the exercise may use a calculator to do so.
- Give students several addition and subtraction questions to complete. Show some answers under a visualiser. Ask students to discuss the method and accuracy.

Section 2.3 Multiplying and dividing fractions

Learning objectives
- Multiply proper fractions
- Multiply mixed numbers
- Divide by fractions

Resources and homework
- Student Book 2.3: pages 42–44
- Practice Book 2.3: pages 14–16

Making mathematical connections
- Rearranging simple formulae containing fractions
- Solving equations containing fractions

Making cross-curricular connections
- **Food Technology** – calculating the required fractions of ingredients
- **Science** – calculating with fractions in physics
- **Relevance** – using fractions in day-to-day calculations

Prior learning
- Students should now the multiplication tables to 10 × 10 and be able to cancel fractions. They should also be familiar with multiplication of fractions.
- Students should also be able to convert between mixed numbers and improper fractions.

Working mathematically
- Students should be able to understand and fluently execute methods involving the four operations with fractions, extending to mixed numbers and questions with more operations.

Common misconceptions and remediation
- Students work out multiplications incorrectly, e.g. $3 \times 3 = 6$, and make errors converting mixed numbers to improper fractions. Stress the importance of knowing the multiplication tables .When multiplying mixed numbers, students may multiply the whole numbers and then the fractions, e.g. giving $1\frac{1}{2} \times 2\frac{1}{4} = 2\frac{1}{8}$ instead of $3\frac{3}{8}$. Point out errors as they occur.
- When dividing fractions, students often simply divide the numerators and denominators (as in multiplying) or find the reciprocal of the wrong fraction (or of both fractions). Encourage students to estimate answers first, e.g. $8\frac{5}{6} \div 1\frac{2}{5} \approx 9 \div 1\frac{1}{2} = 6$.

Probing questions
- Write down two fractions that multiply together to give a bigger answer than either of the fractions you are multiplying. How did you do it?
- What do you know about dividing by a number between 0 and 1?

Literacy focus
- Key term: reciprocal
- Ask students to write a bulleted list of their method for answering this type of question.

Part 1
- Remind students that they learned how to multiply proper fractions in Key Stage 3. They may need further reinforcement of the rule.
- Ask students some quickfire multiplications of fractions, e.g.
$\frac{1}{2} \times \frac{1}{2}\left(\frac{1}{4}\right), \frac{1}{2} \times \frac{1}{3}\left(\frac{1}{6}\right), \frac{1}{5} \times \frac{1}{3}\left(\frac{1}{15}\right), \frac{1}{8} \times \frac{1}{4}\left(\frac{1}{32}\right)$.

- Move on to questions involving non-unit fractions, e.g. $\frac{2}{3} \times \frac{1}{2} \left(\frac{2}{6} = \frac{1}{3} \right)$ and remind students to give all answers in their simplest form.
- Check that students know how to find the reciprocal of fractions and mixed numbers. Ask students for the reciprocal of:

$\frac{1}{3} \left(\frac{3}{1} = 3 \right), \frac{2}{7} \left(\frac{7}{2} \right), \frac{3}{4} \left(\frac{4}{3} \right), \frac{2}{5} \left(\frac{5}{2} \right), 1\frac{1}{4} \left(\frac{4}{5} \right)$, because $1\frac{1}{4} = \frac{5}{4}$ Explain, if necessary, that the reciprocal of a fraction can be found by inverting the fraction.

Part 2

Multiplying fractions

- Draw a 2 by 5 rectangle and shade half of it, as shown.
- Ask students what one-fifth of the half is ($\frac{1}{10}$ or one square) and write $\frac{1}{5} \times \frac{1}{2} = \frac{1}{10}$.
- Ask students how they can get the answer from the fractions. If necessary, prompt **less able** students by writing more fraction calculations on the board.
- Establish that the rule is to multiply the numerators and multiply the denominators, then cancel if possible.
- Ask students how they will deal with multiplying mixed numbers, prompting them to change to improper fractions, then work through Example 6 on page 42 of the Student Book.
- Check that students can change mixed numbers into improper fractions, e.g.

$1\frac{7}{18} \left(\frac{25}{18} \right), 3\frac{1}{3} \left(\frac{10}{3} \right)$ and $1\frac{9}{20} \left(\frac{29}{20} \right)$

Reciprocal of a fraction; Dividing fractions

- Write on the board: $3 \div \frac{3}{4} = 4$ and $3 \times \frac{4}{3} = 4$. Explain that dividing by a fraction is the same as multiplying by its reciprocal.
- Ask: How many halves in 6? ($6 \div \frac{1}{2} = 6 \times 2 = 12$).
- Work through Example 7 on page 43 of the Student Book. Students often find this a difficult concept so give more examples, as required.
- Remind students that, to divide mixed numbers, they must first change the mixed numbers into improper fractions.
- **Students can now do Exercise 2C from the Student Book.**

| N 1–8, 10 | Calculator n/a | CM 9, 11, 13a | MR n/a | PS 12 | EV 13b |

Part 3

- Write on the board: $1\frac{2}{5} \times 2\frac{3}{7} = \frac{7}{5} \times \frac{17}{7}$. Tell students that if they simplify the fractions as soon as possible, they will be working with smaller numbers. Show that they should still get the correct answer if they work out $\frac{7 \times 17}{5 \times 7} = \frac{119}{35}$ and then simplify $\frac{17}{5}$.
- Discuss the following disadvantages: working with large numbers creates more chance of an error; not being able to spot common factors, so the answer is not reduced to its simplest form.
- Students can use calculators to check their answers and correct errors. **Less able** students who have not completed the exercise could use a calculator for any remaining questions.
- Look at the different format of fractions on calculator displays and ensure that students write the fractions as, e.g. $\frac{3}{4}$ and not $3 \rfloor 4$.
- Give students several multiplication and division questions to complete. Show some answers under a visualiser. Ask the class to discuss the method and accuracy.

Section 2.4 Fractions on a calculator

Learning objectives

- Use a calculator to add and subtract fractions
- Use a calculator to multiply and divide fractions

Resources and homework

- Student Book 2.4: pages 44–48
- Practice Book 2.4: pages 16–17

Making mathematical connections

- Efficient use of a calculator

Making cross-curricular connections

- **Food Technology** – calculating the required fractions of ingredients
- **Science** – calculating with fractions in physics
- **Relevance** – everyday calculations of fractions with a calculator

Prior learning

- Students should be able to add and subtract simple fractions without using a calculator.

Working mathematically

- Using a calculator effectively is a valuable skill that students need to learn.
- Make sure that all students have an appropriate calculator.

Common misconceptions and remediation

- The most common mistakes are errors made in keying the calculation and then not checking that the answer is sensible.

Probing questions

- Provide students with some fraction questions and answers with common errors and ask them to identify the mistake in each calculation.
- When would it be appropriate to use a calculator rather than a standard written method?

Literary focus

- Key term: shift key
- Ask students to write a step-by-step guide for using a calculator to answer calculations with fractions.

Part 1

- **Note:** Students must have scientific calculators for this lesson.
- Explain to students how to enter fractions on a calculator. Give them several fractions, including mixed numbers, to key in.

Part 2

Using a calculator to convert improper fractions to mixed numbers

- Go through this section on page 45 of the Student Book. Give students practice converting between improper fractions and mixed numbers. E.g. ask students to key in $\frac{16}{7}$ on their calculators and check that they can convert it to a mixed number ($2\frac{2}{7}$). Repeat with other improper fractions.

- If students do not get the correct answers, ask them to follow the keying instructions.
  Using a calculator to convert mixed numbers to improper fractions
- Go through this section with students. Then give them practice in converting between mixed numbers and improper fractions. E.g. ask students to key in $4\frac{3}{5}$ on their calculators and check that they can convert it to an improper fraction ($\frac{23}{5}$). Ask them to convert it back to a mixed number. Repeat with other mixed numbers.
- If students struggle, ask them to follow the keying instructions.

  Using a calculator to add and subtract fractions
- Go through Examples 8 and 9 and give students some more questions to try. They could display their results on mini whiteboards.

  Using a calculator to multiply and divide fractions
- Go through Examples 10 and 11 with students and give them some more questions to try. Again, they could display their results on mini whiteboards.
- **Students can now do Exercise 2D from Student Book.**

N 1–3, 4a, 5, 7–9	Calculator all	CM 4b	MR 11, 14	PS 6, 12, 13, 15	EV 10

Part 3

- Ask students to key this pattern of multiplications into their calculators.
  $$1\frac{1}{2} \times 2\frac{2}{3} \times 3\frac{3}{4} \times 4\frac{4}{5} \times 5\frac{5}{6} \times 6\frac{6}{7} \dots$$
- Ask students to look at the answers as they are keying in the multiplications and to tell you what they notice. (Every time they multiply a pair of numbers, the answer is a whole number.) With **more able** groups, prove this, using algebra.
  $$1\frac{1}{2} \times 2\frac{2}{3} = 4$$
  $$1\frac{1}{2} \times 2\frac{2}{3} \times 3\frac{3}{4} \times 4\frac{4}{5} = 72$$
  $$1\frac{1}{2} \times 2\frac{2}{3} \times 3\frac{3}{4} \times 4\frac{4}{5} \times 5\frac{5}{6} \times 6\frac{6}{7} = 2880$$
- Give students a quick calculator test to check that they can use the calculator efficiently. Either read out the following questions or write them on the board.

  1 $1\frac{1}{2} + 3\frac{2}{3} \left(5\frac{1}{6}\right)$

  2 $7\frac{5}{12} - 2\frac{1}{4} \left(5\frac{1}{6}\right)$

  3 $1\frac{1}{12} + 2\frac{3}{8} + 1\frac{17}{24} \left(5\frac{1}{6}\right)$

  4 $5\frac{3}{5} + 2\frac{1}{4} - 2\frac{41}{60} \left(5\frac{1}{6}\right)$

  5 $6\frac{3}{4} + 2\frac{1}{6} - 3\frac{2}{3} \left(5\frac{1}{4}\right)$

- Point out to students the potential for errors if they assume they know an answer rather than working it out.

Section 2.5 Increasing and decreasing quantities by a percentage

Learning objectives
- Increase and decrease quantities by a percentage

Resources and homework
- Student Book 2.5: pages 48–51
- Practice Book 2.5: pages 17–18

Making mathematical connections
- Profit and loss
- Compound interest

Making cross-curricular connections
- **Business** – net profit, VAT
- **Geography** – population increase
- **Relevance** – everyday use in calculating VAT, prices of items at sales, etc.

Prior learning
- Students should know how to work out a percentage of a quantity and be able to convert simple percentages to fractions such as $5\% = \dfrac{5}{100}$.

Working mathematically
- The answer to a percentage decrease question is £100. Ask students to make up one easy question and one hard question that gives this answer.
- Repeat for a percentage increase question.

Common misconceptions and remediation
- Students often make errors when asked to increase or decrease a quantity by a percentage, as they may misread the question and simply work out the percentage. For example, when asked to increase 30 by 5%, students work out 5% of 30 but forget to add it on to the original amount to reach the required answer.
- Encourage students to reread the questions to check that they have answered them correctly.

Probing questions
- Explain how you would increase or decrease £170 by 15%. Can you do it in a different way?
- How would you find the multiplier for different percentage increases and decreases?
- How can you tell whether a multiplier will result in an increase or a decrease?

Literacy focus
- Key term: multiplier
- Ask students to write a step-by-step guide on how to increase or decrease by a percentage.
-

Part 1
- Revise the use of percentage multipliers by asking questions such as: What is 2% as a multiplier? (0.02). Include some of the more difficult questions such as: What is 0.8% as a multiplier? (0.008); What is 3.4% as a multiplier? (0.034).
- To check prior knowledge, ask questions about working out a percentage of a quantity, such as: How would you work out 13% of 40? Lead on to questions involving increasing by a percentage, such as: How would you increase an amount by 13%? (Students may suggest working out 13% and adding it on.) Repeat for other values.

- Move on to decreasing by a percentage. Ask students how they would work out 6% of 70. Then ask how they would decrease 70 by 6%.
- Ask students what multiplier they would use to increase an amount by 13% (1.13).

Part 2

Increasing by a percentage

- Display the following table of multipliers.

1.05	0.05	0.95	1.5	0.5
0.85	0.15	1.15	0.25	1.25
0.75	0.55	0.45	1.55	1.45

- Ask students questions about the multipliers, starting with simple percentages: What percentage is equivalent to the multiplier: 0.05? (5%), 0.45? (45%), 0.5? (50%) and so on.
- Now ask what percentage is equivalent to the multiplier 1.25 (125%). Check that students understand that this represents a 25% increase. Repeat for 1.5 (50% increase), 1.15 (15% increase), 1.05 (5% increase) and 1.55 (55% increase).
- Work through Examples 12 and 13 in the Student Book.
- Point out that students can use the 'adding on' or 'subtracting' methods but they also need to understand the 'multiplier' method.

Decreasing by a percentage

- Ask students to identify the multiplier from the table above that represents a 5% decrease (0.95). Repeat for other decreases: 15% decrease (0.85), 25% decrease (0.75).
- Work through Examples 14 and 15 on page 49 of the Student Book.
- **Students can now do Exercise 2E from the Student Book.**

N 1–5, 8a, 9, 12	Calculator all	CM 6, 7, 10, 11, 13	MR n/a	PS 14	EV 8b 8c, 15

Part 3

- Tell students that they have £100.
  - Ask half of the class to increase their £100 by 10%, and then to decrease the answer by 10% (£99).
  - Ask the other half to decrease their £100 by 10%, and then to increase the answer by 10% (£99).
- Ask all students to show their answer on a whiteboard at the same time. Establish that the result is always £99 and ask students why it is not £100. (The decrease is from a larger amount each time.)
- Ask students to calculate the following and display their answers on mini whiteboards:
  - an increase of 12% on an original cost of £150
  - a decrease of 7% on an original cost of 560 g.

Section 2.6 Expressing one quantity as a percentage of another

Learning objectives

- Express one quantity as a percentage of another
- Work out percentage change

Resources and homework

- Student Book 2.6: pages 51–53
- Practice Book 2.6: pages 18–19

Making mathematical connections

- Probability

Making cross-curricular connections

- **All subjects** – working out your percentage exam mark from a raw score
- **Geography** – calculating percentages of sections of population such as different age groups
- **Relevance** – daily use of percentages

Prior learning

- Students should know how to use a percentage multiplier.
- They should also know how to write one quantity as a fraction of another quantity.

Working mathematically

- Ask students to explain a calculation and write down the steps they need to take to get the answer. Ask: How do you know what you have to do first?

Common misconceptions and remediation

- Students frequently forget to make sure the units of the two quantities are the same. Encourage them always to look at units carefully.
- Students often use the new value after the increase or decrease as the denominator rather than the original value. Frequently repeating the formula for percentage change should help students to remember it.

Probing questions

- Provide students with some questions and answers with common errors and ask them to identify the mistake in each calculation.
- Ask students how they would estimate the answer to a question.

Literacy focus

- Key terms: percentage change, percentage decrease, percentage increase, percentage loss, percentage profit
- Ask students to write an explanation for each key term in this section.

Part 1

- Ask mental calculation questions involving increasing or decreasing quantities by a percentage. For example:
  - Increase £50 by 10% (£55)
  - Decrease 40 kg by 25% (30 kg)
  - Increase 100 cm by 2% (102 cm)
  - Decrease 70 g by 50% (35 g)
- Ask more questions, increasing the level of difficulty for **more able** students by including decimals or fractions, e.g. Increase £18.50 by 10% (£20.35).

Part 2

- Explain that to express one quantity as a percentage of another, you write the first quantity as a fraction of the second quantity and then convert to a percentage by multiplying by 100.
- Work through Examples 16 and 17 on page 51 of the Student Book.

Percentage change

- Discuss percentage change and establish that, if the change is an increase, it is called a percentage increase.
- Ask students what they think each of the following percentage changes is called.
  - Decrease 100 cm by 2% (98 cm). Change is a decrease. (percentage decrease)
  - Increase £100 by 5% (£105). Change is a profit. (percentage profit)
  - Decrease £100 by 17% (£83). Change is a loss. (percentage loss)
- Now ask students to look at the table. Ask if they know how to get from £50 and £55 to 10%.

Original amount	Percentage change	New amount	Change
£50	+10%	£55	£5
40 kg	−25%	30 kg	10 kg
100 cm	+2%	102 cm	2 cm
70 grams	−50%	35 grams	35 grams

Add an extra column showing the change for **less able** students and ask them how to get from £5 and £50 to 10% (£5 is 10% of £50).
Repeat for the other rows in the table.

- Now write the formula on the board: Percentage change = $\dfrac{\text{change}}{\text{original amount}} \times 100$
- Show students that the formula works for each row in the table, e.g.
  for £50 to £55 (change = £5), percentage change = $\dfrac{5}{50} \times 100 = 10\%$
- Work through Example 18 on the board.

Using a multiplier (or decimal)

- Explain to students that you can also **express one quantity as a percentage of another** by dividing the first quantity by the second and then multiplying the resultant decimal by 100 to give the percentage.
- Go through Example 19 on page 52 of the Student Book.
- Encourage students to try this method on Examples 16 and 17 in the Student Book.
- **Students can now do Exercise 2F from the Student Book.**

N 1–8	Calculator all	CM 9–11	MR n/a	PS 12	EV 13

Part 3

- Ask the following questions.
  - Express 40p as a percentage of £4. (What are the obvious mistakes?)
  - Sam buys a painting for £1500 and sells it for £2000. What is Sam's percentage profit?
  - Sam buys a painting for £1500 and sells it for £1200. What is his percentage loss?
  Discuss the answers as a class.
- Ask students to write two of their own questions and solve them. Display the questions and solutions under a visualiser. Discuss the questions and answers in the class.

Chapter 3 Statistics: Statistical diagrams and averages

Overview

3.1 Statistical representation	**3.3** Scatter diagrams
3.2 Statistical measures	

Prior learning

Know how to calculate and use the mode, median and mean.
Know how to extract information from tables and diagrams.

Learning objectives

Ensure that students can: draw and interpret pie charts; draw and interpret line graphs; solve problems that use averages; calculate averages from frequency tables; draw scatter diagrams and lines of best fit.

In the examination, students will be expected to:
- draw and interpret bar charts and pie charts
- draw and interpret line graphs
- use averages to solve (more complex) problems
- identify the advantages and disadvantages of each type of average and decide which one to use in a given different situation
- work out and use the range of a set of data
- calculate the mode, the median and the mean from a frequency table
- identify the modal group
- estimate the mean from a grouped frequency table

- draw, interpret and use scatter diagrams
- draw and use a line of best fit.

Extension

Ask students to research 'correlation and causality'. This is an interesting area, which would stimulate **more able** students.
More able students could draw their lines of best fit through the mean points in order to improve accuracy.

Curriculum references

Section	GCSE specification
3.1	S 2
3.2	S 4
3.3	S 6

Route mapping

Exercise	Accessible	Intermediate	Challenging	AO1	AO2 MR CM	AO3 PS EV	Key questions
3A	1–8			1, 2, 3a–d, 4a–c, 5a, 6, 7a	3e, 4d, 7b	5b, 8	5, 7
3B	1–5			1a–c, 2, 3a–b	1d, 3c, 4	5	2, 3
3C	1–7	8–10		1, 5a, 7	2, 4, 6	3, 5b, 8–10	5, 7
3D	1–7	8, 9		1–3a, 4, 5a–d, 6	3b, 5e, f, 8	7, 9	5, 6
3E	1–10			1, 2, 3a–c, 4, 5a–b, 7	3d, 5c, 6, 9, 10	8	2, 3
3F	1–8			1–5a, 6a–d	5b, 6e, 8	7	6

Key questions are those that demonstrate mastery of the concept, or which require a step-up in understanding or application. Key questions could be used to identify the questions that students must tackle, to support differentiation, or to identify the questions that should be teacher-marked rather than student-marked.

About this chapter

Making connections: Statistical diagrams are an important way to view and interpret information.

Relevance: Statistical graphs are seen every day and analysing them is an important skill that is necessary for many jobs. Think how many times you have seen statistical diagrams being shown or interpreted on television.

Working mathematically: Students should understand that pie charts are suited to categorical data, and they should be able to draw pie charts using an electronic device or by hand. Students should also be able to draw compound bar charts with subcategories and use frequency diagrams for continuous data. Students should be able to find the mean from a grouped frequency table. In addition, students should be able to use scatter graphs for continuous data with two variables, showing, for example, height against weight.

Assessment: In each section of this chapter, ensure that students have a good grasp of the key questions in each exercise before moving on. (Refer to the 'Route mapping' table above.) Encourage students to read and think about the 'Ready to progress?' statements on page 82 of the Student Book. Check students' understanding at the end of the chapter, formatively, using peer assessment. Students could do a mini test in the form of the 'Review questions' on pages 82–85 of the Student Book. Follow up the test with an individual target-getting session based on any areas for development that a student may have.

Worked exemplars from the Student Book – suggestions for use

- Present students with the same questions but using different numbers. Students should use the exemplars to mirror their working, in full, or using only the notes.
- Copy and cut the exemplars into cards. Students should match the working with the notes.
- Ask students to write their own questions and set them out as exemplar questions.

Answers to the Student Book questions are available on the CD-ROM provided.

Section 3.1 Statistical representation

Learning objectives

- Draw and interpret bar charts and pie charts
- Draw and interpret line graphs

Resources and homework

- Student Book 3.1: pages 59–65
- Practice Book 3.1: pages 20–21

Making mathematical connections

- Angle theorems
- Linear graphs

Making cross-curricular connections

- **Geography** – various areas including, e.g. representing weather, climate, populations
- **Economics and Business Studies** – interpreting financial graphs
- **Physical education** – interpreting data on sports participation
- **Relevance** – interpreting data in daily life

Prior learning

- Students should know how to extract information from tables and diagrams.
- They should know that there are 360 degrees in a circle and be able to draw a circle using a compass.

Working mathematically

- The questions in Exercise 3A of the Student Book require students to apply their learning to real-life problems involving pie charts and line graphs.
- Students are also required to make links to fractions. You may want to revisit comparing simple fractions if **less able** students struggle with the required comparisons.

Common misconceptions and remediation

- Students struggle to transfer their understanding of angles, fractions and percentages to the interpretation of pie charts. Careful use of the correct mathematical language will help.
- The most common mistake students make with line graphs is the poor choice, or incorrect use, of scales to represent times. Students also often make intermediate or future estimates without giving realistic thought to the data. Point out these errors as soon as they occur.

Probing questions

- What information do you need to work out the angles in each category for a pie chart?

Literacy focus

- Key terms: line graph, trend
- Ask students to use the word 'trend' in a sentence involving statistical interpretation.
- Show students a pie chart and ask them to make up a statement or question for it using one or more of these words: fraction, percentage, proportion.

Part 1

- Write 120 on the board and ask: What is half of 120? (60); What is $\frac{1}{3}$ of 120? (40); What is $\frac{1}{4}$ of 120? (30); What is $\frac{1}{6}$ of 120? (20). Discuss with the class how they worked these out.
- Repeat for 180, then for 300.

Part 2

Bar charts and pie charts

- Work though the text and Examples 1 and 2 on page 60 of the Student Book.
- Draw a circle on the board and introduce the idea of a circle representing data (pie chart).
- Draw some simple radii in the circle and explain that each category is represented by a sector of the circle (a slice of the pie).
- Draw another circle (pie chart) and mark a sector of 90°.
  Say that this pie chart represents the car sales in a showroom on one weekend.
  Label the 90-degree sector 'British' and say: 'This sector represents the British cars sold.'
  Label the rest 'Foreign' and say: 'This sector represents the foreign cars sold.'
- Ask: If 40 cars were sold, how many of them were British?

  The sector shown is one-quarter of the pie, so $\frac{1}{4}$ of the 40 cars that were sold were British.

  What is $\frac{1}{4}$ of 40? (10)
- Ask: How many foreign cars were sold? (The remainder, 30)
- Go through Examples 3 and 4 on pages 61 and 62 of the Student Book, explaining how to calculate the angles in a pie chart.
- **Students can now do Exercise 3A from the Student Book.**

S 1–7	Calculator all	CM n/a	MR 3e, 4d, 7b	PS 8	EV 5b

Line graphs

- Draw a bar chart using the data from Example 5, which represents outside temperatures at various times.
- Ask: Why is this type of bar chart not very helpful?
  Lead to the response that it does not tell you about the temperatures in between the marked points in time.
- Mark a cross on the middle of the top of each bar in the chart and join the crosses. Students should agree that this is better. (If necessary, demonstrate to **less able** students the reason why it is a better method.)
- Explain that line graphs are often used instead of bar charts when time is involved. Point to a position along the line and ask what time it represents for the temperature at that point. On a line graph, it is possible to make estimates between given values.
- Introduce the term 'time series' although students do not need it yet.
- Look at Example 5 again and explain that although the temperature was taken only at certain times, it is still a time series, as time is continuous.
- **Students can now do Exercise 3B from the Student Book.**

S 1–3	Calculator n/a	CM n/a	MR 1d, 3c, 4	PS 5	EV n/a

Part 3

- Lead a class discussion about the value of line graphs. Ask questions such as: When can they be used? Why can they be useful?
- On the board, sketch a pie chart with random angles, and label the sectors, for example: Blue, Red, Green, and so on. Say that this pie chart represents the colours of 100 cars. Ask students to estimate the percentage of each sector.

Learning objectives

- Use averages to solve problems
- Identify the advantages and disadvantages of each type of average and learn which one to use in different situations
- Work out and use the range of a data set
- Calculate the mode, the median and the mean from a frequency table
- Identify the modal group and estimate the mean from a grouped frequency table

Resources and homework

- Student Book 3.2: pages 65–74
- Practice Book 3.2: pages 22–24

Making mathematical connections

- Histograms with unequal class widths

Making cross-curricular connections

- **Geography** – averages of, e.g. temperature, population
- **Science** – averages from experimental data
- **Relevance** – working out averages in daily life

Prior learning

- Students should know how to calculate the mean, mode, median and range from small sets of discrete data.

Working mathematically

- There are several ways to express an average, including mode, median, mean.
- An average must be representative of a set of data. When you need to find an average, you must choose one that accurately represents the data. The wrong average will be misleading.

Common misconceptions and remediation

- Students may confuse the three averages. Regularly remind them of the definitions.
- Students often forget to order data before finding the median or make errors when finding the median of an even set of numbers. Remind them to add the middle two, then halve.
- At Higher level, students often make the error of using $\bar{x} = \frac{\Sigma fx}{\Sigma x}$ rather than $\bar{x} = \frac{\Sigma fx}{\Sigma f}$. If they label columns clearly and write the correct formula, this should not occur.

Probing questions

- Discuss the reasons why group widths of a certain size might be chosen before collecting a sample. (All the same width? When might it make sense to choose different widths?)
- Why can we only estimate the mean (median, range) from grouped data?
- Why do we use the mid-point of the group interval when calculating an estimated mean? Why not use the end of the group interval?

Literacy focus

- Key terms: continuous data, discrete data, estimate of the mean, measure of location, modal group
- Make a list of each key term with its meaning.

Part 1

- Encourage an initial discussion on averages. Establish a single number used to represent all the data. Why is there a need for three types of averages? Describe each type.
- Remind students of the inequality symbols: $<$, $>$, $\geq$ and $\leq$.
- Introduce and explain terms such as 'lower class boundary' and 'upper class boundary' for each interval. Explain why it is best to use inequalities when describing continuous intervals, rather than simply expressing a range such as 0–10, 10–15.

Part 2

Averages; The range

- Write a simple list such as: 2, 2, 2, 3, 3, 4, 4, 4. Ask for the mode (2 and 4). Students may say 'no mode' or 'two modes'. Emphasise that there can be more than one mode and 'no mode' occurs only if every number has the same frequency.
- Write a list with an even number of items and ask for the median. Discuss how to find this (find the mean of the two middle values). Work through another example.
- Using the table on page 66 of the Student Book for reference, discuss each type of average, why we use them, their advantages and disadvantages. Reinforce that only the mean considers every value and this is why we may, incorrectly, call the mean the average.
- Go through Example 6, showing how to calculate the range and explaining why the mean is the best average in this case.
- **Students can now do Exercise 3C from the Student Book.**

S 1, 5, 7	Calculator all	CM n/a	MR 2, 4, 6	PS 3, 8–10	EV 5b

Frequency tables; Using your calculator

- Work through Example 7. Explain that you usually round your answer when you calculate the mean. The degree of accuracy should be to one more sf than the data items. Point out that the mean should always have a unit, e.g. number of people.
- Show students how to use the statistical functions on their calculators to answer Example 7.
- **Students can now do Exercise 3D from the Student Book.**

S 1–6	Calculator all	CM 3b, 5e, 5f	MR 8	PS 7, 9	EV n/a

Grouped frequency tables

- Say: We all spend different amounts of money on lunch, so it would not be practical to set up a table with a row for each amount. It would be better to use ranges, e.g. Less than £1, £1–£1.99... Demonstrate that data must fall into only one group.
- Build a table from the class data and/or work through each step of Example 8.
- Discuss the modal group or modal class (the group with the largest frequency). Why is it not possible to find the mode? (exact numbers within each group are unknown)
- Explain how to estimate the mean. Estimate the total amount of money for each group by multiplying the midpoint amount (assume that all the data values in a group take the midpoint amount – a full range of values is expected within each group, with as many values above the halfway value as below) by the frequency. Total these values then divide by the total frequency and round appropriately.
- **Students can now do Exercise 3E from the Student Book.**

S 1–5, 7	Calculator all	CM 6, 9	MR 3d, 5c, 10	PS 8	EV n/a

Part 3

- Recap how to find a mean using the statistics mode of a scientific calculator. Demonstrate by checking (or asking students to check) relevant answers from the exercises.

Section 3.3 Scatter diagrams

Learning objectives
- Draw, interpret and use scatter diagrams
- Draw and use a line of best fit

Resources and homework
- Student Book 3.3: pages 74–78
- Practice Book 3.3: page 25

Making mathematical connections
- Lines of regression

Making cross-curricular connections
- **Science** – finding a relationship between bivariate data from an experiment
  Relevance – working with related data in daily life

Prior learning
- In terms of statistical work, no prior knowledge is needed for studying the topic in this lesson.
- Students should be able to use appropriate scales on axes and be able to interpret intermediate positions within the scales.

Working mathematically
- It is useful to explain to students that the line of best fit should have as many values above it as below it. **More able** students could plot the mean point and draw their lines of best fit through it.
- No correlation indicates that there is no clear link between the two sets of data, which is sometimes useful to know.

Common misconceptions and remediation
- Students often draw lines of best fit inappropriately. Remind them that the line need not necessarily go through the origin and that, in some cases, it will not go through any plotted points.

Probing questions
- Why might reading a value from a line of best fit be subject to error?
- What problems might you encounter if you extend a line of best fit beyond known values?
- When might it not be sensible to draw a line of best fit on a scatter diagram?

Literacy focus
- Key terms: line of best fit, negative correlation, no correlation, outlier, positive correlation, scatter diagram
- Ask students to describe in words the relationship between the data sets.

Part 1
- Draw a straight-line graph on a coordinate grid. Give the value of one variable and ask students to find the corresponding value of the other variable.

Part 2

- Ask: If you get a good mark in a Mathematics test, are you likely also to get a good mark in an English test? Discuss trends and the fact that some people 'buck the trend'.
- The scatter diagram on page 74 of the Student Book shows Mathematics and English results. Mention that these points have been plotted from data and that the pattern they show clearly demonstrates that, for this group of students, there is a clear link between a good English mark and a good Mathematics mark – the higher the English mark, the higher the Mathematics mark.

Correlation

- Introduce the word 'correlation' and explain that, in this case, the diagram indicates positive correlation – the bigger one variable gets, the bigger the other gets.
- Explain that this is not always the case. Talk about the three diagrams that show positive correlation, negative correlation and no correlation. Ensure that students grasp the clear difference between positive and negative correlation.
- Extend this discussion with **more able** students to include strong positive and weak positive correlation, and the equivalent negative correlations. Some patterns show a slight correlation that can be described as weak, or a clear link, hence strong. Show students some examples.
- Work through Example 9.

Line of best fit

- Direct students to look at the diagrams illustrating lines of best fit on page 76. Ask them to describe the lines. If necessary, explain lines of best fit in more detail. There should be just one straight line that shows the trend. Mention that it does not need to go through any of the given points, nor through the origin, but should be as close to them all as possible, with the same number above as below.
- Explain 'outliers' to **more able** students: these are points that clearly buck the trend. This will sometimes happen and, as long as only one or two are in the data set, they can be ignored. Mention that a line of best fit can be a curve, but it must be only one smooth curve and not an attempt to join every point together.
- Ask questions about missing marks from the set in the diagram such as: What English mark might you expect from the girl who gained 75 marks in the Mathematics test? (73) Ensure that students know how to use the line of best fit to answer such a question and, if necessary, ask and work through further questions explaining the method carefully. Emphasise to **more able** students that this is only an approximation.
- **Students can now do Exercise 3F from the Student Book.**

| S 1–6 | Calculator all | CM 5b, 6e, 8 | MR n/a | PS 7 | EV n/a |

Part 3

- Ask students for examples of variables that would give the different types of correlation. They should provide examples to show: positive, negative and no correlation.

Chapter 4 Algebra: Number and sequences

Overview

4.1 Patterns in number	**4.5** General rules from given patterns
4.2 Number sequences	**4.6** The *n*th term of a quadratic sequence
4.3 Finding the *n*th term of a linear sequence	**4.7** Finding the *n*th term for quadratic sequences
4.4 Special sequences	

Prior learning

Know how to substitute numbers into an algebraic expression.
Know how to state in words a rule for a simple linear sequence.
Know how to factorise simple linear expressions.
Know how to expand a pair of linear brackets to get a quadratic expression.

Learning objectives

Ensure that students can: recognise rules for sequences; express a rule for a sequence, in words and algebraically; generate the terms of linear and quadratic sequences, given a formula for the *n*th term; find the *n*th term of linear and quadratic sequences; find some common sequences of numbers.

In the examination, students will be expected to:
*   recognise patterns in number sequences
*   recognise how number sequences are built up
*   generate sequences, given the *n*th term
*   work out the *n*th term of a linear sequence
*   recognise and continue some special number sequences
*   find the *n*th term from practical problems involving sequences
*   generate the terms of a quadratic sequence, given the *n*th term
*   work out the *n*th term of a quadratic sequence.

Extension

Formally introduce the equations involved in arithmetic and geometric progressions to prepare **more able** students for A Level.

Curriculum references

Section	GCSE specification
4.1	A 23
4.2	A 2, 23, 24
4.3	A 2, 23, 24, 25
4.4	A 2, 23, 24, 25
4.5	A 2, 23, 24, 25
4.6	A 2, 23, 24, 25
4.7	A 2, 23, 24, 25

Route mapping

Exercise	Accessible	Intermediate	Challenging	AO1	AO2 MR CM	AO3 PS EV	Key questions
4A	1–4	5	6, 7	1–4	5, 7	6	7
4B	1–3	4	5–11	1–6	9–11	7, 8	5, 6
4C	1–4	5, 6	7–12	1–7	9, 10a–c, 11	8, 10d, 12	2, 3
4D	1–4	5–14	15–17	1, 3a, 3c, 7–10, 14, 15	2, 3b, 4–6, 11–13	16, 17	7, 9
4E	1–5	6–8	9–13	1–8a, 9a, 9b	8b, 11, 12	9c, 10, 13	11, 12
4F	1	2–5	6–12	1–5, 7	6, 9b, 12	8, 9a, 10, 11	6, 7
4G			1–10	1–4	6	5, 7–10	4

Key questions are those that demonstrate mastery of the concept, or which require a step-up in understanding or application. Key questions could be used to identify the questions that students must tackle, to support differentiation, or to identify the questions that should be teacher-marked rather than student-marked.

About this chapter

Making connections: The chapter covers all the main areas of sequences, including quadratic and graphical representation of sequences. The next step is A Level content.

Relevance: There is an emphasis on the use of logic and thinking in steps. There are applications in engineering, architecture, manufacturing, project management and many other areas; STEM careers are a strong focus.

Working mathematically: How do you know if a sequence is linear or quadratic? Explain to students how they would find the general rule for a linear sequence. Explain how they would find the rule for a quadratic sequence.

Assessment: In each section of this chapter, ensure that students have a good grasp of the key questions in each exercise before moving on. (Refer to the 'Route mapping' table above.) Encourage students to read and think about the 'Ready to progress?' statements on page 114 of the Student Book. Check students' understanding at the end of the chapter, formatively, using peer assessment. Students could do a mini test in the form of the 'Review questions' on pages 114–115 of the Student Book. Follow up the test with an individual target-getting session, based on any areas for development that a student may have.

Worked exemplars from the Student Book – suggestions for use

- Present students with the same question but using different numbers. Students should use the exemplars to mirror the working, in full or only using the notes.
- Copy and cut the exemplar into cards. Students should be able to match the working with the notes. (You may need to remove the words 'first, second', and so on.)
- Ask students to write their own questions and set them out as exemplars.

Answers to the Student Book questions are available on the CD-ROM provided.

Section 4.1 Patterns in number

Learning objectives
- Recognise patterns in number sequences

Resources and homework
- Student Book 4.1: pages 87–88
- Practice Book 4.1: page 26

Making mathematical connections
Binomial expansion

Making cross-curricular connections
- **Science** – using formulae
- **Relevance** – developing logical thinking

Prior learning
- Students should be confident with multiplication tables up to 12×12.
- Students should be able to recognise number patterns.

Working mathematically
- Spotting patterns in numbers is an important part of Mathematics. It will help students to form and see rules when they make calculations.

Common misconceptions and remediation
- Students will need to be accurate at each step when generating number patterns. A single mistake will cause the pattern to go wrong.

Probing questions
- Ask students questions about the $11\times$ table, for example:
  - $11 \times 34 = 374$
  - $11 \times 23 = 253$
- Ask them to identify a pattern in the numbers that they can use to work these out quickly. With reference to $11 \times 23 = 253$:
  - Write down the first digit. (2)
  - Add the digits. $(2 + 3 = 5)$
  - Write down the last digit. (3)
- Will this work when the two digits add up to more than 9? How would you overcome this?

Literacy focus
- Key terms: pattern, sequence
- Ask students to write a step-by-step guide on how one of the four sequences in the Student Book is generated.

Part 1

- Kaprekar's sequence produces some interesting number patterns. Ask students to follow the method and look for patterns throughout the process.
    1. Write down a two-digit number. (e.g. 39)
    2. Reverse the digits. (93)
    3. Subtract the smaller number from the larger number. (93 – 39 = 54)
    4. Repeat steps **2–4** using this as the new starting number. (54 – 45 = 9; 90 – 09 = 81; 81 – 18 = 63…)
- Ask: Can you see any patterns? (9× table)
    Does Kaprekar's sequence work for all numbers? (No, 11, 22, 33, 44 …)
    Why not?
- Now ask students to try the sequence with three-digit numbers. Does the same pattern occur?

Part 2

- Go through Pascal's triangle with students. Start the sequence for students and ask them to finish it, as shown below.

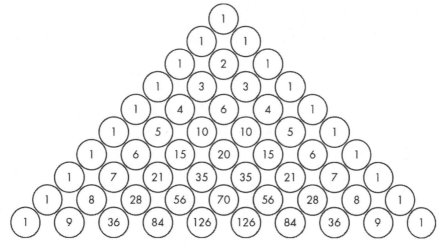

- Now ask students to look for patterns in the sequence, e.g. odd and even numbers, diagonal lines, sum of the numbers in each row.
- Work through the four number patterns on page 87 of the Student Book.
- **Students can now do Exercise 4A from the Student Book.**

A 1–4	Calculator n/a	CM 7	MR 5	PS n/a	EV 6

Part 3

- Ask students to do repeated additions with the number 9. For example:

Multiples of 9
- $9 \times 3 = 27$ Now add the digits $2 + 7 = 9$
- $9 \times 39 = 351$ $3 + 5 + 1 = 9$
- $9 \times 393 = 3537$ $3 + 5 + 3 + 7 = 18$ and again: $1 + 8 = 9$

Powers of 9
- $9^3 = 729$ Now add the digits $7 + 2 + 9 = 18$ and again $1 + 8 = 9$
- $9^5 = 59049$ $5 + 9 + 0 + 4 + 9 = 27$ $2 + 7 = 9$
- $9^9 = 387420489$ $3 + 8 + 7 + 4 + 2 + 0 + 4 + 8 + 9 = 45$ $4 + 5 = 9$
- Ask students to come up with their own ideas for repeated 9 addition.

Section 4.2 Number sequences

Learning objectives

- Recognise how number sequences are built up
- Generate sequences, given the *n*th term

Resources and homework

- Student Book 4.2: pages 89–92
- Practice Book 4.2: pages 26–27

Making mathematical connections

- Substitution into expressions

Making cross-curricular connections

- **Science** – using formulae
- **ICT** – generating number sequence
- **Relevance** – developing logical thinking

Prior learning

- Students need to know how to substitute into simple expressions.

Working mathematically

- Use a spreadsheet to produce sequences and explore term-to-term rules. What happens 'if'?

Common misconceptions and remediation

- Students find sequences accessible and usually do well. They make errors mainly with methods, which can be addressed with more practice.
- **Less able** students may, for example, double the 5th term to work out the 10th term. Point out that this will not work.
- Another common error is to look only at the first two numbers and assume that the rest follow this pattern. Stress the importance of using all the information provided and using this to check that their sequences work.

Probing questions

- The term-to-term rule for a sequence is +5. Is this enough information to generate the sequence? What else do you need?

Literacy focus

- Key terms: coefficient, consecutive, difference, *n*th term, term, term-to-term
- Make sure students are familiar with the other bold words in the text.
- Ask students to describe a sequence in words.

Part 1

- Write the numbers 2 and 4 on the board. Ask students what the next two numbers in the pattern could be. The most likely answer is 6 and 8. Write this on the board and ask how the pattern is building up (+2 each time).
- Now write 2, 4, 8, 16, … on the board and ask how this is building up (×2).
- Write 2, 4, 7, 11, … on the board and ask students how this is building up (+ 2 + 3 + 4 …).
- Repeat with 1, 5, …, asking for more series starting with these numbers and a description of how each one builds up.

Part 2

- Students suggest some sequences and describe how they build up.
- First ask for sequences that increase by a fixed amount, such as +3.
- Then ask for sequences that decrease by a fixed amount, such as –4. Then ask for sequences that increase by a different amount each time, such as +1, +2, +3, ... or +2, +4, +6.
- Next ask for sequences that multiply by a fixed number each time, such as ×2. As these will increase very quickly, keep the starting numbers simple or allow calculators.
- Now ask for sequences that divide by a fixed number each time, such as ÷10. These soon become decimals, often recurring, so stick to ÷2, ÷5 or ÷10.
- Most students can usually see intuitively how these patterns build up.

Differences

- Use the introductory text and Example 1 on page 89 of the Student Book to demonstrate how to use differences. This may confuse some **less able** students, so work through more examples until all students grasp the idea.

Generalising to find the rule

- Work through Example 2. **Less able** students may find the concept of the general term difficult. It might help to present it as: 4, 4 + 1 × 3, 4 + 2 × 3, and so on. It is, essentially, adding a term that is itself increasing by a rule.
- Work through Example 3 to reinforce the concept and method.
- Make sure students understand that the series builds up according to the 'term-to-term rule'.
- **Students can now do Exercise 4B from the Student Book.**
- **Less able** students can complete the questions in pairs, if necessary. Provide support as needed.

A 1–6	Calculator n/a	CM 9–11	MR n/a	PS 7, 8	EV n/a

Part 3

- Write some 'silly' sequences on the board and ask for the next term. For example:
  - 31, 28, 31, 30, 31, 30, ... (31: days in the months)
  - O, T, T, F, F, ... (S: initial letters of the numbers, one, two, three, ...)
  - 1, 2, 5, 10, 20, ... (50: British coins).
- Ask students to think of or find some silly or unusual sequences for a future lesson.
- Challenge students, in pairs, to create their own sequences from a general rule.

Section 4.3 Finding the *n*th term of a linear sequence

Learning objectives

*   Find the *n*th term of a linear sequence

Resources and homework

*   Student Book 4.3: pages 92–95
*   Practice Book 4.3: pages 27–28

Making mathematical connections

*   Equations, expressions identities and functions

Making cross-curricular connections

*   **Computing** – generating number sequences
*   **ICT** – using spreadsheets
*   **Relevance** – developing logical thinking

Prior learning

*   Students should be able to recognise number patterns and know how to find differences between consecutive terms.

Working mathematically

*   Use a spreadsheet to produce sequences and explore the position-to-term rules. What happens 'if'?

Common misconceptions and remediation

*   Students often miscalculate the constant term. Remind students to look carefully at *all* the numbers provided before determining the constant.

Probing questions

*   The term-to-term rule for a sequence is +4. What does that tell you about the position-to-term rule? Is this enough information to find the rule for the *n*th term? What else do you need?
*   What do you look for in a sequence to help you to find the position-to-term (*n*th term) rule?
*   How would you approach finding the position-to-term (*n*th term) rule from the information in the table?

Position	2	7	12
Term	7	22	37

Literacy focus

*   Key terms: arithmetic sequence, linear sequence
*   Explain to students the meaning of the key terms and how they relate to other areas of Mathematics.

Part 1

*   Give students a starting number and an answer, e.g. 3 and 16. Ask for a rule of the form 'multiply by a number, then add or subtract a number' to get from 3 to 16, e.g. × 3 + 7.
*   Write this as a linear expression in *n*, e.g. $3n + 7$.
*   Ask students for similar rules and ask them to write them as linear expressions.
*   This should produce rules such as: $5n + 1$, $2n + 10$, $4n + 4$, $6n − 2$, $7n − 5$.

Part 2

- Point out that the rules written down are *linear expressions* because they contain a single term in the variable n and no powers.
- Ask a student to give a similar linear expression in n and ask the class to substitute $n = 1, 2, 3, \ldots$ into this expression and write the results in a list. For example, if the student says $3n + 2$, the list will be: 5, 8, 11, 14, 17, …
- Can they see any connections with previous work? Establish that the expression generates a sequence with a constant difference.
- Repeat with another linear expression.
- Taking any of the sequences used at the beginning of the lesson, write the linear expression and the series on the board and ask students if they can see any connections.
- The difference and the coefficient of n is the most obvious. Students may also spot that the first term of the sequence is the difference plus or minus the constant term.
- Work through the text and Examples 4, 5, and 6 in the Student Book.
- **Students can now do Exercise 4C from the Student Book.**

| A 1–7 | Calculator n/a | CM 9–11 | MR n/a | PS 10d, 12 | EV 8 |

Part 3

- Write the sequence 2, 4, 8, 16 on the board.
- How is it built up?
- Can they find an nth term? It may help students if you write $2, 2 \times 2, 2 \times 2 \times 2, \ldots$
- The nth term should be recognisable as 2^n.
- This principle similarly applies for the nth term of 10, 100, 1000, 10 000, …
- Ask students to generate their own sequences and find the nth term.

Section 4.4 Special sequences

Learning objectives

- Recognise and continue some special number sequences

Resources and homework

- Student Book 4.4: pages 95–99
- Practice Book 4.4: pages 28–29

Making mathematical connections

- Coordinates and graphs

Making cross-curricular connections

- **Science** – patterns in nature
- **Computing** – coding, loops, binary
- **Relevance** – developing logical thinking

Prior learning

- Students should be able to recognise number patterns.
- Students should be familiar with powers.

Working mathematically

- This section explores different sequences that do not always have a (simple) nth-term rule.
- Students can explore the links between the Fibonacci sequence and nature in more detail.
- Where possible, provide opportunities for students to generate the sequences using a spreadsheet.

Common misconceptions and remediation

- Students often work out powers incorrectly when using calculators, e.g. they may calculate 10^9 instead of 10^{10}.
- Encourage students to practise working with powers on their calculators.

Probing questions

- Could you write down a rule for the Fibonacci sequence? Why?
- Explain how to generate square numbers.

Literacy focus

- Key terms: geometric sequence, powers of 2, powers of 10
- Ask students to write a sentence on how to generate the Fibonacci sequence.

Part 1

- Recall the 'silly sequences' and 'power sequences' activity in Part 3 of section 4.2.
- Ask students if they have thought of or found any other unusual or silly sequences.
- If so, write these on the board and discuss them.
- If not, then other silly sequences include:
  - 3, 3, 5, 4, 4, 3, … (number of letters in numbers as words)
  - 15, 26, 40, 16, 37, … (sums of squares of digits in the previous number)
- Students may have found some other interesting sequences such as Fibonacci or powers series.
- Remind students about 2, 4, 8, 16, … and 10, 100, 1000, … (powers of 2 and of 10).

Part 2

Geometric sequences; Fibonacci sequences; Prime numbers

- Referring to the Student Book (pages 95 and 96), go through the special number sequences.
- Make sure students understand the nth terms for the odd and even number sequences.
- Test the nth term of the square numbers. For example, ask students to test the square number rule for $n = 15$, then show that the 15th square number is 225.
  ($1 \times 1 = 1$, $2 \times 2 = 4$, $3 \times 3 = 9$, $4 \times 4 = 16$, $5 \times 5 = 25$, …, $13 \times 13 = 169$, $14 \times 14 = 196$, $15 \times 15 = 225$)
- Ask students to extend the sequence of triangular numbers to 10 terms.
- Then test the rule for $n = 10$. Both answers should be 55.
  (1, 3, 6, 10, 15, 21, 28, 36, 45, 55)
- Test the rules for power sequences for $n = 10$.
  ($2^{10} = 1024$ and $10^{10} = 10\ 000\ 000\ 000$)
- Remind students about prime numbers.
  (2, 3, 5, 7, 11, 13, 17, 19, 23, 29, 31, 37, 41, 43, …)
  They have no pattern, but it is important to note that 2 is the only even prime number.
- Work through Examples 7 to 9 with students. Example 7 tests knowledge of odd, even and prime numbers.
- **Students can now do Exercise 4D from Student Book.**

A 1, 3a, 3c, 7–10, 14, 15	Calculator 7, 12, 14	CM 3b, 4–6, 11, 12	MR 2, 13	PS 16, 17	EV n/a

Part 3

- Put a copy of the current month's calendar on the screen or board.
- Highlight a row, a column or a diagonal and ask students to name the nth term.
- Ask students on what days the square numbers, triangular numbers, prime numbers and powers of 2 fall.

Section 4.5 General rules from given patterns

Learning objectives
- Find the *n*th term from practical problems involving sequences

Resources and homework
- Student Book 4.5: pages 100–104
- Practice Book 4.5: pages 30–31

Making mathematical connections
- Problem solving
- Coordinates and graphs

Making cross-curricular connections
- **Computing** – efficient coding using 'repeat' or loops
- **Art** – fractals
- **Relevance** – developing logical thinking

Prior learning
- Students should be able to substitute into simple algebraic expressions.
- They should have some experience in continuing a sequence.

Working mathematically
- Suggest to students that they should sift through the words to get to the mathematics, write down the sequence and concentrate on the numbers rather than words such as 'fences' or 'pentagons'.

Common misconceptions and remediation
- Students often make the mistake of attempting to answer the question in their heads rather than writing down the sequence. Remind them that they should always set up a table of results.
- Students should concentrate on working mathematically, that is, with the numbers rather than with the descriptive words.

Probing questions
- Explain how the pattern increases.
- How can you tell that the sequence will be linear?

Literacy focus
- There are no new key terms in this section.

Part 1
- Remind students how to work out the next term in a sequences and its *n*th term.
- Ask students to do this for some sequences, e.g.
  - 7, 9, 11, 13, 15, …
  - 7, 17, 27, 37, …
  - 7, 107, 207, 307, …

Part 2

- Work through Example 10 on page 100 of the Student Book. Draw attention to the method of using a table to record results.
- Extend the table for a few columns (or rows). Test a generalisation to make sure that the rule works.
- Initially, some **less able** students may need help with recording a sequence in this way.
- **Students can now do Exercise 4E from the Student Book.**

A 1–7, 8a, 9a–b	Calculator n/a	CM n/a	MR 8b, 11, 12	PS 9c, 10	EV 13

Part 3

- Draw the following patterns on the board:

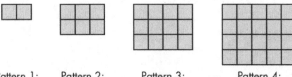

Pattern 1:   Pattern 2:   Pattern 3:   Pattern 4:
2 squares   6 squares   12 squares   20 squares

- Ask students: How many squares in pattern 5? (30)
- Prompt students if they do not spot this at first.
- Ask how they worked this out. (The pattern goes up 4, 6, 8, 10, …)
- Can they give a rule for the nth term?
- Look at the width (number of squares) of each block: 2, 3, 4, 5, … $n + 1$.
- Look at the height (number of squares) of each block: 1, 2, 3, 4, … n.
- The number of squares is: $1 \times 2, 2 \times 3, 3 \times 4, 4 \times 5, n \times (n + 1)$.
- If there is time, ask students to draw their own patterns, and swap with a partner to produce a table and work out the nth term.

Section 4.6 The *n*th term of a quadratic sequence

Learning objectives
* Generate the terms of a quadratic sequence, given the *n*th term

Resources and homework
* Student Book 4.6: pages 105–108
* Practice Book 4.6: page 31

Making mathematical connections
* Quadratic expressions
* Coordinates and graphs

Making cross-curricular connections
* **Computing** – efficient coding using 'repeat' or loops
* **Art** – fractals
* **Relevance** – developing logical thinking

Prior learning
* Students should be able to find the *n*th term of a linear sequence.

Working mathematically
* Students will need to explain how to spot a sequence with a quadratic rule.
* Students will need to understand the similarities and differences between the way they would continue a linear sequence and the way they would continue a quadratic sequence.

Common misconceptions and remediation
* Students do not always identify that a sequence is quadratic and so continue it in a linear fashion.
* Students often miscalculate n^2 when substituting. Use quickfire questions to give regular practice in this skill.

Probing questions
* How do you decide that a sequence is quadratic?
* Write down a quadratic sequence on mini whiteboards.

Literacy focus
* Key terms: first difference, position-to-term rule, quadratic expression, quadratic rule, quadratic sequence, second difference
* Ask students to make a list of the key terms and their definitions.

Part 1
* Check, by using quickfire questions, that students can square numbers fluently.
* Following on from the previous lessons, ask students to find the *n*th term of these sequences.
  o 5, 8, 11, 14 ($3n + 2$)
  o 20, 18, 16, 14, 12 ($22 - 2n$)

Part 2

- Ask students to write down the first difference (differences between the terms) and the second difference (differences between the differences) for each of the two sequences in Part 1.
- Students should discover that the second differences are all 0. Explain that this is a feature of linear sequences.
- Work through Example 11 and Example 12 on page 105 of the Student Book, explaining to students how to accurately generate a quadratic sequence and how to identify a quadratic sequence by looking at the 2nd differences..
- **Students can now do Exercise 4F from the Student Book.**

A 1–5, 7	Calculator n/a	CM 6, 9b, 12	MR n/a	PS 8, 9a, 10, 11	EV n/a

Part 3

- Give students the following expressions and ask them to generate the first five terms on a mini whiteboard.
  - $n^2 + 2$
  - $n^2 + 2n - 1$
- Ask students to show that both sequences are quadratic by finding the second difference.
- Give students a sequence starting 2, 3, … and ask them to continue it so that it has a quadratic nth term.

Section 4.7 Finding the *n*th term for quadratic sequences

Learning objectives
- Work out the *n*th term of a quadratic sequence

Resources and homework
- Student Book 4.7: pages 108–112
- Practice Book 4.7: page 31

Making mathematical connections
- Quadratic expressions
- Coordinates and graphs

Making cross-curricular connections
- **Computing** – efficient coding using 'repeat' or loops
- **Art** – fractals
- **Relevance** – developing logical thinking

Prior learning
- It is essential that students can find the *n*th term of a linear sequence and generate terms for a quadratic sequence.

Working mathematically
- Students will need to explain how to find the *n*th term for a sequence where the rule is quadratic.
- Students will need to understand the similarities and differences between the way they would find the *n*th term for a linear sequence and the way they would find the *n*th term for a quadratic sequence.

Common misconceptions and remediation
- Students do not always identify that a sequence is quadratic and so find a linear expression for the *n*th term.
- Students often miscalculate n^2 when substituting. Use quickfire questions to give regular practice in this skill.

Probing questions
- How do you work out if a sequence is linear or quadratic?
- What methods do you use to work out the *n*th term of a quadratic sequence?
- Compare the way you work out the *n*th term for a linear sequence with the way you work out the *n*th term for a quadratic sequence.
  Which parts of your method are the same?
  Which parts are different?

Literacy focus
- There are no new key terms in this section.
- Ask students to write down a step-by-step guide for their chosen method of finding the *n*th term of a quadratic sequence.

Part 1
- Ask students to write down a quadratic sequence on mini whiteboards.
- Ask them how they know it is a quadratic sequence and not a linear sequence.

Part 2

- Write the sequence 1, 4, 9, 25, 36, … on the board.
- Ask students what the nth term of this sequence is (n^2).
- Now display the sequence 2, 5, 10, 26, 37, …
- Ask what the nth term of this sequence is ($n^2 + 1$).
- Work through Example 13 on page 109 of the Student Book. Explain that spotting the pattern based on the square numbers is often a good way to find the nth term of a quadratic sequence. Remind them always to try this first.
- Demonstrate more methods for finding the nth term by working through Examples 14, 15 and 16 in the Student Book.
- **Students can now do Exercise 4G from the Student Book.**

| A 1–4 | Calculator n/a | CM 6 | MR n/a | PS 5, 7–9 | EV 10 |

Part 3

- Ask students to continue the sequence starting 5, 7, ... so that it is a quadratic sequence.
- Ask them to find the nth term of the sequence using their preferred method.
- Ask students to find the nth term of the following sequences.
  - 6, 17, 34, 57, 86
  - 3, 18, 41, 72, 111
  - 7, 14, 23, 34, 47

Chapter 5 Ratio, proportion and rates of change: Ratio and proportion

Overview

5.1 Ratio	**5.4** Compound measures
5.2 Direct proportion problems	**5.5** Compound interest and repeated percentage change
5.3 Best buys	**5.6** Reverse percentage (working out the original amount)

Prior learning

Know multiplication tables up to 12 × 12.
Know how to simplify fractions.
Know how to find a fraction of a quantity.
Know how to multiply and divide, with and without a calculator.

Learning objectives

Ensure that students can: understand what a ratio is; divide an amount according to a given ratio; solve problems involving direct proportion; compare prices of products; calculate compound measures (rates of pay, speed, density, pressure); calculate compound interest and repeated percentage change; calculate a reverse percentage.

In the examination, students will be expected to:
- simplify a ratio
- express a ratio as a fraction
- divide amounts into given ratios
- complete calculations from a given ratio and partial information
- recognise and solve problems that involve direct proportion
- find the cost per unit mass
- find the mass per unit cost
- use the above to find which product is the cheaper
- recognise and solve problems involving the compound measures of rates of pay, speed, density and pressure
- calculate simple interest
- calculate compound interest
- solve problems involving repeated percentage change
- calculate the original amount, given the final amount, after a known percentage increase or decrease.

Extension

Direct **more able** students towards the more challenging PS and MR questions in the exercises throughout this chapter.

Curriculum references

Section	GCSE specification	Section	GCSE specification
5.1	R 4, 5, 6, 7	5.4	R 11
5.2	R 10	5.5	R 16
5.3	R 11, 12	5.6	R 9

Route mapping

Exercise	Accessible	Intermediate	Challenging	AO1	AO2 MR CM	AO3 PS EV	Key questions
5A	1–10	11–15		1–10	11, 12, 15	13, 14	12, 14
5B	1–9	10–14		1–5a, 6–8a, b, c, 9	8d, 10, 11c, 12, 14	5b, 13	8, 12
5C	1–13	14, 15		1–3, 5, 7, 12, 13	6, 8	4, 9–11, 14, 15	7, 14
5D	1–10	11–15		1–9a	9b, 10, 13, 15	11, 12, 14	6, 9
5E	1–8			1–4	5, 8	6, 7	4, 7
5F	1–7	8–10		1–3, 5–7	4	8–10	4, 5
5G	1–9	10–17		1–8, 12–14	9–11, 16	15, 17	12–14
5H	1–14	15–17		1–8, 10, 12a, c,14	9, 12b, 13, 15, 17	11, 16	6–8, 14
5I	1–9	10–16		1–5a, 6a, 7, 8a, 9a	5b, 6b, 8b, 9b, 10, 16	11–15	4, 11
5J	1	2–17	18–19	1–10a	10b–15	16–19	3, 8

Key questions are those that demonstrate mastery of the concept, or which require a step-up in understanding or application. Key questions could be used to identify the questions that students must tackle, to support differentiation, or to identify the questions that should be teacher-marked rather than student-marked.

About this chapter

Making connections: This chapter starts with the core parts of ratio and proportion before covering more complex areas of percentages (compound interest, reverse percentages). The skills learnt in this chapter will be used in areas of Science (compound measures) and Geography (ratio and proportion).

Relevance: We use fractions, decimals, percentage, ratio and proportion in everyday life to help us calculate quantities or to compare two or more pieces of information.

Working mathematically: How do you find a multiplier to increase or decrease by a percentage? How do you find a multiplier to calculate an original value after a percentage increase or decrease?

Assessment: In each section of this chapter, ensure that students have a good grasp of the key questions in each exercise before moving on. (Refer to the 'Route mapping' table above.) Encourage students to read and think about the 'Ready to progress?' statements on page 148 of the Student Book. Check students' understanding at the end of the chapter, formatively, using peer assessment. Students could do a mini test in the form of the 'Review questions' on pages 148–149 of the Student Book. Follow up the test with an individual target-getting session, based on any areas for development that a student may have.

Worked exemplars from the Student Book – suggestions for use

- Present students with the same question but using different numbers. Students should use the exemplar to mirror the working, in full or only using the notes.
- Copy and cut the exemplars into cards. Ask students to match the working and notes.
- Ask students to write their own questions and set them out as exemplar questions.

Answers to the Student Book questions are available on the CD-ROM provided.

Section 5.1 Ratio

Learning objectives
- Simplify a ratio
- Express a ratio as a fraction
- Divide amounts into given ratios
- Complete calculations from a given ratio and partial information

Resources and homework
- Student Book 5.1: pages 117–125
- Practice Book 5.1: pages 32–34

Making mathematical connections
- Sharing in a ratio
- Simplifying fractions
- Proportion

Making cross-curricular connections
- **Geography** – ratio within population
- **Food Technology** – ratio of ingredients in a recipe
- **Relevance** – using ratio in daily tasks

Prior learning
- Students should know the multiplication tables up to 10 × 10, how to cancel fractions, how to find a fraction of a quantity and how to multiply and divide, both with and without a calculator.

Working mathematically
- Ratio can cause problems for some students, so encourage them to write down or verbalise their methods in order to embed their learning.
- Structure tasks so students can work out the methods for themselves, either by increasing the difficulty incrementally, or through one straightforward and one complex example.

Common misconceptions and remediation
- Students often forget to express all the quantities in the same units. Keep reminding them to address the units first
- When expressing (for example) 3 : 5 as a fraction, students may simply write it as $\frac{3}{5}$.

  Remind them, frequently, that the denominator is the number of parts in the ratio (8), so $\frac{3}{8}$.

Probing questions
- If the ratio of boys to girls in a class is 4 : 1, could there be exactly 35 children in the class? Why? Could there be 7 girls? Why?

Literacy focus
- Key terms: common units, ratio
- Make sure students are clear about what a ratio is. Encourage them to write a practical problem using ratio.

Part 1
- Use quickfire questions to provide practice in converting between metric units, including money, time, measurement and mass. Write down the conversions for **less able** students. Add others such as litres and centilitres, tonnes and kilograms for **more able** students.
- Write pairs of fractions on the board with either the numerator or denominator from one fraction missing. Ask students to provide the missing number to make the fractions equivalent. Challenge **more able** students with improper fractions using large numbers, e.g. $\frac{100}{40} = \frac{?}{5}$ (12.5), $\frac{720}{9} = \frac{?}{3} = \frac{?}{1}$ (240, 80).

Part 2

Common units and Ratios as fractions

- Explain that a ratio is a way of comparing the sizes of two or more quantities with the same units, e.g. compare cm to cm, not cm to m. Remind students that a ratio can also be expressed as a fraction. The denominator is the sum of the numbers in the ratio.
- Ask how many times further 1 km is than 1 m (1000). Write on the board:
  1 m to 1 km = 1 m : 1 km = 1 : 1000
- Explain that ratios do not have units, so when the units of the quantities are different, one unit must be converted before the ratio can be formed.
- Write these ratios on the board and explain that they are all equivalent: 1 : 2, 2 : 4, 3 : 6.
- Now write 4 : 12 on the board and ask for some equivalent ratios (1 : 3, 2 : 6).
  Ask students to draw four squares and shade one. ■ □ □ □

  Ask: What is the ratio of shaded to unshaded? (1 : 3) What fraction are unshaded? $\left(\frac{3}{4}\right)$

  What is the ratio of unshaded to shaded? (3 : 1).

  This reinforces the idea of a corresponding order of the words and the ratio.
- Ask students to draw eight pint glasses, and shade three. Write: 8 pints = 1 gallon.

  Ask: What is the ratio of shaded (drinks) to unshaded (empty)? (3 : 5) What fraction are empty? $\left(\frac{5}{8}\right)$ What fraction of one gallon is three pints? $\left(\frac{3}{8}\right)$.

  This will reinforce the need to work in one unit (pints).
- Work through Examples 1 and 2, which combine the work on units with the work on ratios.
- **Students can now do Exercise 5A from the Student Book.**

R 1–10	Calculator n/a	CM 15	MR 11, 12	PS n/a	EV 13, 14

Dividing amounts in a given ratio

- Hand each student a sheet of paper and ask them to tear or cut it into 16 pieces.
- Write the ratio 1 : 3 on the board and ask the students to share the 16 pieces between two piles in this ratio. They should put three in the second pile for each one in the first pile.
- Ask what fraction of the pieces are: in the first pile $\left(\frac{1}{4}\right)$; the second pile $\left(\frac{3}{4}\right)$.
- Say that $\frac{1}{4}$ of 16 pieces = 4 pieces and $\frac{3}{4}$ of 16 pieces = 12 pieces.
- Demonstrate the different methods by working through Examples 3 and 4.
- **Students can now do Exercise 5B from the Student Book.**

R 1–9, 11	Calculator 4, 5, 8–10, 13	CM 8d	MR 10, 11c, 12, 14	PS 13	EV 5b

Calculating with ratios when only part of the information is known

- Explain that sometimes students will be told the value of only one part of a ratio, rather than the value of the whole amount. For example: I share money with my brother in the ratio 2 : 3. I get £2. How much does my brother get? (£3)
- Say that in Exercise 3B the 'same' question would have been written as: Divide £5 in the ratio 2 : 3. Ask **more able** students to rewrite the questions in Exercise 5B in this way. **Less able** students can decide what information the question is providing.
- Work through Examples 5 and 6 in the Student Book.
- **Students can now do Exercise 5C from the Student Book** using their favoured method. **Less able** students could work in pairs.

R 1–3, 5, 7, 12, 13	Calculator 1, 2, 7, 12, 13, 15	CM 8	MR 6	PS 9–11, 15	EV 4, 14

Part 3

- For each section, check students' understanding by going over the CM, MR, PS and EV questions in Exercises 5A–5C.

Section 5.2 Direct proportion problems

Learning objectives
- Recognise and solve problems that involve direct proportion

Resources and homework
- Student Book 5.2: pages 125–128
- Practice Book 5.2: pages 34–35

Making mathematical connections
- Inverse proportion
- Functions

Making cross-curricular connections
- **Art** – using proportion in paintings and drawings
- **Food technology** –adjusting ingredients in a recipe
- **Relevance** – using proportion in everyday life, e.g. mixing cement

Prior learning
- Students should know how to multiply and divide without using a calculator.

Working mathematically
- How do you know that given sets of numbers are in direct proportion?
- What tips would you give the person next to you to help them solve problems involving direct proportion?
- Talk me through the thinking that enabled you to solve this problem.

Common misconceptions and remediation
- Errors will occur when some information in the question leads to an answer that is not sensible. For example, when adapting a recipe, students may give answers of 1.5 eggs (see Part 2). Point out that in practical situations answers must always be sensible.

Probing questions
- Six apples cost £1.20. Explain how you would work out how much eight apples or twelve apples cost?
- Three books cost £21. Explain how you would work out how much four books cost.

Literacy focus
- Key terms: direct proportion, unit cost, unitary method
- What are the key words in this question? How do the words help you work out the problem?

Part 1
- Write the following on the board and ask students to give an answer:
  Six (of something) cost 36p. How much will five cost?
- Students should have an intuitive idea of this and will answer 30p.
- Discuss the idea of finding the cost of one item and then scaling up to the required number. Repeat with other values such as: Eight cost 56p. How much will six cost?
- For **less able** students, use whole-number answers.
- For **more able** students, use decimals such as: Seven cost £10.50. How much will six cost?

Part 2

- Explain to students that the method they used in Part 1, of finding the cost of one item and then scaling, is called the *unitary method*.
- Write this recipe on the board.
  For four people:
  - o 100 g butter
  - o 300 g flour
  - o 2 eggs
  - o 1 cup milk
- Ask students how they could amend this for three people – do not worry about the eggs at this stage. (Divide by 4 and multiply by 3.)
- Now say that you only have 300 g of butter and 600 g of flour but plenty of eggs and milk. Ask how many you could serve and why. (8, only enough flour for 8)
- Demonstrate other methods by working through Examples 7 and 8 from the Student Book.
- **Students can now do Exercise 5D from the Student Book.**

R 1–9	Calculator all	CM 9b	MR 10, 13, 15	PS 12	EV 11, 14

Part 3

- On the board, write a simple recipe for six people.
- Ask students how much of each ingredient would be needed for one person, two people, twelve people, and so on. Include an item, such as two eggs, which cannot be divided easily.
- Point out that a problem like this would not occur in an examination, but could come up in real life.
- As a lead-in to the next section on best buys, ask students which is better value: three chocolate bars for 90p or five chocolate bars for £1.50. (Neither; both work out at 30p for each bar.)
- Now discuss with students how they would compare values.

Section 5.3 Best buys

Learning objectives

- Find the cost per unit mass
- Find the mass per unit cost
- Use the above to find which product is the cheaper

Resources and homework

- Student Book 5.3: pages 128–131
- Practice Book 5.3: pages 35–36

Making mathematical connections

- Sharing in a ratio
- Simplifying fractions
- Proportion

Making cross-curricular connections

- **Business** – unit cost of items
- **Food Technology** – cost per unit of ingredients in a recipe
- **Relevance** – using ratio in daily tasks

Prior learning

- Students need to know how to multiply and divide, with and without a calculator.

Working mathematically

- What numbers are key to solving this problem? How do they help you to solve it?
- What would your estimate of the answer be? Why?

Common misconceptions and remediation

- Students often forget to express all the quantities in the same unit. Stress to students that they must always compare like with like.
- Students may not comprehend which is the best buy once they have completed the calculations. Careful thought and practice should help students to overcome this problem.

Probing questions

- Can you solve the problem in a different way?
- What do you look for when deciding the most efficient way to solve a problem?

Literacy focus

- Key terms: best buy, better value, mass
- Which words are key to solving this problem? How do they help you to solve it?

Part 1

- Draw two jars of different sizes on the board. Label both jars 'Jam'. Write '250 g' and '£0.55' on one and '600 g' and '£1.20' on the other. Ask students if they can tell which jar is better value for money.
- Explore various methods. For example:
  o Find the cost of 50 g (11p and 10p).
  o Find a common multiple of 250 and 600 (3000), giving 12 × 55 = 660 and 5 × 120 = 600.
- Students may still be confused about which is better value. Emphasise the phrase 'More jam per penny'.
- Point out that this is a clue about how to work out the problem: 'More jam per penny'. Students can work it out as: jam ÷ money, with the word 'per' being replaced with ÷.

Part 2

- Continue with the example used in Part 1.
- Make a list of possible answers for students to write down. Explain that you have written them both in pence to make it easier to do the calculations

	250 g for 55p	**600 g for 120p**	
Dividing by 5	50 g for 11p	50 g for 10p	*Dividing by 12*
Dividing by 250	1 g for 0.22p	1 g for 0.2p	*Dividing by 600*
Multiplying by 12	3000 g for £	3000 for £6	*Multiplying by 5*
Dividing by 55	Number of grams per penny = 250 ÷ 55 = 4.54	Number of grams per penny = 600 ÷ 120 = 5	*Dividing by 120*

- Talk about each answer and how to obtain it.
- Now demonstrate different methods by working through Examples 9, 10, 11 and 12. Explain that different students will prefer different methods and that the more methods with which they are comfortable, the easier they will find this topic.
- **Students can now do Exercise 5E from the Student Book.**

R 1–4	Calculator all	CM 5, 8	MR n/a	PS 6	EV 7

Part 3

- Ask students if they think the larger quantities will be proportionally cheaper than the smaller quantities. Why might it not always be the best option to buy the biggest?
- Discuss the practicalities of buying large quantities to save money. Suggest, for example: Is it worth buying two loaves of bread that are on a special offer when one loaf will be thrown away because it will not get eaten?
- Encourage students to write their own questions and solve them.

Section 5.4 Compound measures

Learning objectives

- Recognise and solve problems involving the compound measures of rates of pay, speed, density and pressure

Making mathematical connections

- Equations, expressions, identities and functions
- Rearranging formula
- Solving equations

Resources and homework

- Student Book 5.4: pages 132–139
- Practice Book 5.4: pages 36–39

Making cross-curricular connections

- **Science** – using compound measures
- **Computing** – formulae in spreadsheets
- **Relevance** – relationships between speed, distance and time, used when travelling; calculating hourly rates of pay

Prior learning

- Students should know how to multiply and divide, with and without using a calculator.
- Students should be familiar with standard units of length, mass, capacity and volume.
- Students should know how to calculate the volumes of cuboids, prisms and cylinders.

Working mathematically

- This section teaches students how to calculate with different measures: rates of pay; the relationships between speed, distance and time; the relationships between mass, density and volume.
- Discuss compound units. What does km/h mean? What does m/s mean?
- Discuss the difference between weight and mass.
- Do two different objects that have the same mass always have the same volume?

Common misconceptions and remediation

- Some students fail to grasp that 30 minutes is not 0.3 of an hour, or that 15 minutes is not 0.15 of an hour. Point out these errors as they occur.
- Students may not relate units to formulae. Explain that 'per' means 'over' in Latin and is related to division. Miles per hour (mph) means 'miles over hours', that is, distance ÷ time. Grams per cubic centimetre (g/cm^3) means 'grams over cubic centimetres', that is mass ÷ volume.
- Students sometimes forget to convert linear measures to appropriate units before calculating with compound measures. Point this out when it occurs.

Probing questions

- What makes questions involving speed easy to solve? What makes them difficult to solve? Write some questions that are easy to solve and some that are difficult to solve.
- Explain why travelling a distance of 60 kilometres in 45 minutes is an average of 80 km/h.
- What makes questions involving density easy to solve? What makes them difficult to solve? Write some questions that are easy to solve and some that are difficult to solve.
- How can you use the units of speed or density to help you solve a problem? How can you use the information given in a problem to help you work out the units for speed or density?

Literacy focus

- Key terms: average speed, compound measure, density
- Students could write a step-by-step guide on how to rearrange the formulae in this section.

Part 1

- Ask students simple quickfire questions about speed. (Write answers on mini whiteboards.)
  - Speed 30 mph. How far in 30 minutes? (15 miles)
  - Distance 40 miles; time 1 hour. What is the average speed? (40 mph)
  - Speed 30 mph; distance 90 miles. How long? (3 hours)

Part 2

Rates of pay

- Using page 132 of the Student Book, introduce the triangle for calculating rates of pay. This shows how the three variables are connected.
- The hourly amount earned is calculated by the rule:
      Pay (P) = Hours worked (H) × hourly rate (R)
- **Students can now do Exercise 5F from the Student Book.**

R 1–3, 5–7	Calculator all	CM 4	MR n/a	PS 8–10	EV n/a

Speed, time and distance

- Revisit the questions in Part 1. Discuss how students worked out the answers. In each case, prompt students to give a formula: Speed × Time = Distance; Distance ÷ Time = Speed; Distance ÷ Speed = Time. Refer to the D, S, T triangle on page 133 of the Student Book.
- Remind students how to convert hours and minutes into hours and vice versa.

  E.g. 20 minutes = 20 ÷ 60 hour = $\frac{1}{3}$ hour, 0.8 of an hour = 0.8 × 60 minutes = 48 minutes

- Work through Examples 14, 15 and 16. Remind students to change hours and minutes into hours each time.
- **Students can now do Exercise 5G from the Student Book.**

R 1–8, 12–14	Calculator all	CM 9, 17	MR 10, 11, 15	PS 16	EV n/a

Density

- Referring to page 137 of the Student Book, discuss the formulae for solving problems involving density, mass and volume using the triangle notation. Discuss how students can rearrange the formula to calculate any one of the three variables, given the other two: $M = D \times V$; $D = M \div V$; $V = M \div D$.
- Work through the following examples (and then Examples 17 and 18) with students:
  - A metal rod has a mass of 4 kg and a volume of 160 cm^3.
    Calculate the density of the rod in g/cm^3.
    Density = Mass (4000 g) ÷ Volume (160 cm^3) = 25 g/cm^3
  - A plank of teak wood is 10 cm by 15 cm by 360 cm. It has a density 0.8 g/cm³. What is the mass of this piece of wood in kilograms?
    First, calculate the volume of the wood in cm^3: 10 cm × 15 cm × 360 cm = 54 000 cm^3
    Then calculate the mass: $M = D$ (0.8) × V (54 000) = 43 200 g = 43.2 kg (43 200 ÷ 1000)

Pressure

- Introduce the pressure triangle, highlighting the similarities with work already covered.
- Work through Example 19.
- **Students can now do Exercise 5H from the Student Book.**

R 1–8, 10, 12, 14	Calculator n/a	CM 9, 12b, 17	MR 13, 15	PS 11, 16	EV n/a

Part 3

- Go through the formulae linking: speed, distance and time; density, mass and volume; pressure, force and area. Reinforce the triangle method with students.

Section 5.5 Compound interest and repeated percentage change

Learning objectives

- Calculate simple interest
- Calculate compound interest
- Solve problems involving repeated percentage change

Making mathematical connections

- Rearranging formula
- Solving equations

Resources and homework

- Student Book 5.5: pages 140–143
- Practice Book 5.5: pages 39–40

Making cross-curricular connections

- **Economics and Business** – interest on loans and savings
- **Computing** – formulae in spreadsheets
- **Relevance** – interest on savings and purchases

Prior learning

- Students should be able to increase an amount by a percentage, preferably using the multiplier method.

Working mathematically

- Students are taught how to solve problems involving compound interest, simple interest and repeated proportional change using multiplicative methods.
- Encourage students to use a spreadsheet to solve problems such as:
  - How long would it take to triple an investment with an interest rate of 6% per annum?
  - A ball is dropped from a height of 16 m. With each bounce, it bounces to $\frac{3}{4}$ of its previous height. How many bounces before it is at half the height from which it first bounced?

Common misconceptions and remediation

- When using the year-by-year method, errors are commonly due to premature or incorrect rounding. Remind students not to round until the last stage.
- When using the compound interest formula for depreciation, students often forget that the '$+ r\%$' becomes a '$- r\%$'.
- Errors are frequently made by not reading the question properly, e.g. does the question ask for the total amount in the bank after n years, or for the total interest received after n years? Encourage students to reread the question and check that their answer is sensible.

Probing questions

- How do you decide on the order of operations for a complex calculation when using a calculator?
- Explain why this calculation gives the solution to this repeated proportional change problem.
- What is the difference between compound interest and simple interest?

Literacy focus

- Key terms: annual rate, compound interest, principal, simple interest
- Ask students to write the meaning of each word. Then discuss the meanings with the class, until you are sure that everyone understands them.

Part 1

- Give the class the following problem.
  Craig invests £100 in a savings account that pays 5% interest per annum.
  - How much does Craig have in the account at the end of the first year? (£105)
  - How much does Craig have in the account at the end of the second year? (£110.25)
  - How much does Craig have in the account at the end of the third year? (£115.76)
- Discuss a quicker method of finding out how much Craig has after 3 years. (100×1.05^3)
- Encourage students to check the calculation on their calculators.
- Discuss the advantage of using the multiplier for an investment of 10 years instead of calculating each year separately. (Only one calculation, so much quicker to work out)

Part 2

- Since the method has already been established in Part 1, check that students can complete the calculations using a calculator. Use the text on page 141 of the Student Book if necessary.
- Write on the board: £3000 investment, 6%, 5 years.
- Ask students to give the multiplier for the calculation. (1.06)
- Now ask students for the calculation to work out the final value of the investment.
  (3000×1.06^5)
- Ask students to do the calculation on their calculators. (£4014.68)
- Ensure that they give the answer in correct money notation.
- Provide a few more calculations for students to work out on their calculators. Use different contexts, for example:
    The population of a village is 10 000. Each year for 3 years it falls by 2% of the amount at the end of the year. What is the population after 3 years? (9411 or 9412)
- Some students will prefer to understand the method to learning a formula.
- Ask **more able** students to put the method into a formula. They may derive the formula shown in the Student Book (page 140). Refer all students to this formulae as an alternative way of working.
- Work through Example 20 and ask students to use their calculators to check the answer.
- **Students can now do Exercise 5I from the Student Book.**

R 1–5a, 6a, 7, 8a, 9a	Calculator all	CM n/a	MR 5b, 6b, 8b, 9b, 10, 16	PS 11–15	EV n/a

Part 3

- Set these problems:
  - Mr Cash invests £1 000 000 for 5 years at an annual compound interest rate of 5%.
    By how much does his money grow? (£276 281.56)
  - Miss Cash buys a car for £100 000 that depreciates by 5% per year.
    By how much has the car depreciated after 5 years? (£22 621.91)
  - Mrs Cash invests £1 000 000 at a rate of 5% per annum, compound interest.
    How many years will it take this money to reach £1.5 million? (9 years)
- For **more able** students, ask:
    Work out the interest rate (to the nearest whole number) needed to double the value of an investment in 5 years. (15%)
- Now give students a set of problems involving compound interest and a set of calculations. Ask students to match the problems to the calculations.

Section 5.6 Reverse percentage (working out the original amount)

Learning objectives

- Calculate the original amount, given the final amount, after a known percentage increase or decrease

Resources and homework

- Student Book 5.6: pages 143–145
- Practice Book 5.6: page 40

Making mathematical connections

- Percentage change

Making cross-curricular connections

- **Economics and Business** – calculating gross income from net
- **Geography** – population calculations
- **Relevance** – calculating prices in sales

Prior learning

- Students should be able to work out a multiplier.
- Students will also need to know that the whole amount is always equivalent to 100%.

Working mathematically

- Students will be taught to solve questions such as:
  o Dave has savings of £2967.85 after 6% interest has been added. How much were his savings before the interest was added?
  o Factory workers get a 3% increase. The new hourly rate is £8.50. What was the hourly rate before the increase?

Common misconceptions and remediation

- A common error is to work out 'the percentage of' rather than 'the percentage *off*', e.g. '10% of' instead of '10% off.' Emphasise that students should always read the text carefully.
- The Part 2 activity provides an opportunity to highlight this.

Probing questions

- Talk me through how you got your answer to this question.
- Explain how you found the multiplier when you solved this question.

Literacy focus

- There are no new key terms in this section.
- Ask students to write down a step-by-step method for solving reverse percentage questions.

Part 1

- Tell students that for each of the following statements they must work out 100%. Start with simple percentages, e.g.

  50% is £3 (100% is £6)   25% is 4 kg (100% is 16 kg)
  20% is 5 cm (100% is 25 cm)   10% is 60p (100% is £6).
- Move on to more difficult percentages, using fractions and decimals for **more able** students. Encourage students to give answers in two or more steps.

  90% is £18 (10% is £2, so 100% is £20)
  75% is 15 kg (25% is 5 kg, so 100% is 20 kg)
  37.5% is 30 cm (12.5 % is 10 cm, 25% is 20 cm, 100% is 80 cm).

Part 2

- Develop the questions to give a real context. Ask students to think about this problem:
  A sale offers 10% off all prices. The sale price of a dress is £18. What was the original price of the dress?
- Point out that '10% off' does not mean '10% of', so they must not work out '10% of' at any time in this question. On the board, write: 10% *off* not 10% *of*.
- Ask students how they would solve the problem.
- Show students both methods. They should choose the approach they prefer and stick with it.

The unitary method

- This involves scaling to obtain 1% and then 100%, as used in Part 1.
- Show students the three steps for the unitary method in the Student Book (page 143). Then work through the dress example.
  - o 10% off means that the sale price is 90%.
  - o 90% is equivalent to £18.
  - o 1% is equivalent to 20p, or 10% is equivalent to £2 (dividing by 90 or 9).
  - o So, 100% (the original price) = £20.
- Now work through Examples 21 and 22 in the Student Book.

The multiplier method

- Show students the two steps of the multiplier method in the Student Book (page 144).
  - o 10% off means a multiplier of 0.9.
  - o Divide by the multiplier to find the original amount: £18 ÷ 0.9 = £20
- Now work through Example 23.
- **Students can now do Exercise 5J from the Student Book.**

R 1–10	Calculator all	CM 10b, 11, 12, 14	MR 13, 15	PS 16, 17, 19	EV 18

Part 3

- Ask students to work through these questions on VAT, salaries and body mass.
  - o An MP3 player costs £176.25, including VAT at 17.5%.
    How much would it have cost without VAT? (£150)
  - o Pam earns £21 840 after being given a 4% pay rise.
    How much did she earn before her pay rise? (£21 000)
  - o Paul has started a new fitness programme and is keeping a diary of his weight. In the first month, he lost 6% of his body mass. The next month, he gained 6% of his body mass.
    Did he gain or lose weight overall? (lose)
    What was the percentage change? (0.36%)
    If his mass now is 75 kg, what was his mass at the start of the first month? (75.3 kg)

Chapter 6 Geometry and measures: Angles

Overview

6.1 Angle facts	**6.5** Angles in parallel lines
6.2 Triangles	**6.6** Special quadrilaterals
6.3 Angles in a polygon	**6.7** Scale drawings and bearings
6.4 Regular polygons	

Prior learning

Know how to use a protractor to measure an angle.
Know the meaning of the terms 'acute', 'obtuse', 'reflex' and 'right' and how to use these terms to describe angles.
Know the names and angle properties of quadrilaterals.
Know what a polygon is and the names of polygons with up to ten sides.
Know that a diagonal is a line joining two non-adjacent vertices of a polygon.
Know the meaning of the terms 'parallel' and 'perpendicular' in relation to lines.

Learning objectives

Ensure that students can: calculate angles on a line and around a point; calculate angles in a triangle and in any polygon; calculate angles in parallel lines; calculate interior and exterior angles in polygons; read scale maps and drawings; use bearings.

In the examination, students will be expected to:
* calculate angles on a straight line and angles around a point
* use vertically opposite angles
* recognise and calculate the angles in different sorts of triangles
* calculate the sum of the interior angles in a polygon
* calculate the exterior angles and the interior angles of a regular polygon
* find angles in parallel lines
* use angle properties in quadrilaterals
* read scale drawings and maps
* draw scale drawings
* use a bearing to specify a direction.

Extension

More able students can design their own questions based on the exercises and share them with the class. Students could also use maps and set bearing questions; then use the maps to design travel plans.

Curriculum references

Section	GCSE specification
6.1	G 1, 3
6.2	G 1, 3, 4
6.3	G 1, 3, 4
6.4	G 1, 3, 4
6.5	G 1, 3
6.6	G 1, 3, 4
6.7	G 1, 3, 15

Route mapping

Exercise	Accessible	Intermediate	Challenging	AO1	AO2 MR CM	AO3 PS EV	Key questions
6A	1–8			1, 2	3, 7	4–6, 8	5, 6
6B	1–5	6–10		1–5	7–10	6	9, 10
6C	1–5			1–5			2, 3, 4
6D	1–5	6, 7		1, 3, 4	2, 6	5, 7	4
6E	1–8	9–12		1–4	5, 6, 9, 12	7, 8, 10, 11	3, 4
6F	1–9			1, 3	2, 6, 8, 9	4, 5, 7	2–4
6G	1–6	7–9		1–4	6, 9	5, 7, 8	2, 3
6H	1–13	14		2, 5, 6, 8, 10, 11	3, 7, 9	1, 4, 12–14	5, 9

Key questions are those that demonstrate mastery of the concept, or which require a step-up in understanding or application. Key questions could be used to identify the questions that students must tackle, to support differentiation, or to identify the questions that should be teacher-marked rather than student-marked.

About this chapter

Making connections: This chapter explores the connections between various shapes and their angles.

Relevance: Angles help us construct many things, from tables to skyscrapers. It is essential that students understand them, as they literally shape our world. There are applications in engineering, architecture and many more areas.

Working mathematically: What do you look for when calculating a missing angle in a shape? What is the least information you need to be able to calculate all the angles in the shape? What do you look for when solving a geometrical problem? How do you decide where to start? How would you explain to somebody that the exterior angles of a polygon add up to 360°?

Assessment: In each section of this chapter, ensure that students have a good grasp of the key questions in each exercise before moving on. (Refer to the 'Route mapping' table above.) Encourage students to read and think about the 'Ready to progress?' statements on page 176 of the Student Book. Check students' understanding at the end of the chapter, formatively, using peer assessment. Students could do a mini test in the form of the 'Review questions' on pages 176–177 of the Student Book. Follow up the test with an individual target-getting session based on any areas for development that a student may have.

Worked exemplars from the Student Book – suggestions for use

- Present students with the same question but using different numbers. Students should use the exemplar to mirror the working, in full or only the notes.
- Copy and cut the exemplar into cards. Students match the working with the notes. (You may need to remove the words 'first, second', and so on.)
- Copy and cut the working into cards, splitting the label/description from the working. Students put the working in order then match this with the descriptions.

Answers to the Student Book questions are available on the CD-ROM provided.

Section 6.1 Angle facts

Learning objectives

- Calculate angles on a straight line and angles around a point
- Use vertically opposite angles

Resources and homework

- Student Book 6.1: pages 151–153
- Practice Book 6.1: pages 41–42

Making mathematical connections

- Bearings
- Trigonometry

Making cross-curricular connections

- **Design and Technology** – using angles when designing
- **Art** – using angle facts in symmetrical designs
- **Relevance** – applications in engineering, manufacturing and architecture

Prior learning

- Students should be able to work out complements to 180° and 360°.

Working mathematically

- Students should be able to calculate angles on a straight line or at a point, for example, the angle between the hands of a clock, or intersecting diagonals in a quadrilateral.

Common misconceptions and remediation

- Students sometimes get confused between angles at a point and angles on a straight line. Reinforce these concepts in order to avoid errors in calculations.

Probing questions

- Why do angles on a straight line add up to 180?
- Why do angles at a point add up to 360?

Literacy focus

- Key terms: angles around a point, angles on a straight line, vertically opposite angles
- Ask students to explain what is meant by each key term.

Part 1

- Invite the class to imagine a square. Now cut off a corner.
- Ask some students to describe the shape that is left.
- Invite the class to imagine another square. Now cut off two corners.
- Ask other students to describe the shape that is now left.
- Repeat by cutting off three or four corners.

Part 2

- Explain that it is not always possible or necessary to measure angles on diagrams. Angles on diagrams can be calculated by using given geometrical information. Angles whose values are not given are denoted by letters (e.g. *a*, *b*, *c* …) and are called *unknown angles*.

Angles on a line

- Draw the diagram shown on the board and explain how to calculate the size of unknown angles on a line using various examples.

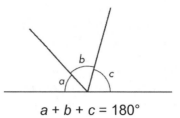

$$a + b + c = 180°$$

Angles around a point

- Draw the diagram shown on the board and explain how to calculate the sizes of unknown angles around a point using various examples.

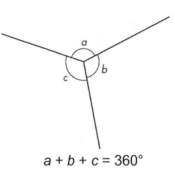

$$a + b + c = 360°$$

Vertically opposite angles

- Draw the diagram shown on the board and explain how to calculate the sizes of unknown angles using various examples.

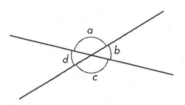

$$a = d \textbf{ AND } b = c$$

- Notice that the adjacent angles add up to 180°: $a + b = 180°$.
- Work through Examples 1, 2 and 3 from the Student Book (pages 151–152).
- **Students can now begin Exercise 6A from Student Book.**

G&M 1, 2	Calculator all	CM 3, 7	MR n/a	PS 4–6, 8	EV n/a

Part 3

- Ask some students to explain the meaning of: angles around a point, angles on a line, angles in a triangle, vertically opposite angles.
- Ask other students to make up an example to illustrate each of the above.

Section 6.2 Triangles

Learning objectives
- Recognise and calculate the angles in different sorts of triangles

Making mathematical connections
- Pythagoras' theorem
- Trigonometry

Resources and homework
- Student Book 6.2: pages 154–156
- Practice Book 6.2: pages 42–44

Making cross-curricular connections
- **Design and Technology** – using triangles when designing
- **Art** – using triangles in symmetrical designs
- **Science** – triangles of forces
- **Relevance** – applications in engineering and architecture

Prior learning
- Students should know the meanings of the terms *acute*, *obtuse*, *reflex* and *right* and be able to use these terms to describe angles.

Working mathematically
- Students will learn the skills required to calculate unknown angles in triangles, including isosceles triangles and right-angled triangles, when only one other angle is given. This will link to Trigonometry in later chapters.

Common misconceptions and remediation
- Students will get confused with all the different names of triangles. Go through the different types in the Student Book and set quickfire questions after students have learned them all.

Probing questions
- Can you draw a triangle with:
  - one acute angle
  - two acute angles
  - one obtuse angle
  - two obtuse angles?

Literacy focus
- Key terms: acute-angled triangle, equilateral triangle, isosceles triangle, obtuse-angled triangle, right-angled triangle, scalene triangle
- Ask students to describe each type of triangle.

Part 1
- Draw some triangles on the board, including right-angled, isosceles, equilateral and scalene. Ask students to compare them and comment on the differences and similarities.
- Now go through the different types of triangles formally, using the Student Book. Students may record them or you could give students a sheet to stick in their books.

Part 2

Special triangles

- Draw the triangle ABC on the board. Remind the class that they already know that the sum of the interior angles of a triangle is 180°. In the diagram on the right: $a + b + c = 180°$

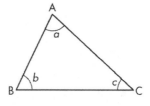

- On the board, draw an isosceles triangle, an equilateral triangle and a right-angled triangle.

 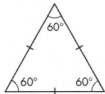 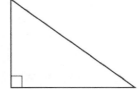

- Ask the class to describe how they can recognise each type of triangle. Make sure students understand that the base angles of an isosceles triangle are equal and that the interior angles of an equilateral triangle are equal (each 60°).
- Next, draw an isosceles triangle with an angle of 40° at the apex.
- Ask the class to work out the base angles. Repeat with other values for the angle at the apex.

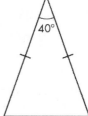

- The angle marked y on the diagram below is known as an **exterior angle** of the triangle. Show the class how to work out the size of such an angle.
  Angles in a triangle add up to 180°, so:
  $x = 180° - 48° - 110°$
  $x = 22°$
  Angles on a straight line add up to 180°, so:
  $y = 180° - 22°$
  $x = 158°$
- Now work through Example 4.
- **Students can now do Exercise 6B from the Student Book.**

G&M 1–5	Calculator all	CM 7, 8	MR 9, 10	PS n/a	EV 6

Part 3

- Ask the class to explain how to find an unknown angle in a triangle.
- Ask a student to explain how to find an exterior angle of a triangle.
- Draw several different triangles on the board, including some isosceles triangles. After annotating the angles, ask individual students to work out the unknown angles.
- Ask students to learn the different types of triangles and their properties for homework. Follow this up by testing them. (Students should use mini whiteboards.)

Section 6.3 Angles in a polygon

Learning objectives

- Calculate the sum of the interior angles in a polygon

Making mathematical connections

- Locus
- 3D shapes

Resources and homework

- Student Book 6.3: pages 157–159
- Practice Book 6.3: pages 44–46

Making cross-curricular connections

- **Science** – geometric shapes in chemistry
- **Design and Technology** – constructing models of designs
- **Geography** – identifying locations on maps by descriptions of the 2D representation of man-made objects
- **Relevance** – applications in engineering and architecture

Prior learning

- Students should know that the sum of the interior angles of a triangle is 180° and the sum of the interior angles in a quadrilateral is 360°.

Working mathematically

- How could you explain to someone how to find the sum of the interior angles of a polygon?
- Does this work for all polygons? Why?
-

Common misconceptions and remediation

- Students often think that the sum of an exterior angle and an interior angle is 360°. Throughout the lesson, reinforce that it is 180°.

Probing questions

- What clues do you look for when solving a geometrical problem?
- How do you decide where to start? Is it possible to solve the problem in a different way?
- How would you convince a friend that each of the angles in a … is equal to …?

Literacy focus

- Key terms: interior angle, polygon
  Ask students to make up sentences or questions using these words.

Part 1

- Ask: What is a three-sided shape called? … a four-sided shape? … a five-sided shape? … a 10-sided shape? (Note that students are expected to know the names of these polygons for GCSE examinations.)
- **More able** students might want to know about polygons with more than 10 sides. Students could do their own research into this. (*hendecagon* (11 sides), *dodecagon* (12 sides), *icosagon* (20 sides))

Part 2

Angle sums from triangles
- Draw a quadrilateral and a pentagon on the board.
- Show students how to split them into triangles from one vertex to find the sum of the interior angles.
- Ask students to do the same for a hexagon and a heptagon. They should use convex polygons, but not regular ones.
- Encourage students to draw their own polygons and split them into triangles.
- Ensure that students draw all the diagonals from one vertex of the polygon.
- You could provide **less able** students with a worksheet of ready-drawn polygons.
- **Students can now do Exercise 6C from the Student Book.**

G&M 1–5	Calculator n/a	CM n/a	MR n/a	PS n/a	EV n/a

n-sided polygon
- Next ask students to work out the sum of the interior angles for octagons, nonagons and decagons without drawing the shapes. Ask them to record their results in a table.
- **Less able** students should notice the formula in words:

  sum of interior angles = 180 × (2 less than the number of sides)
- **More able** students should write down this algebraic formula:

  $S = 180 (n - 2)°$

  where S is the sum of the interior angles and n is the number of sides.
- **Students can now do Exercise 6D from the Student Book.**

G&M 1, 3, 4	Calculator all	CM 2	MR 6	PS 5, 7	EV n/a

Part 3

- Display a table for regular polygons with the column headings: 'Number of sides', 'Exterior angle' and 'Interior angle'.
- Encourage individuals to complete rows of the table for shapes with 3 to 10 sides, and with *n* sides.
- Ask: What happens to the interior angle of a regular polygon as the number of sides increases? Why?

Section 6.4 Regular polygons

Learning objectives
- Calculate the exterior angles and the interior angles of a regular polygon

Resources and homework
- Student Book 6.4: pages 160–163
- Practice Book 6.4: pages 46–47

Making mathematical connections
- Locus
- 3D shapes

Making cross-curricular connections
- **Science** – geometric shapes in chemistry
- **Design and Technology** – constructing models of designs
- **Geography** – identifying locations on maps by descriptions of the 2D representation of man-made objects
- **Relevance** – applications in engineering and architecture

Prior learning
- Students should know that the sum of the interior angles of a triangle is 180° and the sum of the interior angles in a quadrilateral is 360°.
- Students should also know how to calculate the sum of interior angles in a polygon.

Working mathematically
- Students work to understand the logic rather than try to learn justifications of this type by memory. This way they see the transferable nature of the thinking process.
- Discuss this with students and provide opportunities to identify the steps in the process and use similar logic in different contexts.

Common misconceptions and remediation
- Make sure students are clear in their understanding of regular and irregular polygons and how this translates into calculating angles.

Probing questions
- What happens to the interior angle of a regular polygon as the number of sides increases? Why?

Literacy focus
- Key term: exterior angle
  Ask students to explain the difference between an exterior angle and an interior angle.

Part 1
Guess the shape
- Tell the class that you are thinking of a 2D shape (e.g. a square, an isosceles triangle, a trapezium, a regular decagon, a circle).
- Tell students that they can ask 10 closed questions to guess exactly what the shape is and that you will answer only 'Yes' or 'No'.
- Repeat this activity regularly, adjusting the questions to suit the ability of the students.

Part 2

- Define a regular polygon as one in which all the sides are equal and all the angles are equal.
- Display diagrams of a square, a regular pentagon and a regular hexagon.
- Ask students to find the size of each interior angle for the regular polygons and record their results in a table.

Interior and exterior angles of regular shapes

- Remind students what an exterior angle is and that the sum of an interior angle and its exterior angle is 180°. Referring to the Student Book text, ask students to find the size of each exterior angle for the regular polygons in their tables.
- **Less able** students should notice that the formula in words for finding each exterior angle and interior angle in a regular polygon is:
  - exterior angle = 360° ÷ number of sides
  - interior angle = 180° – exterior angle
- **More able** students should write down the algebraic formulae for any regular polygon:

$$E = \frac{360°}{n} \qquad\qquad I = 180° - E$$

$$= 180° - \frac{360°}{n}$$

where E is the exterior angle, I is the interior angle, and n is the number of sides.
- Point out that when students need to work out the size of an interior angle of a regular polygon, it is more straightforward to find the size of the exterior angle first.
- Work through Example 6 with students.
- **Students can now do Exercise 6E from the Student Book.**

G&M 1–4	Calculator all	CM 5, 6	MR 9, 12	PS 7, 8, 10, 11	EV n/a

Part 3

- Display a table for regular polygons with the column headings: 'Number of sides', 'Exterior angle' and 'Interior angle'.
- Encourage individuals to complete rows of the table for shapes with 3 to 10 sides, and with n sides.
- Give students a few regular polygons and ask them to calculate the interior and exterior angles of these polygons.

Section 6.5 Angles in parallel lines

Learning objectives
- Find angles in parallel lines

Resources and homework
- Student Book 6.5: pages 163–165
- Practice Book 6.5: pages 47–48

Making mathematical connections
- Trigonometry
- Bearings

Making cross-curricular connections
- **Science** – forces
- **Art** – designs involving parallel lines and angles
- **Relevance** – applications in engineering and architecture

Prior learning
- Students should understand the nature of parallel lines and be able to calculate complements of 180 confidently.

Working mathematically
- Students work to understand the logic rather than try to learn justifications of this type by memory. This way they see the transferable nature of the thinking process.
- Discuss this with students and provide opportunities to identify the steps in the process and use similar logic in different contexts.

Common misconceptions and remediation
- Some students may be confused between alternate and corresponding angles. Constant reference to them during the lesson is usually beneficial.
- **Note:** Remind students that referring to alternate angles as Z angles, or corresponding angles as F angles, will not be acceptable in examinations.

Probing questions
- Refer to a geometrical diagram with parallel lines and lines that intersect them.
  - o Explain how you would use the information given to you in this diagram.
  - o How do you decide where to start in order to find the missing angles?

Literacy focus
- Key terms: allied angles, alternate angles, corresponding angles
- Consistent reference to these key terms during the lesson will help students to remember the correct terms.

Part 1
- Write this grid of numbers on the board.

90	70	50	30	60	58	73
45	105	32	17	127	15	165
63	87	25	120	148	20	3
163	135	75	110	130	65	40

- Ask students to: choose a number from the board and subtract it from 180; find two numbers that add up to 180; add together two numbers to give a total less than 180 and subtract the result from 180; find two numbers that add up to 90; find three numbers that add up to 180.

Part 2

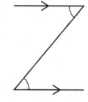

- Explain to the class that the lesson is about solving problems using alternate, corresponding and allied angles within parallel lines.
- Draw the letter Z on the board (top right). Ask students what happens to the letter Z when the card is rotated through 180°. (Students should be specific about what happens to the two angles.)
- Demonstrate, by measuring, that the top and bottom angles are equal.
- Now ask the class what happens to the two angles if a letter Z is drawn without the top and bottom lines being *parallel*. (Ensure that students recognise that if the lines are parallel, then the angles are equal, but if they are not parallel, then the angles will be different.)
- Point out that the correct name for angles of this type is *alternate angles*.
- Draw a letter F on the board (middle right) and establish the rules for corresponding angles.
- Point out that the correct name for angles of this type is *corresponding angles.*
- Now draw the diagram as shown (bottom right) and establish the rules for *co-interior* or *allied angles*.
- Students should now add the following text to their notes.

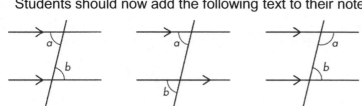

a and *b* are equal	*a* and *b* are equal	*a* + *b* = 180°
a and *b* are alternate angles	*a* and *b* are corresponding angles	*a* and *b* are allied angles

- Work through Example 7 in the Student Book.
- **Students can now begin Exercise 6F from the Student Book.**

G&M 1, 3	Calculator all	CM 2, 6, 8, 9	MR n/a	PS 4, 5	EV 7

Part 3

- Summarise the lesson by pointing out that, in questions with many parallel lines, many of the angles will often be the same and many others will be the supplement of the first angle.
- Remind the class that they need to be able to work out angles *and* remember the correct terminology.
- Draw a set of parallel lines intersected by a transversal. Point out some angle pairs and ask students to identify the pairs and display their answers on mini whiteboards.

Section 6.6 Special quadrilaterals

Learning objectives
- Use angle properties in quadrilaterals

Resources and homework
- Student Book 6.6: pages 166–168
- Practice Book 6.6: pages 48–49

Making mathematical connections
- Symmetry
- Trigonometry

Making cross-curricular connections
- **Science** – forces
- **Art** – designs involving quadrilaterals
- **Relevance** – applications in engineering and architecture

Prior learning
- Students should know that the sum of the angles in any triangle is 180°, that two of the sides of an isosceles triangle are equal, and that the sum of the angles in a quadrilateral is 360°.
- Students should also know that when a transversal cuts parallel lines, the alternate angles are equal, the corresponding angles are equal and the allied (or co-interior) angles are supplementary (have a sum of 180°).

Working mathematically
- Students should, by the end of the lesson, understand and be able to recall the properties of the following shapes:
  - parallelogram
  - rectangle
  - rhombus
  - square
  - kite
  - trapezium.

Common misconceptions and remediation
- Some students may be confused about the difference between alternate and corresponding angles. Constant reference to them during the lesson is usually beneficial.
- **Note:** Again remind students that, in examinations, it is not acceptable to refer to alternate angles as Z angles or corresponding angles as F angles.

Probing questions
- What information would you need about a quadrilateral in order to classify it as a: parallelogram, rectangle, rhombus, square, kite, trapezium?
- Can you explain why a rhombus must be a parallelogram, but a parallelogram is not necessarily a rhombus?
- Why can't a trapezium have three acute angles?

Literacy focus
- Key term: bisect
- Students work in pairs. One student describes a shape and the other student tries to draw it.

Part 1

- On the board, draw a pair of parallel lines cut by a transversal.
- Ask a student to mark a pair of alternate angles on the diagram.
- Repeat for a pair of corresponding angles and a pair of allied angles.

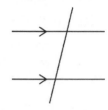

Part 2

- Draw an equilateral triangle and an isosceles triangle on the board. Go through the geometrical properties of both shapes, ensuring that students are familiar with them.

  Parallelogram; Rectangle; Rhombus; Square; Kite; Trapezium
- Draw a parallelogram on the board. Go through the geometrical properties of the parallelogram and encourage students to record all the facts for future reference.
- Remind **less able** students about the mathematical conventions for parallel lines, equal sides and naming angles. Talk to **more able** students about the angles created by diagonals in a parallelogram (alternate angles, vertically opposite angles).
- Draw each of the following shapes on the board in turn and go through its geometrical properties:
  - a rectangle
  - a rhombus
  - a square
  - a kite
  - a trapezium*.
- Encourage students to record all the facts for future reference.
- *For the trapezium, tell **more able** students that if the sloping sides are equal, the shape is an *isosceles trapezium*.
- Briefly revise the symmetry of the less familiar quadrilaterals, since this is often a problem area for **less able** students.

Shape	Number of lines of symmetry	Order of rotational symmetry
Parallelogram	0	2
Rhombus	2	2
Kite	1	0
Trapezium	0	0

- **Students can now begin Exercise 6G from the Student Book.**

G&M 1–4	Calculator all	CM 6, 9	MR n/a	PS 7, 8	EV 5

Part 3

- On the board, draw an isosceles triangle, a trapezium, a parallelogram, a kite and a rhombus. Do not mark the identical angles and sides.
- Ask students (in turn) to mark pairs of identical angles or sides on the diagrams until all possibilities have been covered.
- Draw the six quadrilaterals (parallelogram, rectangle, rhombus, square, kite, trapezium) on the board and ask students first to identify, and then to describe, as many properties of each quadrilateral as they can.

Section 6.7 Scale drawings and bearings

Learning objectives
- Read scale drawings and maps
- Draw scale drawings
- Use a bearing to specify a direction

Resources and homework
- Student Book 6.7: pages 168–173
- Practice Book 6.7: pages 50–54

Making mathematical connections
- Trigonometry
- Coordinates
- Ratio

Making cross-curricular connections
- **Geography** – maps and bearings
- **Design and Technology** – scale drawings
- **Relevance** – applications in engineering navigation and architecture

Prior learning
- Students should know how to simplify a ratio into the form 1 : *n*.
- Students should also be familiar with the directions on a compass.

Working mathematically
- Explain to students that a *scale drawing* is an accurate representation of a real object.
- Scale drawings are usually smaller than the original objects. All the measurements must be in proportion to the corresponding measurements of the original. All the angles must be equal to the corresponding angles on the original.

Common misconceptions and remediation
- Students often calculate bearings incorrectly. Reinforce that the bearing is measured clockwise from the north line to the direction of travel and that the bearing must always be written as three figures.
- When making a scale drawing, remind students to express *all* measurements in the *same* unit.

Probing questions
- Why is it important to write bearings as three figures?
- Why do you think map scales are given as a ratio? What are the advantages of this?

Literacy focus
- Key terms: scale drawing, scale factor, three-figure bearing
- Discuss the key terms with students to make sure that they understand the meanings.

Part 1
- Show the class a map of Britain or a local map of your area. Ask the students about the scale for the map. Using the map, lead the discussion to scale drawing, map scales and bearings.
-

Part 2
Scale drawings
- On the board, make a scale drawing of the *plan* dimensions of a room in school, e.g. a classroom, hall or gym.

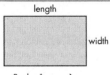

Scale: 1 cm = 1 m

- Explain the importance of choosing a sensible *scale*. If you double the scale, the scale drawing is halved in size.
- Show the class how to use the scale to work out the actual length and width of the room.
- Work through Example 8 in the Student Book.
- Explain that maps are scale drawings used to represent areas of land in subjects such as Geography. Show the class various maps and the different *map scales* that are used.
- Show students how to work out the actual direct distance ('as the crow flies') between two places on the map. E.g. if the direct distance between A and B on a map with a scale of 1 cm to 10 km is 4 cm, the actual direct distance between A and B is 4 × 10 km = 40 km.
- Explain that a *map ratio* is an alternative to a map scale. It is the ratio of a distance on the map to the actual distance it represents on the ground. Map ratios are given in the form 1 : *x* and have no units. You can think of a map ratio as a *scale factor*.
  For example, a map scale might of 1 cm to 5 km is equivalent to a map ratio of 1 : 500 000. This is because 1 km = 100 × 1000 cm so 1 cm to 5 km is the same as 1 cm to 500 000 cm.
- Work through Example 9 from the Student Book.

Bearings
- Draw the main compass points on the board or show an actual compass.
- North (N), south (S), east (E) and west (W) are examples of *compass bearings*.
- A *bearing* is a specified direction in relation to due *north*. The symbol for north is: Students will have probably seen this symbol on maps in Geography.
- Explain that bearings are used for navigation (air and sea) and in sports like orienteering.
- Students can copy into their books: A bearing is measured in degrees (°). The angle is always measured *clockwise* from the north line. A bearing is always given using three digits and is referred to as a *three-figure bearing*. For example, the bearing for an easterly direction is 090°. (This is pronounced as 'a bearing of zero nine zero'.)
- Draw the first bearing diagram on the board. Explain that the three-figure bearing of B from A is 040°. The three-figure bearing of A from B is 220°.
- Draw the second bearing diagram, on the board. Explain how to find the bearing of Leeds from Manchester (050°).
- To find the bearing of Manchester from Leeds (often referred to as the *back bearing*), use the broken line to find the alternate angle of 50° and then add 180°. The bearing is 230°. (The difference between the two bearings is 180°.)
- Work through Example 10 in the Student Book.

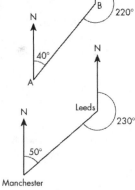

- **Students can now work through Exercise 6H from the Student Book.**

| G&M 2, 5, 6, 8, 10, 11 | Calculator n/a | CM 7 | MR 3, 9 | PS 1, 4, 12–14 | EV n/a |

Part 3
- Ask students to write each of the following scales as a map ratio.
  1 cm to 2 m   1 cm to 5 m   2 cm to 1 m   1 cm to 10 km   1 cm to 200 km
- A map ratio is 1 : 250 000. The distance between two towns on the map is 12 cm. What is the actual distance between the two towns?

Chapter 7 Geometry and measures: Transformations, constructions and loci

Overview

7.1	Congruent triangles	**7.5**	Bisectors
7.2	Rotational symmetry	**7.6**	Defining a locus
7.3	Transformations	**7.7**	Loci problems
7.4	Combinations of transformations	**7.8**	Plans and elevations

Prior learning

Know how to find the lines of symmetry of a 2D shape.
Know how to draw the lines with equations $x = \pm a$, $y = \pm b$, $y = x$ and $y = -x$.
Know how to measure lines and angles.
Know how to use scale drawings.

Learning objectives

Ensure that students can: show that two triangles are congruent; find the order of rotational symmetry of a 2D shape; know what is meant by a transformation; translate, reflect, rotate and enlarge 2D shapes; bisect a line and an angle; construct perpendiculars; define a locus; solve locus problems; construct and interpret plans and elevations of 3D shapes.

In the examination, students will be expected to:
* demonstrate that two triangles are congruent
* find the order of rotational symmetry for a 2D shape
* recognise shapes with rotational symmetry
* translate, reflect, rotate and enlarge a 2D shape
* combine transformations
* construct the bisectors of lines and angles
* construct angles of 60° and 90°
* draw a locus for a given rule
* solve practical problems using loci
* construct and interpret plans and elevations of 3D shapes.

Extension

More able students could start to transform quadratic curves.

Curriculum references

Section	GCSE specification
7.1	G 5
7.2	G 7
7.3	G 7
7.4	G 7
7.5	G 2
7.6	G 2
7.7	G 2
7.8	G 13

Route mapping

Exercise	Accessible	Intermediate	Challenging	AO1	AO2 MR CM	AO3 PS EV	Key questions
7A		1–8		1, 3, 4	2, 5–7	8	8
7B	1–8			1, 2	4, 6	3, 5, 7, 8	6
7C	1–9			1–3	5, 6, 9	4, 7, 8	1
7D	1–11			1, 6–8	2, 3, 5, 11	4, 9, 10	8
7E	1–14			1, 4, 5, 9, 12, 13	6–8, 10, 14	2, 3, 11	4, 13
7F	1–5	6–9		1–4, 6	5, 9	7, 8	6, 7
7G	1–8	9–13		1, 4, 7, 12	2, 3, 5, 6, 8, 10, 13	9, 11	10, 12
7H	1–14			2–5, 7–9, 12–14	11	1, 6, 10	6, 13, 14
7I	1–10			1, 2, 4, 6	5, 9	3, 7, 8, 10	3, 7
7J	1–17			1–5, 9–15,	7, 8	6, 9c, 16, 17	9, 11
7K	1–4	5, 6		1, 2, 4	3, 5	6	1, 2, 4

Key questions are those that demonstrate mastery of the concept, or which require a step-up in understanding or application. Key questions could be used to identify the questions that students must tackle, to support differentiation, or to identify the questions that should be teacher-marked rather than student-marked.

About this chapter

Making connections: Explain that when a point moves according to certain specified conditions, the path traced out is called a *locus* (plural *loci*). This is a Latin word, which means 'place'. This section links in to later work on vectors.

Relevance: Loci have a range of practical applications, including helping to decide on suitable routes for a new train line or the path of an object that follows a rule, such as a piston. This chapter shows students how to change the position of shapes according to certain rules and how to construct loci from given criteria.

Working mathematically: Find the result of translating, reflecting, rotating or enlarging a shape. Trace the path of a point on a wheel as it rotates. Trace the path of an object as it moves, equidistant from two points. Find the locus of points: equidistant from two points, from a line, and from a point.

Assessment: In each section of this chapter, ensure that students have a good grasp of the key questions in each exercise before moving on. (Refer to the 'Route mapping' table above.) Encourage students to read and think about the 'Ready to progress?' statements on page 214 of the Student Book. Check students' understanding at the end of the chapter, formatively, using peer assessment. Students could do a mini test in the form of the 'Review questions' on pages 214–215 of the Student Book. Follow up the test with an individual target-getting session, based on any areas for development that a student may have.

Worked exemplars from the Student Book – suggestions for use
* Present students with the same question but using different numbers. Students should use the exemplar to mirror the working, in full or only the notes.
* Copy and cut the exemplar into cards. Ask students to match the working with the notes.
* Copy and cut the working into cards, splitting the label/description from the working. Ask students to put the working in order then match with the descriptions.

Answers to the Student Book questions are available on the CD-ROM provided.

Section 7.1 Congruent triangles

Learning objectives

- Demonstrate that two triangles are congruent

Resources and homework

- Student Book 7.1: pages 179–181
- Practice Book 7.1: page 55

Making mathematical connections

- Cosine rule
- Sine rule

Making cross-curricular connections

- **Art** – congruent shapes in designs
- **Design and Technology** – congruent shapes in designs
- **Relevance** – applications in engineering and architecture

Prior learning

- Students should be able to recognise congruent shapes and understand the meaning of congruency.
- They should also be able to use tracing paper to check if shapes are congruent.

Working mathematically

- Students learn to describe the four conditions for congruence of triangles by the end of this section.
- Remind them that if three corresponding measurements (including one side) are the same in two triangles, then the triangles are congruent.

Common misconceptions and remediation

- Students often think three identical angles is enough to prove congruency in two triangles. This only shows that the two triangles are similar. It is important to reinforce, regularly, the four conditions that establish congruency.

Probing questions

- Are two triangles with equal angles always congruent?
- What is the minimum information you need to show that two triangles are congruent?

Literacy focus

- Key term: congruent
- Ask students to write a question using the key term to show that they understand it.

Part 1

NB: *This section may take more than 1 hour.*

- Remind students of the definition of congruent, that is, identical.
- Draw these two triangles on the board and ask if the shapes are congruent. Most students will say yes.
- Draw another pair of triangles, one a reflection of the other. Students may be unsure as to whether these triangles are congruent or not.
- Establish that they are. Use this to emphasise the importance of clearly understanding what congruent means. Stress that it does not matter that one triangle is reflected; the sides and angles remain identical and therefore these triangles are congruent.

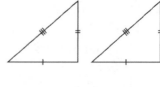

Part 2

Conditions for congruent triangles

- Remind students that two congruent triangles are identical: that is, three corresponding angles are equal and three corresponding sides are equal.
- Tell students that there are four conditions to prove congruency: each requires three identical measurements on the triangles to be known.

Condition 1: SSS

- Work through Condition 1 using the Student Book. Draw the triangles on the board and label them ABC and XYZ. Ask students to list the pairs of equal angles. Show **more able** students the convention for showing congruent triangles for Condition 1: $\triangle ABC \equiv \triangle XYZ$ (SSS).

Condition 2: SAS

- Now work through Condition 2. Again draw the triangles on the board and label them ABC and XYZ. Ask for pairs of equal sides and angles. Show **more able** students the convention for showing congruent triangles for Condition 2: $\triangle ABC \equiv \triangle XYZ$ (SAS).

Condition 3: ASA or AAS

- Draw both pairs of triangles for Condition 3 on the board. Label the triangles ABC and XYZ and ask for the third angle and pairs of equal sides. Show **more able** students the convention for showing congruent triangles for Condition 3: $\triangle ABC \equiv \triangle XYZ$ (ASA) or $\triangle ABC \equiv \triangle XYZ$ (AAS).

Condition 4: RHS

- Finally work through Condition 4, again displaying the triangles and labelling them ABC and XYZ. Ask the students to give the pairs of equal angles and sides. Show **more able** students the convention for showing congruent triangles for Condition 4: $\triangle ABC \equiv \triangle XYZ$ (RHS).

Notation

- Discuss the text in the Student Book and then look at Example 1 with students.
- Show **more able** students how to prove and set out a geometrical problem using congruent triangles:

  In the diagram on the right, AB is parallel to CD and AE = ED.

  Prove that triangles ABE and CDE are congruent.

  AE = ED (given)

  $\angle BAE = \angle CDE$ (alternate angles)

  $\angle AEB = \angle CED$ (opposite angles)

  So, $\triangle ABE \equiv \triangle CDE$ (ASA)

  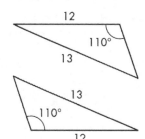

- **Students can now do Exercise 7A from the Student Book.**

| G&M 1, 3, 4 | Calculator n/a | CM 5, 6 | MR 2, 7 | PS n/a | EV 8 |

Part 3

- Ask students to consider whether the triangles on the right are congruent.
- The answer is not obvious as, initially, none of the congruency rules seem to fit. However, the remaining angles to be found must both be acute so that there will be no ambiguity when calculating the non-included angle, and hence none regarding the included angle. So, according to the SAS rule, these triangles are congruent.

Section 7.2 Rotational symmetry

Learning objectives
- Find the order of rotational symmetry for a 2D shape
- Recognise shapes with rotational symmetry

Resources and homework
- Student Book 7.2: pages 181–183
- Practice Book 7.2: page 56

Making mathematical connections
- Transformations
- Line symmetry

Making cross-curricular connections
- **Art** – symmetry
- **ICT** – to use software such as Logo
- **Relevance** – applications in Art and design, and architecture

Prior learning
- Students should be familiar with line symmetry.

Working mathematically
- By the end of this section, students should be able to write down the order of rotational symmetry of a 2D shape with confidence. Encourage students to draw their own shapes on squared paper, with 'x' lines of symmetry, or order of rotational symmetry 'x'.

Common misconceptions and remediation
- A common misconception is to think that all polygons have the same number of lines and order of rotational symmetry as they do number of sides and/or angles. To address this, make sure students find lines of symmetry on regular and irregular shapes.

Probing questions
- What is the order of rotational symmetry of a:
  - regular hexagon
  - regular octagon
  - regular pentagon
- Can you name any shapes that have rotational symmetry but no lines of symmetry or lines of symmetry but no rotational symmetry?

Literacy focus
- Key terms: order of rotational symmetry, rotational symmetry
- Ask students to write a definition for each key term to show that they understand it.

Part 1
- Ask students to imagine a square.
- Now ask them to imagine rotating it about its centre point and count how many times it looks exactly the same.
- Repeat the task with a rectangle and then a parallelogram.

Part 2

- The students will require tracing paper and squared paper for this lesson.
- Explain that there are two types of symmetry for 2D shapes: line symmetry and rotational symmetry. A plane shape has rotational symmetry if it can be rotated about a point and is exactly the same in a new position.
- Ask students to draw a square. Demonstrate how to trace the shape and then turn the tracing paper until the tracing fits exactly on top of the original square. Encourage students to put an arrow at the top of the tracing paper so that it is easy to see when it has been rotated through 360°.
- Establish that the square has rotational symmetry of order 4. (This should be the same as for the imaginary square the students rotated in Part 1.)
- Repeat with a rectangle (rotational symmetry of order 2) and a kite (no rotational symmetry). Tell students that a shape with no rotational symmetry is said to have rotational symmetry of order 1.
- Work through Example 2 in the Student Book with the class.
- **Students can now do Exercise 7B from the Student Book.**

| G&M 1, 2 | Calculator n/a | CM n/a | MR 4, 6 | PS 3, 5 | EV 7, 8 |

Part 3

- Show students a set of shapes such as triangles, quadrilaterals and circles. These could be cut from old magazines or displayed on a visualiser or IWB.
- Ask students to give the order of rotational symmetry for each shape.
- Establish that a circle has an infinite number of lines of symmetry and its order of rotational symmetry is also infinity. (Some students may think that it has 360.) Ask them to explain 'infinity'. (Introduce the symbol for infinity, ∞, if appropriate.)

Section 7.3 Transformations

Learning objectives

- Translate, reflect, rotate and enlarge a 2D shape

Resources and homework

- Student Book 7.3: pages 183–195
- Practice Book 7.3: pages 57–62

Making mathematical connections

- Mappings, coordinates and graphing vectors

Making cross-curricular connections

- **Science** – vectors
- **ICT** – using programs such as Logo
- **Relevance** – applications in Art and design, and architecture

Prior learning

- Students need to be familiar with equations of lines, of the type:
  $y = x$, $y = -x$, $y = a$ and $x = b$.

Working mathematically

- To build confidence, encourage students to use the terms, 'transformation' and 'translation', in the correct context.
- Remind them that when a triangle has been translated, it has not been reflected or rotated.
- When reflecting shapes in diagonal lines, it is easier if students turn the page so that the mirror line is horizontal or vertical.

Common misconceptions and remediation

- **Translation: Less able** students may confuse the terms 'transformation' and 'translation'. Reinforce that a translation is a specific type of transformation (like a rotation or a reflection).
- **Reflection:** When reflecting shapes in diagonal lines, students often draw the image and the object at different distances from the mirror line. Using tracing paper will help.
- **Rotation:** Students often forget to provide all the required information when describing a rotation. Stress that they need the centre, the angle and the direction of the rotation.
- **Enlargement:** It often occurs that students do not use the centre of enlargement that is provided. Encourage them to mark the given centre clearly each time.

Probing questions

- What changes and what stays the same when you: translate; rotate; reflect; enlarge a shape?
- When is the image congruent to the original shape? How do you know?

Literacy focus

- Key terms: angle of rotation, centre of enlargement, centre of rotation, enlargement, image, invariant, mirror line, object, reflection, rotation, transformation, translation, vector
- Ask students to describe transformations in words.

Part 1

- Discuss the general idea of the transformation of an object and what it means. Students will have come across different types of transformations, so ask them to name specific types.

Part 2

Translation

- Discuss how to describe different translations on a coordinate grid.
- Put a cross on a vertex on both triangles. Explain that to move from its position in triangle A to triangle B, the cross moves 3 squares to the right and 2 squares up. Demonstrate that the movement is the same for all vertices and that it can be represented by the vector $\binom{3}{2}$.

- Work through Example 3 from the Student Book.
- **Students can now do Exercise 7C from the Student Book.**

G&M 1–3	Calculator n/a	CM 5, 9	MR 6	PS 4, 7, 8	EV n/a

Reflections

- Discuss how to describe different reflections on a coordinate grid.
- Establish the best way is to give the equation of the mirror line.
- Explain how to count across the squares from a vertex to the mirror line, and then count across the same number of squares to find the position of the reflection of that vertex.
- Demonstrate with this example: Triangle B is the reflection of triangle A in the line $x = -1$; Triangle C is the reflection of triangle A in the line $y = 1$.
- **Students can now do Exercise 7D from the Student Book.**

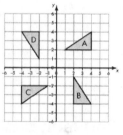

G&M 1, 6–8	Calculator n/a	CM 2, 3, 11	MR 5	PS 4	EV 9, 10

Rotations

- Discuss how to describe different rotations on a coordinate grid.
- Establish the best way is to give coordinates of the centre of rotation.
- Demonstrate with this example, using tracing paper.
  Triangle B is a rotation of triangle A by 90° clockwise about (0, 0) or the origin; Triangle C is a rotation of triangle A by 180° about (0, 0) (note that there is no need for a direction for a 180° rotation); Triangle D is a rotation of triangle A by 90° anticlockwise about (0, 0) (note that 270° clockwise is also acceptable).
- **Students can now do Exercise 7E from the Student Book.**

G&M 1, 4, 5, 9, 12, 13	Calculator n/a	CM 10, 14	MR 6–8	PS 2, 3	EV 11

Enlargements

- An enlargement is a transformation that changes the size of a shape.
- Discuss how to describe enlargements on a coordinate grid. Establish that it is best to give the coordinates as the centre of enlargement.
- Demonstrate with an example: Triangle Y is an enlargement of triangle X of scale factor 3, about (0, 0).
- Demonstrate the ray method and then show students how to count squares from (0, 0) to each vertex of X; and repeat three times from (0, 0) to each vertex of Y. The centre of enlargement is the origin, so multiplying the coordinates of the vertices of X by 3 gives the vertices of Y.
- Work through the text in the Student Book which covers both methods as well as negative and fractional enlargements.
- **Students can now do Exercise 7F from the Student Book.**

G&M 1–4, 6	Calculator n/a	CM 9	MR 5	PS 7, 8	EV n/a

Part 3

- Ask students what they notice about the coordinates of the object and image points when they: rotate some points through 180° about the origin; reflect some points in the line $y = x$.
- Ask students why, if point (a, b) is rotated through 180° about the origin, the image point is $(-a, -b)$.

Section 7.4 Combinations of transformations

Learning objectives
* Combine transformations

Resources and homework
* Student Book 7.4: pages 195–197
* Practice Book 7.4: pages 62–63

Making mathematical connections
* Mappings, coordinates and graphing vectors

Making cross-curricular connections
* **Science** – vectors
* **ICT** – using programs such as Logo
* **Relevance** – applications in Art and design, and architecture

Prior learning
* Students should have covered section 7.3 on translation, reflections, rotations and enlargements.

Working mathematically
* You often have to use more than one transformation in a question. In this exercise, you will practise combining the transformations you have met so far.
* Remember:
  o To describe a translation fully, you need to use a vector.
  o To describe a reflection fully, you need to use a mirror line.
  o To describe a rotation fully, you need to give a centre of rotation, an angle of rotation and the direction of turn.
  o To describe an enlargement fully, you need to give a centre of enlargement and a scale factor.

Common misconceptions and remediation
* Students often miss some of the information required to explain rotations and enlargements fully. Throughout the lesson, reinforce the information in the table.
* Always have tracing paper available.

Transformation	Information needed
Translation	column vector
Reflection	equation of mirror line
Rotation	angle, direction, centre of rotation
Enlargement	scale factor, centre of enlargement

Probing questions
* What changes and what stays the same when you, for example, combine transformations such as a reflection followed by a rotation?

Literacy focus
* There are no new key terms in this section.

Part 1
* Display a coordinate grid, with x-axis and y-axis labelled appropriately. Draw on two squares: A with vertices at (–2, 0), (–2, 2), (0, 0) and (0, 2), and B with vertices at (0, 0), (0, 2), (2, 2), (2, 0).
* Ask students: Is B is a transformation of A? If so, describe the transformation.

- Ask: Is it possible to describe it as a translation? Can it be described as: a reflection, a rotation: an enlargement?' Expected answers include:

  o translation by the vector $\begin{pmatrix} 2 \\ 0 \end{pmatrix}$

  o reflection in the line $x = 0$ or the y-axis

  o rotation of 90° clockwise about the origin, or 90° anticlockwise about (0, 2)

  o no enlargement, as B is not enlarged.

Part 2

- Say that this lesson covers all the transformations they have met and combinations of them.
- Consider enlargements first. If the object and the image are a different size, there has been an enlargement. Consider a translation next.
- A shape may have been transformed more than once, by combined transformations. Work through the examples below. In each case, give **less able** students a copy of the diagram or let them draw it themselves on squared paper.
  Example 1: Display this diagram.
- Ask students to describe fully the single transformation that maps triangle A onto triangle B: a rotation of 90° clockwise about the origin or (0, 0).
- Now ask students to describe fully the single transformation that maps triangle B onto triangle C: a reflection in the line $x = 0$ or the y-axis.
- Explain that the combined transformation that maps triangle A onto triangle C is a rotation of 90° clockwise about the origin, followed by a reflection in the line $x = 0$.
- Now ask students to give the single transformation that maps triangle C onto triangle A. Make sure they give a full description of the reflection: a reflection in the line $y = -x$.
  Example 2: Display this diagram.
- Ask students to describe the single transformation that maps triangle A onto triangle B: a translation by the vector $\begin{pmatrix} 4 \\ -2 \end{pmatrix}$.
- Now ask students to describe fully the single transformation that maps triangle B onto triangle C: an enlargement by scale factor 2 about the origin or (0, 0).
- Explain that the combined transformation that maps triangle A onto triangle C is: a translation by the vector $\begin{pmatrix} 4 \\ -2 \end{pmatrix}$ followed by an enlargement by scale factor 2 about the origin.
- Now ask students to give the single transformation that maps triangle C onto triangle A: an enlargement by scale factor $\frac{1}{2}$ about (–8, 4).
- **Students can now do Exercise 7G from the Student Book.**

G&M 1, 4, 7, 12	Calculator n/a	CM 3, 5, 6, 8, 10	MR 2, 13	PS 9	EV 11

Part 3

- Ask students to work in pairs to design a poster to summarise all the transformations they have covered. If they need help, show this thought-process diagram and ask students to complete it.

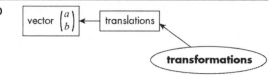

Section 7.5 Bisectors

Learning objectives

- Construct the bisectors of lines and angles
- Construct angles of 60° and 90°

Resources and homework

- Student Book 7.5: pages 198–201
- Practice Book 7.5: pages 63–64

Making mathematical connections

- Loci
- Scale drawings

Making cross-curricular connections

- **Design technology** – Graphics
- **Art** – geometric designs
- **Relevance** – applications in Art and design, architecture and engineering

Prior learning

- Students should be able to use compasses to draw arcs and circles accurately.

Working mathematically

- To **bisect** means to divide in half. So a bisector divides something into two equal parts.
- A **line bisector** divides a straight line into two equal lengths.
- An **angle bisector** is the straight line that divides an angle into two equal angles.

Common misconceptions and remediation

- Students may just measure lengths rather than construct them. Some students erase the construction lines. Remind student about these things frequently.

Probing questions

- Why do we use compasses for constructions?
- For which constructions is it important to get two lines the same length using arcs?

Literacy focus

- Key terms: angle bisector, line bisector, perpendicular bisector
- Students could write down the key steps needed to bisect a line and an angle as part of their notes.

Part 1

- Discuss how to bisect a line (cut it into two equal parts), then demonstrate the wrong way to bisect a line. (Draw a straight line, measure half-way along and make a mark. Use a protractor, centred on this mark, to make an angle of 90°.)
- Stress that in an examination, if students use this incorrect method to bisect a line, they would not get any marks for the question.
- Now demonstrate on the board the correct method to bisect a straight line, using a pair of compasses and a straight edge.

Part 2

- Make sure that each student has a pair of compasses fitted with a sharp pencil, a straight edge, another sharp pencil for drawing and plenty of plain paper.
- Work through each construction as detailed in the Student Book.

To construct a line bisector

- Go through the text in the Student Book and demonstrate how to construct a line bisector, reminding students that the arcs drawn are construction lines and so should be faint, but still visible. Ask students to draw a few straight lines and then bisect them all.

To construct an angle bisector

- Next talk about angle bisectors and demonstrate how to construct them. Students will need to draw quite a few angles of their own to practise this skill. They should use a protractor to check their accuracy.

To construct an angle of 60°

- Go through the text in the Student Book and demonstrate how to construct an angle of 60°. **More able** students could try to construct an angle of 30° at this point by constructing an angle of 60° and then bisecting it.

To construct a perpendicular from a point on a line (an angle of 90°); To construct a perpendicular from a point to a line

- Go through the text under these two headings and then show all students how to construct a perpendicular line from a point on a line. Practise this with a few perpendiculars from various lines on their plain paper.
- **Less able** students may omit drawing a perpendicular from a point to the line at this stage, but **more able** students should attempt it.
- **Students can now do Exercise 7H from the Student Book.**

G&M 2–5, 7–9, 12–14	Calculator n/a	CM 11	MR n/a	PS 10	EV 1, 6

Part 3

- Provide a board pen that is attached to a piece of string at least 50 cm long. Draw an angle of 120° and ask a volunteer to bisect it, using the board pen and the string.
- Ask another volunteer to bisect one of the resulting 60° angles.
- Ask a third volunteer to bisect one of the 30° angles, and a fourth to use a board protractor to check the size of the 15° angle produced.
- Draw a horizontal line (40–50 cm long) on the board. Ask another volunteer to bisect the line, again using the board pen and string.
- Ask a final volunteer to bisect one of the two halves.

Section 7.6 Defining a locus

Learning objectives
- Draw a locus for a given rule

Resources and homework
- Student Book 7.6: pages 201–203
- Practice Book 7.6: page 64

Making mathematical connections
- Scale drawings

Making cross-curricular connections
- **Design technology** – graphics
- **Art** – geometric designs
- **Science** – Physics dynamics
- **Relevance** – applications in Art and design, and architecture

Prior learning
- Students need to be able to construct the perpendicular bisector of a line. They should also be able to bisect an angle, although it will frequently be shown as two points, without the line joining them.

Working mathematically
- A locus (plural loci) is the movement of a point according to a given rule.

Common misconceptions and remediation
- Students may not recognise the difference between the distance 'from a point' and the distance 'from a line'.
- They may not be accurate enough in their constructions.
- Remind students to be aware of these things.

Probing questions
- How can you tell if the path of points of a locus is equidistant from another point or a line?
- What is the same or different about the path traced out by the centre of a circle being rolled along a straight line and the centre of a square being rolled along a straight line?

Literacy focus
- Key terms: equidistant, locus (loci)
- Encourage students to identify the key words from each question.

Part 1
- Pick a point in the classroom, or go outside if space is limited.
- Ask a student to move in such a way as to stay 2 m from the point.
- Discuss the shape of the path traced out.
- Now choose two points.
- Ask a student to move so that he or she remains the same distance from the two points.
- Discuss the shape of the path traced out.
- Now choose three points, A, B and C, and repeat, then discuss.

Part 2

- Provide plain paper and make sure that all students have rulers.
- Ask them to mark a dot (labelled C) on the paper, about 10 cm down from the top and in from the left-hand side.
- Now ask students to mark four more dots on the paper, all 4 cm away from point C.
- Check that students have the right idea.
- Now ask them to mark another four points, each 4 cm away from point C; then ask them to mark four more points.
- Unless a student has already remarked on this, ask what is so special about this set of points they are marking. (They are making a circle around point C.)
- Confirm this fact and explain that this circle is the path or locus (plural loci).
- Ask students to mark two points, A and B, on their paper and find the locus of a point that is always the same distance (equidistant) from A and B.
- Lead them so that they see that this will be a line perpendicular to the imaginary line joining the two points, the perpendicular bisector.
- Work through Examples 4 to 7 in the Student Book.
- **Students can now begin Exercise 7I from the Student Book.**

| G&M 1, 2, 4, 6 | Calculator n/a | CM 9 | MR 5 | PS 3, 7, 8 | EV 10 |

Part 3

- Ask students to imagine a bird tethered by a leash 1 m long to a point on a perch at least 1 m high.
- What is the locus of the possible points that the bird can reach in flight?
  (a sphere, radius 1 m)
- Now ask students to imagine the bird tethered by a leash 1 m long to a perch 3 m long. This time, the tether is attached to a ring that can slide along the full length of the perch.
- What is the locus of the possible points that the bird can reach in flight now?
  (a cylinder, radius 1 m and length 3 m, with a hemisphere, radius 1 m, on each end)

Section 7.7 Loci problems

Learning objectives
- Solve practical problems using loci

Resources and homework
- Student Book 7.7: pages 203–207
- Practice Book 7.7: pages 65–67

Making mathematical connections
- Scale drawings
- Shading regions

Making cross-curricular connections
- **Design technology** – graphics
- **Art** – geometric designs
- **Science** – dynamics of Physics
- **Relevance** – applications in Art and design, and architecture

Prior learning
- Students should be able to use a pair of compasses to draw a circle and know that the distance from the centre to any point on the circumference is the same, equal to the radius.

Working mathematically
- Students are solving practical problems with loci. They will need to work accurately, identify the key words in each question and apply the techniques learned in the previous lesson.

Common misconceptions and remediation
- Students may have problems with scale, and so need to take care to ensure that they use the correct scale.
- They should also take care to interpret 'closer to' and 'further away' correctly.

Probing questions
- What key words do you look for in a question to help you draw the locus?
- Describe a locus that requires you to bisect an angle.
- Describe a locus that requires you to bisect a line.
- Describe a locus that requires you to draw a circle.

Literacy focus
- There are no new key terms in this section.

Part 1
- Provide plain paper and ask students to put three small crosses on their paper, to represent local towns, for example, Barnsley, Rotherham and Doncaster.
- Make sure students choose places that are not all in a line. Accuracy at this stage is not really important.
- Ask students to label the points, then to find all the points that are the same distance between, say, Barnsley and Rotherham. This will be the perpendicular bisector of the line drawn between Barnsley and Rotherham.
- Then ask students to find all the points that are the same distance from Rotherham and Doncaster.
- Discuss the lines they have drawn and talk about what is special about the point of intersection of the two lines.
- Establish that this point is *equidistant* from all three towns.

Part 2

- Ensure that every student has a pair of compasses fitted with a sharp pencil, as well as another sharp pencil and a ruler.
- Talk through Example 8 to demonstrate a practical locus problem.
- Make sure that students understand what the problem is asking, before going to the solution. Working through the problem on their own sheet of paper will help **less able** students with their understanding. They can trace the points of the towns onto their plain paper.
- Talk through Example 9, which is a different type of locus problem. Again, it will help **less able** students to draw this solution for themselves.
- Finally, work through Example 10, which is a classic locus problem.
- **Students can now do Exercise 7J from the Student Book.**

| G&M 1–5, 9–15 | Calculator n/a | CM 7, 8 | MR n/a | PS 6, 16, 17 | EV 9c |

Part 3

- To provoke discussion and comment, ask: What is the locus of a point that is one metre away from the walls, ceiling and floor of this classroom?
- There are two regions to consider, one inside the room, which will give a locus of a smaller cuboid shape, and the other outside the room (over and under), which will give an interesting shape of a cuboid with rounded corners. Discuss the shape of these corners, which will be quarter spheres.

Section 7.8 Plans and elevations

Learning objectives
- Construct and interpret plans and elevations of 3D shapes

Resources and homework
- Student Book 7.8: pages 208–211
- Practice Book 7.8: pages 67–68

Making mathematical connections
- Isometric drawings
- Oblique drawings

Making cross-curricular connections
- **Design and Technology** – graphics
- **Art** – 3D drawings
- **Relevance** – applications to manufacturing, engineering and design

Prior learning
- Students will need to understand scales and be able to draw accurately.

Working mathematically
- Plans and elevations are 2D drawings representing 3D shapes as seen from specific directions.
- The **plan** is a view looking down from above.
- The **front elevation** is the view looking horizontally at the shape from the front.
- The **side elevation** is the view looking horizontally at the shape from the side.

Common misconceptions and remediation
- Students sometimes get mixed up between the different types of elevations. Reinforce the elevations with students using mini whiteboards and a variety of shapes, for example: Draw the front elevation of this shape, draw the plan, and so on.

Probing questions
- Starting from a 2D representation of a 3D shape:
  - How many faces will the 3D shape have? How do you know?
  - What will be opposite this face in the 3D shape? How do you know?

Literacy focus
- Key terms: front elevation, plan, side elevation
- Ask students to write questions using the key terms, to show that they understand the words.

Part 1
- Ask students to imagine a large cube. Ask: How many faces does it have? (6) How many edges does it have? (12)
- Now ask students to imagine a cube on which the top and front faces are coloured in red and the other faces are coloured in blue. Ask:
  - How many edges are there where a red face touches another red face? (1)
  - How many edges are there where a blue face touches another blue face? (5)
  - How many edges are there where a red face touches a blue face? (6)
  - You could show the class a model of the cube to help explain the answers.

Part 2

- On the board, draw a copy of the 3D shape show on the right. (You could also make the shape from multi-link cubes.)
- Ask the class to copy it onto isometric paper.
- Show students the correct way to use isometric paper. Explain that the dots must always be in vertical columns.
- Explain that a 3D shape can be viewed from different angles:
  A **plan** is the view of a 3D shape when it is looked at from above (a bird's-eye view).
  An **elevation** is the view of a 3D shape when it is looked at from the front or from the side.
- The class can now draw the plan and the two elevations, as shown, on squared paper:
- Work through Examples 11, 12 and 13 from the Student Book.
- **Students can now begin Exercise 7K from the Student Book.**

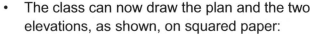

| Plan from A | Front elevation from B | Side elevation from C |

| G&M 1, 2, 4 | Calculator n/a | CM n/a | MR 3, 5 | PS n/a | EV 6 |

Part 3

- Ask individual students to explain the following terms: plan, front elevation and side elevation.
- Discuss with the class what would happen if they were to view any of the 3D shapes that they have drawn from below (a worm's-eye view) or from the back.
- Ask students to draw an accurate copy of the cuboid shown on an isometric grid.

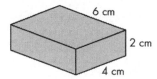

6 cm

2 cm

4 cm

- For each of the following 3D shapes, ask students to draw, on centimetre-squared paper:
  i   the plan
  ii the front elevation
  iii the side elevation.

a

b

c

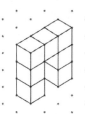

Chapter 8 Algebra: Algebraic manipulation

Overview

8.1 Basic algebra	**8.5** More than two binomials
8.2 Factorisation	**8.6** Quadratic factorisation
8.3 Quadratic expansion	**8.7** Factorising $ax^2 + bx + c$
8.4 Expanding squares	**8.8** Changing the subject of a formula

Prior learning

Know how to use letters to represent numbers.
Know the basic language of algebra.
Know how to collect together like terms.
Know the BIDMAS/BODMAS rule.
Know how to solve basic linear equations.

Learning objectives

Ensure that students can: substitute numbers into expressions and formulae; simplify expressions by collecting like terms; expand and factorise expressions; expand two or more binomials; factorise quadratic expressions; rearrange formulae.

In the examination, students will be expected to:
- recognise expressions, equations, formulae and identities
- substitute into, manipulate and simplify algebraic expressions
- factorise an algebraic expression
- expand two binomials to obtain a quadratic expression
- expand the square of a binomial
- expand more than two binomials
- factorise a quadratic expression of the form $x^2 + ax + b$ into two linear brackets
- factorise a quadratic expression of the form $ax^2 + bx + c$ into two linear brackets
- change the subject of a formula.

Extension

Much of this content will be new to students. Make sure that even the **more able** students have the techniques embedded before moving on. Factorising quadratics is a vital an important skill to secure for A Level study.

Curriculum references

Section	GCSE specification
8.1	A 1, 2, 4, 6
8.2	A 1, 3, 4
8.3	A 1, 3, 4
8.4	A 1, 3, 4
8.5	A 1, 3, 4
8.6	A 1, 3, 4
8.7	A 1, 3, 4
8.8	A 1, 3, 5

Route mapping

Exercise	Accessible	Intermediate	Challenging	AO1	AO2 MR CM	AO3 PS EV	Key questions
8A	1–12			1–5, 11	7–9	6, 10, 12	2, 3, 10, 11
8B	1–12			1,5–9	4, 11	2, 3, 10, 12	6, 7
8C	1–6	7		1,3	4, 5, 7	2, 6	3, 6
8D	1–3			1, 2		3	1
8E	1–3			1–3			1
8F	1–5	6, 7		1, 2	5, 6, 7	3, 4	2, 6
8G		1–7		1, 3	2, 6	4, 5, 7	1
8H	1	2–6		1, 2	6	3, 4, 5	2, 6
8I		1–8	9–11	1–3, 9–11	5, 7, 8	4, 6	1, 2
8J		1–5	6	1, 2	4, 5	3, 6	1, 2
8K		1–3	4–7	1, 4	3, 6, 7	2, 5	1, 4
8L		1–4	5–7	1, 4, 5	3, 6	2, 7	1
8M	1–11	12–19	20	1–10, 14–19	12, 20	11, 13	1–9, 14–19

Key questions are those that demonstrate mastery of the concept, or which require a step-up in understanding or application. Key questions could be used to identify the questions that students must tackle, to support differentiation, or to identify the questions that should be teacher-marked rather than student-marked.

About this chapter

Making connections: Algebra is the way that the language of Mathematics is expressed. Algebra comes from the Arabic *al-jabr,* which means something similar to 'completion'. It was used in a book written in 820AD by a Persian mathematician called al-Khwārizmī. The use of symbols then developed until the middle of the 17th century, when René Descartes developed what is regarded as the basis of the algebra we use today. This chapter covers the key areas of Higher Level algebra; the next step is A Level content.

Relevance: There is an emphasis on the use of logic and thinking in steps. There are applications in engineering, architecture, manufacturing, project management and many other areas; STEM careers are a strong focus.

Working mathematically: This chapter starts with basic algebra such as substituting into expressions. It moves on to expanding brackets and factorising, including expanding binomials and factorising quadratics. Finally, students are taught how to rearrange formula.

Assessment: In each section of this chapter, ensure that students have a good grasp of the key questions in each exercise before moving on. (Refer to the 'Route mapping' table above.) Encourage students to read and think about the 'Ready to progress?' statements on page 246 of the Student Book. Check students' understanding at the end of the chapter, formatively, using peer assessment. Students could do a mini test in the form of the 'Review questions' on pages 246–247 of the Student Book. Follow up the test with an individual target-getting session, based on any areas for development that a student may have.

Worked exemplars from the Student Book – suggestions for use
*   Present students with the same question but using different numbers. Students should use the exemplar to mirror the working, in full or only the notes.
*   Copy and cut the exemplars into cards. Students match the working with the notes.
*   Copy and cut the working into cards, splitting the label/description from the working. Students put the working in order, then match with the descriptions.

Answers to the Student Book questions are available on the CD-ROM provided.

Section 8.1 Basic algebra

Learning objectives

- Recognise expressions, equations, formulae and identities
- Substitute into, manipulate and simplify algebraic expressions

Resources and homework

- Student Book 8.1: pages 217–223
- Practice Book 8.1: pages 69–72

Making mathematical connections

- Solving equations
- Using formula

Making cross-curricular connections

- **Science** – substituting into scientific formulae
- **Relevance** – developing logical thinking

Prior learning

- Students should: be familiar with the basic language of algebra; be able to multiply together algebraic terms; understand BIDMAS/BODMAS; be able to multiply negative numbers.

Working mathematically

- Encourage students to use brackets when substituting numbers into an expression.
- Tell students that, when doing simple calculations with direct numbers, it is sometimes helpful to 'say the problem to yourself'.
- Write on the board: + 2 − −3 and ask students to display their answers on mini-whiteboards. Now say the calculation as 'plus two minus minus three' and again, ask students to display their answers. You should find that there are fewer errors this time.
- Stress that, when they are multiplying one term outside the brackets by one or more terms inside the brackets, they must multiply everything inside the brackets by the number or algebraic term outside the brackets.
- Structure tasks so students can work out the methods for themselves, either by increasing the difficulty incrementally or through one straightforward and one complex example.

Common misconceptions and remediation

- Students often forget to follow BIDMAS rules or misunderstand algebraic conventions, e.g. when substituting $t = 4$ into the expression $2t + 7$, they get $24 + 7$ instead of $2 \times 4 + 7$.
- Students may try to oversimplify by combining unlike terms, e.g. $2t + 7 = 9t$.
- When expanding brackets, students may multiply the first term but then write the next terms without multiplying them; e.g. $5(3a + 2b) = 15a + 2b$ (instead of $15a + 10b$).

Probing questions

- What steps do you follow when substituting values into an expression or a formula? What would you do first? Why?
- Give students examples of expanding brackets with mistakes and ask them to identify the errors. For example:
  $3(x + 2) = 3x + 2$ $\qquad$ $3(x − 5) = 3x − 8$ $\qquad$ $−2(6 − x) = −12 − 2x$ $\quad$ $12 − (x − 3) = 9 − x$
- Can you give me an expression that is equivalent to, for example, $6x + 4y − 3$?
- What do you look for when you have an expression to simplify

Literacy focus

- Key terms: equation, expand, expression, formula, identity, like terms, simplify, substitute, variable
- Be explicit about the language of algebra; encourage the use of the correct terms.

Part 1

NB: *This section may take more than 1 hour*

- Draw a grid on the board as shown, but without answers. Ask students to fill in the values using a formula, e.g. $2a + b$.
- Explain, if needed, that $2a + b$ is 2 lots of a, plus b.
- For **more able** students, use fractional or negative values for a and b or a quadratic rule with negative values for a and b. Set a time limit or make it a race.

	a		
	2	3	5
2	6	8	12
b 4	8	10	14
6	10	12	1

Part 2

- Work through the introductory text and Example 1 with the class.

Substitution

- Work though this, encouraging students to always: substitute values into the expression, replace letters with numbers in brackets; evaluate each term; work out the final answer.
  - Ask students to work out the value of, for example, $3a + 2b = 3c$ when $a = 2$, $b = -4$ and $c = -5$. Collect answers and methods. It is unlikely that everyone will get the correct answer, and methods will vary. Do not reveal the correct answer is at this stage.
  - Write $3(2) + 2(-4) -3(-5)$ on the board and ask students to work it out. Gauge the number of students that now have a different answer, but still do not give the correct answer.
  - Write $6 - 8 + 15$ and ask students to work it out. Check students' answers and give the correct answer (+13). Discuss which calculation they found easiest.
- **More able** students may feel this is a waste of time; warn them that errors that the examiner cannot see could mean zero marks, so showing the method – at least the first step – is vital.
- Work through Examples 2 and 3, highlighting the use of BIDMAS/BODMAS.
- **Students can now do Exercise 8A from the Student Book.**

A 1–5, 11	Calculator n/a	CM n/a	MR 7–9	PS 6, 10	EV 12

Expansion

- Write on the board: $3 \times 4 + 3 \times 5$ and $3 \times (4 + 5)$ and ask students to work out these calculations. They should get '27' both times. Write on the board: $3 \times (4 + 5) = 3 \times 4 + 3 \times 5$
- Now write $2 \times (x + 5)$ and ask students to write this without brackets, using the previous example as a clue ($2 \times x + 2 \times 5$). Simplify to $2x + 10$. Repeat with $3(y - 6)$, reminding **less able** students of the invisible multiplication sign between the number outside the brackets and the opening bracket. Show this as $3 \times (y - 6)$ $(= 3 \times y - 3 \times 6 = 3y - 18)$
- Introduce the term 'expansion'.

Collecting like terms

- Ask students to simplify: $3a + 5b + 2a + 4b$. If this leads to answers such as $14ab$ as well as the correct answer, $5a + 9b$, explain 'like terms' and say that only these can be combined.
- **Less able** students may prefer to rewrite the calculation as: $3a + 2a + 5b + 4b$. Point out that once they have identified the like terms, they only need to combine the coefficients.
- Repeat with: $6a + 2b - 3a + 5b$ $(3a + 7b)$ and $5a - 4b + 9a + 5b$ $(13a + b)$. Rewrite $5a - 4b + 9a + 5b$ as $5a + 9a - 4b + 5b$, if necessary.

Expand and simplify

- Go through Example 4 from the Student Book, which brings together the above processes.
- **Students can now do Exercise 8B from the Student Book.**

A 1, 5–9	Calculator 10	CM n/a	MR 4, 11	PS 2, 10, 12	EV 3

Part 3

- Write on the board: $3 \times 4 + 3 \times 5 = 3 \times (4 + 5)$ and $2x + 10 = 2(x + 5)$
- Explain that this shows the reverse process of expanding – *factorisation*.
- Ask the students to 'reverse' $3x - 18$, $4x - 20$ and $4y + 6x$.

Section 8.2 Factorisation

Learning objectives
- Factorise an algebraic expression

Resources and homework
- Student Book 8.2: pages 223–225
- Practice Book 8.2: pages 72–73

Making mathematical connections
- HCF
- Rearranging formulae
- Solving equations

Making cross-curricular connections
- **Science** – using formulae
- **Relevance** – developing logical thinking

Prior learning
- Students must be able to expand brackets confidently before starting this work.
- Students should be able to find the highest common factor (HCF) of two or more numbers.

Working mathematically
- Factorisation is the opposite of expansion. It puts an expression back into the brackets it may have come from.
- In factorisation, you have to look for the common factors in *every* term of the expression.
- To factorise the expression $6t + 9m$:
  - first look for the HCF of the numerical coefficients 6 and 9 (3)
  - then look for any factors of the letters, t and m (none)
- So, $6t + 9m = 3 \times 2t + 3 \times 3m = 3(2t + 3m)$
- **Note:** You can always check a factorisation by expanding the answer.

Common misconceptions and remediation
- Students may find a factor, but not the *highest* factor.
- In a question such as $4xy + 2x$, students may write $2x(2y + 0)$ as they think that there is nothing left when $2x$ is taken from the second term. Stress that they are dividing, not subtracting.

Probing questions
- What steps do you follow when factorising?
- What would you do first? Why?
- Give students examples of factorising with mistakes and ask them to identify the errors. E.g. $4x + 2 = 4(x + 2)$ $x - 15 = 5(x - 10)$ $-12 - 6x = -2(6 + 3x)$

Literacy focus
- Key terms: common factor, factorisation
- Ask students to write questions using the key terms, to show their understanding.

Part 1

- Ask students to give the HCF of:
  - ○ 6 and 9 (3)
  - ○ 6a and 9 (3)
  - ○ 6a and 9a (3a)
  - ○ a^2 and 9a (3a)
  - ○ 6a^2 and 9a^2 (3a^2)
- **Less able** students may find it easier to see the common factors if the expressions are broken down into products, e.g. 6 and 9 become 3 × 2 and 3 × 3, 6a and 9 become 3 × 2a and 3 × 3, 6a and 9a become 3a × 2 × 3a × 3, and so on.

Part 2

- Write some expansions on the board, such as:
  - ○ $2(x + 5) = 2x + 10$
  - ○ $3(x - 2) = 3x - 6$
  - ○ $5(x + 3) = 5x + 15$
- Now write $2x + 14 = \dots$ and ask students if they can write down the expansion from which it comes. Most students should be able to work out that the answer is $2(x + 7)$.
- Repeat with other examples such as $5x - 15$ and $6x + 18$.
- Explain that what they have been doing is called *factorisation* and it is the reverse of expanding.
- Now ask students to factorise $4x + 12$. Some students may answer $2(2x + 6)$. Explain that this is a partial factorisation; that they must take the HCF out of each term. The full factorisation is $4(x + 3)$.
- Now ask for the factorisation of $x^2 + 3x$. [$x(x + 3)$]
- Prompt, if necessary by rewriting as: $x \times x + 3 \times x$
- Work through the different factorisations in Example 5.
- Emphasise to students that they can multiply out the factorised expression to check that it is the same as the original expression.
- Many students find this topic difficult. It may help to restrict **less able** students to examples with positive values and numerical factors initially. Alternatively, encourage these students to write terms as products, as in Part 1.
- **Students can now do Exercise 8C from the Student Book.**

A 1, 3	Calculator n/a	CM 4, 5	MR 7	PS 6	EV 2

Part 3

- Ask students to supply expressions with terms that have an HCF of 6, 6a, 6a^2, 6ab, 6ab^2, and so on.
- Ask for several expressions for each HCF. (This is the reverse of Part 1.)

Section 8.3 Quadratic expansion

Learning objectives
- Expand two binomials to obtain a quadratic expression

Resources and homework
- Student Book 8.3: pages 225–230
- Practice Book 8.3: pages 73–76

Making mathematical connections
- Solving quadratic equations
- Rearranging formulae

Making cross-curricular connections
- **Science** – using formulae
- **Relevance** – developing logical thinking

Prior learning
- Students should be able to multiply out a single set of brackets.

Working mathematically
- A quadratic expression is one where the highest power of the variables is 2. For example: y^2 $3t^2 + 5t$ $5m^2 + 3m + 8$
- You can expand an expression such as $(3y + 2)(4y - 5)$ to give a quadratic expression. $(3y + 2)$ and $(4y - 5)$ are examples of binomials. A binomial is the sum of two terms.
- Multiplying out pairs of these brackets is usually called *quadratic expansion*.
- The rule for expanding expressions such as $(t + 5)(3t - 4)$ is similar to the rule for expanding single brackets: *Multiply everything in one set of brackets by everything in the other set of brackets.*

Common misconceptions and remediation
- Students make errors with signs, particularly when multiplying two negatives $(- \times -)$; remind students of the conventions for multiplying like and unlike signs.
- Students may make mistakes by not writing down the brackets twice when expanding the square of an expression in brackets; remind them to make sure that they have the same numbers of opening and closing brackets.

Probing questions
- Write down two expressions that, when you expand them, have:
  - a positive x coefficient
  - a negative x coefficient
  - no x coefficient.
- Explain how you multiply out two brackets.

Literacy focus
- Key term: binomial
- Make sure students understand the meaning of the key term, as well as *quadratic expression* and *expansion*.
- Encourage students to write a step-by-step guide for their chosen method.

Part 1
- Revise multiplying out a single set of brackets, e.g. $5(2x + 3)$, $x(2x + 3)$, $5x(2x + 3)$.

Part 2

- Ask how students worked out the expansions. Some may have done these mentally, while others may have used jottings. If there were errors (which is very likely if powers and negative numbers were used), ask what caused them to make errors.
- Write on the board: $(8 + 2)(7 - 3)$. Ask students to work out the value of this expression.
- They should work out the brackets and calculate $10 \times 4 = 40$.
- Write down: $8 \times 7 + 2 \times 7 + 8 \times -3 + 2 \times -3$. Ask students to work out: $56 + 14 - 24 - 6 = 40$.
- Ask students for the connections between the two calculations (apart from the obvious one that the answer is the same).
- Write $(x + 2)(x \times 3)$ on the board and ask students to expand this in the same way.
  $x \times x + 2 \times x + x \times 3 + 2 \times 3$
- Simplify and evaluate this to: $x^2 + 2x + 3x + 6 = x^2 + 5x + 6$.
- Demonstrate the three methods for expanding quadratics.
- Demonstrate the **expansion method**:
  $(x - 3)(x + 4) = x(x + 4) - 3(x + 4) = x^2 + 4x - 3x - 12 = x^2 + x - 12$
- Work through Example 6 from the Student Book.
- **Students can now do Exercise 8D from the Student Book.**

A 1, 2	Calculator n/a	CM n/a	MR n/a	PS n/a	EV 3

- Demonstrate the **FOIL method**:
  - Multiply the **F**irst terms: $x \times x = x^2$
  - Multiply the **O**uter terms: $x \times -2 = -2x$
  - Multiply the **I**nner terms: $-3 \times x = -3x$
  - Multiply the **L**ast terms: $-3 \times -2 = 6$
  - Combine the terms: $x^2 - 5x + 6$

- Work through Example 7 from the Student Book.
- **Students can now do Exercise 8E from the Student Book.**

A 1–3	Calculator n/a	CM n/a	MR n/a	PS n/a	EV n/a

- Demonstrate the **Box method** for expanding $(x - 5)(x + 4)$
- Multiply each term and collect the x terms 'diagonally': $x^2 - x - 20$
- Now work through Examples 8 and 9 from the Student Book.
- **Students can now do Exercise 8F from the Student Book.**

$\times$	x	-5
x	x^2	$-5x$
$+4$	$4x$	-20

A 1, 2	Calculator n/a	CM 7	MR 5, 6	PS 3, 4	EV n/a

Quadratic expansion with non-unit coefficients

- Once students have mastered a method, work through this section. Examples 10 and 11 use the box method and split brackets method. Students can use FOIL if this is their preferred method.
- Work through Example 12.
- **Students can now do Exercise 8G from the Student Book.**

A 1, 3	Calculator n/a	CM 2	MR 6	PS 4, 5, 7	EV n/a

Part 3

- Ask students if they can work out the brackets that lead to $x^2 + 12x + 27$. [$(x + 3)(x + 9)$]
- Repeat with $2x^2 + 7x + 3$. [$(2x + 1)(x + 3)$]

Section 8.4 Expanding squares

Learning objectives
- Expand the square of a binomial

Resources and homework
- Student Book 8.4: pages 231–232
- Practice Book 8.4: page 76

Making mathematical connections
- Solving quadratic equations
- Rearranging formulae

Making cross-curricular connections
- **Science** – using formulae
- **Relevance** – developing logical thinking

Prior learning
- Students should be able to expand a pair of linear brackets.

Working mathematically
- Whenever you see a linear bracketed term squared, such as $(x - 2)^2$, write the brackets twice, and then expand using whichever method you prefer.

Common misconceptions and remediation
- Students may use two negatives in the difference of two squares.
- Students check that the 'x^2' part and the '+ number' part are correct, but forget to check that the 'x' part is correct.

Probing questions
- What can you tell me about the x^2 coefficient when you square a bracket?
- What can you tell me about the constant term when you square a bracket?
- What can you tell me about the x coefficient when you square a bracket?
- Does this always happen when you square a bracket?

Literacy focus
- Key terms: There are no new key terms in this section.

Part 1
- Ask students to expand the following brackets using their preferred method:
  - $(x + 5)(x + 4)$
  - $(x - 2)(x + 3)$
  - $(2x + 4)(x - 6)$
  - $(2x - 3)(3x - 4)$

Part 2
- Encourage students always to write down the brackets twice, and then use their preferred expansion method.
- Work through Examples 13 and 14.
- **Students can now do Exercise 8H from Student Book.**

A 1, 2	Calculator n/a	CM n/a	MR 6	PS 4, 5	EV 3

Part 3

- Give students a calculation such as $(3x + 2)^2$.
- After they have worked out the answer $(9x^2 + 12x + 4)$, ask them to do the following:
  - Square the first term: $(3x)^2 = 9x^2$
  - Double the product of the two terms: $2(3x \times 2) = 12x$
  - Square the last term: $2^2 = 4$
  - Put it all together: $9x^2 + 12x + 4$

  What do they notice? (This is equal to the square of the expression.)
- Does this work when squaring any similar expression?
- Multiply out these brackets and simplify the result:
  - $(x + 3)(x - 3)$
  - $(x + y)^2$
  - $(x - y)^2$
  - $(5x + 1)^2$
  - $(x + y)(x - y)$

Section 8.5 More than two binomials

Learning objectives
- Expand more than two binomials

Resources and homework
- Student Book 8.5: pages 232–234
- Practice Book 8.5: pages 76–77

Making mathematical connections
- Solving quadratic equations
- Rearranging formulae

Making cross-curricular connections
- **Science** – using formulae
- **Relevance** – developing logical thinking

Prior learning
- Students should be able to expand two linear brackets and square a bracket.

Working mathematically
- When more than two binomials are multiplied together, you multiply one pair of binomials together first, then multiply the result by the next binomial, and so on.
- Students use an extension of the expansion and box method techniques they have met already. (FOIL would need extra letters for the middle term.)

Common misconceptions and remediation
- Students sometimes leave out terms when multiplying. Remind them of the general rule: *Multiply everything in one pair of brackets by everything in the other pair of brackets, and then continue this for each additional pair of brackets.*

Probing questions
- Why is the FOIL method not suitable for these questions?
- Could you make up a similar method to FOIL that would work?
- Try your method to see if it will work.

Literacy focus
- Key terms: There are no new key terms in this section.
- Ask students to write a step-by-step guide explaining how to expand more than two brackets.

Part 1
- Give students the following brackets to expand:
  - $(2x + 3)(3x - 4)$
  - $(2x + 1)^2$
  - $(x - y)^2$
  - $(5x - 3)^2$
  - $(2x + y)(2x - y)$

Part 2

- Remind students that FOIL will not work for these and to apply the general rule, which is to multiply everything in one pair of brackets by everything in the other pair of brackets, and then continue this for additional pairs of brackets.
- Demonstrate the **expansion method** for: $(x-3)(x+4)(x+2)$
- Expand the first pair of brackets: $\quad x(x+4) - 3(x+4) = x^2 + 4x - 3x - 12$
$$= x^2 + x - 12$$

- Expand this with the final bracket:
$$x(x^2 + x - 12) + 2(x^2 + x - 12) = x^3 + x^2 - 12x + 2x^2 + 2x - 24$$
$$= x^3 + 3x^2 - 10x - 24$$

- Work through Example 15 in the Student Book.
- Demonstrate the **Box method** for: $(x-1)(2x+3)(x+4)$
- Expand the first pair of brackets using the box method:

×	2x	+3
x	$2x^2$	+3x
−1	−2x	−3

$(x-1)(2x+3) = 2x^2 + x - 3$
- Expand $(2x^2 + x - 3)(x + 4)$ using the box method:

×	$2x^2$	+x	−3
x	$2x^3$	$+x^2$	−3x
+4	$8x^2$	+4x	−12

$(2x^2 + x - 3)(x + 4) = 2x^3 + 9x^2 + x - 12$
- Work through Examples 16 and 17 from the Student Book.
- **Students can now do Exercise 8I from the Student Book.**

A 1–3, 9–11	Calculator n/a	CM 7	MR 5, 8	PS 6	EV 4

Part 3

- Give students the following brackets to expand:
  - $(x + 3)(x - 4)(x + 2)$
  - $(2x + 1)^3$
  - $(x - y)^3$
  - $(5x - 3)^3$
  - $(x + y)(x - y)(x + y)$

Section 8.6 Quadratic factorisation

Learning objectives
*   factorise a quadratic expression of the form $x^2 + ax + b$ into two linear brackets

Resources and homework
*   Student Book 8.6: pages 235–238
*   Practice Book 8.6: pages 77–78

Making mathematical connections
*   Solving quadratic equations

Making cross-curricular connections
*   **Science** – working with formulae
*   **Relevance** – applications in engineering and Physics

Prior learning
*   Students should be confident in factorising simple expressions such as $5x + 10$, $5x^2 + 10x$ and $5xy - 20x$.
*   Students should also be able to expand and simplify two linear brackets.

Working mathematically
*   Quadratic factorisation involves putting a quadratic expression into brackets (where possible).
*   Start by factorising quadratic expressions of the type $x^2 + ax + b$, where a and b are integers.

Common misconceptions and remediation
*   Students may use two negatives in the difference of two squares.
*   Students check that the 'x^2' part and the '+ number' part are correct, but forget to check that the 'x' part is correct.

Probing questions
*   What is the most important information for factorising a quadratic expression?
*   Explain how you go about factorising a quadratic expression.

Literacy focus
*   Key term: difference of two squares
*   Students could write a step-by-step guide on how to solve quadratic equations, including a section on the difference of two squares.

Part 1
*   Ask students to factorise these expressions:
    o $8r + 2t$
    o $4a - 12ab$
    o $7acd - 5abc$
    o $12ab^2 + 24b$
    o $12s + 6t$
    o $16ab + 12b$
    o $3t^2 + 6t$
    o $9x^3 - 27xy$
*   Ask students to expand expressions such as $(2x)^2$, $(4y)^2$ and $(3p)^2$.

Part 2

- Refer back to the previous lesson. Explain that this lesson is about reversing the process in which two linear brackets are expanded.
- Start with $x^2 + 5x + 6$. Students should see that this will have two sets of brackets, each of which will start with x, so $(x\ .....)(x\ .....)$.
- They should also spot that the two numbers in brackets multiply to give the constant term. **More able** students may spot that the sum of the numbers is the coefficient of x, and the rules about signs.
- Write down the answer to the factorisation: $(x + 2)(x + 3)$
- Drawing on the rules already given, work through the text in the Student Book to formalise the rules of factorisation.
- Work through Examples 18 and 19.
- **Students can now do Exercise 8J from the Student Book.**

| A 1, 2 | Calculator n/a | CM 4, 5 | MR n/a | PS 3, 6 | EV n/a |

Difference of two squares

- Ask students to look back at their answers for Exercise 8G. Ask: What rule did you spot? They should say $(x + y)(x - y) = x^2 - y^2$, or similar.
- Explain that this is called the difference of two squares and that the process can be reversed.
- The factorisation of $x^2 - y^2$ is $(x + y)(x - y)$.
- Talk through the text in the Student Book and then work through Examples 20 and 21.
- **Less able** students may find the square roots of terms such as $4x^2$ difficult to recognise, so provide practice, as in the Part 1.
- **Students can now do Exercise 8K from the Student Book.**

| A 1, 4 | Calculator n/a | CM 3 | MR 6, 7 | PS 2, 5 | EV n/a |

Part 3

- Give students some factorised expressions that are the difference of two squares, such as $(x - 2)(x + 2)$. Ask them to reverse the process and expand the brackets without using the FOIL method ($x^2 - 4$).

Section 8.7 Factorising $ax^2 + bx + c$

Learning objectives

- Factorise a quadratic expression of the form $ax^2 + bx + c$ into two linear brackets

Making mathematical connections

- Solving quadratic equations

Resources and homework

- Student Book 8.7: pages 239–240
- Practice Book 8.7: pages 78–79

Making cross-curricular connections

- **Science** – Working with formulae
- **Relevance** – applications in engineering and Physics

Prior learning

- Students must be able to factorise expressions of the form $x^2 + bx + c$ before starting this section.

Working mathematically

- Adapt the method for factorising $x^2 + ax + b$ to allow for the factors of the coefficient of x^2.

Common misconceptions and remediation

- Remind students always to check their expansions and factorisations by doing the reverse each time. This should always equal the original expression.

Probing questions

- How can you check if you have factorised correctly?
- What effect does the non-unit coefficient of x^2 have on your solution?

Literacy focus

- Key terms: There are no new key terms in this section.
- Ask students to write a step-by-step guide on how to factorise quadratic expressions.

Part 1

- Give students some questions to factorise that involve a unit coefficient of x^2 such as:
  - $x^2 + 5x + 6$
  - $x^2 - 8x - 20$
  - $x^2 - 9x + 14$
  - $x^2 + 21x - 22$

Part 2

- Ask students if they can factorise $2x^2 - x - 1$.
- The process of factorising equations with a non-unit coefficient of x^2 is not as easy as with a unit coefficient of x^2. It depends on intelligent guesswork and experience.
- Show the method by working through the factorisation of $2x^2 - x - 1 = (2x + 1)(x - 1)$.
- If students are struggling, you can show them the method in Part 3, below.
- Then work through Examples 22 to 24 from the Student Book.
- **Less able** students will find it difficult to match the factors of the coefficient of x^2 and the constant term, especially if there is a minus sign. Explain that practice is the best way to overcome their difficulties.

Students can now do Exercise 8L from the Student Book.

| A 1, 4, 5 | Calculator n/a | CM 3 | MR 6 | PS 2, 7 | EV n/a |

Part 3

- If **less able** students are struggling, demonstrate the method shown below.
  Factorise $6x^2 - 7x - 10$.

Identify a, b and c	$a = 6$, $b = -7$, $c = -10$
Multiply the a and c terms	$6 \times -10 = -60$
Since $-12 \times 5 = -60$ (ac) and $12 + 5 = -7$ (b), rewrite $-7x$ as $-12x + 5x$	$6x^2 - 12x + 5x - 10$
Factor in pairs **Note:** that the two brackets will always be equal if you have correctly factorised, in this case, both $(x - 2)$	$6x(x - 2) + 5(x - 2)$
Put the $6x + 5$ together and the common factor $(x - 2)$	$(6x + 5)(x - 2)$

Section 8.8 Changing the subject of a formula

Learning objectives
- Change the subject of a formula

Resources and homework
- Student Book 8.8: pages 241–243
- Practice Book 8.8: pages 79–80

Making mathematical connections
- Solving equations
- Working with formulae

Making cross-curricular connections
- **Science** – rearranging formulae
- **Relevance** – applications to engineering

Prior learning
- Students will need to be able to use brackets, factorise and manipulate algebraic fractions. This lesson will support developing confidence in these areas.

Working mathematically
- The subject is the variable (letter) in a formula or equation which stands on its own, usually on the left-hand side of the equals sign. For example, x is the subject of each of the following equations:

$$x = 5t + 4 \qquad x = 4(2y - 7) \qquad x = \frac{1}{t}$$

- To change the existing subject to a different variable, you have to rearrange (transpose) the formula to get that variable on its own on the left-hand side. Do this by using inverse operations.
- The main difference between rearranging formulae and solving equations is that when you solve an equation, each step gives a numerical value and when you rearrange a formula, each step gives an algebraic expression.

Common misconceptions and remediation
- Students make most errors because of poor algebraic skills.
- They often do not 'do the opposite', e.g. for $a + b = c$, they wrongly write $a = c + b$.
- They may not use brackets or clear division correctly, e.g. for $2a + b = c$, students may incorrectly write $a = c - b \div 2$ instead of either $a + (c - b) \div 2$, or $a = \dfrac{c - b}{2}$.
- Extra practice and worked examples should help students reduce the frequency of these errors.

Probing questions
- Give students examples of the steps towards the solution of a rearrangement with typical mistakes in them. Ask them to identify the mistakes and explain how to correct them.
- Talk me through the steps involved in rearranging this equation.
- What tells you the order of the steps?

Literacy focus
- Key terms: inverse operations, rearrange, subject, transpose
- Ask students to describe how they change the subject of a formula.

Part 1

What is my rule?

- Say that you have a simple rule in your head and it, for example, involves adding a number to a starting number. You will give a final number and they must guess the starting number. For example, if the rule is $y = x + 6$:
  - Say: My final number is 13. What number did I start with?
  - Once a student guesses the correct answer (7), record it and say:
    Now my final number is 20. What number did I start with? (14)
  - After several examples, some students will realise the rule. Ask them to give the rule, or continue until more students spot it.
- If students do not spot the rule, make it easier. Start with the result for 1 (7), then 2 (8).
- If answers are sequential, students will spot the rule more easily.
- Make the rules less or more complex depending on students' ability.
- Straightforward rules include $x - 3$, $2x$ and $x \div 5$.
- Challenge **more able** students with more complex rules such as $2x + 1$, $3x - 2$ and even $\frac{x}{2} + 1$, $\frac{x + 1}{5}$ or $x^2 + 3$, if appropriate.

Part 2

- Ask students to rearrange the formula $y = 2x + 3$ to make x the subject. They will have met this before, but remind them of the process.
- Work through Examples 25 to 28 in the Student Book. Point out the similarities to solving an equation (the same rules about rearranging apply, so apply the inverse operation, or 'do the same thing to both sides').
- Remind students that the result will be an expression rather than a number.
- Now write on the board: $y + 2x = x + 7$ and say: Make x the subject.
- Ask students why this is different from previous examples. (The subject appears twice.)
- Discuss what to do to rearrange to make x the subject. (Students should spot that they can simplify the xs by taking one x off each side.)
  - The subject term must be taken out of at least two terms as a common factor.
  - All terms containing the subject term will need to be collected on one side of the equals sign and all other terms on the other side.
- Students may be let down by poor algebraic skills so, before these students try this topic, give them some practice in basic algebra (expanding brackets, collecting terms, factorising).
- **Students can now begin Exercise 8M from the Student Book.**

$$y = 2x + 3$$
$$y - 3 = 2x$$
$$x = \frac{y - 3}{2}$$

$$y + 2x = x + 7$$
$$y + x = 7$$
$$x = 7 - y$$

| A 1–10, 14–19 | Calculator n/a | CM 12 | MR 20 | PS 11 | EV 13 |

Part 3

- Recall the method for adding and subtracting fractions, such as: $\frac{2}{3} + \frac{1}{4}$, $\frac{4}{5} - \frac{1}{3}$.

Chapter 9 Geometry and measures: Length, area and volume

Overview

9.1 Circumference and area of a circle	**9.6** Cylinders
9.2 Area of a parallelogram	**9.7** Volume of a pyramid
9.3 Area of a trapezium	**9.8** Cones
9.4 Sectors	**9.9** Spheres
9.5 Volume of a prism	

Prior learning

Know the formula for the area of a rectangle: area = length × width or $A = lw$

Know the formula for the area of a triangle: area = $\frac{1}{2}$ × base × height or $A = \frac{1}{2}bh$

Know the formula for the volume of a cuboid: volume = length × width × height *or* $V = lwh$

Know the common metric units to measure area, volume and capacity shown in this table:

Area	Volume	Capacity
100 mm^2 = 1 cm^2	1000 mm^3 = 1 cm^3	1000 cm^3 = 1 litre
10 000 cm^2 = 1 m^2	1 000 000 cm^3 = 1 m^3	1 m^3 = 1000 litres

Learning objectives

Ensure that students can: calculate the circumference and area of a circle; calculate the area of a parallelogram and a trapezium; calculate the length of an arc; calculate the area and angle of a sector; calculate the volume of a prism and a pyramid; calculate the volume and surface area of a cylinder, a cone and a sphere.

In the examination, students will be expected to:
- calculate the circumference and area of a circle
- calculate the area of a parallelogram and a trapezium
- calculate the length of an arc
- calculate the area and angle of a sector
- calculate the volume of a prism
- calculate the volume and surface area of a cylinder
- calculate the volume of a pyramid
- calculate the volume and surface area of a cone
- calculate the volume and surface area of a sphere.

Extension

More able students could explore more complex shapes, for example, volumes and surface areas of frustums.

Curriculum references

Section	GCSE specification	Section	GCSE specification
9.1	G 9, 14	9.6	G 14, 16
9.2	G 14, 16	9.7	G 14, 17
9.3	G 14, 16	9.8	G 14, 17
9.4	G 14, 17, 18	9.9	G 14, 17
9.5	G 14, 16		

Route mapping

Exercise	Accessible	Intermediate	Challenging	AO1	AO2 MR CM	AO3 PS EV	Key questions
9A	1–13	14		1–3, 6, 7, 10	11, 14	4, 5, 8, 9, 12, 13	8, 10, 11
9B	1–4			1	3	2, 4	1
9C	1–10	11, 12		1, 3, 6	2, 4, 7, 10	5, 8, 9, 11, 12	3, 6, 7
9D		1–8	9–13	1–3, 5, 6	4, 7, 9, 13	8, 10–12	1, 10, 11
9E	1–6	7–11		1, 2, 6	3, 5	4, 7–11	1, 2, 8, 9
9F		1–9	10	1, 2	3, 6	4, 5, 7–10	1, 6, 8
9G		1–9	10	1, 5	2, 3, 7, 8	4, 6, 9, 10	1, 5
9H		1–5	6–10	1, 4, 5	3, 7	2, 6, 8–10	1, 4
9I		1–6	7–10	1–3	5, 7, 10	4, 6, 8, 9	1, 5, 7

Key questions are those that demonstrate mastery of the concept, or which require a step-up in understanding or application. Key questions could be used to identify the questions that students must tackle, to support differentiation, or to identify the questions that should be teacher-marked rather than student-marked.

About this chapter

Making connections: This chapter starts by reviewing how to calculate the circumference and area of a circle and the area of a parallelogram and a trapezium, which many students will have met before. It then introduces more complex formulas for areas and volumes, including calculating the length of an arc and the area and angle of a sector. It also covers the volumes of prisms, pyramids, cylinders, cones and spheres.

Relevance: There are many everyday uses of area and volume calculations such as in decorating. There are also applications in manufacturing, plumbing and general engineering.

Working mathematically: What information is required in order to find both the volume and surface area of a cylinder? How can you which tell the difference between the formulae for the circumference and the formula for the area of a circle? What about the difference between the formula for the surface area of a cube and the volume of a cube?

Assessment: In each section of this chapter, ensure that students have a good grasp of the key questions in each exercise before moving on. (Refer to the 'Route mapping' table above.) Encourage students to read and think about the 'Ready to progress?' statements on page 272 of the Student Book. Check students' understanding at the end of the chapter, formatively, using peer assessment. Students could do a mini test in the form of the 'Review questions' on pages 272–273 of the Student Book. Follow up the test with an individual target-getting session, based on any areas for development that a student may have.

Worked exemplars from the Student Book – suggestions for use

- Present students with the same question but using different numbers. Students should use the exemplar to mirror the working, in full or only the notes.
- Copy and cut the exemplars into cards. Students match the working with the notes.
- Copy and cut the working into cards, splitting the label/description from the working. Students put the working in order then match with the descriptions.

Answers to the Student Book questions are available on the CD-ROM provided.

Section 9.1 Circumference and area of a circle

Learning objectives

- Calculate the circumference and area of a circle

Resources and homework

- Student Book 9.1: pages 249–251
- Practice Book 9.1: pages 81–82

Making mathematical connections

- Volumes of cylinders
- Surface areas of cylinders
- Areas of sectors

Making cross-curricular connections

- **Science** – using formulae
- **Relevance** – applications in many career pathways

Prior learning

- This lesson is likely to be revision as students should have learned how to calculate the area and circumference of a circle previously.

Working mathematically

- Encouraging students to show their workings clearly at each step of the problem.
- Challenge **more able** students by asking, for example:
  - A circle has an area of 50 cm^2. What is its diameter?
  - A car has wheels with a diameter of 45 cm. How many rotations does each wheel make during a 10-km journey?

Common misconceptions and remediation

- **Less able** students may confuse πr^2 and $(\pi r)^2$. Encourage them to write the formula for the area of the circle in the form $A = \pi \times r \times r$ until they are confident using the formula (and their calculator).
- Some students do not round numerical answers to an appropriate degree of accuracy. Remind them of this periodically.

Probing questions

- What is the least information you would need, to find the circumference and area of a circle?
- Explain the steps you would follow to find the circumference of a circle given the area.

Literacy focus

- Key terms: circumference, π (pi)
- Check students' understanding by asking them to write questions using the key terms.

Part 1

- Draw a suitable circle and ask students to label the important features such as circumference, radius and diameter.

Part 2

Circumference of a circle

- Revise the formula for the circumference of a circle ($C = 2\pi r$) and ask students to calculate the circumference of circles given the radius or the diameter.
- Work through Example 1 from the Student Book.

Area of a circle

- Work through the sketch proof of $A = \pi r^2$ shown in the Student Book.
  - o Show a circle divided into slices.

  - o Rearrange the slices so that they form a parallelogram (approximately), as shown.

    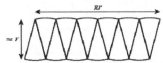

  - o The top and bottom of the parallelogram together equal the circumference of the circle, $2\pi r$, so each side must be πr.
  - o The height of each triangular section is approximately r.
  - o Therefore, the area of a circle is approximately $\pi r \times r = \pi r^2$.
- **More able** students should be able to see how the diagrammatical approximation improves as the circle is divided into more slices.
- Work through Example 2 from the Student Book.
- **Students can now do Exercise 9A from the Student Book.**

G&M 1–3, 6, 7, 10	Calculator n/a	CM n/a	MR 11, 14	PS 4, 5, 8, 13	EV 9, 12

Part 3

- The bull's-eye illusion consists of five concentric circles.
- Draw it on the board and ask students which is larger: the shaded inner area or the shaded outer area. Most think that the inner area is larger.
- Tell them that the innermost ring has a radius of 1 cm, the next ring has a radius of 2 cm … the outer ring has a radius of 5 cm.
- Work out the two areas. (They are both the same, 28.27 cm².)
- Say: You want to draw a circle with a circumference of 20 cm. To what radius should you open your compasses? (3.2 cm)
- On the board, write the solutions to some area and circumference questions with mistakes in them. Ask students to identify the errors.

Section 9.2 Area of a parallelogram

Learning objectives
- Calculate the area of a parallelogram

Resources and homework
- Student Book 9.2: pages 252–253
- Practice Book 9.2: page 82

Making mathematical connections
- Areas of 2D shapes
- Volumes and surface areas of 3D shapes

Making cross-curricular connections
- **Design and Technology** – calculating areas of shapes as part of the design aspect of a project
- **Relevance** – everyday applications of area, e.g. in manufacturing, design

Prior learning
- Students should be able to calculate the area of a rectangle.

Working mathematically
- Students should have a good grasp of this concept from Key Stage 3. The practical demonstration showing why you use the perpendicular height in Part 2 will be useful for **less able** pupils.
- **More able** students could explore the link between the area of a parallelogram and the area of a trapezium.

Common misconceptions and remediation
- **Less able** students will often confuse slant height with perpendicular height. Stress to students that when the height of a parallelogram refers to its perpendicular height, not the length of a slanted side.

Probing questions
- Why do we find the area of a parallelogram by multiplying the base by the perpendicular height?
- Convince me that a rhombus must be a parallelogram, but that a parallelogram is not necessarily a rhombus.

Literacy focus
- Key terms: There are no new key terms in this section.
- Ask students to explain in words why the area of a parallelogram is base × perpendicular height.

Part 1
This activity will check students' understanding of the area of a triangle.
- On the board, draw a set of triangles (right-angled and non-right-angled) with the same area, including one with a different area.
- Ask students, in pairs, to identify the odd one out and explain why all the other triangles are the same and the odd triangle is not.

Part 2

- For this activity, the class needs coloured card or gummed paper and scissors.
- Ask the class to draw and cut out a parallelogram. You may want to provide a template.
- Ask them to mark a right-angled triangle, as shown, cut it, and attach it to the other side of the shape.

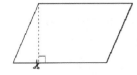 

This shows that the area of the parallelogram is the same as the area of a rectangle with the same base and height.

- The area of a parallelogram is given by the formula: $A = b \times h = bh$

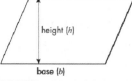

- Demonstrate how to use this formula to calculate the area of a parallelogram.
  On the diagram, $b = 8$ cm and $h = 5$ cm
  So, $A = 8 \times 5 = 40$ cm²
- Work through Example 3 from the Student Book.
- **Students can now do Exercise 9B from the Student Book.**

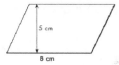

G&M 1	Calculator all	CM 3	MR n/a	PS 4	EV 2

Part 3

- Ask the class to work in pairs or small groups to explain how to find the area of a parallelogram, by drawing diagrams on individual mini whiteboards or on A4 paper.
- Ask different groups to show their explanations to the rest of the class.

Section 9.3 Area of a trapezium

Learning objectives
- Calculate the area of a trapezium

Resources and homework
- Student Book 9.3: pages 253–256
- Practice Book 9.3: pages 83–84

Making mathematical connections
- Areas of 2D shapes
- Volumes and surface areas of 3D shapes

Making cross-curricular connections
- **Design and Technology** – calculating areas of shapes as part of the design aspect of a project
- **Relevance** – everyday applications of area in, e.g. manufacturing, design

Prior learning
- Students should know how to find the areas of triangles, rectangles and parallelograms.

Working mathematically
- Discuss what distances should be measured to find the area in the examples students drew in the starter. In some examples, the height may not be obvious (when there is no perpendicular line joining the two parallel sides).
- Challenge **more able** students to find the area of these examples.
- Use the examples as a teaching point.

Common misconceptions and remediation
- The most common error is not identifying the height correctly. Give students plenty of examples in different orientations to make sure they can identify the height confidently.
- Emphasise that squares and rectangles are special cases of trapeziums. In Part 2, show students that the formula for the area of a trapezium works for these shapes.

Probing questions
- Why do you have to add the parallel sides when finding the area of a trapezium?
- Write down all the formulae for the areas of 2D shapes that you know.
- Can you draw a 2D shape that does not have a formula to work out the area?

Literacy focus
- Key terms: There are no new key terms in this section.
- Ask students to explain, in words, the formula for the area of a trapezium.

Part 1
- Ask students to draw a trapezium on their mini whiteboards or plain paper.
- Ask them to draw a second trapezium that is very different.
- Then ask them to draw a third trapezium that is different again.
- Share examples with the whole class and discuss what the examples have in common.

Part 2

- Explain that the area of a trapezium is given by:
  A = half the sum of the parallel sides × height.

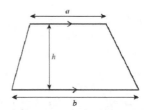

- Tell students that this can be derive this formula by splitting a trapezium into two triangles, as shown.

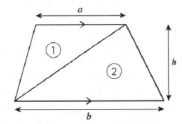

Area of triangle 1 = $\frac{1}{2}$ × base × height = $\frac{1}{2}ah$

Area of triangle 2 = $\frac{1}{2}$ × base × height = $\frac{1}{2}bh$

Therefore, total area = $\frac{1}{2}ah + \frac{1}{2}bh = \frac{1}{2}h(a + b) = \frac{1}{2}(a + b)h$

- Make sure that students understand that height refers to perpendicular height, and that they must add the two parallel sides.
- Tell students that they should give final answers to a suitable degree of accuracy, usually three significant figures.
- Work through Example 4 from the Student Book with the class.
- **Students can now do Exercise 9C from the Student Book.**

G&M 1, 3, 6	Calculator all	CM 4	MR 2, 7, 10	PS 5, 8, 9, 11	EV 12

Part 3

- Draw the following diagrams on the board:

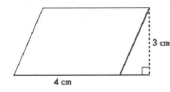

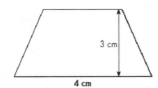

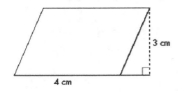

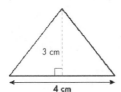

- Ask: Which has the largest area? (They are all the same except the triangle, which is half the size.)

Section 9.4 Sectors

Learning objectives
- Calculate the length of an arc
- Calculate the area and angle of a sector

Resources and homework
- Student Book 9.4: pages 256–258
- Practice Book 9.4: pages 84–85

Making mathematical connections
- Trigonometry
- Areas of segments
- Rearranging formula

Making cross-curricular connections
- **Science** – using formulae
- **Relevance** – working with formulae

Prior learning
- Students must know and be able to use the formulae for the area and circumference of a circle.

Working mathematically
- Following revision of calculating the area and circumference of circles, most students should be in a position to begin to discover the formulae for the arc length and area of a sector.
- Ask students to write down the formula for the circumference of a circle.
- Then ask them to write a formula for the curved part of a semi-circle and then for the curved part of a quarter circle.
- Can they make the leap to finding the formula for the arc length of a sector, given a sector angle?

Common misconceptions and remediation
- Students often forget that the perimeter of a sector is the sum of the arc length plus two radii, not the arc length alone. Emphasise this point.

Probing questions
- Talk me through calculating the arc length/area of this sector.
- Why do we divide the sector angle by 360°?

Literacy focus
- Key terms: arc, sector, subtend
- Be explicit about the language used in this section. Go through the key words with students and make sure they understand their meaning

Part 1
- Recap students' knowledge of circles.
- Draw circles with radii of 5 cm and 10 cm on the board.
- Ask students what they can tell you about their circumferences.
- They may tell you how to work them out. Try to elicit that one circumference is double the length of the other.
- Establish that whenever the radius of a circle is doubled, the circumference will also double.
- Move on to the areas. Is the same thing true? (No, when the radius is doubled, the area becomes four times greater.)

Part 2

- Work through the initial text in the Student Book to help students understand the language of this topic.

  Length of an arc and area of a sector
- Explain that if an arc subtends an angle $\theta°$ at the centre of a circle:

  length of the arc $= \dfrac{\theta}{360} \times 2\pi r$

  area of the sector $= \dfrac{\theta}{360} \times 2\pi r^2$
- Make sure students understand that the angle tells you what fraction of a whole circle you are considering. Remembering the formula is less important.
- Work through Examples 5 and 6 from the Student Book.
- **Students can now do Exercise 9D from the Student Book.**

G&M 1–3, 5, 6	Calculator all	CM 7, 9, 13	MR 4	PS 8, 10–12	EV n/a

Part 3

- Draw two sectors: one with an angle of 90° and radius 4 cm, the other with an angle of 45° and radius 8 cm.
- Ask: Which sector had the longer length of arc? Which sector has the larger area?
- Allow students to think about this in pairs for a couple of minutes. Then take their comments. (They have the same arc length. The area of the second sector is twice the area of the first.)
- Ask students to suggest other sectors with the same arc length as those given above. (Other examples are: 180° and 2 cm, 60° and 6 cm, 120° and 3 cm, 22.5° and 16 cm)

Section 9.5 Volume of a prism

Learning objectives
* Calculate the volume of a prism

Resources and homework
* Student Book 9.5: pages 259–261
* Practice Book 9.5: pages 85–86

Making mathematical connections
* Areas of 2D shapes
* Volumes of 3D shapes
* Dimensions
* Density

Making cross-curricular connections
* **Science** – volumes of prisms in experiments
* **Food Technology** – volumes of containers
* **Relevance** – applications to manufacturing, engineering and design

Prior learning
* Students need to be able to calculate areas of rectangles, triangles, trapeziums and compound shapes.

Working mathematically
* Draw a rectangle, triangle, circle and trapezium on the board and ask students to recall the areas of these shapes.
* Extend the diagrams into 3D prisms by adding depth.
* Ask what the rectangular prisms and circular prisms are more commonly called (cuboid, cylinder).
* Why is it that the other two prisms do not have special names?

Common misconceptions and remediation
* Students will sometimes mistake the length of the prism for a length occurring in the common cross-section. Encourage them to sketch a good diagram and solve the problem in two distinct stages to avoid making this error.

Probing questions
* How do you go about finding the volume of a prism?

Literacy focus
* Key terms: cross-section, prism
* Encourage students to write a short sentence using the key words to describe what makes a prism a prism.

Part 1
* Ask students if they have heard the word 'prism' before and what they understand by it.
* Show students as many examples of prisms as you can find (including packaging boxes and pictures).
* Discuss what they have in common (a constant cross-section parallel to one plane).
* Include some examples that are not prisms to make the point.

Part 2

- Explain that the volume of a prism is given by the product of the area of its cross-section and its length:

  $V = Al$

  where A is the area of the cross-section and l is the length of the prism.
- Stress to the students that to work out most problems, the first step will usually be to calculate the cross-sectional area of the prism.
- Students will probably be familiar with the formula for the area of a cuboid. Show them the equivalence and explain that the formula for the volume of a prism is a generalisation of this formula.
- Work through Example 7 in the Student Book with the class.
- If you have some real boxes, ask students to make appropriate measurements and calculate their volume.
- **Students can now do Exercise 9E from the Student Book.**

| G&M 1, 2, 6 | Calculator all | CM 3 | MR 5 | PS 4, 7–10 | EV 11 |

Part 3

- Ask students to sketch a prism with a volume of 60 cm³. This could be done in pairs, using mini whiteboards if you have them. Ask one or two students who have drawn interesting prisms to show them to the class.
- For a given prism volume (e.g. 24 cm²), find as many possible prisms with whole-number dimensions as you can.

Section 9.6 Cylinders

Learning objectives

- Calculate the volume and surface area of a cylinder

Making mathematical connections

- Areas of 2D shapes
- Volumes of 3D shapes
- Dimensions
- Density

Resources and homework

- Student Book 9.6: pages 262–263
- Practice Book 9.6: pages 86–87

Making cross-curricular connections

- **Science** – volumes of cylinders used in experiments
- **Food Technology** – volumes and surface areas of cylindrical containers
- **Relevance** – applications to manufacturing, engineering and design

Prior learning

- Students should know how to find the volume of a prism and the area of a circle.

Working mathematically

- Ask students to work out the formulae for surface area and volume based on their mathematical knowledge of the areas of circles and the volumes of prisms.

Common misconceptions and remediation

- **Less able** students may be confused between $\pi r^2 h$ and $(\pi r)^2 h$. Encourage them to use a simpler version of the formula – $V = \pi \times r \times r \times h$ – until they are more confident.

Probing questions

- What is the minimum information you need to be able to find the volume and surface area of a cylinder?
- How would you go about finding the volume of a cylinder if you know the circumference and the height?

Literacy focus

- Key terms: cross-section, prism
- Ask students to list the key terms and their definitions.

Part 1

- Take a trundle wheel into the class or display a picture of a trundle wheel.
- Explain that a trundle wheel is used to measure distances. It has a wheel with a circumference of 1 metre.
- Ask students, in pairs, to work out the diameter of the wheel (31.8 cm) and its area (796 cm^2).
- This serves to revise the formulae that they will need for this lesson.

Part 2

Volume

- Using an A4 sheet of paper, make a hollow cylinder by bending the long edges together.
- Remind students that a cylinder is a circular prism.
- Tell them that the sheet of paper is 29.7 cm long and 21.0 cm wide and set them the task of finding the volume of the cylinder (1040 cm³ to 3 sf).
- Prompt them to use their knowledge of prisms to work out the formula for the volume of a cylinder.
- If they have not worked out the formula, display it and show them how it can be derived from the formula for the volume of a prism:
  Volume = $\pi r^2 h$
- You could set an extension task of finding the volume of the cylinder formed by putting the shorter edges together. Is it the same? (No, 1470 cm³ to 3 sf)
- Work through Example 8 with students.

Surface area

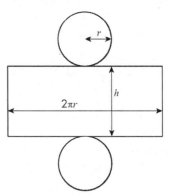

- Revisit the curved A4 sheet and ask how they can find the area of the curved surface of the cylinder.
- This should be easy: 29.7 × 21.0 cm².
- Now consider a cylinder with two circular ends, as shown.
- The total surface area consists of a rectangle and two circles.
- Demonstrate that the curved surface area is πdh or $2\pi rh$ and the total surface area is $\pi dh + 2\pi r^2$ or $2\pi rh + 2\pi r^2$.
- You could show **more able** students that this is equivalent to $2\pi r(r + h)$.
- Work through Example 9 with students.
- **Students can now do Exercise 9E from the Student Book.**

G&M 1, 2	Calculator all	CM 6	MR 3	PS 4, 8, 9	EV 5, 7, 10

Part 3

- Ask students, individually or in pairs, to work out the amount of metal that is used to make a 2p coin.
- Discuss students' answers. (Based on a thickness of 2 mm and a diameter of 26 mm, the volume is approximately 1060 mm³.)
- Discuss the accuracy of the measurement of the coin's 'thickness'.
- What is the effect of the rim and the pattern?

Section 9.7 Volume of a pyramid

Learning objectives
- Calculate the volume of a pyramid

Resources and homework
- Student Book 9.7: pages 264–266
- Practice Book 9.7: pages 87–88

Making mathematical connections
- Areas of 2D shapes
- Volumes of 3D shapes
- Dimensions
- Density

Making cross-curricular connections
- **Science** – density of objects
- **Food Technology** – volumes of packaging materials
- **Relevance** – applications to manufacturing, engineering and design

Prior learning
- Students should know how to calculate the areas of simple shapes such as circles, rectangles and triangles.

Working mathematically
- Show students a picture of the Great Pyramid of Giza. Say that the base was originally a square of side 230.4 m and the height was 146.6 m. Its mass is estimated as 5.9 million tonnes.
- Ask students to estimate the volume. You are not looking for accuracy, just a reasonable guess, so suggest that they compare it with a cuboid of a similar size. (about 2.5 million m³)
- Ask students to calculate the value of: $\dfrac{\text{side}}{\text{height}} \times 2$.
- Where have they seen this number before? (It is extremely close to π.)
- The ratio of its side to its height is $\dfrac{\pi}{2}$. Is this a coincidence? Nobody knows.

Common misconceptions and remediation
- Students sometimes assume that the height is given by the length of a sloping edge rather than the vertical height. Pointing out this error whenever it occurs should minimise it.

Probing questions
- What is the minimum information you need to be able to find the volume of a pyramid?
- Talk me through how you would you go about finding the volume of a pyramid.

Literacy focus
- Key terms: apex, edge, frustum, pyramid, vertex, vertices
- Ask students to define each of the key terms. They will need a clear understanding of each of these terms to answer questions on this topic.

Part 1
- Review the previous lesson by giving students some questions on the surface area and volume of cylinders.

Part 2

- Explain that the formula to calculate the volume of a pyramid involves its base area and height.
- Write on the board: Volume = ? × area of base × height and explain that the question mark stands for a number. Ask: What number? $\left(\dfrac{1}{3}\right)$. (Part 3 should help to reinforce this).
- Compare this to the formula for the area of a triangle: area = $\dfrac{1}{2}$ × length of base × height
- Use the formula to calculate the volume of the Great Pyramid.
- Explain that not all pyramids have a square base, although this is the most common type. The formula for the volume is the same, whatever the shape of the base.
- If you have any models of pyramids, show them and ask students to show the dimensions they would need to measure to calculate the volumes.
- They can then measure these dimensions and use them to calculate the volumes.
- Work through Examples 10 and 11 with students.
- **Students can now begin Exercise 9G from the Student Book.**

G&M 1, 5	Calculator all	CM 3	MR 2, 7, 8	PS 4, 6, 9	EV 10

Part 3

- Ask students to sketch a pyramid with a volume of 64 cm³.
- Collect students' suggestions.
- Three possibilities are:
  - o base 4 × 4, height 12
  - o base 8 × 8, height 3
  - o base 2 × 2, height 48.

Section 9.8 Cones

Learning objectives
- Calculate the volume and surface area of a cone

Resources and homework
- Student Book 9.8: pages 266–268
- Practice Book 9.8: pages 89–90

Making mathematical connections
- Areas of 2D shapes
- Volumes of 3D shapes
- Dimensions
- Density

Making cross-curricular connections
- **Science** – density of objects
- **Food Technology** – volumes of packaging materials
- **Relevance** – applications to manufacturing, engineering and design

Prior learning
- Students should know how to find the volume of a pyramid.

Working mathematically
- How would you help someone to distinguish between the formula for the surface area of a cone and the volume of a cone?
- Ask students to talk you through how the formula for the surface area of a cone is derived.

Common misconceptions and remediation
- Students often confuse the height and the slant height. Make sure they understand the difference between them.

Probing questions
- What is the minimum information you need to be able to find the volume and surface area of a cone?
- Talk me through how you would you go about finding the volume and surface area of a cone.

Literacy focus
- Key terms: slant height, vertical height
- Make sure students become familiar with the key terms and understand their meaning.

Part 1
- Give students a circular piece of paper (or a circle printed on paper for them to cut out).
- Ask students to find the centre. (They can do this by folding the circle in half in two different ways and finding where the diameters cross, but give students a chance to work out a method by themselves.)
- Ask them to draw in any two radii and cut along them. They now have two sectors.
- Show them how to tape or glue the straight edges to make a cone and ask them to do this with both sectors.
- Ask students to describe the similarities and differences. Establish:
  - All have the same slant height – introduce this terminology and distinguish it from the (actual) height.
  - They have different heights and bases. Make it clear that the height is measured perpendicular to the base.
  - The greater the height, the smaller the base area/diameter, and vice versa.
- Ask them to measure the height and base diameter of each cone.

Part 2

- Ask students how they can find the volume of a cone. They should realise that a cone is a pyramid with a circular base, so they can use the formula: $\frac{1}{3}$ × area of base × height.

  Volume of a cone = $\frac{1}{3} \times \pi r^2 \times h$ or $V = \frac{1}{3}\pi r^2 h$

- Ask them to calculate the volume of each cone they made in the starter.
- Now ask them how they can find the area of the curved surface of the cone. Through discussion, establish:
  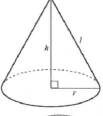
  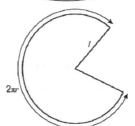
  - The curved surface area is the same as the area of the original sector.
  - The radius of the original sector is the slant height of the cone (*l*).
  - The area of the original circle is πl^2.
  - The circumference of the original circle is $2\pi l$
  - The length of the arc of the sector is $2\pi r$, where *r* is the radius of the circular base of the cone.

  - The sector is a fraction of the original circle, namely $\frac{2\pi r}{2\pi l} = \frac{r}{l}$.

  - The area of the curved surface is $\frac{r}{l} \times \pi l^2 = \pi r l$.

- Emphasise the final result as some students will find the details of this demanding.
- Ask students to find the area of the curved surface of each of their cones.
- Finally, ask students to imagine that they have added a circular base to their cone. What is the total surface area of each one? (curved surface + base)
- Show **more able** students the formula for the total surface area of a cone:
  $A = \pi r l + \pi r^2 = \pi r(l + r)$.
- Discuss Example 12 with students.
- **Students can now do Exercise 9H from the Student Book.**

| G&M 1, 4, 5 | Calculator all | CM 7 | MR 3 | PS 2, 8–10 | EV 6 |

Part 3

- Look at students' answers to question 5. Ask: Is there connection between the angle of the sector and the diameter of the base?

- The connection is $d = \frac{\text{angle}}{180} \times l$, but students may express this in different ways.

Section 9.9 Spheres

Learning objectives
- Calculate the volume and surface area of a sphere

Resources and homework
- Student Book 9.9: pages 268–269
- Practice Book 9.9: page 90

Making mathematical connections
- Areas of 2D shapes
- Volumes of 3D shapes
- Dimensions
- Density

Making cross-curricular connections
- **Science** – density of objects, working with formulae
- **Relevance** – applications to manufacturing, engineering and design

Prior learning
- Students should be confident with the work on pyramids and cones from the preceding lessons.

Working mathematically
- Demonstrate that the volume of a cylinder is greater than the volume of a sphere as the sphere fits inside the cylinder with space around it. You could show this with a clear tennis ball tube and some tennis balls. You could also show students that the volume of a sphere is two-thirds the volume of the cylinder that contains it.

Common misconceptions and remediation
- Students may make errors keying $\frac{4}{3}$ in the volume formula into their calculators. Make sure students can use their own calculators efficiently and correctly.
- Tell students that using an approximation such as 1.33 leads to errors so should be avoided.

Probing questions
- What is the minimum information you need to be able to find the volume and surface area of a sphere?
- Talk me through how you would you go about finding the volume and surface area of a sphere.

Literacy focus
- Key term: sphere
- Write a step-by-step guide explaining how to calculate the surface area and volume of a sphere.

Part 1
- Revise the formulae covered so far by drawing shapes and asking students for the formulae to work out the area or volume as appropriate.

Part 2

- Explain that to conclude their work on volume and surface area, they will be looking at the sphere. Give them the following formulae:
  - Volume = $\frac{4}{3}\pi r^3$
  - Surface area = $4\pi r^2$
- Show students a football made up of many hexagons.
- Ask what measurements they need to find the volume and surface area.
- The radius is difficult to measure, but the diameter is possible if you have callipers or put a book on top and a table below and then measure the gap.
- Ask students to calculate the volume and surface area, remembering to include units.
- Ask them to check that their results seem reasonable.
- To estimate the surface area of the football, calculate the area of one hexagon by splitting it into two trapeziums; multiply this by the number of hexagons that make up the football. Check that it is close to the calculated value.
- Discuss what 'close' means in this context.
- Work through Example 13 with students.
- **Students can now begin Exercise 9I from the Student Book.**

| G&M 1–3 | Calculator all | CM n/a | MR 5, 7, 10 | PS 4, 6, 9 | EV 8 |

Part 3

- Set this question for students to tackle in pairs:
  The Earth is approximately spherical. The length of the equator is 40 000 km. Two-thirds of the Earth's surface is covered with water. What area of the Earth's surface is covered with water? (about 340 million km²)
- Discuss how they worked out the answer and the appropriate degree of accuracy for the area. (Two-thirds is an approximation, so the answer should also be an approximation.)

Chapter 10 Algebra: Linear graphs

Overview

10.1 Drawing linear graphs from points	**10.5** Real-life uses of graphs
10.2 Gradient of a line	**10.6** Solving simultaneous equations using graphs
10.3 Drawing graphs by gradient-intercept and cover-up methods	**10.7** Parallel and perpendicular lines
10.4 Finding the equation of a line from its graph	

Prior learning

Know how to plot coordinates in all four quadrants.
Know how to substitute numbers into a formula.
Know how to read and estimate from scales.
Know how to plot a graph from a given table of values.
Know how to plot equations of horizontal and vertical lines.

Learning objectives

Ensure that students can: draw a straight-line graph from its equation; find the equation of a linear graph; read information from a conversion graph; use graphs to find formulae and solve simultaneous linear equations; draw linear graphs parallel or perpendicular to other lines.

In the examination, students will be expected to:
* draw linear graphs by finding points
* find the gradient of a straight line and draw a line with a certain gradient
* draw graphs using the gradient-intercept method
* draw graphs using the cover-up method
* find the equation of a line, using its gradient and intercept
* find the equation of a line given two points on the line
* convert from one unit to another unit by using a conversion graph
* use straight-line graphs to find formulae
* solve simultaneous linear equations using graphs
* draw linear graphs parallel or perpendicular to other lines and passing through a specific point.

Extension

Explore more complex graphs such as quadratic graphs and use these to solve an equation with a straight line.

Curriculum references

Section	GCSE specification
10.1	A 8, 9
10.2	A 10
10.3	A 8, 9
10.4	A 10

Section	GCSE specification
10.5	A 14
10.6	A 19
10.7	A 9, 10

Route mapping

Exercise	Accessible	Intermediate	Challenging	AO1	AO2 MR CM	AO3 PS EV	Key questions
10A	1–9	10		1–3	4, 5	6–10	1–3
10B	1–7	8, 9		1, 2, 9	5–8	3, 4	1, 7, 9
10C	1–3	4		1, 2	3	4	1
10D		1–8		1, 2, 5	3, 4, 6	7, 8	1
10E		1–11		1, 4, 7, 8, 10, 11	3, 6, 9	2, 5	1, 2, 4
10F	1, 2	3–7		3–5	2, 6	1, 7	2, 3
10G		1–13		1–9	12, 13	10, 11	1–9
10H		1–5	6–11	2, 4, 5, 7	1, 6, 10	3, 8, 9, 11	4, 5

Key questions are those that demonstrate mastery of the concept, or which require a step-up in understanding or application. Key questions could be used to identify the questions that students must tackle, to support differentiation, or to identify the questions that should be teacher-marked rather than student-marked.

About this chapter

Making connections: The chapter starts with students reviewing how to draw a straight-line graph from its equation. Students will then relate this to finding the equation of a linear graph. The next area covered involves everyday uses of conversion graphs before students are shown how to solve simultaneous equations graphically. Finally, students are taught how to draw linear graphs that are parallel or perpendicular to other lines.

Relevance: A linear graph (often called a straight-line graph) shows two variables that increase at a constant rate. You will meet linear graphs and the relationships they represent in various situations in daily life, for example, exchange rates and the cost of hiring a vehicle, along with many other situations.

Working mathematically: Explain how to plot the graph $y = 3x + 2$. What are the initial steps? Is the point (2, 4) on the line $y = x + 2$? How do you know? Write down some equations that pass through these points. How can you solve these equations graphically?

Assessment: In each section of this chapter, ensure that students have a good grasp of the key questions in each exercise before moving on. (Refer to the 'Route mapping' table above.) Encourage students to read and think about the 'Ready to progress?' statements on page 302 of the Student Book. Check students' understanding at the end of the chapter, formatively, using peer assessment. Students could do a mini test in the form of the 'Review questions' on pages 302–303 of the Student Book. Follow up the test with an individual target-getting session, based on any areas for development that a student may have.

Worked exemplars from the Student Book – suggestions for use

* Present students with the same question but different numbers. They should use the exemplar to mirror the working, in full or just the notes.
* Copy and cut the exemplars into cards. Students match the working with the notes.
* Copy and cut the working into cards, splitting the label/description from the working. Students put the working in order then match with the descriptions.

Answers to the Student Book questions are available on the CD-ROM provided.

Section 10.1 Drawing linear graphs from points

Learning objectives
- Draw linear graphs by finding points

Resources and homework
- Student Book 10.1: pages 275–277
- Practice Book 10.1: pages 91–92

Making mathematical connections
- Quadratic graphs
- Graphs of trigonometric functions
- Statistical graphs

Making cross-curricular connections
- **Science** – representing experimental results graphically
- **Relevance** – uses in engineering, manufacturing and business

Prior learning
- Students must be able to read and plot coordinates, including coordinates given in tables of values.
- Students must also be able to substitute into simple algebraic functions.

Working mathematically
- Remind students that they should always use a sharp pencil when drawing linear graphs.
- Mention that if a point does not fit on a straight line, it has been calculated or plotted incorrectly.

Common misconceptions and remediation
- Students often work out two points and draw the line, rather than checking a third point to see that the line is correct.
- Inadequate algebra skills can lead to mistakes.

Probing questions
- Explain how you would draw the straight line graph of: $y = 3x + 2$.
- How do you determine the scale on the x- and y-axis? Do the scales have to be the same?

Literacy focus
- Key term: linear graph
- Make sure that students know the meaning of the word 'linear' as used in algebraic contexts.

Part 1
- Write a rule on the board, for example: × 2 + 1.
- Ask for the results for inputs of 0, 1, 2, 3 and 4.
- Give other rules and ask students to find the results for the same input numbers, for example: × 4 – 5, ÷ 2 – 3.
- Provide other input numbers for these rules and ask students to work out the results, for example: –3, –2, –1.

Part 2

- Introduce or revise linear graphs by plotting graphs for some of the sets of values generated in Part 1.
- Emphasise these points:
  - They need a minimum of two points to draw a straight line. They should use a third point as a check.
  - They should use a sharp pencil. (Thick lines makes it difficult to read values accurately and will not gain full marks in an examination.)
  - They should look directly down at the paper. This will help them plot points and draw lines accurately.
  - A tolerance of 1 mm is usually allowed in an examination.
- Work through Example 1 from the Student Book.
- Discuss the hints that follow the example in the Student Book.
- **Students can now do Exercise 10A from the Student Book.**

| A 1–3 | Calculator n/a | CM 4, 5 | MR n/a | PS 8–10 | EV 6, 7 |

Part 3

- Draw a set of axes on the board.
- Ask a student to draw the line with the equation: $y = 2x + 1$.
- If it seems correct, ask for the coordinates of the points where the line crosses the x-axis and the y-axis.
- Repeat with other lines, for example: $y = 3x - 2$; $y = 6x$; $y = \frac{1}{2}x + 4$.

Section 10.2 Gradient of a line

Learning objectives

- Find the gradient of a straight line
- Draw a line with a certain gradient

Making mathematical connections

- Gradients of quadratic graphs
- Gradients from statistical graphs

Resources and homework

- Student Book 10.2: pages 278–282
- Practice Book 10.2: pages 92–94

Making cross-curricular connections

- **Science** – analysing experimental results graphically
- **Relevance** – uses in engineering, manufacturing and business

Prior learning

- Students must have completed the previous section and be able to read and plot coordinates, including those from tables of values.
- Students must also be able to substitute into simple algebraic functions.

Working mathematically

- Is the gradient of a linear graph the same at all points on the line? In what types of graphs might the gradient change? Can you draw a graph with gradient of 0?
- Show **more able** students quadratic graphs. Ask the class: How would you find the gradient at a point?

Common misconceptions and remediation

- Students often get the x and y distances the wrong way around when calculating gradients. Tell students that a good way to remember this is: x is a cross and goes *across*.

Probing questions

- Talk me through how you found the gradient of this line.
- Does it matter if the x-axis scale is different to the y-axis scale?

Literacy focus

- Key term: gradient
- Encourage students to write a step-by-step guide explaining how to work out the gradient of a linear graph.

Part 1

- Review the previous section by asking students to draw the graphs of: $y = 2x + 3$ and $y = x + 2$ for x-values from −4 to 4.
- Ask students about the steepness of the lines.
- Explain that the steepness is called the *gradient* of the line.

Part 2

- Work through the introductory text at the beginning of this section in the Student Book.
- Emphasise these points:
  - When drawing a triangle to calculate the gradient, use integer grid lines.
  - Always divide the distance in the y-direction by the distance in the x-direction.
  - Lines that slope from top left to bottom right have a negative gradient.
- Work through Example 2 from the Student Book.

Drawing a line with a certain gradient

- Discuss the text under this heading in the Student Book.
- Work through Example 3.
- **Students can now do Exercise 10B from the Student Book.**

A 1, 2, 9	Calculator n/a	CM 7, 8	MR 5, 6	PS n/a	EV 3, 4

Part 3

- Ask students to look back at the graphs they drew in Part 1.
- Ask them to tell you the gradient and the intercept of each line with the y-axis.
- Can they see a connection?

Section 10.3 Drawing graphs by gradient-intercept and cover-up methods

Learning objectives

- Draw graphs using the gradient-intercept method
- Draw graphs using the cover-up method

Resources and homework

- Student Book 10.3: pages 282–286
- Practice Book 10.3: pages 94–95

Making mathematical connections

- Quadratic graphs
- Graphs of trigonometrical functions
- Statistical graphs

Making cross-curricular connections

- **Science** – representing experimental results graphically
- **Relevance** – uses in engineering, manufacturing and business

Prior learning

- Students must have completed the previous two sections and be able to read and plot coordinates, including those from tables of values.
- Students must also be able to substitute into simple algebraic functions.

Working mathematically

- Remind students always to start with the intercept. Drawing a line passing through the correct intercept may earn them one mark in an examination, even if the gradient is wrong.

Common misconceptions and remediation

- Students often calculate gradients incorrectly, for example, they calculate x-step ÷ y-step rather than y-step ÷ x-step.
- Students may omit the minus sign from a negative gradient.
- When using the cover-up method to draw graphs with a negative constant term, students misinterpret the intercept or misunderstand and plot a point on the wrong axis.
- To remediate these problems, provide additional practice and worked examples.

Probing questions

- What is the effect on a graph of increasing/decreasing the value of m?
- What is the effect on a graph of changing the value of c?
- What have you noticed about the graphs of functions of the form $y = mx + c$?
- What are the similarities and differences?

Literacy focus

- Key terms: constant term, cover-up method, gradient-intercept, intercept, $y = mx + c$
- Make sure students link m to the gradient and c to the y-intercept.
- Encourage students to make study notes based on this section, and to include all the key terms.

Part 1

- Show some graphs or refer to graphs that students have already seen.
- Establish the links between their equations and their gradients and y-intercepts.
- Students should spot that the coefficient (the number in front) of x is the same as the gradient, and the point where the graph crosses the y-axis is given by the constant term.

Part 2

Gradient-intercept method

- The principle of the first part of this section has been covered in Part 1.
- Work through Example 4 from the Student Book.
- Check that all students can find the intercept with the y-axis.
- If **less able** students have trouble drawing the gradients, a printed sheet showing the x-step and y-step of the necessary gradients may be helpful.
- **Students can now do Exercise 10C from the Student Book.**

A 1, 2	Calculator n/a	CM n/a	MR 3	PS 4	EV n/a

Cover-up method

- Show students a set of axes.
- Ask them to give you coordinates of different points on the y-axis.
- Write these on the board and ask students what they have in common.
- Students should spot that the x-value is 0. Recall that the y-axis has the equation $x = 0$.
- Repeat with points on the x-axis or ask students for the equation of the line ($y = 0$).
- Work through the text in this section and Example 5 from the Student Book.
- **Less able** students may need support, especially when the equation involves a negative value. Remind these students that, when dividing a positive by a negative, the result is negative, and that when dividing a negative by a negative, the result is positive.
- Challenge **more able** students to find the equation (in the form $ax + by = c$) for lines passing through two points such as (5, 0) and (0, −3).
- **Students can now do Exercise 10D from the Student Book.**

A 1, 2, 5	Calculator n/a	CM n/a	MR 3, 4, 6	PS 7	EV 8

Part 3

- Write this equation on the board: $4x + 3y = 12$.
- Use the cover-up rule to plot the graph.
- Work through rearranging the equation so that it is in the form $y = mx + c$. (Students may have some experience of rearranging formulae.)

$$4x + 3y = 12$$
$$3y = -4x + 12$$
$$y = -\frac{4}{3}x + 4$$

- Link this to the graph. It should have the same gradient and intercept.
- Tell students that they can always use the gradient-intercept method to draw a graph if they rearrange the equation so it is in the form $y = mx + c$.

Section 10.4 Finding the equation of a line from its graph

Learning objectives

- Find the equation of a line, using its gradient and intercept
- Find the equation of a line given two points on the line

Resources and homework

- Student Book 10.4: pages 286–289
- Practice Book 10.4: pages 96–97

Making mathematical connections

- Quadratic graphs
- Graphs of trigonometric functions
- Statistical graphs

Making cross-curricular connections

- **Science** – analysing experimental results graphically
- **Relevance** – uses in engineering, manufacturing and business

Prior learning

- Students should know how to draw a line using the gradient-intercept method.
- Students should also know how to find the gradient of a straight line.

Working mathematically

- Suggest that students write down the equation as $y = mx + c$, then substitute the y-intercept value as the constant and work from there.

Common misconceptions and remediation

- Students often fail to recognise a negative gradient. Remind them (if necessary, every time they begin to answer questions about a graph) that lines that slope from top left to bottom right always have a negative gradient. Say: forward slope equals positive, backward slope equals negative.

Probing questions

- What effect does changing the value of m have on the graph?
- What effect does changing the value of c have on the graph?
- What is the same and what is different about the graphs of functions of the form $y = mx + c$?

Literacy focus

- Key terms: There are no new key terms in this section.

Part 1

- Write on the board: $y = 2x - 1$ $4x - 2y = 2$ and $x = \dfrac{y + 1}{2}$
- Ask students to say which method they would use to plot the graphs of each equation.
- Expect them to choose the gradient-intercept method for $y = 2x - 1$ and the cover-up method for $4x - 2y = 2$.
- They may not be sure of a method for the third equation, so may choose to create a table of values (e.g. $y = 3$, $x = 2$ and $y = 9$, $x = 5$).
- Plot these lines together. They are all the same.

Part 2

- Show an accurate but unlabelled graph, e.g. $y = 3x + 1$.
- Ask students what the equation of the line is. They should be able to reverse the gradient-intercept method. If not, prompt them by asking them for the standard form of the equation of a line ($y = mx + c$).
- Write down the equation for this line.
- Work through the text and Example 6 from the Student Book with the class to consolidate the link between the gradient and m, and the y-intercept and c.
- **Students can now do Exercise 10E from the Student Book.**

| A 1, 4, 7, 8, 10, 11 | Calculator n/a | CM 3, 9 | MR 6 | PS 2, 5 | EV n/a |

Part 3

This links with the next section (Real-life uses of graphs).

- Show a sketch of a 'gas bill' graph, which consists of a basic charge and a price per unit.
- Do not add any values to the graph.

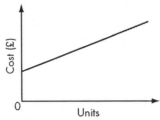

- Ask students how they can find the basic charge from the graph (the intercept).
- Then ask students how they can find the price per unit (the gradient).

Section 10.5 Real-life uses of graphs

Learning objectives

- Convert from one unit to another unit by using a conversion graph
- Use straight-line graphs to find formulae

Resources and homework

- Student Book 10.5: pages 290–294
- Practice Book 10.5: pages 97–98

Making mathematical connections

- Quadratic graphs
- Graphs of trig functions
- Statistical graphs

Making cross-curricular connections

- **Science** – finding the formula linked to an experiment graphically
- **Relevance** – uses in engineering, manufacturing and business

Prior learning

- Students should know how to draw a line using the gradient-intercept and cover-up methods.
- Students should also know how to find the gradient of a straight line.

Working mathematically

- Students draw the horizontal and vertical 'tracking' lines on conversion graphs, where possible, for maximum accuracy.

Common misconceptions and remediation

- Students often plot a point on the wrong axis when using the cover-up method. Additional practice examples should reduce the frequency of this error.

Probing questions

- For everyday problems explore questions such as:
  - What is the relationship between the gradient and the problem?
  - What is the relationship between the intercept and the problem?

Literacy focus

- Key term: conversion graph
- Ask students to write a sentence describing the relationship between variables on some conversion graphs.

Part 1

- Start this topic by revisiting the work covered in Part 3 of the previous section.
- Again, show the sketch of the 'gas bill' graph, which consists of a basic charge and a price per unit and do not add any values to the graph.
- Ask students to produce an equation for the graph using their own charges.

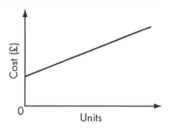

Part 2

- Explain that you will be looking at using graphs in practical situations.
- Discuss the text and work through Example 7 from the Student Book with the class.
- Emphasise these points:
  - The intercept on the vertical axis is the value of the function at zero.
  - Although this is usually zero on conversion graphs, it can be any value on a 'charges for services' graph. It is often called the basic charge or call-out fee.
  - The gradient of the line is the value per unit.
  - Again, this may be called something slightly different.
- **Students can now do Exercise 10F from the Student Book.**

| A 3–5 | Calculator all | CM n/a | MR 2, 6 | PS 1, 7 | EV n/a |

Part 3

- Display the £ to € conversion graph and discuss it with the students. Ask questions such as:
  - How many euros is 10 pounds?
  - Why does the graph go through the origin?
  - What is the equation of the line?
  - Can you use the equation of the line to convert the £ to € or € to £?

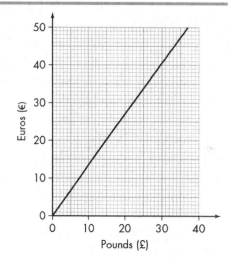

Section 10.6 Solving simultaneous equations using graphs

Learning objectives
- Solve simultaneous linear equations using graphs

Resources and homework
- Student Book 10.6: pages 295–296
- Practice Book 10.6: pages 98–99

Making mathematical connections
- Drawing linear graphs
- Solving simultaneous equations algebraically

Making cross-curricular connections
- **Science** – finding experimental results using graphs
- **Relevance** – applications to manufacturing, engineering and business

Prior learning
- Students should be able to draw a line from its equation using the gradient-intercept or cover-up method and work out the gradient of a line.
- Exercise 10G (Student Book, page 296) is better completed if students have already learned how to solve simultaneous equations algebraically (Chapter 15).

Working mathematically
- Two different straight lines that are not parallel will intersect at one point. This point is the solution of the equations of the lines, or the simultaneous equations.
- You can solve simultaneous equations algebraically (as shown in Chapter 15), or graphically.
- To solve simultaneous equations using this method, students must be able to draw graphs accurately.

Common misconceptions and remediation
- Students often plot a point on the wrong axis when using the cover-up method. Additional practice examples should reduce the frequency of this error.

Probing questions
- Explain how to solve two simultaneous linear equations graphically.
- Is it possible for two simultaneous linear equations to have more than one pair of solutions or to have no solution? Explain why.

Literacy focus
- Key term: simultaneous equation
- Ask students to write a step-by-step method for solving simultaneous equations graphically.

Part 1

- Write the equation $y = 2x + 1$ on the board and ask students for pairs of (x, y) values that will lie on the graph, for example: (1, 3), (0, 1), (3, 7).
- Now write $x + y = 10$ and students for pairs of (x, y) values that will lie on this graph, for example: (0, 10), (1, 9).
- If it has not already been found, ask what pair of values is true for both equations. (3, 7)
- Repeat for a different pair of equations such as $y = 3x - 1$ and $x - 2y = 5$. (1, −2)

Part 2

- Refer back to Part 1 and ask students if they can find the pair of (x, y) values that are true for both $y = 3x - 2$ and $2x - 3y = 6$. (0, −2)
- If students have already covered simultaneous equations, solve this algebraically by the substitution method:

$$2x - 3(3x - 2) = 6$$
$$2x - 9x + 6 = 6$$
$$-7x = 0$$
$$x = 0, y = -2$$

- Explain that graphs can be used to solve problems like this.
- Demonstrate by working through Example 8 from the Student Book with the class.
- **Students can now do Exercise 10G from Student Book.**

| A 1–9 | Calculator n/a | CM 13 | MR 12 | PS 10, 11 | EV n/a |

Part 3

- On the board, write the equation: $y = \frac{3}{4}x - 6$.
- Explain that mathematicians prefer equations without fractions and with as few minus signs as possible.
- Show students how to rearrange the equation:

	$y = \frac{3}{4}x - 6$
(Multiply both sides by 4)	$4y = 3x - 24$
(Subtract $3x$ from both sides)	$4y - 3x = -24$
(Multiply both sides by −1)	$3x - 4y = 24$

- Repeat with $y = 2 - \frac{2}{3}x$ ($3y + 2x = 6$) and $y = \frac{3}{5}x + 2$ ($5y - 3x = 10$).

Section 10.7 Parallel and perpendicular lines

Learning objectives
- Draw linear graphs parallel or perpendicular to other lines and passing through a specific point

Resources and homework
- Student Book 10.7: pages 297–299
- Practice Book 10.7: page 100

Making mathematical connections
- Drawing linear graphs
- Quadratic graphs
- Solving simultaneous equations algebraically

Making cross-curricular connections
- **Science** – finding experimental results using graphs
- **Relevance** – applications to manufacturing, engineering and business

Prior learning
- Students should be able to draw a line from its equation using the gradient-intercept or cover-up method and work out the gradient of a line.

Working mathematically
- If two lines are parallel, their gradients are equal.
- If two lines are perpendicular, their gradients are negative reciprocals of each other.

Common misconceptions and remediation
- Students often make errors as a result of poor algebraic skills.
- They also forget the negative when finding the gradient of a perpendicular line, that is, they find the reciprocal instead of the negative reciprocal.
- Extra practice and worked examples should help to remediate these problems.

Probing questions
- How can you tell if two lines are parallel by looking at their equations?
- How can you tell if two lines are perpendicular by looking at their equations?

Literacy focus
- Key term: negative reciprocal
- Ask students to write a sentence describing the relationships between the gradients of perpendicular lines, and a sentence describing the relationship between the gradients of parallel lines.

Part 1

- Write the equation $y = 3x - 5$ on the board and ask students to give you the equation of a line parallel to this line.
- They should provide equations such as $y = 3x + c$.
- Now ask for a line parallel to $3x + 2y = 6$.
- Students may say they don't know, or attempt to rearrange into the form $y = \dots$
- Point out, if necessary, that any equation of the form $3x + 2y = c$ is parallel to the example given.
- Ask students what it means if the lines are perpendicular to each other.
- Draw a pair of perpendicular lines on a coordinate grid on the board.
- Discuss their gradients.
- Ask students to measure the gradients of the two lines and comment on what they notice.

Part 2

- Students will need to be confident with drawing lines and calculating gradients. Revise these skills if necessary.
- Recap the significance of the values of m and c in graphs of the form $y = mx + c$.
- Explain that they will be learning to work out the equations of lines that are parallel to or perpendicular to given lines.

Finding the equation of a parallel line

- Recap the conditions for parallel lines.
- Work through the text from the Student Book.
- Students are expected to calculate the equations of parallel lines using algebraic methods. However, it may help **less able** students to draw the required lines on grids.

Finding the equation of a perpendicular line

- Work through the text and Examples 9 and 10 from the Student Book.
- **Students can now do Exercise 10H from the Student Book. Less able** students are likely to need support throughout this exercise.

A 2, 4, 5, 7	Calculator n/a	CM 1, 6, 10	MR n/a	PS 3, 8, 9, 11	EV n/a

Part 3

- Recall with students:
  - methods for drawing graphs by the gradient-intercept and the cover-up methods
  - solving simultaneous equations by drawing graphs
  - the uses of graphs to solve 'charges for services' type problems
  - the principles of finding the equations of lines parallel or perpendicular to other lines.

Chapter 11 Geometry and measures: Right-angled triangles

Overview

11.1 Pythagoras' theorem	**11.8** Using the sine and cosine functions
11.2 Finding the length of a shorter side	**11.9** Using the tangent function
11.3 Applying Pythagoras' theorem in real-life situations	**11.10** Which ratio to use
11.4 Pythagoras' theorem and isosceles triangles	**11.11** Solving problems using trigonometry
11.5 Pythagoras' theorem in three dimensions	**11.12** Trigonometry and bearings
11.6 Trigonometric ratios	**11.13** Trigonometry and isosceles triangles
11.7 Calculating angles	

Prior learning

Know how to find the square and square root of a number.
Know how to round numbers to a suitable degree of accuracy.

Learning objectives

Ensure that students can: use Pythagoras' theorem in right-angled triangles; use Pythagoras' theorem to solve problems; use Pythagoras' theorem in three dimensions; use trigonometric ratios in right-angled triangles; use trigonometry to solve problems.

In the examination, students will be expected to:
* calculate the length of the hypotenuse and a shorter side in a right-angled triangle
* use Pythagoras' theorem to solve problems in two and three dimensions
* find lengths of sides and angles in right-angled triangles using the sine, cosine and tangent functions
* decide which trigonometric ratio to use in a right-angled triangle
* solve practical problems and bearing problems using trigonometry
* solve problems using an angle of elevation or an angle of depression
* use Pythagoras' theorem and trigonometry to solve problems involving isosceles triangles.

Extension

Much of this material is new. **More able** students who find the work easy could move on to the sine and cosine rules, or complete a discovery exercise on radians.

Curriculum references

Section	GCSE specification		Section	GCSE specification
11.1	G 20		11.8	G 20
11.2	G 20		11.9	G 20
11.3	G 20		11.10	G 20
11.4	G 20		11.11	G 20
11.5	G 20		11.12	G 20
11.6	G 20		11.13	G 20
11.7	G 20			

Route mapping

Exercise	Accessible	Intermediate	Challenging	AO1	AO2 MR CM	AO3 PS EV	Key questions
11A	1–3	4, 5		3	1, 4, 5	2	3, 4
11B	1–5	6–8		1–3	8	4–7	3, 5
11C	1–13			2	9, 11	1, 3–8, 10, 12, 13	1, 4, 7
11D		1–12		1, 2, 9	4, 5, 7, 8	3, 6, 10–12	1, 7, 9, 10
11E		1–6	7–9	1, 7	5, 8	2–4, 6, 9	1, 3, 7
11F		1–15	16	1, 2, 5, 6, 8–15	3, 4, 16	7	1, 2, 15
11G		1–8	9, 10	1–6	7, 9, 10	8	
11H		1–6	7, 8	1–6	7, 8		1–4
11I		1–6	7, 8	1–6	7, 8		1–4
11J		1–6	7, 8	1–6	7, 8		1–4
11K		1–3	4, 5		4, 5		1–3
11L		1–9	10	1, 3, 4, 7	8, 10	2, 5, 6, 9	3, 8, 9
11M		1–9	10	1–3, 5, 6	4, 8	7, 9, 10	4, 5, 9
11N		1–8	9	1, 2, 4, 5, 7, 8	3	6, 9	5, 9
11P		1–4	5, 6	1, 2	6	3–5	1, 2, 3

Key questions are those that demonstrate mastery of the concept, or which require a step-up in understanding or application. Key questions could be used to identify the questions that students must tackle, to support differentiation, or to identify the questions that should be teacher-marked rather than student-marked.

About this chapter

Making connections: The chapter covers all the basic work on trigonometry, including Pythagoras' theorem and trigonometrical ratios. It moves on to calculating and problem solving in two and three dimensions (2D and 3D). The next step is the sine and cosine rules.

Relevance: There is an emphasis on problem solving and reasoning. There are applications in many areas, especially STEM careers such as engineering and architecture.

Working mathematically: How do you decide if a problem can be solved using trigonometry? Talk me through the information you need in order to calculate the shorter side of a right-angled triangle. Talk me through how you would decide whether to use Pythagoras or trigonometric ratios to work out a problem.

Assessment: In each section of this chapter, ensure that students have a good grasp of the key questions in each exercise before moving on. (Refer to the 'Route mapping' table above.) Encourage students to read and think about the 'Ready to progress?' statements on page 342 of the Student Book. Check students' understanding at the end of the chapter, formatively, using peer assessment. Students could do a mini test in the form of the 'Review questions' on pages 342–343 of the Student Book. Follow up the test with an individual target-getting session, based on any areas for development that a student may have.

Worked exemplars from the Student Book – suggestions for use

- Present students with the same question but using different numbers. Students should use the exemplar to mirror the working, in full or only using the notes.
- Copy and cut the exemplars into cards. Students match the working with the notes.
- Ask students to write their own exemplar questions based on those in the Student Book.

Answers to the Student Book questions are available on the CD-ROM provided.

Section 11.1 Pythagoras' theorem

Learning objectives

- Calculate the length of the hypotenuse in a right-angled triangle

Resources and homework

- Student Book 11.1: pages 305–307
- Practice Book 11.1: page 101

Making mathematical connections

- Square roots
- Sine and cosine rule
- Solving equations

Making cross-curricular connections

- **Science** – using formulae, particles moving on inclined planes
- **Relevance** – applications in architecture and engineering

Prior learning

- Students should be familiar with square numbers and know how to find the square and square root of a number.
- Students should also know how to round numbers correctly and understand the concept of an appropriate level of accuracy in the context of a problem.

Working mathematically

- Pythagoras' theorem can be stated as follows:
  For any right-angled triangle, the area of the square drawn on the hypotenuse is equal to the sum of the areas of the squares drawn on the other two sides.
- The form of the rule that most people remember is:
  In any right-angled triangle, the square of the hypotenuse is equal to the sum of the squares of the other two sides.
- Pythagoras' theorem is usually written as a formula: $c^2 = a^2 + b^2$

Common misconceptions and remediation

- Students often forget to find the final answer by taking the square root. Laying out solutions logically can help prevent this error.
- Students try to apply the theorem in unsuitable situations such as when the triangle in the question is not known to be a right-angled triangle. Emphasise that Pythagoras' theorem only applies to right-angled triangles.

Probing questions

- How do you know which side is the hypotenuse when solving a problem using Pythagoras' theorem?

Literacy focus

- Key terms: hypotenuse, Pythagoras' theorem, Pythagorean triple
- Make sure that students know what the hypotenuse is and how to identify it.
- Ask students to define *square numbers*.

Part 1

- Display a target board of whole numbers and ask students to identify the square numbers.
- Ask for any known square numbers that are missing from the board.
- Try to elicit the first 12 square numbers, with some other commonly known square numbers such as 400, 625, 1 000 000.
- Ask for squares of some simple decimal numbers such as 0.5 and 0.1.

Part 2

- Ask students if they have heard of Pythagoras' theorem.
- Students might remember it in the form $a^2 + b^2 = c^2$ or as a fact about squares. Encourage a clear and precise description.
- Now ask students how they know it is true. They are unlikely to recall a proof.
- Give students copies of the dissection on the right. Make sure they understand that it shows squares on the sides of a right-angled triangle.
- To help **less able** students, the class can work in pairs to cut out the five smaller pieces and fit them into the largest square. This demonstrates Pythagoras' theorem. By labelling the sides of a right-angled triangle as a, b and c, deduce that $a^2 + b^2 = c^2$.

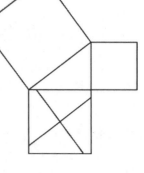

Finding the length of the hypotenuse

- Draw a triangle on the board and label it with the dimensions shown.
- Discuss how to calculate the length of the unknown side, or *hypotenuse*.
- Ask students to do the required calculation:
  $5.4^2 (29.16) + 7.3^2 (3.29) = \sqrt{82.45} = 9.080\ 198\ 236$

5.4 cm

7.3 cm

- Discuss the appropriate way to round the calculator answer. In this case, rounding to 1 dp is appropriate, because this is the degree of accuracy of the other lengths (9.1 cm).
- Work through Example 1 from the Student Book with the class.
- **Students can now do Exercise 11A from the Student Book.**

G&M 3	Calculator all	CM 4	MR 1, 5	PS 2	EV n/a

Part 3

- Draw a right-angled triangle with a semi-circle on each side.
- Ask if Pythagoras' theorem is true for semi-circles as well as squares. (it is)
- If students want to check a numerical example, give the sides as 6 cm, 8 cm and 10 cm. Encourage discussion and ask students to justify their answers.
- Challenge **more able** students with the question: Is it true for any other shapes? (Yes, it is true for any similar shapes.)

Section 11.2 Finding the length of a shorter side

Learning objectives
- Calculate the length of a shorter side in a right-angled triangle

Resources and homework
- Student Book 11.2: pages 307–309
- Practice Book 11.2: pages 102–103

Making mathematical connections
- Square roots
- Sine and cosine rule
- Solving equations

Making cross-curricular connections
- **Science** – using formulae, particles moving on inclined planes
- **Relevance** – applications in architecture and engineering

Prior learning
- Students should be familiar with square numbers and know how to find the square and square root of a number.
- Students should also know how to round numbers correctly and understand the concept of an appropriate level of accuracy in the context of a problem.
- Students should also be able to use Pythagoras' theorem to work out the length of the hypotenuse of a right-angled triangle.

Working mathematically
- Students will need to be comfortable with rearranging formulae.

Common misconceptions and remediation
- Students often confuse the methods for finding the hypotenuse (11.1) and finding a shorter side. Encourage students to label the hypotenuse first so they are clear which side they need to work out.
- Continue to remind students that Pythagoras' theorem can only be applied to right-angled triangles and that laying out their working carefully will help make sure they have completed all the necessary steps.

Probing questions
- How do you know when to add the squares of the sides and when to subtract them?

Literacy focus
- Key terms: There are no new key terms in this section.
- Ask students to write a step-by-step guide explaining how to solve questions using Pythagoras' theorem.

Part 1
- Draw these diagrams as accurately as possible on the board.
- Ask: How do these diagrams show that Pythagoras' theorem is true? (The diagram on the right can be divided into two squares.)
- Make sure all students can see that these are the squares on the shorter sides of the triangle.

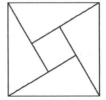 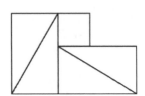

Part 2

- Draw a right-angled triangle and label the hypotenuse 13.6 cm and shortest side 8.4 cm.
- Ask: How can we work out the length of the missing side? Make sure students understand that they need to **subtract** the square of the shorter side from the square of the hypotenuse.
- Work through the calculation:

missing side² $= 13.6^2 - 8.4^2$
$= 184.96 - 70.56$
$= 114.4$
missing side $= \sqrt{114.4}$
$= 10.7$ cm (to 1 dp)

- Work through Example 2 from the Student Book.
- **Students can now do Exercise 11B from the Student Book.**

G&M 1–3	Calculator all	CM 8	MR n/a	PS 4–7	EV n/a

Part 3

- Draw a triangle and label the sides 8 cm, 15 cm and 17 cm. Do not mark any angles.
- Show that $8^2 + 15^2 = 17^2$.
- Ask: Is the triangle right angled? (yes)
- This is the inverse of Pythagoras' theorem. Students often do not realise that this is different.

    Right-angled triangle → sum of squares property
    is different from:
    sum of squares property → right-angled triangle.

Section 11.3 Applying Pythagoras' theorem in real-life situations

Learning objectives

- Use Pythagoras' theorem to solve problems

Resources and homework

- Student Book 11.3: pages 309–311
- Practice Book 11.3: pages 103–104

Making mathematical connections

- Square roots
- Sine and cosine rule
- Solving equations

Making cross-curricular connections

- **Science** – using formulae, particles moving on inclined planes
- **Relevance** – applications in architecture and engineering

Prior learning

- Students should know how to use Pythagoras' theorem to find either the hypotenuse or a shorter side.
- This lesson presents problems that can be solved using Pythagoras' theorem in a wide range of contexts. Students will need to know how to use compass bearings, coordinates and find the area of a rectangle.

Working mathematically

- Pythagoras' theorem can be used to solve some practical problems.
- When a problem involves only two lengths:
  - o Draw a diagram that includes a right-angled triangle.
  - o Decide which side you need to find: the hypotenuse or one of the shorter sides.
  - o Label the unknown side x.
  - o If it is the hypotenuse: square both numbers; add the squares and take the square root of the sum. If it is one of the shorter sides: square both numbers; subtract the smaller square from the larger square and take the square root of the difference.
  - o Round the answer to a suitable degree of accuracy.

Common misconceptions and remediation

- Mistakes can arise when students do not correctly identify a right-angled triangle and/or the hypotenuse correctly. Tell students that drawing a clear diagram at the start will help to avoid these mistakes.

Probing questions

- What do you look for in a problem to decide whether it can be solved using Pythagoras' theorem?
- What is the same or different about a right-angled triangle with sides of 3 cm, 4 cm and an unknown hypotenuse, and a right-angled triangle with sides of 3 cm, 4 cm and an unknown shorter side?

Literacy focus

- Key terms: There are no new key terms in this section.

Part 1

- Tell students that when builders want to construct a wall that is perpendicular to an existing wall, they use the '3, 4, 5 rule'.
- Ask students for suggestions as to how this rule works.
- Explain that builders generally use a rod such as a metre ruler as a measuring unit. They mark off 3, 4 and 5 lengths in a triangle with the 3 or 4 along the existing wall, which gives the required right angle. (Remember that a 3, 4, 5 triangle is right-angled.)
- You could demonstrate this in the classroom using string instead of rods.
- Tell the class that scientists believe that the Egyptians used this method to get the base edges perpendicular when building the pyramids and this method is still used today.

Part 2

- Start by working through Example 3 from the Student Book.
- Show students how to draw a diagram to represent the information from the initial statement of the problem.
- Ask students to identify and label the required side and then demonstrate the use of the appropriate form of Pythagoras' theorem to calculate the missing length.
- **Students can now do Exercise 11C from Student Book.**

| G&M 2 | Calculator all | CM 9, 11 | MR n/a | PS 1, 3–8, 10, 12 | EV 13 |

Part 3

- Ask students, in pairs, to design a practical question that can be solved using Pythagoras' theorem.
- Share the problems with the class.

Section 11.4 Pythagoras' theorem and isosceles triangles

Learning objectives

- Use Pythagoras' theorem in isosceles triangles

Resources and homework

- Student Book 11.4: pages 311–313
- Practice Book 11.4: pages 104–105

Making mathematical connections

- Square roots
- Sine and cosine rule
- Solving equations

Making cross-curricular connections

- **Science** – using formulae, particles moving on inclined planes
- **Relevance** – applications in architecture and engineering

Prior learning

- Students should know how to use Pythagoras' theorem to find either the hypotenuse or a shorter side.
- They also need to know the properties of isosceles triangles.

Working mathematically

- Students use the symmetrical properties of isosceles triangles to form two congruent right-angled triangles. They use with Pythagoras' theorem to solve problems involving isosceles triangles.

Common misconceptions and remediation

- Mistakes can arise when students do not correctly identify a right-angled triangle and/or the hypotenuse correctly. Tell students that drawing a clear diagram at the start will help to avoid these mistakes.

Probing questions

- Talk me through how you drew and labelled the triangle for this problem.
- How can you use Pythagoras' theorem to work out if an angle in a triangle is acute, obtuse or a right angle?

Literacy focus

- Key terms: There are no new key terms in this section.

Part 1

- Draw and label several triangles and ask students to calculate the area of each one.

Part 2

- Draw an equilateral triangle on the board and label the side lengths as shown.
- Ask students how they can work out the area.
- Discuss students' suggestions. Remind them, if necessary, that they need to calculate the perpendicular height.
- Work through the calculation:

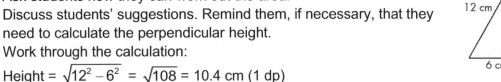

Height = $\sqrt{12^2 - 6^2}$ = $\sqrt{108}$ = 10.4 cm (1 dp)

Area = $\frac{1}{2}$ × 12 × 10.4 cm = 62.4 cm²

- Explain that this method can be used in any isosceles triangle.
- Work through Example 4 from the Student Book.
- **Students can now do Exercise 11D from the Student Book.**

G&M 1, 2, 9	Calculator n/a	CM 7, 8	MR 4, 5	PS 3, 6, 10, 11	EV 12

Part 3

- Discuss students' answers to question 7 in Exercise 11D of the Student Book.
- Encourage **less able** students to try different examples until they can see that the equilateral triangle has the largest area.

Section 11.5 Pythagoras' theorem in three dimensions

Learning objectives

- Use Pythagoras' theorem to solve problems involving three dimensions

Making mathematical connections

- Square roots
- Sine and cosine rule
- Solving equations

Resources and homework

- Student Book 11.5: pages 314–316
- Practice Book 11.5: pages 105–106

Making cross-curricular connections

- **Science** – using formulae, particles moving on inclined planes
- **Relevance** – applications in architecture and engineering

Prior learning

- Students need to know how to use Pythagoras' theorem to find any missing side of a right-angled triangle.

Working mathematically

- Some questions involve applying Pythagoras' theorem in 3D situations. A clearly labelled diagram will help students to identify the required dimensions to calculate the solutions.
- Students approach 3D problems in the same way as 2D problems:
  - Identify a right-angled triangle that contains the length they need.
  - Redraw this triangle and label it with the given lengths and the length to be found – usually x or y.
  - Decide whether the unknown length is the hypotenuse or one of the shorter sides.
  - Calculate the required length and round to a suitable degree of accuracy.
- There is often more than one calculation required when solving 3D problems. Remind students to round answers only at the final stage.

Common misconceptions and remediation

- Mistakes can arise when students do not identify a right-angled triangle from the 3D shape or do not identify the hypotenuse correctly. Tell students that drawing a clear diagram of each triangle needed will help to avoid these mistakes.

Probing questions

- Talk me through how you drew and labelled the triangle for this problem.

Literacy focus

- Key terms: There are no new key terms in this section.
- Ask students to write a step-by-step guide explaining how to solve 3D Pythagoras' problems.

Part 1

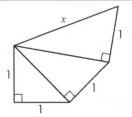

- Draw the diagram shown on the board.
- Challenge students to work out the length of x.
- Suggest **less able** students work in pairs.
- After a short time, ask for answers and methods.
- Establish that x can be found by using Pythagoras' theorem three times ($x = 2$).

- Discuss the intermediate lengths: $\sqrt{2}$ and $\sqrt{3}$. Use this opportunity to stress that, if students round their answers at each stage, their final answer will not be exact.
- Ask students to generalise the result. (If 1 is replaced by a, then x will equal $2a$.)

Part 2

- Ask students to imagine a wire going from the bottom right corner of the classroom to the top left corner of the classroom. (Choose another room if the classroom is not a cuboid!) Tell them that you know the length, width and height of the classroom. Ask: How can you work out the length of the wire?
- Take students' suggestions and establish that they can find the length by using Pythagoras' theorem twice:

$$\text{diagonal of the floor} = \sqrt{\text{length}^2 + \text{width}^2}$$

$$\text{length of wire} = \sqrt{\text{diagonal}^2 + \text{height}^2}$$

Show students how to draw and label appropriate diagrams.
- Work through Example 5 in the Student Book, drawing attention to the correct way to set out a solution.
- **Students can now do Exercise 11E from the Student Book.**

G&M 1, 7	Calculator all	CM 5, 8	MR n/a	PS 2–4, 6, 9	EV n/a

Part 3

- Have an unopened drinks can available. Ask students how long a drinking straw must be so that it does not disappear inside the can.
- Measure any lengths students suggest on the unopened can and when the correct ones are suggested, use them to calculate the minimum length. (The triangle is formed by the height and the diameter of the can.)

Section 11.6 Trigonometric ratios

Learning objectives
- Use the three trigonometric ratios

Resources and homework
- Student Book 11.6: pages 316–319
- Practice Book 11.6: page 107

Making mathematical connections
- Pythagoras' theorem
- Solving equations
- Substituting into equations
- Using a calculator

Making cross-curricular connections
- **Science** – using formulae, particles moving on inclined planes
- **Relevance** – applications in architecture and engineering

Prior learning
- Students should be able to round numbers to a given number of significant figures.

Working mathematically
- Trigonometry is concerned with the calculation of sides and angles in triangles. It involves the use of three important ratios: sine, cosine and tangent.
- These ratios are defined in terms of the sides of a right-angled triangle and an angle.

Common misconceptions and remediation
- Students make errors keying calculations on their calculators. Make sure that students know how to set their calculators to degrees.

Probing questions
- Why are similar triangles important when using trigonometric ratios (sine, cosine and tangent)?

Literacy focus
- Key terms: adjacent side, opposite side, tangent, cosine, sine, trigonometry
- Encourage students to come up with a mnemonic for remembering the trigonometric ratios such as:

Some **O**ld **H**ens **C**ackle **A**ll **H**ours **T**il **O**ld **A**ge

Part 1
- Show students the same diagram as in Part 1 of 11.5, but labelled as shown.
- Ask them about the angles at P.
  - Are they all the same size?
  - What can they say about the sizes?
- Ensure that you make the following points:
  - They are not all the same size.
  - The first one is 45°.
  - They get smaller as you go around the spiral.
  - If the spiral were to continue, the angles would become smaller and smaller.

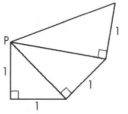

Part 2

- Ask students to draw a right-angled triangle with another angle of 40°, as shown. The triangles should be reasonably large but you want them to be different sizes.
- Ask students to label the 'Hypotenuse'.
- Point out that the other two sides are either opposite the 40° angle or adjacent to it. Students should label these 'Opposite' and 'Adjacent'.
- Ask them to measure the three sides and write the lengths on their triangles.
- Collect the measurements from each student and record them in a table with the headings shown below. (A spreadsheet is ideal.)

Opposite	Adjacent	Hypotenuse	$\dfrac{\text{Opposite}}{\text{Hypotenuse}}$	$\dfrac{\text{Adjacent}}{\text{Hypotenuse}}$	$\dfrac{\text{Opposite}}{\text{Adjacent}}$

Using your calculator

- Use the spreadsheet to work out the ratios in the last three columns and round them to 2 dp.
- Although the sides vary, the ratios should be similar. If any ratios are very different, check the accuracy of the measurements. (The effect of small inaccuracies in measures will be greater for smaller diagrams than larger diagrams.)
- Use the spreadsheet to calculate the average of the values in each column. These should be $\dfrac{\text{Opposite}}{\text{Hypotenuse}}$ 0.64, $\dfrac{\text{Adjacent}}{\text{Hypotenuse}}$ 0.77 and $\dfrac{\text{Opposite}}{\text{Adjacent}}$ 0.84.
- Discuss why these might be better values to use as the 'correct' value for these ratios.
- Explain that these ratios are called the sine, the cosine and the tangent of 40°, and that their abbreviations are sin, cos and tan. They are written as sin 40°, cos 40° and tan 40°.
- Make sure students can use a calculator correctly and check against the values in the table.
- Ask them to find the ratios for other angles.
- Show students how to work out calculations such as 7.2 sin 35° and $\dfrac{7.2}{\sin 35°}$. Check to see that **less able** students can do this efficiently.
- Work through Example 6 from in the Student Book.
- **Students can now do Exercise 11F from the Student Book.**

G&M 1, 2, 5, 6, 8–15	Calculator all	CM n/a	MR 3, 4, 16	PS n/a	EV 7

Part 3

- Return to the triangle students drew at the start of Part 2.
- Ask how this could be used to find the sine, cosine and tangent of 50° (third angle in triangle).
- Then ask students to do the relevant calculations and to check their accuracy using a calculator.

Section 11.7 Calculating angles

Learning objectives

- Use the trigonometric ratios to calculate an angle

Resources and homework

- Student Book 11.7: pages 319–320
- Practice Book 11.7: pages 107–108

Making mathematical connections

- Pythagoras' theorem
- Solving equations
- Substituting into equations
- Using a calculator

Making cross-curricular connections

- **Science** – using formulae, particles moving on inclined planes
- **Relevance** – applications in architecture and engineering

Prior learning

- Students should be able to calculate values of trigonometric ratios to a given degree of accuracy.

Working mathematically

- Students need to think about what angle has a cosine of 0.6. Students should remember that the angle with a cosine of 0.6' is written as $\cos^{-1} 0.6$. This is called the 'inverse cosine of 0.6'. Find out where $\cos^{-1}$ is on your calculator.

Common misconceptions and remediation

- As the notation $\sin^{-1} 0.6$ is new t students, they may get easily confused. Make sure students understand that it cannot be written as $0.6 \sin^{-1}$.
- Make sure students know how to use their calculators to correctly calculate trigonometric ratios.

Probing questions

- What is the largest value you can get from the sine/cosine of an angle? What angle gives this value?
- What is the smallest value you can get from the sine/cosine of an angle? What angle gives this value?

Literacy focus

- Key term: inverse
- Ask students to write a sentence or question that demonstrates their understanding of the key term.

Part 1

- Draw a 3, 4, 5 triangle on the board. Mark the smallest angle x.
- Ask students to write down the sine, cosine and tangent of x.

$$\left(\sin x = \frac{3}{5}, \cos x = \frac{4}{5}, \tan x = \frac{3}{4}\right)$$

- Mark the other angle y and repeat the exercise.

$$\left(\sin y = \frac{4}{5}, \cos x = \frac{3}{5}, \tan x = \frac{4}{3}\right)$$

- Reinforce the three ratios and tell students that they need to learn these.

Part 2

- Following on from Part 1, point out to students that they know that $\sin x = 0.6$. In other words, the angle x has a sine of 0.6.
- Introduce the notation $x = \sin^{-1} 0.6$ and show students how to work this out using a calculator (36.9° or 37°). Make sure that each student can do this on their own calculator.
- Ask students to try and calculate the value of x using the inverse of the cosine and tangent functions.
- Work through angle y in the same way.
- Work through one or both of Examples 7 and 8 from the Student Book, as necessary.
- **Students can now do Exercise 11G from the Student Book.**

G&M 1–6	Calculator all	CM 7, 9, 10	MR n/a	PS n/a	EV 8

Part 3

- Ask students what they would expect to find if they calculated $\sin \sin^{-1} 0.6$. (0.6)
- What about $\sin^{-1} \sin 0.6$? (0.6)
- Ask students to suggest other similar results.
- Why does this happen?
- Now ask students to find $\sin \cos^{-1} 0.6$. (0.8)
- Can they explain the result?

Section 11.8 Using the sine and cosine functions

Learning objectives
- Find lengths of sides and angles in right-angled triangles using the sine and cosine functions

Resources and homework
- Student Book 11.8: pages 321–325
- Practice Book 11.8: pages 108–109

Making mathematical connections
- Pythagoras' theorem
- Solving equations
- Substituting into equations
- Using a calculator

Making cross-curricular connections
- **Science** – using formulae, particles moving on inclined planes
- **Relevance** – applications in architecture and engineering

Prior learning
- Students should be familiar with the sine and cosine functions.
- They should be able to evaluate simple expressions involving the sine/cosine and inverse sine/cosine functions using their calculators.

Working mathematically
- This section will show students how to use the sine and cosine functions to calculate the length of a side.
- It may be useful to show students the graphs of the sine and cosine functions.

Common misconceptions and remediation
- Students find greatest difficulty when the unknown side is in the denominator. Working carefully through Example 10 from the Student Book will help them learn the method.
- Encourage students to check whether their answer is reasonable in the context of the question. For example, the hypotenuse should always be the longest side.

Probing questions
- How do you know when to use sine and when to use cosine?

Literacy focus
- Key terms: There are no new key terms in this section.

Part 1
- Display these equations.

$$\frac{x}{4} = 12 \qquad \frac{x}{12} = 4 \qquad \frac{12}{x} = 4 \qquad \frac{4}{x} = 12$$

Ask students to work in pairs to solve them.

- When they have finished, ask for their answers and working (48, 48, 3, $\frac{1}{3}$).

- Encourage students to come to an agreement if different answers are offered.
- The last equation is the most difficult. Ask for methods to use to solve it. (For example:

$4 = 12x; x = \frac{4}{12} = \frac{1}{3}$)

- Check that students have a good understanding by asking them to writing and solving a similar set of four questions using different numbers.
- Ask one or two pairs with good examples to share them with the class.

Part 2

Sine function

- Display these three diagrams side by side.

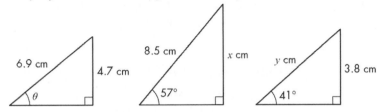

- Identify and label the 'opposite' and 'hypotenuse' in each triangle.
- Now ask students to write the sine ratio for each one and write it underneath the appropriate triangle.

  ($\sin \theta = \dfrac{4.7}{6.9}$; $\sin 57° = \dfrac{x}{8.5}$; $\sin 41° = \dfrac{3.8}{y}$)

- Ask students to solve each equation. Again, if there are different answers, encourage them to work together to identify the correct solution.
- Refer back to Part 1 if students are unsure about the last equation.
- Work through Examples 9 and 10 from the Student Book.
- **Students can now begin Exercise 11H from the Student Book.**

G&M 1–6	Calculator 1–6, 8	CM n/a	MR 7, 8	PS n/a	EV n/a

Cosine function

- Show a copy of the triangle on the right.
- Ask students which ratio they could to find x.
- Establish cosine, because the known value is the hypotenuse and the value to be found is adjacent to the known angle.
- Ask students to work out the value of x using a similar method to that used for sine in the previous section (39 cm)
- Work through Examples 11 and 12 from the Student Book.
- **Students can now begin Exercise 11I from the Student Book.**

G&M 1–6	Calculator 1–7	CM n/a	MR 7, 8	PS n/a	EV n/a

Part 3

- Ask students to look again at the right-angled triangle with a second angle of 62° again.
- Ask: Could you have used sine instead of cosine to find x? (yes) How? (by using the third angle of 28°)
- Ask them to check the answer is the same using this method.
- Can you always use sine instead of cosine? (Yes, in the questions they have seen so far.)
- Tell students that, when there is a choice, they can use whichever they prefer.

Section 11.9 Using the tangent function

Learning objectives
- Find lengths of sides and angles in right-angled triangles using the tangent function

Resources and homework
- Student Book 11.9: pages 326–328
- Practice Book 11.9: page 110

Making mathematical connections
- Pythagoras' theorem
- Solving equations
- Substituting into equations
- Using a calculator

Making cross-curricular connections
- **Science** – using formulae, particles moving on inclined planes
- **Relevance** – applications in architecture and engineering

Prior learning
- Students should have covered the previous lessons in this section and be familiar with the tangent function.
- They should be able to evaluate simple expressions involving the tangent and inverse tangent functions using their calculators.

Working mathematically
- Students will be shown how to use the tangent function to calculate the length of a side.
- It may be useful to show the graph of the tangent function.

Common misconceptions and remediation
- As with cosine and sine, students find greatest difficulty when the unknown side is in the denominator. Monitor this carefully.
- Encourage students to check whether their answer is reasonable in the context of the question. For example, the hypotenuse should always be the longest side.
- Students may find it difficult to decide which is the divisor when they are given two sides. Encourage students to draw clearly labelled diagrams to help with this.

Probing questions
- How do you know when to use sine, when to use cosine and when to use tangent?

Literacy focus
- Key terms: There are no new key terms in this section.
- Ask students to design a simple poster that captures the essential facts or techniques of the trigonometry studies so far.

Part 1
- Show a triangle with angles 45°, 45° and 90°. Ask students to explain why the tangent of 45° must be 1.
- What can they say about the tangent of an angle greater than 45°? (It will be larger than 1.)
- What is the largest value a tangent can have? (There is no limit.)

Part 2

- Draw these two triangles on the board.

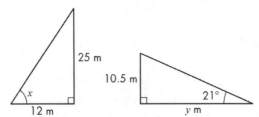

- Tell students that tangents can be used to find the lettered angle and side.
- Ask for suggestions on the method and work through students' solutions.
- Work through Examples 13 and 14 from the Student Book.
- **Students can now do Exercise 11J from the Student Book.**

G&M 1–6	Calculator all	CM n/a	MR 7, 8	PS n/a	EV n/a

Part 3

- Review the work from this lesson and the previous lesson on sine, cosine and tangent ratios.
- Ask students to list the main points that they need to remember.
- Use the key questions to assess this section.

Section 11.10 Which ratio to use

Learning objectives
- Decide which trigonometric ratio to use in a right-angled triangle

Resources and homework
- Student Book 11.10: pages 328–331
- Practice Book 11.10: pages 110–111

Making mathematical connections
- Pythagoras' theorem
- Solving equations
- Substituting into equations
- Using a calculator

Making cross-curricular connections
- **Science** – using formulae, particles moving on inclined planes
- **Relevance** – applications in architecture and engineering

Prior learning
- Students should be familiar with calculating missing sides and angles of right-angled triangles using the trigonometric ratios (sine, cosine and tangent).

Working mathematically
- The key to any trigonometric problem is identifying the correct ratio to solve it.
- To find an unknown side length in a triangle:
  Step 1 Identify the information you have been given and the information you need to find.
  Step 2 Decide which ratio to use.
  Step 3 Substitute into the equation for this ratio.
  Step 4 Solve.

Common misconceptions and remediation
- Selecting the correct ratio is the main stumbling block for students. Advocate a neat and clearly labelled diagram as an invaluable tool in making this choice.

Probing questions
- Talk me through how you decide if a problem can be solved using trigonometry.
- What is the minimum information about a triangle you need to be able to calculate a side?

Literacy focus
- Key terms: There are no new key terms in this section.
- Encourage students to write a step-by-step guide explaining how to solve these problems. (**Less able** students could use the Student Book text as a template.)

Part 1

- Draw this triangle on the board.
- Ask students to discuss, in pairs, how they can find the missing side and angles.
- Is there more than one method?
- Mention that they are looking for methods, not answers.
- After a few minutes, gather suggestions.
  - Use tangent to find one of the angles.
  - Angle sum of a triangle will give the third angle.
  - Use Pythagoras' theorem to find the third side.
  - Find the hypotenuse; then use sine or cosine to find an angle.
- Make sure you mention Pythagoras' theorem to remind students of previous work.

Part 2

- Demonstrate the method by working through Examples 15 to 17 from the Student Book. In each case:
  - draw the triangle on the board
  - label the sides H, O and A
  - identify the two relevant sides
  - write down the appropriate equation.
- Then, ask students to solve the equations in the same way as in the previous two sections.
- Tell students that the text in the Student Book lists the steps in detail. They should refer to this, as necessary, when working through the exercise.
- **Students can now do Exercise 11K from the Student Book.**

| G&M 1–3 | Calculator all | CM 4, 5 | MR n/a | PS n/a | EV n/a |

Part 3

- Look back at Question 4 of Exercise 11K. Ask students to give their explanations of parts **a** and **b**.
- Encourage clear reasoning and precise use of language.
- Make sure that **less able** students understand the explanations.
- Use students' numerical examples from part **c** of question 4 to reinforce what they have found.

Section 11.11 Solving problems using trigonometry

Learning objectives

- Solve practical problems using trigonometry
- Solve problems using an angle of elevation or an angle of depression

Resources and homework

- Student Book 11.11: pages 332–335
- Practice Book 11.11: pages 111–113

Making mathematical connections

- Pythagoras' theorem
- Solving equations
- Substituting into equations
- Using a calculator

Making cross-curricular connections

- **Science** – using formulae, particles moving on inclined planes
- **Relevance** – applications in architecture and engineering

Prior learning

- Students should be familiar with calculating missing sides and angles of right-angled triangles using the trigonometric ratios sine, cosine and tangent.
- They should be able to recognise which trigonometric ratio is required in each situation.

Working mathematically

- Often, trigonometry problems are not presented as straightforward triangle problems. Identifying and solving a triangle problem may be part of solving a practical problem.
- Students should follow these steps when solving a practical problem using trigonometry:
  - o Draw the triangle required.
  - o Label the given information (angles and sides) and label the unknown side or angle x.
  - o Label the O, A and H.
  - o Choose which ratio to use and write it down.
  - o Substitute the numbers into the ratio to form an equation.
  - o Solve the equation.
  - o Round your answer to a sensible degree of accuracy.

Common misconceptions and remediation

- Students often do not identify a right-angled triangle and choose the incorrect ratio. Encourage students to draw the relevant triangle and label the three sides to avoid this error.

Probing questions

- How do you decide whether a problem requires a trigonometric relationship or Pythagoras' theorem to solve it?
- You can use trigonometry to find missing lengths and/or angles in all triangles. True or false?

Literacy focus

- Key terms: angle of depression, angle of elevation
- Ask students to draw a labelled diagram explaining the meaning of 'angle of depression' and 'angle of elevation'.

Part 1

- Lean a long object (e.g. a window pole or ladder) against a classroom wall.
- This will form a right-angled triangle (three sides and three angles).
- Say that, with as few measurements as possible, you want to find all the sides and angles.

- Discuss the lowest number of measurements required and which measurements are easiest to make.
- Students will probably decide that it is easiest to measure two of the lengths.
- Make the two measurements they suggest and ask them to do the necessary calculations.
- Afterwards, discuss how accurate their answers will be.
- Real objects have thickness, which limits the accuracy of results. Students should think about this when answering questions, and round calculator answers sensibly.

Part 2

- Explain that the Health and Safety Executive guidelines recommend the '1 in 4 rule' for ladders.
- Ask: What is the recommended safe angle (with the ground) for ladders?
- Model the following procedure.
  - o Identify the right-angled triangle.
  - o Identify the angle you want.
  - o Label the sides you know (O and A in this case).
  - o Decide on the ratio you want (tangent in this case).
  - o Write down the appropriate equation and solve it.
- Confirm that the angle with the ground is 76° (to the nearest degree).
- Work through Example 18 from the Student Book, if required.
- **Students can now do Exercise 11L from the Student Book.**

| G&M 1, 3, 4, 7 | Calculator all | CM 8, 10 | MR n/a | PS 2, 5, 9 | EV 6 |

Angles of elevation and depression

- Ask: When you look up at an aircraft in the sky, can you tell how far away it is? What can you measure?
- Discuss the meaning of an angle of elevation and an angle of depression.
- Model how to solve the problem in Example 19 from the Student Book, paying particular attention to identifying a right-angled triangle from the initial sketch of the situation.
- **Students can now begin Exercise 11M from the Student Book.**

| G&M 1–3, 5, 6 | Calculator all | CM 4, 8 | MR n/a | PS 10 | EV 7, 9 |

Part 3

- Show students this picture of a person between two tall buildings.
- Ask: If the angle of elevation of the top of each building is the same, what can you say about the heights of the buildings?
  (Adding lines will show that the triangles are similar. One height will be double the other.)
- Then tell students that the angle of elevation is 60° and ask them to work out the heights. (17.3 m and 34.6 m)

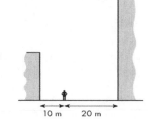

Section 11.12 Trigonometry and bearings

Learning objectives
- Solve bearing problems using trigonometry

Resources and homework
- Student Book 11.12: pages 336–337
- Practice Book 11.12: pages 113–114

Making mathematical connections
- Pythagoras' theorem
- Solving equations
- Substituting into equations
- Using a calculator

Making cross-curricular connections
- **Science** – using formulae, particles moving on inclined planes
- **Relevance** – applications in architecture and engineering

Prior learning
- Students should be able to calculate the missing sides and angles of right-angled triangles using trigonometric ratios.
- They should be able to identify which trigonometric ratio is required in each situation.

Working mathematically
- A bearing is the direction of one place from another. It is given as an angle measured from north in a clockwise direction.
- It is always written as a three-digit number, known as a three-figure bearing.
- Students should follow these three rules when working with bearings:
  o Always start from *north*.
  o Always measure *clockwise*.
  o Always give bearings in degrees as a *three-figure bearing*.
- Tell students that it might help to remember the rules as: NC3.

Common misconceptions and remediation
- Students often do not identify a right-angled triangle and choose the incorrect ratio. Encourage students to draw the relevant triangle and label the three sides to avoid this error.

Probing questions
- How do you know which angle to substitute into your chosen trigonometric ratio?
- Will the angle always be less than 90°?
- Talk me through how you sketched your diagram for this question.

Literacy focus
- Key terms: There are no new key terms in this section.
- Ask students to write out the three rules they should follow when working with bearings.

Part 1
- Explain to students that a bearing is a way of giving a direction. Make the following points.
  o It is measured clockwise from the north.
  o It is always given as three digits.
- Say that a bearing is used for all directions for ships and planes. It is always read over a radio as three digits: 127 will be one, two, seven and not one hundred and twenty-seven. This is to avoid errors if reception is poor.

- Ask students to draw a compass with the main eight points marked and to write in the bearings.
- Set this question and ask students to solve it, working in pairs:
    A yacht is sailing in a square in a race. The first leg is 5 km on a bearing of 070°. What are the bearings of the other three legs?
- Remind them to start by sketching a diagram.
- Since the boat can turn clockwise or anti-clockwise, there are two possible answers. (160°, 250°, 340° or 340°, 250°, 160°)
- As an extension, set a similar question with the boat sailing in an equilateral triangle. (190°, 310° or 310°, 190°)

Part 2

- A plane flies 85 km at a bearing of 213°.
- Ask students to make a scale drawing of this and use it to work out how far south the plane has travelled.
- Ask: Can you calculate this distance south, using trigonometry?
- The first step is to identify a right-angled triangle to use. There are two possibilities. Use whichever students suggest (or both) and demonstrate how to reach the solution (71 km).
- Ask students to compare this answer with the answer from their scale drawing.
- Work through Example 20 from the Student Book.
- **Students can now begin Exercise 11N from the Student Book.**

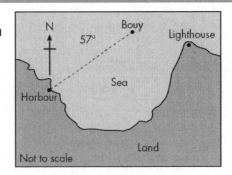

G&M 1, 2, 4, 5, 7, 8	Calculator all	CM 3	MR n/a	PS 6, 9	EV n/a

Part 3

- Display the diagram.
- Tell students that the buoy is 8 km to the east and 5 km to the north of the harbour.
- Ask students to calculate:
    o the shortest distance between the buoy and the harbour
    o the bearing on which the boat sails.

Section 11.13 Trigonometry and isosceles triangles

Learning objectives

- Use trigonometry to solve problems involving isosceles triangles

Resources and homework

- Student Book 11.13: pages 338–339
- Practice Book 11.13: page 115

Making mathematical connections

- Pythagoras' theorem
- Solving equations
- Substituting into equations
- Using a calculator

Making cross-curricular connections

- **Science** – using formulae, particles moving on inclined planes
- **Relevance** – applications in architecture and engineering

Prior learning

- Students should be able to calculate the missing sides and angles of right-angled triangles using trigonometric ratios.
- They should be able to identify which trigonometric ratio is required in each situation.

Working mathematically

- Isosceles triangles often feature in trigonometry problems because they can be split into two congruent right-angled triangles.

Common misconceptions and remediation

- Students often do not identify a right-angled triangle and choose the incorrect ratio. Encourage students to draw the relevant triangle and label the three sides to avoid this error.

Probing questions

- Talk me through how you solved this problem.
- Explain why you need to split the triangle into two in order to solve the problem.

Literacy focus

- Key terms: There are no new key terms in this section.
- Encourage students to write down the properties of an isosceles triangle.

Part 1

- Review the properties of isosceles triangles by asking students some relevant questions, e.g. Work out the values of the lettered angles in these diagrams.

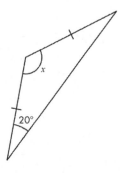
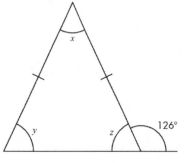

Part 2

- Explain that isosceles triangles occur frequently in problems.
- Use the example of a roof truss, used in constructing houses.
- Ask: If the angle of each sloping piece is 36°, what is the height of the roof?

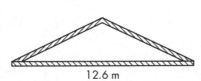 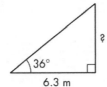

- Show how a right-angled triangle can be formed by dividing the triangle in half. Discuss how trigonometry can be used to find the height of the triangle.
- Demonstrate: $\tan 36° = \dfrac{?}{6.3} = 4.6$ m
- Ask: How can you work out the area enclosed by the roof truss?
  (Area = 0.5 × 12.6 × 4.6 ≈ 29 m^2)
- Ask: How can you work out the volume of the roof space.
  (triangular prism, so area of cross-section × length)
- Work through Example 21 in the Student Book.
- **Students can now do Exercise 11P from the Student Book.**

G&M 1, 2	Calculator all	CM 6	MR n/a	PS 3–5	EV n/a

Part 3

- Discuss students' methods and solutions to question 4 of Exercise 11P. (Find the height of the central triangle using Pythagoras' theorem or trigonometry.)
- Did they notice that all four triangles have the same area?
- Ask how the diagram shows this. (Prompt, if necessary, by drawing a line dividing the top triangle in half. They should look at the angles and put the two halves together in a different way.)
- This means that they only need to calculate the area of the central triangle and one square to be able to answer the question.
- Extend by asking:
  - o Is it is a regular hexagon? (No)
  - o What is the perimeter of the hexagon? (82 cm)

Chapter 12 Geometry and measure: Similarity

Overview

12.1 Similar triangles

12.2 Areas and volumes of similar shapes

Prior learning

Know how to use and simplify ratios.
Know how to enlarge a shape by a given scale factor.

Learning objectives

Ensure that students can: work out the scale factor for two similar shapes; work out lengths of sides in similar shapes; work out areas and volumes of similar shapes.

In the examination, students will be expected to:
* show that two triangles are similar
* work out the scale factor between similar triangles
* solve problems involving the area and volume of similar shapes.

Extension

Explore more complex similar triangles, along with areas and volumes of similar shapes.

Curriculum references

Section	GCSE specification
12.1	G 19, R 12
12.2	G 19, R 12

Route mapping

Exercise	Accessible	Intermediate	Challenging	AO1	AO2 MR CM	AO3 PS EV	Key questions
12A	1–4	5–9		5	1–3, 8	4, 6, 7, 9	5
12B		1–9		1, 2	4, 8	3, 5–7, 9	7, 8, 9
12C	1–2			1	2		1
12D		1–13		1–3, 5, 6, 10	7, 9, 13	4, 8, 11, 12	3–6
12E			1–15	2–4, 6, 7, 9–12	5, 14	1, 8, 13, 15	2, 3, 8

Key questions are those that demonstrate mastery of the concept, or which require a step-up in understanding or application. Key questions could be used to identify the questions that students must tackle, to support differentiation, or to identify the questions that should be teacher-marked rather than student-marked.

About this chapter

Making connections: This chapter introduces similar triangles and shapes and explains how to use these properties to solve problems.

Relevance: The emphasis is on deriving information from diagrams and applying this in theory and contextually. There are applications in engineering, architecture and manufacturing.

Working mathematically: How can you tell if two triangles are similar? Are they always congruent? What is the difference between similarity and congruence? If you double the length of each side of a cuboid, will its volume also double? If not, why?

Assessment: In every section of this chapter, ensure that students have a good grasp of the key questions in each exercise before moving on. (Refer to the 'Route mapping' table above.) Encourage students to read and think about the 'Ready to progress?' statements on page 361 of the Student Book. Check students' understanding at the end of the chapter, formatively, using peer assessment. Students could do a mini test in the form of the 'Review questions' on page 361 of the Student Book. Follow up the test with an individual target-getting session, based on any areas for development that a student may have.

Worked exemplars from the Student Book – suggestions for use

- Present students with the same question but using different numbers. Students should use the exemplar to mirror the working, in full or only using the notes.
- Copy and cut the exemplars into cards. Students to match the working with the notes.
- Ask students to write their own questions and set them out as exemplars.

Answers to the Student Book questions are available on the CD-ROM provided.

Learning objectives
- Show that two triangles are similar
- Work out the scale factor between similar triangles

Resources and homework
- Student Book 12.1: pages 345–350
- Practice Book 12.1: pages 116–119

Making mathematical connections
- Ratio
- Congruence
- Solving equations
- Fractions

Making cross-curricular connections
- **Technology** – scaled models in resistant materials or graphics
- **Relevance** – scale models in architecture

Prior learning
- Students should have covered work on scale factors and enlargements, simplifying ratios and solving equations.

Working mathematically
- Students will need to apply their learning of ratio, fractions and solving equations.

Common misconceptions and remediation
- Students are often unsure of the side they need to find. Unless a missing length is already labelled with an algebraic unknown on the diagram, encourage students to identify the 'missing' length and label it, using a letter such as x, and mark all corresponding sides.

Probing questions
- Talk me through how you decide whether two triangles are similar.
- What do you look for in the question to help you decide?

Literacy focus
- Key terms: similar, similar triangles
- To ensure that students understand 'similar' in a mathematical context, ask them to write down a question and swap with a partner to solve.

Part 1
- Draw two triangles on the board: 4 × 3 × 6 cm and 8 × 6 × 12 cm. Discuss the similarities and differences between the two triangles.
  - Similarities: the angles are the same and corresponding angles are the same, e.g. the smallest angle is opposite the smallest side.
  - Differences: the lengths of the sides in the second triangle are double those in the first; one is an enlargement of the other.
- Explain that the second triangle is an enlargement of the first by a scale factor of 2.
- Hence, all the corresponding sides are in the same ratio of 1 : 2 (3 : 6 = 4 : 8 = 6 : 12) and we can say that the triangles are mathematically similar.
- Two shapes are similar if all the corresponding sides are in the same ratio (one is an enlargement of the other).
- Stress that all corresponding angles in similar shapes are equal.

Part 2

- Draw the two similar triangles on the board. Tell the students that Triangle ABC is similar to triangle XYZ and demonstrate how you can use this to find the length of the side marked x.

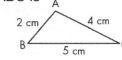

- Since the triangles are similar, triangle XYZ must be an enlargement of triangle ABC.

- Ask students to give the scale factor of the enlargement and say how they worked it out.

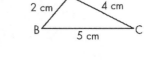

- Show students how this can be set up as an equation with x as a numerator:

$$\frac{x}{5} = \frac{6}{2} \text{ so } x = \frac{6 \times 5}{2} = 15 \text{ cm}$$

- Work through another example on the board: Triangles ABC and ADE are similar. AC = 7 cm, BC = 4 cm, DE = 6 cm. Find the length of CE.

- Show that redrawing the similar triangles separately, labelling CE as x, makes the solution easier to follow.

- Set up and solve an equation using the corresponding sides.

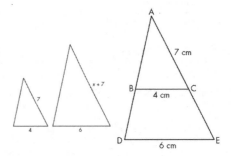

$$\frac{x + 7}{7} = \frac{6}{4} \rightarrow 4(x + 7) = 42 \rightarrow 4x + 28 = 42 \rightarrow 4x = 14$$

So $x = 3.5$ cm

- Work through Example 1 in the Student Book, if required.

- **Students can now do Exercise 12A from the Student Book.**

G&M 5	Calculator n/a	CM 1–3	MR 8	PS 4, 6, 7	EV 9

Further examples of similar triangles

- Work through Examples 2 and 3 from the Student Book.

- If students are still unsure, work through finding the length marked x in the diagram on the right.

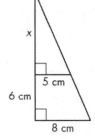

- First, discuss why the two triangles are similar.

- Then set up an equation using the corresponding sides.

$$\frac{x + 6}{x} = \frac{8}{5} \rightarrow 5x + 30 = 8x \rightarrow 3x = 30$$

So $x = 10$ cm

- **Students can now do Exercise 12B from the Student Book.**

G&M 1, 2	Calculator n/a	CM 4	MR 8	PS 3, 5–7	EV 9

More complicated problems

- Work through Example 4 in the Student Book with the class.

- **Students can now do Exercise 12C from the Student Book.**

G&M 1	Calculator all	CM n/a	MR 2	PS n/a	EV n/a

Part 3

- Draw pairs of similar triangles on the board, but in different orientations.

- Ask students to provide the information to show similarity.

Section 12.2 Areas and volumes of similar shapes

Learning objectives

- Solve problems involving the area and volume of similar shapes

Resources and homework

- Student Book 12.2: pages 351–357
- Practice Book 12.2: pages 119–121

Making mathematical connections

- Ratio
- Congruence
- Solving equations
- Fractions
- Area and volume

Making cross-curricular connections

- **Technology** – scaled models in resistant materials or graphics
- **Relevance** – scaled models in architecture

Prior learning

- Students should be familiar with finding squares, cubes, square roots and cube roots of numbers on their calculators. They should also be confident in solving linear equations.

Working mathematically

- Draw two rectangles on the board: 3 by 5 cm and 6 by 10 cm. Why they are similar? What is the scale factor of the enlargement? Compare and discuss the areas.

Common misconceptions and remediation

- Students often form a ratio from sides that do not correspond. Stress the importance of marking the corresponding sides on the diagram.
- Students also make errors setting up, or solving, the equation to work out the missing side.

  Write on the board   If $a : b = c : d$ then $\dfrac{a}{b} = \dfrac{c}{d}$ or $\dfrac{b}{a} = \dfrac{d}{c}$

Probing questions

- Talk me through how you decide if two 3D shapes are similar.
- Two shapes are similar and the scale factor is 2. What is the relationship between their areas? What is the relationship between their volumes?

Literacy focus

- Key terms: area scale factor, linear scale factor, volume scale factor
- Students will need to be familiar with the language of similar shapes. Ask them to read through the questions in the exercises to find the key terms.

Part 1

- Introduce this lesson using the investigation in the introduction of the Student Book.

Part 2

- Draw and label the two rectangles shown on the board.
- Tell students that the shapes are similar, so corresponding sides are in the same ratio.
- The *length ratio* is 1 : 2; the *linear scale factor* is 2.
- The areas of the two rectangles are 15 cm² and 60 cm².
- The *area ratio* is 1 : 4; the *area scale factor* is 4.

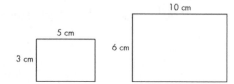

- Explain that this is always the case for similar shapes.
  For two similar shapes, if the length ratio is $a : b$, then the area ratio is $a^2 : b^2$.
- Show students some examples to demonstrate that this idea can be used to find areas for any two similar shapes.

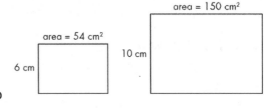

area = 54 cm² 6 cm

area = 150 cm² 10 cm

- Work through Example 5 in the Student Book.
- Explain that the same idea can be used with volumes of similar 3D shapes.
- Draw two similar cuboids on the board. Stress that they are similar because all corresponding sides are in the same ratio. Here the length ratio is 1 : 2 and the linear scale factor is 2.
- The volumes of the two cuboids are 24 cm³ and 192 cm³.
  So the *volume ratio* is 24 : 192 = 1 : 8 and the *volume scale factor* is 8.
- Ask students if they can spot the pattern for volume scale factors.
- Explain that this is always the case for similar 3D shapes.
  For two similar 3D shapes, if the length ratio is $a : b$, then the volume ratio is $a^3 : b^3$.
- Work through Examples 6 and 7. Highlight the working, and ask students to work in the same way.
- **Students can now do Exercise 12D from the Student Book.**

| G&M 1–3, 5, 6, 10 | Calculator all | CM 9, 13 | MR 7 | PS 4, 8, 12 | EV 11 |

More complex problems using area and volume ratios
- Explain that if an area ratio for two similar shapes is $a : b$, then the length ratio is $\sqrt{a} : \sqrt{b}$
  Similarly, if a volume ratio for two similar 3D shapes is $a : b$, then the length ratio is $\sqrt[3]{a} : \sqrt[3]{b}$
- Demonstrate how this can be applied to problems.
  The two hexagons A and B are similar.
  The area of A is 90 cm² and 200 cm².
  Work out the height, h, of hexagon A.
  The area ratio is 90 : 200, so the length ratio is $\sqrt{90} : \sqrt{200}$. (Do not work these out yet.)
  The length ratio is $h : 15$.
  Set up an equation with h as a numerator: $\dfrac{h}{15} = \dfrac{\sqrt{90}}{\sqrt{200}}$

  So $h = \dfrac{15\sqrt{90}}{\sqrt{200}} = 10.1\,\text{cm}$ (3 sf)

- Work through one or more of Examples 8, 9 and 10 from the Student Book.
- **Students can now do Exercise 12E from the Student Book.**

| G&M 2–4, 6, 7, 9–12 | Calculator all | CM 14 | MR 5, 14 | PS 1, 8, 13 | EV 15 |

Part 3

- Ask students to summarise what they have learned in the lessons by copying and completing a table, similar to the one on the left, below.
- **More able** students could copy and complete a table such as that on the right.

Length ratio	Area ratio	Volume ratio
1 : 2		
2 : 3		
4 : 5		
4 : 3		

Volume ratio	Length ratio	Area ratio
1 : 8		
1 : 1000		
8 : 27		
12 : 25		

Chapter 13 Probability: Exploring and applying probability

Overview

13.1 Experimental probability	**13.4** Probability and two-way tables
13.2 Mutually exclusive and exhaustive outcomes	**13.5** Probability and Venn diagrams
13.3 Expectation	

Prior learning

Know that the probability scale goes from 0 to 1.
Know how to use the probability scale to assess the likelihood of outcomes, depending on their position on the scale.
Know how to cancel, add and subtract fractions.

Learning objectives

Ensure that students can: work out the probabilities of outcomes of events, using theoretical or experimental models; recognise mutually exclusive, exhaustive and complementary outcomes; predict the likely number of successful outcomes, given the number of trials and the probability of any one outcome; use two-way tables to solve probability problems; use Venn diagrams to solve probability problems.

In the examination, students will be expected to:
- calculate experimental probabilities and relative frequencies
- estimate probabilities from experiments
- use different methods to estimate probabilities
- recognise mutually exclusive, exhaustive and complementary outcomes
- predict the likely number of successful outcomes, given the number of trials and the probability of any one outcome
- read two-way tables and use them to work out probabilities
- use Venn diagrams to solve probability questions.

Extension

Explore more complex probability questions involving harder conditional probability. **More able** students could explore the next stage (which is A level content) with Venn diagrams by including De Morgan's laws.

Curriculum references

Section	GCSE specification
13.1	P 1, 3, 5
13.2	P 4
13.3	P 2
13.4	P 1, 6, 7
13.5	P 6

Route mapping

Exercise	Accessible	Intermediate	Challenging	AO1	AO2 MR CM	AO3 PS EV	Key questions
13A	1–7	8–10		1–4	5–7, 10	8, 9	5, 8, 9
13B	1–8	9–12		1–7	8, 9, 12	10, 11	6, 7, 11
13C	1–9	10–12		1–7, 9	8, 11	10, 12	5, 7, 10
13D	1–8			1–5, 8	6	7	7, 8
13E	1–9	10–12	13	1–6, 12	8, 11, 13	7, 9, 10	4, 5, 8

Key questions are those that demonstrate mastery of the concept, or which require a step-up in understanding or application. Key questions could be used to identify the questions that students must tackle, to support differentiation, or to identify the questions that should be teacher-marked rather than student-marked.

About this chapter

Making connections: Students will already be familiar with basic probability. This chapter extends this knowledge with the introduction of relative frequency, mutually exclusive and exhaustive events, before moving on to possibility spaces and, finally, Venn diagrams and set notation.

Relevance: There are applications for probability in engineering, marketing, manufacturing and finance (insurance). It is important for students to understand the applications of probability in the real world, as they are many and varied.

Working mathematically: Give some examples of mutually exclusive and exhaustive events. Explain how you would identify all the mutually exclusive outcomes from an experiment. Explain how you use the fact that the sum of probabilities of all mutually exclusive events is one to help you solve a problem.

Assessment: In every section of this chapter, ensure that students have a good grasp of the key questions in each exercise before moving on. (Refer to the 'Route mapping' table above.) Encourage students to read and think about the 'Ready to progress?' statements on page 384 of the Student Book. Check students' understanding at the end of the chapter, formatively, using peer assessment. Students could do a mini test in the form of the 'Review questions' on pages 384–385 of the Student Book. Follow up the test with an individual target-getting session, based on any areas for development that a student may have.

Worked exemplars from the Student Book – suggestions for use

- Present students with the same question using different numbers. They should use the exemplar to mirror the working, in full or only the notes.
- Copy and cut the working into cards, splitting the label/description from the working. Students put the working in order then match with the descriptions.

Answers to the Student Book questions are available on the CD-ROM provided.

Section 13.1 Experimental probability

Learning objectives

- Calculate experimental probabilities and relative frequencies
- Estimate probabilities from experiments
- Use different methods to estimate probabilities

Resources and homework

- Student Book 13.1: pages 363–367
- Practice Book 13.1: pages 122–124

Making mathematical connections

- Tree diagrams
- Conditional probability

Making cross-curricular connections

- **Science** – probability of a reaction from an experiment
- **Geography** – probabilities of natural disasters occurring
- **Relevance** – uses in manufacturing

Prior learning

- Students should know how to find the probability of an event, using formula:

$$P(A) = \frac{\text{number of ways A can happen}}{\text{number of possible outcomes}}, \text{ where A is an event.}$$

Working mathematically

- Students learn the vocabulary or probability. For example:
  - An 'event' is an activity that may have several possible results. It can also be described as a set of outcomes.
  - A 'trial' is one attempt at performing an event, for example, throwing a die or tossing a coin. If you throw a die 10 times, you perform 10 trials.
  - An 'outcome' is one result of an event. (You will usually be interested in the probability of one or more outcomes occurring.)
  - At 'random' means 'without knowing what the outcome is in advance'.

Common misconceptions and remediation

- When data is presented in tabular form, students often have difficulty in identifying the correct information. Make it clear to them that they should use 'number of desired results' and 'number of trials' in all cases, but they need to be able to interpret a table to find these values. Stress to students that they should read tables carefully.

Probing questions

- What effect does increasing the number of trials have on the relative frequency?
- Talk me through an event where you would use experimental probability rather than theoretical probability.

Literacy focus

- Key terms: event, experimental probability, outcome, random, relative frequency, theoretical probability, trial
- Make sure that students are familiar with the key terms from this section. See the 'Working mathematically' section.

Part 1

NB: This section may take more than 1 hour.

- Prepare a bag or box containing a number of different-coloured balls, counters, or similar.
- Ask students to select one without looking and then put it back. Ask a different student to collect the data as it is generated.
- At different stages, e.g. after four selections and again after ten, ask for suggestions (supported by reasons) as to the mix of items in the bag.

Part 2

Terminology; Probability facts

- Work through the text in these sections and Example 1 from the Student Book.
- Ask: What is the probability of throwing a coin and getting a head? Most students will know this. ($\frac{1}{2}$ or 0.5)
- Explain that this is the theoretical probability and ask: Does it a work in practice?
- Ask all students to throw a small-value coin and record the number of heads and the total number of throws in a table like the one below.

Number of throws	Number of heads	Probability
30	18	$\frac{18}{30} = 0.6$

- Show how to find the probability and explain the need to express it as a decimal for comparison as more coins are tossed. Remind **less able** students how to do this, by dividing the numerator by the denominator, and explain that no more than four decimal places are needed.
- Ask students to throw their coins again, count the number of heads and add the results to the table.

Number of throws	Number of heads	Probability
30	18	$\frac{18}{30} = 0.6$
30 + 30 = 60	18 + 14 = 32	$\frac{32}{60} = 0.5333$

- Continue with more throws and add these to the table. Tell students that they should notice that the probability gets closer and closer to 0.5.
- Explain that this is experimental probability and that it is often the only way to find a probability. For example, finding the probability that when dropped, a slice of bread spread with jam will land jam side down!
- Explain that historical data is used to find probabilities of events where experiments are impossible, for example, the probability of asteroids hitting Earth or volcanoes erupting.
- Discuss Example 2 in the Student Book.

Finding probabilities

- Work through this section and Example 3 from the Student Book.
- **Students can now do Exercise 13A from the Student Book.**

P 1–4	Calculator n/a	CM 7	MR 5, 6, 10	PS 8	EV 9

Part 3

- Ask students to explain their reasoning for part **c** of question 6 in Exercise 13A.

Section 13.2 Mutually exclusive and exhaustive outcomes

Learning objectives
- Recognise mutually exclusive, exhaustive and complementary outcomes

Resources and homework
- Student Book 13.2: pages 368–371
- Practice Book 13.2: pages 124–125

Making mathematical connections
- Tree diagrams
- Conditional probability

Making cross-curricular connections
- **Science** – probability from an experiment
- **Relevance** – uses in manufacturing

Prior learning
- Remind students (or explain) how a pack of cards is made up. While this may have been common knowledge at one time, it cannot be assumed that all students will be familiar with using a pack of cards today. Say that, unless stated otherwise, students should assume that a pack of cards consists of 52 cards, with no jokers.

Working mathematically
- Examples of *mutually exclusive* outcomes are 'throwing a head' and 'throwing a tail' with a coin and 'throwing an even number' and 'throwing an odd number' with dice. Outcomes are called mutually exclusive because they can never happen at the same time.
- In the examples given above, there are no other possibilities, so the outcomes are also exhaustive. The probabilities of *exhaustive outcomes* add up to 1.
- 'Drawing a red card' and 'Drawing a king' from a pack of cards are not mutually exclusive. There are two red kings, so both outcomes could occur at the same time.

Common misconceptions and remediation
- Mistakes or misunderstandings inevitably occur with fractions.
- For questions involving mutually exclusive outcomes, ensure that students are comfortable with calculations that require the application of $P(B) = 1 - P(A)$.
- Run through a few examples, and encourage students to evaluate subtractions such as:
$$1 - \frac{7}{12} \ \left(\frac{5}{12}\right) \text{and } 1 - \frac{13}{25} \ \left(\frac{12}{25}\right)$$

Probing questions
- Explain how you know that these outcomes are mutually exclusive.
- Give me an outcome that is not mutually exclusive. Why isn't it?

Literacy focus
- Key terms: complementary, exhaustive, mutually exclusive
  Ensure that students are familiar with the key terms from this section. See the 'Working mathematically' section.

Part 1

- Ask students simple probability questions based on a pack of cards. For example, suppose a single card is taken from a pack. What is the probability that it is:

  a the 2 of clubs $\left(\frac{1}{52}\right)$ **c** red card $\left(\frac{26}{52} = \frac{1}{2}\right)$ **e** an ace $\left(\frac{4}{52} = \frac{1}{13}\right)$

  b a spade $\left(\frac{13}{52} = \frac{1}{4}\right)$ **d** a royal card $\left(\frac{12}{52} = \frac{3}{13}\right)$ **f** an odd-numbered card? $\left(\frac{26}{52} = \frac{1}{2}\right)$

- Ask for all probabilities to be given as fractions in their simplest form.

Part 2

- Ask students if a card can be both a club and a king. (yes, the king of clubs)
- Now ask if a card can be a club and a heart at the same time. (no)
- Point out that it could be either a club or a heart. Explain that this means the two outcomes – 'picking a club' and 'picking a heart' – are *mutually exclusive*. Emphasise the importance of this concept and write the expression on the board so that it is visible throughout the lesson.
- Ask the class to suggest other events that are mutually exclusive (e.g. any two suits or two numbers at the same time, a head and a tail at the same time when throwing a coin).
- Now ask students to suggest events that are not mutually exclusive (e.g. 'picking a 6' and 'picking a diamond', throwing a die and getting a score higher than 1 and an even number, selecting at random a student from the class who is male and has brothers).
- Work through Example 4, which also introduces *exhaustive events* – events that cover all possibilities. Add this expression to the list.
- Now work through Example 5 from the Student Book. You may need to revise fractions with **less able** students.

Complementary outcomes

- Ask: What is the probability of scoring a 3 on a dice? $\left(\frac{1}{6}\right)$ What is the probability of not scoring a 3? $\left(\frac{5}{6}\right)$ Are they mutually exclusive? (yes).
- Write the fractions on the board next to each other.
- Explain that these are *complementary events* – one event happening and another event not happening. Add this expression to the list on the board.
- What is the probability of cutting a pack of cards and getting an ace? $\left(\frac{4}{52}\right)$

  What is the probability of cutting a pack of cards and not getting an ace? $\left(\frac{48}{52}\right)$

  Write these fractions next to each other.
- Now ask students to add together the fractions in each pair. (1)
- Say that the probability of an event and its complement will always total 1.
- **Students can now do Exercise 13B from the Student Book.**

P 1–7	Calculator n/a	CM 8	MR 9, 12	PS 10, 11	EV n/a

Part 3

- Ask students to pick a single card from a pack, at random.
- Ask for descriptions of two events that are:
  - mutually exclusive and exhaustive
  - mutually exclusive and not exhaustive
  - not mutually exclusive.

Section 13.3 Expectation

Learning objectives
- Predict the likely number of successful outcomes, given the number of trials and the probability of any one outcome

Resources and homework
- Student Book 13.3: pages 372–373
- Practice Book 13.3: pages 125–126

Making mathematical connections
- Tree diagrams
- Conditional probability

Making cross-curricular connections
- **Science** – probability of a reaction from an experiment
- **Relevance** – uses in manufacturing

Prior learning
- Students should know how to find the probability of an event, and also how to calculate a fraction of a quantity.

Working mathematically
- When you know the probability of an outcome, you can predict how many times you would expect that outcome to occur in a certain number of trials. This is called *expectation*. Note that this is what you expect. It may not be what actually happens.

Common misconceptions and remediation
- Some students may work out the required probability incorrectly.
- Others may work out the fraction of the number of trials incorrectly.
- Provide plenty of practice and work through any errors with individual students.

Probing questions
- How many times would you expect an event with a probability of 0.25 to occur in 100 trials? Why?

Literacy focus
- Key term: expectation
- Ask students to make a list of all the key terms in this topic so far and then add descriptions or definitions to show that they understand each one.

Part 1
- Recap, or ask a student to explain, how to find a fraction of a quantity.
- Display the number 240 and ask students to choose a fraction of this number and work it out.
- It may be more appropriate to limit the choice of fractions to halves, thirds, quarters, fifths, sixths, eighths, tenths and twelfths.

Part 2
- Ask: If you roll a die 600 times, how many times would you expect to roll the number 5? Discuss this with the class and ensure that they would expect 100 of each of the six numbers.
- Ask: If you cut a pack of cards 100 times, how many times would you expect to cut the ace of diamonds? This is more awkward as there are 52 cards in a pack and not 50, so you will

need to lead the class to an expected value close to 2, since if you cut the pack 104 times, you might expect to have each card twice.

- Explain to **more able** students that, although it is common to refer to an expected number, in practice this exact number rarely occurs. The result is, however, usually close to it. Expected numbers are always an estimate.
- Using the dice example, show the class that they can find the expected number by multiplying the theoretical probability by the number of rolls, i.e. $\frac{1}{6} \times 600 = 100$.
- Ask them to work out the theoretical probability of cutting the ace of diamonds in the cards example ($\frac{1}{52} \times 100 = 1.9231$). You would expect to get the card approximately 1.9 times, which rounds to 2.
- Ensure that students understand the term *expectation*.
- Talk through Examples 6 and 7 from the Student Book.
- **Students can now do Exercise 13C from the Student Book.**

| P 1–7, 9 | Calculator n/a | CM n/a | MR 8, 11 | PS 10, 12 | EV n/a |

Part 3

- Display a table of the total scores from throwing two dice.
- Ask students how many times they would expect to get different scores (such as 4, 12, 5, less than 4), from 360 trials.
- Which score would they expect to get most often?
- Ask why you picked 360 trials.

Section 13.4 Probability and two-way tables

Learning objectives
- Read two-way tables and use them to work out probabilities

Resources and homework
- Student Book 13.4: pages 374–377
- Practice Book 13.4: pages 127–128

Making mathematical connections
- Tree diagrams
- Conditional probability

Making cross-curricular connections
- **Science** – probability tables from an experiment
- **Relevance** – uses in manufacturing

Prior learning
- Students should know how to work out the probability of an event, be able to find the expected number of outcomes given the total number of trials and the probability of the outcome in question.
- They should also be able to read and interpret information from tables.

Working mathematically
- What are the advantages of using a two-way table to show outcomes of two events?
- Explain how you would use a two-way table to show all the outcomes of two six-sided dice being thrown and their scores added.

Common misconceptions and remediation
- Most mistakes will come from misunderstandings in how to read the data from a two-way table. Work through lots of examples with two-way tables, with as much discussion as possible, to support students.

Probing questions
- How can you use a two-way table to calculate probability?
- Do you need the table to be exhaustive? Why?

Literacy focus
- Key terms: two-way table
- Ask students to write down the meaning of the key term to show their understanding.

Part 1

- Collect some data from the class that can be tallied into a two-way table, e.g. favourite pop group, football team or sport, from a shortlist drawn up before the lesson. Use the results to construct a two-way table with column headings 'Male' and 'Female', and up to four row headings. (In a single-sex class, find an alternative way to divide the class into two groups.)
- Ask the class to work out the probabilities of selecting different classes of people (e.g. a girl that supports Manchester United, a boy whose favourite sport is golf).
- Choose a relatively simple multiple of the number of students in the class, and ask how many of this total they would expect to be in each category in the table.

Part 2

- Explain that two-way tables are used to display information about groups, and can be used to calculate probabilities as well as to estimate numbers in larger groups.
- Work through Example 8 with the class.
- **Students can now do Exercise 13D from the Student Book.** Earlier questions will provide **less able** students with plenty of practice. **More able** students can move quickly to the more challenging MR and PS questions.

| P 1–5, 8 | Calculator n/a | CM n/a | MR 6 | PS 7 | EV n/a |

Part 3

- Revisit the information in Part 1 of this section.
- Ask students to suggest how to calculate the percentages of the total that each represents.

Section 13.5 Probability and Venn diagrams

Learning objectives

- Use Venn diagrams to solve probability questions

Resources and homework

- Student Book 13.5: pages 377–381
- Practice Book 13.5: pages 128–129

Making mathematical connections

- Tree diagrams
- Conditional probability

Making cross-curricular connections

- **Science** – Venn diagrams in Biology, e.g. comparisons between different animals
- **Relevance** – logical thought processes; uses in manufacturing and engineering

Prior learning

- Students should know how to find the probability of an event.

Working mathematically

- Students learn set notation. Explain that a *set* is a collection of objects or elements. Capital letters are often used to represent a set. For example, the set of odd numbers less than 10 could be represented by A.

    $A = \{1, 3, 5, 7, 9\}$
- Remind students that the probability of outcome A occurring is written as: $P(A)$.
- Suppose outcome A does not happen. This is the complement of A. It is written as A' and read as 'A dash'.
- The probability of A not happening is written as: $P(A')$.
- The universal set is a set that contains all elements used and is represented as ξ.

Common misconceptions and remediation

- Students often forget to place the events that do not fit into the circles into the set box. Make this really clear in Part 1.

Probing questions

- Can you draw a Venn diagram to show $(A \cup B)' = A' \cap B'$?
- Can you draw a Venn diagram to show $(A \cap B)' = A' \cup B'$?
- These are De Morgan's laws. Ask **more able** students to research these laws.

Literacy focus

- Key terms: element, set, universal set, intersection, union, Venn diagram
- Ask students to write an explanation of each union/intersection type with a diagram.

Part 1

- Draw the Venn diagram shown on the board and ask students to place each sport in the correct place on the diagram.
- The sports are: rugby, football, tennis, basketball, cricket, hockey, fencing, volleyball, cycling.
- Now ask students some questions on probability, for example: What is the probability that one of the sports represented uses a net?

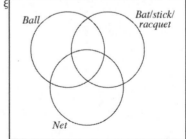

Part 2

- By working through the text in the Student Book, or otherwise, introduce the relevant set notation.
- Work through Example 9 and Example 10, explaining the terminology clearly. Ensure that students understand *intersection*, *union*, etc.
- Work through the example below with students. (It adds another element to this type of question as it combines algebra with Venn diagrams.)
- Tell students that the Venn diagram shows the number of students from a year group of 120 that study French (F) and Art (A).
- Ask: What is the probability that a student studies French?
  First, form an equation in x: $5(x + 6) + 4x + 4x + 15 + 2x = 120$
  Then, solve to find x: 5
  Students that study French: $5(x + 6) + 4x = 55 + 20 = 75$
  $P(F) = \frac{75}{120} = \frac{5}{8}$

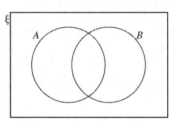

- **Students can now do Exercise 13E from the Student Book.**

| P 1–6, 12 | Calculator n/a | CM 11, 13 | MR 8 | PS 7, 9, 10 | EV n/a |

Part 3

- Shade regions of the Venn diagram shown and ask students to name the region using the correct mathematical terminology.

Chapter 14 Number: Powers and standard form

Overview

14.1 Powers (indices)	**14.3** Standard form
14.2 Rules for multiplying and dividing powers	

Prior learning

Know how to multiply and divide by 10, 100, 1000, …
Know the meaning of the terms *square root* and *cube root*.

Learning objectives

Ensure that students can: calculate using powers (indices); write numbers in standard form; calculate with standard form.

In the examination, students will be expected to:
* use powers (also known as indices)
* multiply and divide by powers of 10
* use rules for multiplying and dividing powers
* change a number into standard form
* calculate using numbers in standard form.

Extension

Students could explore more complex uses of standard form in calculations and decide on a suitable degree of accuracy for presenting a solution.

Curriculum references

Section	GCSE specification
14.1	N 6
14.2	N 6, N7
14.3	N 9, N15

Route mapping

Exercise	Accessible	Intermediate	Challenging	AO1	AO2 MR CM	AO3 PS EV	Key questions
14A	1–5	6–15		1–6, 8, 10–12	7, 13, 14	9, 15	4, 7, 14
14B	1–4	5–10	11–12	1–3, 5–9, 12	4, 10	11	4, 9, 10
14C	1–9	10–13	14–15	1–2, 6–12	3, 13, 14	4, 5, 15	4, 7, 9
14D	1–5	6–10	11–12	1–2, 4–7	8–11	3, 12	5, 6, 11
14E		1	2–14	1–6, 8–11	13	7, 12, 14	5, 6, 12

Key questions are those that demonstrate mastery of the concept, or which require a step-up in understanding or application. Key questions could be used to identify the questions that students must tackle, to support differentiation, or to identify the questions that should be teacher-marked rather than student-marked.

About this chapter

Making connections: The chapter brings together the concepts of indices and evaluating numbers with indices, multiplying and dividing indices, and working with powers of 10. When combined, these produce the powerful method of standard form. It is important to work through the exercises in each section in a linear progression, as each one builds on the work in the previous exercise.

Relevance: This topic has applications in any subject where either very large or very small numbers are used, whether recording or calculating. Examples are Physics, Chemistry, Biology, Engineering and Astronomy.

Working mathematically: How can you, quickly and successfully, carry out calculations on very large or very small numbers? How can you compare them easily? Break these into a number multiplied by a multiple of 10; then change the multiple of 10 into a power of 10.

Assessment: In each section of this chapter, ensure that students have a good grasp of the key questions in each exercise before moving on. (Refer to the 'Route mapping' table above.) Encourage students to read and think about the 'Ready to progress?' statements on page 400 of the Student Book. Check students' understanding at the end of the chapter, formatively, using peer assessment. Students could do a mini test in the form of the 'Review questions' on pages 400–401 of the Student Book. Follow up the test with an individual target-getting session, based on any areas for development that a student may have.

Worked exemplars from the Student Book – suggestions for use

- Use these examples to show progression from working with indices in order to evaluate an expression, to using them for simplifying a complex question.
- Present students with a table similar to the one in exemplar 1, but showing the powers of another number, e.g. 5. Ask similar questions to those in 1a, 1b and 1c.
- Rework exemplar 2, for example: Use another fact such as the mass of one grain of rice is 0.020 mg.

Answers to the Student Book questions are available on the CD-ROM provided.

Section 14.1 Powers (indices)

Learning objectives
- Use powers (also known as indices)

Resources and homework
- Student Book 14.1: pages 387–388
- Practice Book 14.1: page 130

Making mathematical connections
- Multiplication of integers

Making cross-curricular connections
- **Science** – evaluation of expressions, problem solving
- **Relevance** – links to geometry (area and volume), solving algebraic equations

Prior learning
- Students should know the square numbers (power 2) up to $15^2 = 225$, and the cubes of the numbers 1 (1), 2 (8), 3 (27), 4 (64), 5 (125) and 10 (1000).

Working mathematically
- Encourage students to write out power terms in full before working out the answers on a calculator. This will remind them that the calculation is repetitive multiplication.

Common misconceptions and remediation
- Students may ignore powers of 1, for example, by giving $2^5 \times 2$ as 2^5 instead of 2^6. Students can avoid this error if they write the power 1 on their copy of the question.
- Students may assume that anything to the power 0 gives an answer of 0. Test students by asking questions using power 0 regularly.

Probing questions
- Why does a negative number that has an odd number as a power, always give a negative answer, but a number that has an even number as a power, always gives a positive answer?

Literacy focus
- Key terms: index (indices), power
- Ask students to write a set of instructions that describe how to use the power button on their calculators.

Part 1
Revise working with squares and cubes.
- Display a copy of the puzzle on the right. The number in each circle can be found by multiplying together the numbers in the squares either side of it. Ask students to work out and fill in the numbers in the circles.
- Ask students to find the number in the centre. This is the sum of the numbers in each of the four circles. Ask them to estimate the square root of the number in the middle. (Answer = 1313, square root ≈ 36)
- Explain that powers are a shorter way of writing repeated multiplications.
- Introduce cubes of numbers. Ask students the value of: $10 \times 10 \times 10$ (1000).
- Ask students how they can write it using powers (10^3).
- Make sure students know to read this as: '10 cubed', 'the cube of 10' or '10 to the power 3'.
- Repeat for the other cubes that students are expected to know:
  $1^3 = 1$; $2^3 = 8$; $3^3 = 27$; $4^3 = 64$; $5^3 = 125$.

Part 2

- Use this example to demonstrate how quickly powers grow:
  Ask students to imagine a chess (or draughts) board with 64 small squares. Ask them to imagine putting 1p on the first square, 2p on the second square, 4p on the next square and so on, doubling the number each time.
  Ask students to write down (without discussion) how much money they think will be on the board when all 64 squares have been covered.
  Most students will underestimate the answer (over £18 million trillion, or 1.8×10^{19}).
- Explain that a power defines how many times to multiply a number by itself.
  4^5 means $4 \times 4 \times 4 \times 4 \times 4$ and is expressed as 'four to the power of five'.
- Work through Example 1 from the Student Book.

  Working out powers on your calculator; Two special powers
- Ask students to input **7** into their calculator, press **=** , then press **×** **7** and repeatedly press **=** . This will display powers of 7: 7, 49, 343 …
- For **less able** students start with 2, to give the powers of 2, and link this to the work on doubling the money on the chessboard.
- Show students how to use the **x²** button, the **x³** button and the **x■** button on their calculator.
- Finally, check that students know that any number to the power 1 is itself and any number to the power zero is equal to 1.
- **Students can now do Exercise 14A from the Student Book.**

N 1–6, 8, 10–12	Calculator 3, 4, 12, 14		CM 7	MR 13, 14	PS 15	EV 9

Part 3

- The number 531 441 is a power of 3. It is also a power of 9 and 27.
- Ask students to write 521 441 as powers of 3, 9 and 27 (3^{12}, 9^6, 27^4).
- **Less able** students could find the powers of 2 and 4 that create an answer of 1024 (2^{10}, 4^5).

Section 14.2 Rules for multiplying and dividing powers

Learning objectives
- Use rules for multiplying and dividing powers

Making mathematical connections
- Using powers (indices)
- Algebraic fractions
- Adding and subtracting positive and negative integers

Resources and homework
- Student Book 14.2: pages 389–391
- Practice Book 14.2: page 131

Making cross-curricular connections
- **Science** – evaluation of expressions; solving problems
- **Relevance** – links to algebraic fractions

Prior learning
- Students should be able to add and subtract positive and negative integers.
- They should also be familiar with creating the reciprocal of a number.

Working mathematically
- Encourage students to write out the power terms in the calculation fully before working out the answer. Doing this will remind students of why the resulting power is generated.

Common misconceptions and remediation
- Students often struggle to remember the term *reciprocal*. Reciprocal appears in section 14.3, so use the term regularly to establish familiarity.
- Some students will assume that a negative power implies a negative answer, for example, they think that 3^{-2} means $-3^2 = -9$, when in fact, it is $\frac{1}{3^2} = \frac{1}{9}$.

Probing questions
- Use the ideas in this section to prove why the value of any number to the power 0 is 1 and any number to the power 1 is the same as the original number.

Literacy focus
- Key terms: There are no new key terms in this section.
- Ensure that student are familiar with term terms *power*, *indices* and *reciprocal*.
- Ask students to create a chart that contains all the key ideas (with examples) from the first two sections of this chapter.

Part 1
- Ensure that students know that the value of the index number tells them how many 'lots' of a number to multiply together.
  Revise forming the reciprocal of a number.

Part 2

- Ask students to use their calculators to find these values.
  - $2^5, 2^4, 2^3, 2^2, 2^1, 2^0, 2^{-1}$ (32, 16, 8, 4, 2, 1, $\frac{1}{2}$)
  - $3^5, 3^4, 3^3, 3^2, 3^1, 3^0, 3^{-1}$ (243, 81, 27, 9, 3, 1, $\frac{1}{3}$)
- Discuss what is happening with each pattern.
- Introduce the rules for multiplying or dividing numbers in index form by working through the bullet points below.
- Give students a number with a power (e.g. 5^3) and ask them to work out the value (125). Give them the same number with a different power (e.g. 5^5) and ask them to work out that value (3125).
  Ask them to multiply the first number by the second number (390 625).
  Ask students to convert the result to a power of their original numbers (5^8)
  Ask students to make a connection between 5^8, 5^5 and 5^3.
- Give students a different number with a power (e.g. 6^7) and ask them to work out the value (279 936).
  Give them the same number with a smaller power (e.g. 6^3) and ask them to work out that value (216).
  Ask students to divide the first number by the second number (1296).
  Ask students to convert this to a power of their original numbers (6^4).
  Ask students to make a connection between 6^7, 6^4 and 6^3.
- Give students a number with a power (e.g. 4^3) and ask them to work out the value (64).
  Ask them to work out the cube of the result (262 144).
  Ask students to work out the power of 4 that gives this result (4^9).
- Work through the material on page 389 of the Student Book. Use students' results from the above work to support and reinforce the rules of adding, subtracting and multiplying indices.
- Work through the examples at the top of page 390 in the Student Book.
- **Students can now do Exercise 14B from the Student Book. Less able** students may need support for questions 6–9 and could work with a partner to complete them. You could give **more able** students some additional work on mixed multiplication and division, e.g. $27 \times 23 \div 24$ in preparation for Part 3.

| N 1–3, 5–9, 12 | Calculator n/a | CM n/a | MR 4, 10 | PS 11 | EV n/a |

Part 3

- Ask students to create questions in a similar style to questions 8 and 9 of Exercise 14B, but with the answer $\dfrac{3a}{b}$.
- Compile a list of answers.
- Repeat for an answer of $\dfrac{a}{2b}$.
- Again, compile a list of answers.

Learning objectives

- Change a number into standard form
- Calculate using numbers in standard form

Resources and homework

- Student Book 14.3: pages 391–398
- Practice Book 14.3: pages 132–134

Making mathematical connections

- Multiplication of integers
- Powers (indices)
- Multiplying and dividing by powers of 10

Making cross-curricular connections

- **Science** – evaluation of expressions/ solving problems
- **Computing** – expressions of memory size
- **Relevance** – expression of very large or very small numbers

Prior learning

- Students should be able to multiply and divide by 10, 100 and 1000. They should know powers of 10 such as: $10^5 = 10 \times 10 \times 10 \times 10 \times 10 = 100\,000$.
- Students should also be able to convert numbers (e.g. 10 000) back to a power of 10 (10^4).

Working mathematically

- Encourage students to record all stages of working. This will help them see the progression of ideas that have been presented and remind them of the processing that is taking place.

Common misconceptions and remediation

- When inputting numbers on a calculator, students often insert an extra [× 1 0], e.g. to key in 1.3×10^6 they key in [1 • 3 × 1 0 ×10ʸ 6], giving an answer that is 10 times larger than required. Highlighting this error should help students avoid making it.
- Students may also leave answers that are not in standard form, e.g. 23×10^7. Remind students to check that the first number is between 1 and 10.

Probing questions

- How large or how small does a number have to be before it becomes more useful to write it in standard form?
- At what point does your calculator 'switch' from showing numbers as ordinary numbers to showing numbers in standard form?

Literacy focus

- Key terms: standard form, standard index form
- Ask students to create a small poster that explains how to enter a number in standard form into their calculator.

Part 1

NB: *This section may take more than 1 hour.*

- Ask some quickfire questions to familiarise students with multiplications by powers of 10.
  5×10 (50), $5 \times 10 \times 10$ (500); $5 \times 10 \times 10 \times 10$ (5000) 10^1 (10); 10^2 (100); 10^3 (1000)
  $5 \div 10$ (0.5); $5 \div 10 \div 10$ (0.05); $5 \div 10 \div 10 \div 10$ (0.005) 10^{-1} (0.1); 10^{-2} (0.01); 10^{-3} (0.001)
- Now ask some quickfire questions using decimals, e.g. 3.6 instead of 5. Repeat for numbers with two decimal places, e.g. 9.27.

Part 2

Multiplying and dividing by powers of 10; Multiplication by powers of 10; Division by powers of 10; Working with multiples of powers of 10

- Work through the text in the Student Book, including the calculator tasks and Examples 2, 3, 4 and 5.
- **Students can now do Exercise 14C from Student Book. Less able** students could work with a partner to complete questions 13–15.

N 1–2, 6–12	Calculator n/a	CM 14	MR 3, 13	PS 4, 5, 15	EV n/a

Standard form

- Emphasise the format of standard form number as:
  $A \times 10^n$ where $1 \leq A < 10$, and n is an integer.

Standard form on a calculator; Standard form for numbers less than 1

- Write 171 798 691 84 on the board and ask students to key this into their calculator and press **=**. The display should show: $1.717986918 \times 10^{10}$.
  Tell students that this number is displayed in standard form.
  You will need to explain that the calculator has rounded the number because it can only display a certain number of digits. This means that the standard form number displayed could originally have been between 171 798 691 80 and 171 798 69184.
- Reiterate the format of a standard form number: $A \times 10^n$, where $1 \leq A < 10$ and n is an integer.
- Show students the **×10ˣ** key and input **4** **.** **5** **×** **×10ˣ** **6** **=** (4500000).
- Repeat for other numbers.
- **Students can now do Exercise 14D from the Student Book. Less able** students may need support with questions 11–12.

N 1–2, 4–7	Calculator 3, 5, 10–12	CM 8–10	MR 11	PS 3, 12	EV n/a

Calculating with standard form

- Write $2 \times 10^7 \times 6 \times 10^3$ on the board and discuss ways of working it out. Work towards multiplying 2 and 6 and multiplying the powers of 10 leading to 12×10^{10}. Ask students if this is in standard form (no). Ask them to convert it to standard form (1.2×10^{11}). Tell students they will need to be careful with this.
- Repeat for division, e.g. $4 \times 10^3 \div 8 \times 10^5$ (5×10^{-3}). Discourage students from writing the numbers as ordinary numbers and then completing the calculation. Although this is a valid method, it can lead to errors with so many digits.
- Work through Examples 6 and 7, highlighting again the need to check that the final answer is in standard form.
- **Students can now do Exercise 14E from the Student Book. Less able** students may need help with questions 14–17.

N 1–6, 8-11	Calculator 3	CM n/a	MR 13	PS 7, 12, 14	EV n/a

Part 3

- Allow students to check answers to non-calculator questions in Exercise 14E by using their calculators.
- **More able** students can experiment with the 'scientific notation' button to convert from ordinary numbers to standard form. **SHIFT SETUP 7 SCI**

Chapter 15 Algebra: Equations and inequalities

Overview

15.1 Linear equations	**15.5** Using simultaneous equations to solve problems
15.2 Elimination method for simultaneous equations	**15.6** Linear inequalities
15.3 Substitution method for simultaneous equations	**15.7** Graphical inequalities
15.4 Balancing coefficients to solve simultaneous equations	**15.8** Trial and improvement

Prior learning

Know the basic language of algebra.
Know how to collect together like terms.
Know to solve basic linear equations.

Learning objectives

Ensure that students can: set up and solve linear equations with fractions, brackets and variables on both sides; solve linear simultaneous equations; solve a linear inequality and represent the solution on a number line; find a region on a graph that obeys a linear inequality in two variables; use trial and improvement to solve non-linear equations.

In the examination, students will be expected to:
- solve equations in which the variable appears as part of the numerator of a fraction
- solve equations where you have to expand brackets first
- solve equations where the variable appears on both sides of the equals sign
- set up equations from given information and then solve them
- solve simultaneous linear equations in two variables using the elimination method
- solve simultaneous linear equations in two variables using the substitution method
- solve simultaneous linear equations by balancing coefficients
- solve problems using simultaneous linear equations
- solve a simple linear inequality and represent it on a number line
- show a graphical inequality
- find regions that satisfy more than one graphical inequality.
- estimate the answers to some questions that do not have exact solutions, using the method of trial and improvement.

Extension

Solve more complex equations involving a mixture of features: fractions, brackets, variables on both sides. Incorporate these into simultaneous equations. Consider a strategy using trial and improvement that will solve quickly to two decimal places.

Curriculum references

Section	GCSE specification
15.1	A 5
15.2	A 19
15.3	A 19
15.4	A 19

Section	GCSE specification
15.5	A 21
15.6	A 22
15.7	A 14
15.8	A 20

Route mapping

Exercise	Accessible	Intermediate	Challenging	AO1	AO2 MR CM	AO3 PS EV	Key questions
15A	1–5			1	2	3–5	1, 3
15B	1–7			1	2, 6	3–5, 7	1, 5
15C	1–8	9		1, 3	4, 7	2, 5, 6, 8, 9	3, 4, 6
15D	1–3			1–3			3
15E	1–3			1–3			3
15F	1–2			1–2			2
15G		1–12	13, 14	3	4	1, 2, 5–14	8, 12, 14
15H	1–4	5–9		1, 6–8	2, 4, 5	3, 9	1, 7
15I	1–6	7, 8		1–3, 8	5, 7	4, 6	3, 7
15J	1–3	4–13	14	1–9	10–12	13, 14	4, 8, 11
15K	1–6	7–11		1–3, 5, 6	4, 10	7, 8, 11	2, 6

Key questions are those that demonstrate mastery of the concept, or which require a step-up in understanding or application. Key questions could be used to identify the questions that students must tackle to support differentiation, or to identify the questions that should be teacher-marked rather than student-marked.

About this chapter

Making connections: The chapter introduces methods for solving more complex algebraic equations containing: fractional components, terms within brackets, an unknown variable on both sides, simultaneous equations. There is a strong link to linear graphs (Chapter 10) and inequalities. These are all essential skills that students need to master before the more challenging algebraic manipulation in Chapter 24.

Relevance: There is an emphasis on the use of logic and thinking in steps. These skills are transferable to a whole range of subjects and careers.

Working mathematically: Are any of the equations and inequalities in this chapter not solvable by graphical method? What are the advantages of solving algebraically rather than graphically? Are there any advantages of solving graphically rather than algebraically?

Assessment: In each section of this chapter, ensure that students have a good grasp of the key questions in each exercise before moving on. (Refer to the 'Route mapping' table above.) Encourage students to read and think about the 'Ready to progress?' statements on page 432 of the Student Book. Check students' understanding at the end of the chapter, formatively, using peer assessment. Students could do a mini test in the form of the 'Review questions' on pages 432–435 of the Student Book. Follow up the test with an individual target-getting session, based on any areas for development that a student may have.

Worked exemplars from the Student Book – suggestions for use
- For question 1, students could create their own scenario with three inequalities, one true, one maybe true and one false.
- For questions 2 and 3, copy and cut up the exemplar into cards. Students match the working with the notes. (Remove any unnecessary words, e.g. 'first, second'.)
- Copy and cut the working into cards, splitting the label/description from the working. Students put the working in order then match with the descriptions.

Answers to the Student Book questions are available on the CD-ROM provided.

Section 15.1 Linear equations

Learning objectives

- Solve equations in which the variable appears as part of the numerator of a fraction
- Solve equations where you have to expand brackets first
- Solve equations where the variable appears on both sides of the equals sign
- Set up equations from given information and then solve them

Resources and homework

- Student Book 15.1: pages 403–408
- Practice Book 15.1: pages 135–137

Making mathematical connections

- Simplifying and solving linear equations that involve fractions and brackets
- Connection expanding and factorising

Making cross-curricular connections

- **Science** – using formulae
- **Relevance** – developing logical thinking

Prior learning

- Students must be able to calculate confidently with numerical fractions. If you feel that students need a refresher, set this as a homework task before the lesson.
- Students should be able to expand brackets, simplify expressions and solve linear equations.

Working mathematically

- Encourage students to articulate their methods for numerical fractions (equivalence – including cancelling, addition and subtraction – multiplication and division) and then to apply these to algebraic fractions.
- Structure tasks so students can work out the methods for themselves, either by increasing the difficulty incrementally or through one straightforward and one complex example.

Common misconceptions and remediation

- Make sure students understand that they must expand brackets before they can solve the equation. When doing this, students often multiply only the first term inside a bracket, forgetting subsequent terms. Remind students to take care when dealing with negative numbers.
- Students often do not identify the correct order for processes when they solve equations involving fractions. For example, when solving $\frac{x+5}{3} = 7$, students may try to subtract 5 before multiplying by 3. Stress that terms such as $x + 5$ must remain together until the denominator is removed.

Probing questions

- When expanding, why is it necessary to multiply the term outside the bracket by everything inside the brackets?
- When solving, why is it necessary to balance things on both sides of the equals sign?

Literacy focus

- Key terms: There are no new key terms in this section.
- Make sure students are familiar with 'brackets', 'rearrange' and 'do the same to both sides'.
- Be explicit about the language of equivalence – avoid talking about 'cross-multiplication' or 'moving across the equal sign'. Talk about 'balancing' 'doing the same to both sides'.

Part 1

NB: This section may take more than 1 hour.

- Review equations by asking students to solve:

  $x - 4 = 6$ $2x - 4 = 6$ $2x + 5 = 6$ $\dfrac{x}{3} = 6$

- Discuss the methods used to solve the equations.
- Review expanding brackets by asking the following quickfire questions:
  What is $3 \times £4.25$? (£12.75)
  What is $3 \times £4 + 3 \times 25p$? (£12 + 75p = £12.75)
  What is $3 \times (£4 + 25p)$? (£12 + 75p = £12.75)
  What is $3(£4 + 25p)$? (£12 + 75p = £12.75)
  Is $5(2 + 4p) = £10.20$? (No, 10 + 20p)
  Is $5(2x + 3y) = 10x + 3y$? (No, 10x + 15y)
- Discuss the methods used to solve these questions.

Part 2

Fractional equations

- Discuss Examples 1 and 2 in the Student Book, highlighting the need to do the same thing to both sides.
- **Students can now do Exercise 15A from the Student Book.**

A 1	Calculator n/a	CM n/a	MR 2	PS 4, 5	EV 3

Brackets

- Remind students again that they must multiply the term outside the bracket by every term inside the bracket. Work through Example 3 in the Student Book.
- **Students can now do Exercise 15B from the Student Book.**

A 1	Calculator all	CM 6	MR 2	PS 3–5, 7	EV n/a

Equations with the variable on both sides

- Work through Examples 4 and 5. Example 5 demonstrates interpreting some narrative and setting up an equation to represent it. This is a vital skill, so provide more practice if necessary.
- **Students can now do Exercise 15C from the Student Book.**

A 1, 3	Calculator n/a	CM 4	MR 7	PS 2, 5, 6, 8, 9	EV n/a

Part 3

- Ask students to work in pairs to write a narrative question (along the lines of question 2 of Exercise 15C), formulate an equation to represent it and solve it algebraically.
- Share the questions as a class.

Section 15.2 Elimination method for simultaneous equations

Learning objectives

- Solve simultaneous linear equations in two variables using the elimination method

Making mathematical connections

- Rearranging simple formulae
- Solving equations

Resources and homework

- Student Book 15.2: pages 408–410
- Practice Book 15.2: page 137

Making cross-curricular connections

- **Science** – using formulae
- **Business** – optimisation of resources
- **Relevance** – linear programming; comparison of scenarios such as best deals for mobile phone contracts; developing logical thinking

Prior learning

- Students should be able to solve equations and rearrange simple formulae using the concept of 'balance'.

Working mathematically

- This problem has a specific order to the steps needed for solution: combine equations; solve for one variable; substitute that variable; solve for the second variable.

Common misconceptions and remediation

- Students often make errors when expanding brackets with negative terms, either inside or outside of the bracket. Suggest that students revisit Exercise 15B if they are unsure.
- Errors are often made when equations are not labelled and steps are not explained. Encourage good practice: students should label equations and explain each step of their working.

Probing questions

- Ask students to solve the equations in question 3 of Exercise 15D using elimination *and* substitution. Does it seem that one method might be better than the other? Why? Could they make a decision on a method to use before they start to solve? How?

Literacy focus

- Key term: eliminate
- Ensure that students understand the terms *coefficient* and *substitute*.
- Ask students to work in pairs to create a 'Hints and tips' box that outlines the 'rule' for deciding whether the two equations should be added or subtracted.

Part 1

- Remind students that 'simultaneous' means *at the same time*, *together* and that two equations will be solved so that one solution is true for both equations. Work through the first part of the text in the Student Book, up to the heading 'Elimination method'.
- Give students the equations $x - y = 3$ and $2x - y = 7$. Ask them to come up with a range of solutions for each equation. Can they find a solution that satisfies both? ($x = 4$, $y = 1$)

Part 2

Elimination method

- Demonstrate this method by working through Examples 6 and 7 from the Student Book. Make sure that students can see the six steps being applied in Example 7.
- Tell students that they should substitute both values into *both original* equations to check that they are correct.
- Tell students that they should label equations AND write down the operations performed on each one. This will help them keep track of their work and help examiners follow their work.
- **Students can now do Exercise 15D from the Student Book.**

A 1–3	Calculator n/a	CM n/a	MR n/a	PS n/a	EV n/a

Part 3

- Present students with ten additional pairs of simultaneous equation to solve. There should be a mix of each of the two variables having balanced coefficients with different combinations of negative and positive values.
- Ask students to decide whether each pair should be added or subtracted, justifying their decision.

Section 15.3 Substitution method for simultaneous equations

Learning objectives

- Solve simultaneous linear equations in two variables using the substitution method

Resources and homework

- Student Book 15.3: pages 410–411
- Practice Book 15.3: page 137

Making mathematical connections

- Rearranging simple formulae
- Solving equations
- Substitution

Making cross-curricular connections

- **Science** – using formulae
- **Business** – optimisation of resources
- **Relevance** – linear programming; comparison of scenarios such as best deals for mobile phone contracts; developing logical thinking

Prior learning

- Students should be able to rearrange equations, substitute terms into an equation and solve equations.

Working mathematically

- This problem has a specific order to the steps needed for solution: rearrange one equation; substitute that equation into the other equation; solve for one variable; substitute that variable; solve for the second variable.

Common misconceptions and remediation

- Students often forget to multiply everything within the bracket when expanding, so refer back to Exercise 15B for review.
- Substitution is often a source of errors. Make a clear distinction between the methods used when replacing a single term with a new expression at the start of the solution and substituting values towards the end of the solution.

Probing questions

- Is it possible to decide which method (elimination or substitution) will be most straightforward before starting a solution?
- Ask students to look at the equations in parts a and b of question 3, Exercise 15E. Ask students to solve each pair of equations by elimination *and* substitution. Is one method easier than the other? Why?

Literacy focus

- Key terms: There are no new key terms in this section.
- Ensure that students understand the terms *substitution* and *rearrange*.

Part 1

- Prepare a list of questions that can be solved using substitution, for example:
- If $2x + 6y = 10$ and $x = 2y$ find the value of x and y. ($x = 2$, $y = 1$)
- Ask students to work in pairs and consider how to solve each question.

Part 2

- Demonstrate how to use the substitution method by working through these, or similar, examples:

$$4x + 3y = 18 \quad (1)$$
$$y = 5 - x \quad (2)$$

Sub (2) into (1) $4x + 3(5 - x) = 18$
Multiply out $4x + 15 - 3x = 18$
$$x = 3$$
Sub $x = 3$ into (1) $y = 2$
Check in (1) $4 \times 3 + 3 \times 2 = 18$

$$2x + 3y = 8$$
$$x = y - 8 \qquad (x = -2, y = 4)$$

- As you work, remind students that it is important that they substitute both values into *both* of the *original* equations to check that they are correct.
- Again, emphasise the need to label equations and write down the operations performed on each equation.
- Work through Example 8.
- **Students can now do Exercise 15E from the Student Book.**

A 1–3	Calculator n/a	CM n/a	MR n/a	PS n/a	EV n/a

Part 3

- Present students with ten additional pairs of simultaneous equations to solve. There should be a mix of each of the two variables having balanced coefficients with different combinations of negative and positive values. In some pairs, one or the equations should be in the form $y = \ldots$ or $x = \ldots$
- Challenge students to decide quickly which method (elimination or substitution) should be used to solve them, justifying their decision.

Section 15.4 Balancing coefficients to solve simultaneous equations

Learning objectives
- Solve simultaneous linear equations by balancing coefficients

Resources and homework
- Student Book 15.4: pages 411–412
- Practice Book 15.4: page 138

Making mathematical connections
- Rearranging simple formulae
- Solving equations

Making cross-curricular connections
- **Science** – using formulae
- **Business** – optimisation of resources
- **Relevance** – linear programming; comparison of scenarios such as best deals for mobile phone contracts; developing logical thinking

Prior learning
- Students should be able to rearrange equations and confidently use the elimination method.

Working mathematically
- This method adds an important opening step that students need to consider before they begin the elimination method.
- There is no need to consider this method if substitution will be carried out, but substitution often poses problems by creating fractional terms, and students should have already discovered that elimination is usually the easiest method of solution.

Common misconceptions and remediation
- Errors are often made when equations are not labelled and steps are not explained. Encourage good practice.
- Students often fail to multiply through the entire equation by their chosen factor. Encourage students to check each time that corresponding equations are equivalent.
- Students often make errors when expanding brackets with negative terms, either inside or outside of the bracket. Suggest that students revisit Exercise 15B if they are unsure.

Probing questions
- Why does substitution pose problems?
- Why is it better to find the LCM of the coefficients rather than simply multiply the coefficients together?

Literacy focus
- Key terms: There are no new key terms in this section.
- Ask students to create a flowchart to guide someone through the steps required to solve a pair of simultaneous equations. This should bring together the processes of: elimination, substitution and balancing coefficients.

Part 1

- Revise the process of elimination by recapping a few questions from Exercise 15D of Section 15.2.
- Introduce the concept of creating an equivalent equation by asking students to explain the differences or similarities between, for example:

  (a) $y = 2x + 6$ (b) $2y = 4x + 12$

  (c) $y = 4x + 12$ (d) $y = x + 3$

  [(b) = 2 × (a), (c) ≠ 2 × (a) because the left-hand side has not been multiplied by 2;

  (d) is not $\frac{1}{2}$ × (a) because the left-hand side has not been divided by 2]

Part 2

Balancing coefficients in one equation only

- Work through the text in the Student Book, ensuring the students understand the concept of creating an equivalent equation. Ensure they understand that it does not matter which variable they choose as the one to be balanced, although one may be more straightforward.
- Work through the additional example below, if necessary.

$$4x + 2y = 24 \quad (1)$$
$$3x + 4y = 23 \quad (2)$$

(1) × 2 $8x + 4y = 48 \quad (3)$

(3) − (2) $5x \quad = 25$

[÷5] $x \quad = 5$

Sub in (1) $4 × 5 + 2y = 24; 2y = 4; y = 2$

Substitute into (2) to check the values.

Balancing coefficients in both equations

- Carefully work through the next section of text and Example 9 from the Student Book. Make sure students understand that the calculations will use smaller numbers if they find the LCM of the coefficients.
- **Students can now do Exercise 15F from the Student Book.**

A 1, 2	Calculator n/a	CM n/a	MR n/a	PS n/a	EV n/a

Part 3

- Present students with ten additional pairs of simultaneous equations to solve. There should be a mix of each of the two variables having unbalanced coefficients with different combinations of negative and positive values.
- Challenge students to decide quickly which multiplying factors will be used to balance out one of the variables, and then whether the equations should be added or subtracted, justifying their decision.

Section 15.5 Using simultaneous equations to solve problems

Learning objectives
- Solve problems using simultaneous linear equations

Resources and homework
- Student Book 15.5: pages 413–415
- Practice Book 15.5: pages 138–139

Making mathematical connections
- Sequences
- Creating and solving equations

Making cross-curricular connections
- **Business** – optimisation of resources
- **Relevance** – linear programming; developing logical thinking; applications to manufacturing and project management

Prior learning
- Students should be confident with solving simultaneous equations by either elimination (balancing coefficients where necessary) or substitution.
- Students should also be able to create an equation from information written as narrative.

Working mathematically
- This section builds on the skills learned in the previous sections and now adds another skill – that of creating a pair of simultaneous equations from a narrative scenario, and then solving them. This is a vital interpretive skill.

Common misconceptions and remediation
- Students often create equations that are too simplistic by dropping values from the text into an equation without looking carefully for connections between the variables in the text. Encourage students to read and mark the text with the letter they want to use as a variable. Suggest that, unless they are given a letter, they use the initial letters of the objects.
- Students often stop once the equations have been solved; then they do not refer back and answer what the question asks. Stress that they should reread the question to check that their values are appropriate and that they have provided all the answers that are required.

Probing questions
- What is the minimum required number of pieces of information that can be placed in two simultaneous equations?

Literacy focus
- Key terms: There are no new key terms in this section.
- Ask students to choose a question from Exercise 15F in Section 15.4 and to invent a scenario from which the two equations could have been created.

Part 1

- Ask the class to solve the following simultaneous equations:
  $5x + 2y = 26$ $3x + y = 15$ $(x = 4, y = 3)$
- If £x is the cost of a cup of coffee what might £y represent? (Tea?)
- How much would an order of three cups of coffee and four cups of tea cost?
- Write the equation that represents this order.

Part 2

- Explain that students will set up a pair of simultaneous equations from a practical problem. Once students have done this step, they need to use the skills they have already learned to solve the equations.
- Give students the following problem: Four gobstoppers and six chews cost 76p. How much does each cost?
- Clearly this has no unique solution, but students will probably suggest at least one valid answer such as 10p and 6p, or 7p and 8p.
- Add the following information: Three gobstoppers and five chews cost 60p. How much does each cost? If students suggested the previous answers, they will realise that 10p and 6p are the correct answers.
- Now set this up as a pair of equations: $4g + 6c = 76$, $3g + 5c = 60$; solve in the usual way.
- Work through Example 10 from the Student Book, making sure that all students can set up the equation.
- **Students can now do Exercise 15G from the Student Book. Less able** students may require help to set up the equations from the information provided.

| A 3 | Calculator n/a | CM 4 | MR n/a | PS 1, 2, 5–13 | EV 14 |

Part 3

- Use a graph-drawing programme to demonstrate the connection between graphs and simultaneous equations.
- In particular, show students that equations such as $2x + 5y = 10$ and $4x + 10y = 15$ are parallel, and so will not intersect.

Section 15.6 Linear inequalities

Learning objectives

- Solve a simple linear inequality and represent it on a number line

Resources and homework

- Student Book 15.6: pages 416–421
- Practice Book 15.6: pages 139–141

Making mathematical connections

- Solving linear equations

Making cross-curricular connections

- **Computing** – efficient coding using 'repeat' or loops
- **Business** – optimisation of resources
- **Relevance** – applications to manufacturing and project management

Prior learning

- Students should be able to solve linear equations, including those with the variable occurring on both sides of the equation.
- Students should also be able to place a number on a number line accurately.

Working mathematically

- Ensure that students are confident with using the symbols: $<$, $\leq$, $>$, $\geq$ and that they are familiar with the concept of a number line to represent or identify values.

Common misconceptions and remediation

- Students often solve these as equations and do not use the inequality sign in the answer. Encourage students to keep the inequality in the solution at each step.
- Stress that an inequality can have more than one solution. Encourage students to check that the answer(s) they find are suitable for the question asked.

Probing questions

- What is wrong with this solution? $-5x > 12$, $x > -2.4$
- How could you adjust your working to reach the correct solution? ($x < -2.4$)

Literacy focus

- Key terms: inequality, inclusive inequality, strict inequality
- Ask students to describe a visual picture of how they remember that an open (empty) circle represents $<$ or $>$ and that a closed (shaded) circle represents $\leq$ or $\geq$. (For example, an empty circle does not hold the value; a shaded circle contains the value.)

Part 1

- Write on the board: $x < 5$. Ask students to say what it means. (x is less than 5)
- Then ask: What is the biggest value of x you can find that obeys the rule?
- Many will say 4, then 4.9. Keep going until you establish that x can be as large as 4.999… Use the notation for recurring decimal notation if students are familiar with it.
- Now ask students for the smallest value that obeys $x > 3$. This is more difficult, and the answer is 3.00000…0000001, where there is an infinite number of zeros.
- Write on the board: $x \leq 5$. Ask students to say what it means. (x is less than or equal to 5)
- Ask: What is the biggest value of x you can find that obeys the rule? (The answer is, of course, 5.)
- Now ask students: What is the smallest value that obeys $x \geq 3$? (The answer this time is 3.)

Part 2

- Ask students if they can give the values of x that are true for $x + 3 > 7$.
- Work through 5, 4.5, 4, 4.1 and 4.05 to find the smallest possible value of x for which this is true. Establish that a value just bigger than 4 will work, so $x > 4$.
- Now show students how to solve this inequality:

$$x + 3 > 7$$
$$[- 3 \text{ from both sides}] \quad x > 7 - 3$$
$$x > 4$$

- Students should instantly recognise this as being the same basic method as solving an equation. Say that the methods are the same, but that the equals sign is replaced with an inequality sign.
- Work through the introductory text and Examples 11, 12 and 13 from the Student Book.
- **Students can now do Exercise 15H from the Student Book.**
- **Less able** students may find this topic difficult, but if they can solve equations they should make progress with this work. Revise solving simple equations to increase confidence.

| A 1, 6–8 | Calculator n/a | CM 4 | MR 2, 5 | PS 3, 9 | EV n/a |

The number line

- Work through the text in this section and Examples 14 and 15.
- Go back to question 1 of Exercise 15H. Ask students to produce a number line to represent the solution to each inequality.
- **Students can now do Exercise 15I from the Student Book.** Most students will find this accessible.

| A 1–3, 8 | Calculator n/a | CM 7 | MR 5 | PS 4, 6 | EV n/a |

Part 3

- Write $2x + y \leq 7$ on the board and ask for values of x and y that make it true.
  For example: $x = 3$, $y = 1$ or $x = 0$, $y = 0$.
- Repeat with $3x + 4y > 12$.

Section 15.7 Graphical inequalities

Learning objectives
- Show a graphical inequality
- Find regions that satisfy more than one graphical inequality

Resources and homework
- Student Book 15.7: pages 421–426
- Practice Book 15.7: pages 141–142

Making mathematical connections
- Graphs of linear equations
- Venn diagrams

Making cross-curricular connections
- **Business** – optimisation of resources
- **Relevance** – applications to manufacturing and project management

Prior learning
- Students should know how to plot the line of a line of an equation and to substitute into simple expressions.

Working mathematically
- Suggest to students that whatever the inequality, draw as though the inequality is an '=' sign.
- Then, if the sign is > or <, draw a dotted line, and if the sign is ≤ or ≥, draw a solid line.
- Think carefully about whether you want the region above or below the line.

Common misconceptions and remediation
- Students often do not draw the correct line, or they are confused about whether the line should be dotted or solid. They also choose the incorrect side of the line as the region required. Testing a point to check, should help to eliminate these mistakes.
- Students often plot points on the wrong axes using the cover-up rule. They may also shade the wrong side of the line or not define clearly the required region. To help to prevent these mistakes, work through some examples and highlight potential pitfalls.

Probing questions
- Plot these three inequalities: $y < 2x + 2$, $x > 4$, $y > 5 - x$
  Shade the region that satisfies all three inequalities.
- When plotted, it appears as if one inequality is incorrectly expressed. Which one? Why?
- What is the minimum number of inequalities that will define an enclosed region?

Literacy focus
- Key terms: boundary, origin, region
- Ask students to describe how to decide which side of a plotted line is included in a region and is likely to provide a solution to the problem.

Part 1
- Recall the cover-up method for drawing linear graphs.
- Write $2x + 3y = 6$ on the board. Remind students that the x-axis is the line $y = 0$, so, covering up the y-term and solving the remaining linear equation, $2x = 6$, gives the point (3, 0). Similarly, the y-axis is the line $x = 0$, which gives the point (0, 2).
- Repeat with other similar lines if necessary. Note that there is no need for negative values, although you could cover this with **more able** students.

Part 2

- Ask students to sketch the graph of $2x + 3y = 6$.
- Ask which side of the line would satisfy $2x + 3y \leq 6$.
- The natural instinct, as the sign is 'less than or equal to', is to go for the region under the line. This is correct, but ask: How can you be sure? (test a point)
- Ask students: Which is an 'obvious' point to test? (the origin, if it is not on the line: $2 \times 0 + 3 \times 0 \leq 6$)
- Make sure that students realise that the answer to $2x + 3y \leq 6$ is a region and that it is infinitely large.
- Repeat with the inequality $x > 2$. Ask why this is different. Students should realise that there is only one variable and the inequality is a 'strict' inequality.
- Tell students that we represent the strict inequality by drawing the boundary line as a dashed line.
- Sketch the region, highlighting that it is still a region.
- Ensure that students are aware of the steps involved in drawing a graphical inequality:
  Step 1: Draw the boundary line (dashed or solid as appropriate).
  Step 2: Test a point not on the line to establish which side of the line is required.
- Students are often confused by how to mark a region. Questions will usually state whether they need to shade or, for example, mark the region clearly with an R. There is no established convention.
- Work through Example 16, checking that students have understood the principles.

More than one inequality
- Introduce the idea that some regions may be bound by more than one line.
- Sketch a pair of coordinate axes with two lines drawn on them.
- Indicate the area between the lines and ask students to identify some points in this region.
- Repeat with other pairs of lines.
- Use a similar method to show regions enclosed by three or more lines.
- Work through the text in this section and Example 17 from the Student Book.
- **Students can now do Exercise 15J from the Student Book.** Students may benefit from having pre-printed graph spaces with axes marked on them.

A 1–9	Calculator n/a	CM 12	MR 10, 11	PS 13, 14	EV n/a

Part 3

- Write these inequalities on the board: $y < 2x + 2$, $x < 4$, $y \geq 5 - x$
- Ask students, in pairs, to draw these on a set of axes and shade the region they bound.
- How many coordinate points satisfy all three inequalities? (9)

Section 15.8 Trial and improvement

Learning objectives
- Estimate the answers to some questions that do not have exact solutions, using the method of trial and improvement

Resources and homework
- Student Book 15.8: pages 426–429
- Practice Book 15.8: page 143

Making mathematical connections
- Solving equations
- Approximation/estimation
- Iteration

Making cross-curricular connections
- **Computing** – data sorting methods
- **Relevance** – applications to manufacturing and project management

Prior learning
- Students should understand approximation and estimation.
- They should be able to apply BIDMAS/BODMAS, particularly working out a power before a multiplication or division.

Working mathematically
- Students should work in pairs, developing a strategy and a method of recording their progress through a solution.
- Students should constantly revise their mental estimation of the solution.

Common misconceptions and remediation
- Students often do not test the halfway value, as they think the answer is obvious. Remind them of the need to do this whenever errors arise.
- Students tend to keep improving their guesses until the answer is within one decimal place of the target value. Tell students they only need to check the bounds to the same degree of accuracy that is required and then test the halfway value.

Probing questions
- Why is it necessary to use the halfway rule as the final step in the solution?
- Why is it important to record your route to a solution in a structured way?

Literacy focus
- Key terms: trial and improvement
- Ask students to create a number line on which they eliminate the values that are not part of the solution after they make each 'guess'. This gives a visual illustration of how the search for an answer is being accomplished, a process in computing terms known as *binary chop*.

Part 1
- Write this calculation on the board: $2.7^3 - 2 \times 2.7$
- Ask students to work it out. (14.283)
- It is unlikely that everyone in class will have obtained the correct value.
- Draw attention to the cube button or the power key. (On older calculators the power key often involves '2nd function' keys which can cause difficulties form some students.)
- Another way to do the calculation is: $2.7 \times 2.7 \times 2.7 - 2 \times 2.7$. Make sure students understand that 2.7^3 means $2.7 \times 2.7 \times 2.7$.
- Repeat with similar calculations until students can do these.

Part 2

- Write the following on the board: $x^2 + x = 12$.
- Ask students if they can solve it for x. If they need a clue, say that it is a whole number.
- Establish the answer 3 and show that $3 \times 3 + 3 = 12$.
- Below the first equation, write: $x^2 + x = 20$ and repeat the process (4).
- Now, below the other two equations, write: $x^2 + x = 15$. Ask students if this can be solved. Some may say no, as solutions of 3 and 4 have already been used. Others may say that the answer is between 3 and 4. Ask students how they can be sure of this.
- Explain that (at this level), the equation cannot be solved, so the only method is guesswork.
- Ask students to find the answer by guessing a number between 3 and 4 and trying it out. Say that if their first guess does not work, they should guess again.
- Point out that there is no exact answer so, as soon as they get an answer very close to 15, they can give you the value (3.405… or 3.4).
- Check the solutions in the original equation ($3.4^2 + 3.4 = 14.96$).
- Explain that this is called 'trial and improvement' and that it is used to find the answer to certain types of equations that cannot be solved using 'rearrangement'.
- Ask students if they can see any significant differences between this type of equation and the ones that they have solved using rearrangement (an x term with a power).
- Explain that to use this process efficiently, they must work in a systematic way and use a table.
- Work through the text in the Student Book, up to Example 18. Emphasise the need to record the way the solution is progressing systematically.
- Explain that they need to test the midpoint of the two 1-dp values (4.6 and 4.7) because, as we are dealing with curves, there is no guarantee that an x value that gives an answer closest to the target value is closest to the real answer.
- Work through Examples 18 and 19 in the Student Book. Focus particularly on why the concept of rounding is important in Example 18.
- **Students can now do Exercise 15K from the Student Book.**
- Remind them to set out their working in a table. Be prepared to support **less able** students using their calculators. **Less able** students could work in pairs, possibly with a **more able** student, to complete the questions 4 onwards.

A 1–3, 5, 6	Calculator 1–4, 6–11	CM 4, 10	MR n/a	PS 7, 8, 11	EV 9

Part 3

- Ask students to find the solution to $x^5 = 100$ using trial and improvement (2.5 to 1 dp).
- Then write the following on the board:
  $x^2 = 100, x = 10$ $x^3 = 100, x = 4.6$ $x^4 = 100, x = 3.2$ $x^5 = 100, x = 2.5$
- Ask students to guess the answer to $x^6 = 100$ and then try it out (2.15 or 2.2).

Chapter 16 Number: Counting, accuracy, powers and surds

Overview

16.1 Rational numbers, reciprocals, terminating and recurring decimals	**16.5** Limits of accuracy
16.2 Estimating powers and roots	**16.6** Problems involving limits of accuracy
16.3 Negative and fractional powers	**16.7** Choices and outcomes
16.4 Surds	

Prior learning

Know how to round numbers to the nearest 10, 100 or 1000.
Know how to round numbers to a given number of decimal places.
Know how to round numbers to a given number of significant figures.
Know squares of integers up to 15 × 15 = 225 and corresponding roots.
Know cubes of integers 1, 2, 3, 4, 5 and 10 and corresponding roots.
Know what indices, square roots and cube roots are.
Know how to divide by a fraction.
Know what terminating and recurring fractions are.

Learning objectives

Ensure that students can: work out a reciprocal; convert fractions to terminating or recurring decimals, and vice versa; estimate powers and roots of positive numbers; work with negative and fractional powers; calculate with surds; work out the error interval for rounded numbers; use limits of accuracy in calculations; use the product rule for counting.

In the examination, students will be expected to:
- recognise rational numbers, reciprocals, terminating decimals and recurring decimals
- convert terminal decimals to fractions
- convert fractions to recurring decimals
- find reciprocals of numbers or fractions
- how to estimate powers and roots of any given positive number
- apply the rules of powers to negative and fractional powers
- find and use the relationship between negative powers and roots
- simplify surds
- calculate and manipulate surds, including rationalising a denominator
- find the error interval or limits of accuracy of numbers that have been rounded to different degrees of accuracy
- combine limits of two or more variables to solve problems
- work out the number of choices, arrangements or outcomes when choosing from lists or sets.

Extension

Encourage students to work with surds and fractions for as long as possible throughout a solution. Working with surds and fractions (or terms of π) provides greater accuracy than using recurring decimals, rounding or limits of accuracy.

Curriculum references

Section	GCSE specification
16.1	N 10
16.2	N 6
16.3	N 7
16.4	N 8

Section	GCSE specification
16.5	N 16
16.6	N 16
16.7	N 4

Route mapping

Exercise	Accessible	Intermediate	Challenging	AO1	AO2 MR CM	AO3 PS EV	Key questions
16A		1–11	12–17	1, 3–8, 14, 15	2, 9–11, 17	12, 13, 16	5, 12, 15,
16B	1–4	5		1, 3–5		2	3, 4
16C		1–10		1–6	8, 9	7, 10	3, 10
16D			1–6	1–3	4, 5	6	2
16E			1–9	1–6	7, 8	9	7
16F		1–3	4–16	1–11, 13		12, 14–16	6, 12, 13
16G			1–14	1–7, 14	8, 9, 11, 12	10, 13	5, 6, 14
16H	1–3	4–9		1–3, 6, 7	9	4, 5, 8	3, 8
16I		1–9	10–19	1, 2, 5–8, 11–18	3, 9	4, 10, 19	3, 6, 14
16J		1–9	10–23	3, 6–11, 14–17, 22	2, 4, 5, 12, 18, 23	1, 11c, 11e, 13, 19, 20, 21b, 22b	4, 22

Key questions are those that demonstrate mastery of the concept, or which require a step-up in understanding or application. Key questions could be used to identify the questions that students must tackle, to support differentiation, or to identify the questions that should be teacher-marked rather than student-marked.

About this chapter

Making connections: The chapter builds on the previous work on rounding and estimating and prepares the way for extending other skills.

Relevance: There is an emphasis on students' consideration of required accuracy. Sometimes an answer can be stated very accurately, e.g. if left as a surd or in terms of π. However, at other times, the degree of accuracy can be managed, e.g. a recurring decimal into a fraction, or by specifying a lower and upper bound for an answer.

Working mathematically: How do you get the most accurate answer to a problem? Does keeping stages of working in fraction or surd form help? Why? How can powers be manipulated without using a calculator?

Assessment: In each section of this chapter, ensure that students have a good grasp of the key questions in each exercise before moving on. (Refer to the 'Route mapping' table above.) Encourage students to read and think about the 'Ready to progress?' statements on page 468 of the Student Book. Check students' understanding at the end of the chapter, formatively, using peer assessment. Students could do a mini test in the form of the 'Review questions' on pages 468–469 of the Student Book. Follow up the test with an individual target-getting session, based on any areas for development that a student may have.

Worked exemplars from the Student Book – suggestions for use

* Present students with the same questions but using different numbers. They should use the exemplar to mirror the working, in full or only the notes.

Answers to the Student Book questions are available on the CD-ROM provided.

Section 16.1 Rational numbers, reciprocals, terminating and recurring decimals

Learning objectives

- Recognise rational numbers, reciprocals, terminating decimals and recurring decimals
- Convert terminal decimals to fractions
- Convert fractions to recurring decimals
- Find reciprocals of numbers or fractions

Resources and homework

- Student Book 16.1: pages 437–440
- Practice Book 16.1: pages 144–145

Making mathematical connections

- Simplifying fractions

Making cross-curricular connections

- **Science** – using formulae
- **Relevance** – developing logical thinking

Prior learning

- Students will need to know how to round decimals and how to convert fractions into decimals using a calculator.
- Students also need to be able to simplify fractions by cancelling.

Working mathematically

- Encourage students to articulate their methods for numerical fractions, especially when converting from one format to another, e.g. from a recurring decimal to a fraction.
- Structure tasks so that students can refine the methods for themselves, either by increasing the difficulty incrementally or through one straightforward and one complex example.

Common misconceptions and remediation

- With recurring decimals, students make the mistake of multiplying by the wrong power of 10.
- In the GCSE examination, the question involving changing a recurring decimal to a fraction is often a 'prove' or 'show that' question, and students do not always show sufficient or clear workings for an examiner to follow. Tell students to set out work with comments, as in Examples 1 and 2 in the Student Book, so that examiners can follow each step clearly and award marks even when students make errors. Encourage students to give reasons for each step of their working.

Probing questions

- You have seen what a rational number is. What do you think an irrational number is?
- How could you define an irrational number? What is the most well-known irrational number?

Literacy focus

- Key terms: rational number, recurring decimal, terminating decimal
- Ask students to list the steps required to convert a recurring decimal into a fraction.

Part 1

NB: *This section may take more than 1 hour.*

- Ask students what $\frac{1}{2}$ is as a decimal? (0.5) $\frac{1}{4}$? (0.25) $\frac{1}{8}$? (0.125)
- Point out what is happening to the decimal fraction as the denominator doubles.
- Say that knowing $\frac{1}{2} = 0.5$ can help them to work out other decimals. Ask: What is $\frac{3}{8}$? (0.375); $\frac{5}{8}$? (0.625); $\frac{1}{40}$? (0.025); $\frac{1}{80}$? (0.0125) $\frac{1}{16}$? (0.0625) Discuss the answers.

- Write fractions on the board and discuss them with the class, e.g. ask what $\frac{1}{3}$ is as a decimal (0.333…). Make sure that students understand the difference between $\frac{1}{3}$ and $\frac{3}{10}$ (0.333… and 0.3).

Part 2

Rational numbers

- Remind students that they are expected to recall simple, common conversions such as $\frac{1}{2}$, $\frac{1}{3}$, $\frac{1}{4}$, $\frac{1}{10}$, $\frac{3}{4}$ and know how to convert the others.
- Refer back to $\frac{3}{10}$ = 0.3 and $\frac{1}{3}$ = 0.333… Point out that although $\frac{1}{3}$ = 0.33 (to 2 dp), 0.33 is actually $\frac{33}{100}$. Explain that $\frac{1}{3}$ is a recurring decimal and is written as $0.\dot{3}$. Show other recurring decimals, e.g. 0.181818… = $0.\dot{1}\dot{8}$ Be clear about the dot notation.

Converting fractions into decimals

- Demonstrate how to convert fractions into decimals using division on a calculator, e.g. with $\frac{2}{11}$ as 2 ÷ 11, or using the fraction keys.
- Discuss the text under this heading in the Student Book.

Converting terminal decimals into fractions

- Remind students of place values that follow the decimal point: $\frac{1}{10}$, $\frac{1}{100}$, $\frac{1}{1000}$ and so on.
- Discuss the text under this heading in the Student Book.

Converting recurring decimals into fractions

- Write 0.7 = $\frac{7}{10}$ and $0.\dot{7}$ = $\frac{7}{9}$ on the board. Now write 0.18 = $\frac{18}{100}$ and $0.\dot{1}\dot{8}$ = $\frac{18}{99}$ on the board.
- Ask students what they think $0.\dot{1}2\dot{3}$ is as a fraction $\left(\frac{123}{999}\right)$.
- Point out that while it is good to use patterns to spot answers, they need a formal method to prove the results. Work through Example 1 and Example 2.
- Ask them to show that $0.\dot{1}\dot{8}$ = $\frac{18}{99}$.

Finding reciprocals of numbers or fractions

- Explain that a reciprocal is 1 divided by the number and show examples.
- Explain that dividing 1 by a fraction inverts the fraction, e.g. $\frac{2}{3}$ is the reciprocal of $\frac{3}{2}$.
- Show students the reciprocal button on a calculator. $\boxed{x^{-1}}$
- **Students can now do Exercise 16A from the Student Book. Less able** students may need help with questions 12–17.

N 1, 3–8, 14, 15	Calculator 1–7, 9, 15, 16b, 17	CM 10, 17	MR 2, 9, 11	PS n/a	EV 12, 13, 16

Part 3

- Students will have found out that $\frac{1}{9}$ = 0.111… and $\frac{2}{9}$ = 0.222… Establish that $\frac{3}{9}$ = 0.333…
- Ask what other common fraction this recurring decimal represents.
- Show students that $\frac{3}{9}$ cancels to $\frac{1}{3}$.
- Carry on with $\frac{4}{9}, \frac{5}{9}, \frac{6}{9}$ (= $\frac{2}{3}$), $\frac{7}{9}, \frac{8}{9}$ and $\frac{9}{9}$ (= 1).
- Leave students with the apparent fallacy that 1 = 0.9999… since $0.\dot{9}$ is the same as $\frac{9}{9}$ = 1.

Section 16.2 Estimating powers and roots

Learning objectives
- How to estimate powers and roots of any given positive number

Resources and homework
- Student Book 16.2: pages 440–442
- Practice Book 16.2: page 145

Making mathematical connections
- Working with known powers and roots
- Rounding to one significant figure
- Working with surds

Making cross-curricular connections
- **Science** – using formulae
- **Relevance** – approximations involving area and volume

Prior learning
- Students should be confident in rounding numbers to 1 significant figure (sf).
- Students should be able to recall the first 15 squares (and their square roots), the first five cubes (and cube roots), and 10 cubed (and root), as well as use the terms 'square', 'square root', 'cube' and 'cube root', and their symbols.

Working mathematically
- Encourage students to use a number line. You could copy and then photocopy those on page 441 of the Student Book, and students can glue them into their books.

Common misconceptions and remediation
- Students sometimes think of approximating as guessing, and may replace a number that should be rounded to 1 sf with one rounded to the nearest whole unit.
- Remind students that estimating is actually quite a precise method.
- Reinforce the rules of rounding and, if necessary, look back at Section 1.3 of Chapter 1, which deals with approximation and rounding.

Probing questions
- Explain, without using a calculator for checking, whether the following approximations are true or false:

  $\sqrt{1440} = 120$ $\sqrt{380} \approx 19$ (to 2 sf)

  $\sqrt[3]{47000} \approx 34$ (to 2 sf) $2.5^4 = 36$

Literacy focus
- Key terms: There are no new key terms in this section.
- Ask students to describe and write down the steps they would need to take to get results for Exercise 16B, questions 5a i and iv (5a i $\sqrt{6600}$ iv 5.8^4)

Part 1

- Give students a quickfire mental test on the first 15 squares (and their roots), the cubes 1 to 5, 10 (and their cube roots), and rounding a variety of numbers (>1 and <1) to 1 sf.

Part 2

- Give students a copy of the number lines on page 441 to glue into their books.
- Work through the text and Example 3 and Example 4 from the Student Book, referring to the number line when necessary.
- **Students can now do Exercise 16B from the Student Book.**

| N 1, 3–5 | Calculator 5 | CM n/a | MR n/a | PS 2 | EV n/a |

Part 3

- Ask students to work in pairs and set each other questions similar to those in question 5 of Exercise 16B in the Student Book.
- One partner should set the question; the other partner should explain how he or she arrives at an answer, justifying each step.

Section 16.3 Negative and fractional powers

Learning objectives

- Apply the rules of powers to negative and fractional powers
- Find and use the relationship between negative powers and roots

Resources and homework

- Student Book 16.3: pages 442–446
- Practice Book 16.3: pages 146–147

Making mathematical connections

- Powers and roots
- Reciprocals

Making cross-curricular connections

- **Science** – using formulae
- **Relevance** – developing logical thinking

Prior learning

- Students should be comfortable with the way in which positive powers are manipulated.
- Students should also recall how to make the reciprocal of a number.

Working mathematically

- Students need to be able to see the connection between negative numbers and reciprocals, between fractional indices and roots, and mixtures of these.

Common misconceptions and remediation

- Students often assume that the value represented by a negative index is a negative number. Emphasise that a negative index represents a number that needs to have a reciprocal formed.

Probing questions

- Can you 'prove' to yourself that a negative index will result in the reciprocal of that number?

Literacy focus

- Key terms: There are no new key terms in this section.
- Ask students to refer back to the chart they made in Section 14.2 showing examples of powers (indices) and the rules for multiplying and dividing powers. Suggest students add some more 'rules' and 'facts' to the chart.

Part 1

- Remind students of the rules covered so far, as these can be used to explain the workings of the rules students will meet in this section.
- Present students with a range of expressions to evaluate. They should require them to multiply and divide by integer powers and include division problems that result in a negative index number.

Part 2

- Introduce the central concept that $x^{-a} = \dfrac{1}{x^a}$.
- Consider the questions in Example 5 carefully and work through it with the class.
- **Students can now do Exercise 16C from the Student Book.**

| N 1–6 | Calculator n/a | CM n/a | MR 8, 9 | PS 7, 10 | EV n/a |

Indices of the form $\frac{1}{n}$

- Ask students for the value of $\sqrt{5} \times \sqrt{5}$ (5).
- Repeat for other numbers, e.g. $\sqrt{6} \times \sqrt{6}$ (6). Then generalise: $\sqrt{x} \times \sqrt{x}$ (x).
- Now write $x^{\frac{1}{2}} \times x^{\frac{1}{2}}$ and remind students of the rules for multiplying indices (x^1 or x).
- Write these expressions, aligning those in the second row under those in the top row.

$$\sqrt{x} \times \sqrt{x} = x$$
$$x^{\frac{1}{2}} \times x^{\frac{1}{2}} = x$$

- Ask: What does this tell you? ($x^{\frac{1}{2}} = \sqrt{x}$)
- Repeat, using cube roots and the power $\frac{1}{3}$, in order to establish that $x^{\frac{1}{3}} = \sqrt[3]{x}$.
- **Students can now do Exercise 16D from the Student Book.**

| N 1–3 | Calculator n/a | CM 5 | MR 4 | PS 6 | EV n/a |

Indices of the form $\frac{a}{b}$

- Work carefully through Example 6 from the Student Book, explaining the significance of each part of the power. Work through each of the four steps looking at each part of the power in turn.
- Tell students that showing their working is important as, in examinations, credit is given for showing understanding of each step.
- **Students can now do Exercise 16E from the Student Book.**

| N 1–6 | Calculator n/a | CM 8 | MR 7 | PS 9 | EV n/a |

Part 3

- Ask students to write numbers to a power so that the value of every term is 4.
- **Less able** students will need examples to help them start, e.g. $2^2, 8^{\frac{2}{3}}, \left(\dfrac{1}{2}\right)^{-2}$
- Compile a list of answers.
- Repeat for numbers written to powers that equal 9.

Section 16.4 Surds

Learning objectives
- Simplify surds
- Calculate and manipulate surds, including rationalising a denominator

Resources and homework
- Student Book 16.4: pages 447–452
- Practice Book 16.4: pages 147–149

Making mathematical connections
- Equations, expressions identities and functions
- Working with powers (indices) and roots

Making cross-curricular connections
- **Science** – using formulae
- **Relevance** – developing logical thinking

Prior learning
- Students need to know the square numbers, be able to identify factors and know how to expand brackets.

Working mathematically
- Students need to take care with notation and make sure that they annotate the steps they are taking. This will help to reduce the common errors described below.

Common misconceptions and remediation
- Students may forget to simplify surds that have a square number as a factor, e.g. either leaving $\sqrt{24}$ unsimplified or simplifying to $4\sqrt{6}$ instead of $2\sqrt{6}$. Encourage students to write intermediate steps, e.g. $\sqrt{4} \times \sqrt{6}$. Also encourage students to square the unsimplified and simplified expressions to check that they are the same.

Probing questions
- Which method is best for finding composite functions in simple cases? Does it change if one function has more operations? If the second (last) function has more than one x?

Literacy focus
- Key terms: exact value, rationalise, surd
- Ask students to create a table like the one on page 447 of the Student Book listing the four general rules. They should list two of their own examples for each rule: one in terms of x, and one with numbers that can be evaluated.

Part 1
- Ask the class these quickfire questions:
  $\sqrt{100}$ (10) $\sqrt{4}$ (2)
  $\sqrt{100} \times \sqrt{100}$ (100) $\sqrt{4} \times \sqrt{4}$ (4) $\sqrt{7} \times \sqrt{7}$ (7)
- Ask students to break these numbers into a factor multiplied by a square number:
  98 (2×49)   75 (3×25)   200 (2×100)   112 (7×16)
- Now write on the board: $\sqrt{12} = 3.464\ldots$ and $\sqrt{3} = 1.732\ldots$
- Ask students if they can see a link. ($\sqrt{12} = 2\sqrt{3}$)

Part 2

- Tell students that the first step when working with surds is to simplify where possible.
- Work through the examples in the table on page 447 of the Student Book.
- Now ask students if they can identify any square numbers that are factors of 12 (4).
- Write: $\sqrt{12} = \sqrt{4} \times \sqrt{3}$
  $= 2\sqrt{3}$
- Repeat with other examples: $\sqrt{8}$ ($2\sqrt{2}$), $\sqrt{18}$ ($3\sqrt{2}$), $\sqrt{24}$ ($2\sqrt{6}$), $\sqrt{40}$ ($2\sqrt{10}$), $\sqrt{28}$ ($2\sqrt{7}$), $\sqrt{48}$ ($4\sqrt{3}$), $\sqrt{54}$ ($3\sqrt{6}$)
- Now ask students to compare these three examples.
  - $\sqrt{2} \times \sqrt{2}$ (= 2, whole-number answer)
  - $\sqrt{2} \times \sqrt{3}$ (= $\sqrt{6}$, a surd answer)
  - $\sqrt{2} \times \sqrt{6}$ (= $\sqrt{12}$, so will simplify)
- Show that the last example can be split into $\sqrt{2} \times \sqrt{2} \times \sqrt{3}$, giving $2\sqrt{3}$.
- Show students a division and encourage them to write these in fraction form, for example:

$$\sqrt{6} \div \sqrt{2} = \frac{\sqrt{6}}{\sqrt{2}} = \sqrt{3}$$

- Students have now looked at all the basic ways of simplifying surds.
- Display a more complex question, for example: $3\sqrt{20} \times 4\sqrt{12} \div 2\sqrt{15}$
- Work through this showing each step. (360)
- **Students can now do Exercise 16F from the Student Book. Less able** students need support.

| N 1–11, 13 | Calculator n/a | CM n/a | MR n/a | PS 12, 15, 16 | EV 14 |

Calculating with surds

- Use Examples 7 and 8 from the Student Book to demonstrate how surds feature in solving problems.
- You may need to remind students about how Pythagoras' theorem works (Section 11.1).

Rationalising a denominator

- Tell students that a surd is an irrational number and it is not good practice to write a fraction with an irrational number in the denominator.
- Explain that the process of removing a surd from the denominator of a fraction is called rationalising the denominator.
- Work through Example 9 to demonstrate the process. Encourage the use of the alternative method for part **b** as it reinforces the idea of simplifying surds when possible.
- **Students can now do Exercise 16G from the Student Book.** Support **less able** students as needed.

| N 1–7, 14 | Calculator n/a | CM 11, 12 | MR 8, 9 | PS 10, 13 | EV n/a |

Part 3

- Use this section to look at approximate values of square roots, for example, ask for two consecutive numbers between which each of the following square roots lie:
  $\sqrt{6}$, $\sqrt{60}$, $\sqrt{90}$, $\sqrt{65}$, $\sqrt{130}$
- Challenge **more able** students with larger numbers.

Section 16.5 Limits of accuracy

Learning objectives
*   Find the error interval or limits of accuracy of numbers that have been rounded to different degrees of accuracy

Resources and homework
*   Student Book 16.5: pages 452–455
*   Practice Book 16.5: pages 149–150

Making mathematical connections
*   Rounding

Making cross-curricular connections
*   **Business** – cost effectiveness/efficiency
*   **Relevance** – applications in manufacturing and project management

Prior learning
*   Students should be familiar with rounding to the nearest 1, 10, 100… and to a given number of decimal places or significant figures.
*   Students should also know the difference between discrete and continuous data.

Working mathematically
*   Student should be comfortable with the distinction between discrete and continuous data and be able to demonstrate this by using the correct symbols for inequality.

Common misconceptions and remediation
*   Students often give an incorrect upper bound, for example, saying that the upper bound of 22 cm is 22.49 cm or 22.4 cm (rather than $22.4\dot{9}$ or 22.5 cm). Minimise this error by pointing it out to students every time it occurs.

Probing questions
*   A farmer has 870 sheep (s), counted to the nearest 10. Explain why the limits of s cannot be $865 \le s \le 875$.

Literacy focus
*   Key terms: error interval, limits of accuracy, lower bound, upper bound
*   Ask students to describe the difference between discrete data and continuous data and how the limits of accuracy differ between these data types.

Part 1
*   Give students a number such as: 6513.9604
*   Ask them to round it to the nearest 1000, 100, 10, 1, 1 dp, 2 dp, 3 dp, 1 sf, 2 sf, 3 sf, 4 sf, as a check of their prior knowledge. (7000, 6500, 6510, 6514, 6514.0, 6513.96, 6513.960, 7000, 6500, 6510, 6514)
*   Repeat with other numbers such as 9178.276 and 999.99
*   Check that students know the difference between discrete data and continuous data.
*

Part 2
Discrete data
*   Work through Example 10 in the Student Book, ensuring that students fully understand the concept and the use of the inequality symbols.
*   Say: To the nearest 10, there are 30 students in the next room. How many people could be in the room? (25 to 34 inclusive)

- Ask students to clarify why it could not be 35 students ($25 \le$ number of people ≤ 34, it could not be 35 students because 35 rounds to 40). Check that all students have used the inequality symbols correctly.
- For **less able** students, illustrate the answer using a number line. Point out that, as the data is discrete, only the whole numbers are considered – you cannot have 25.3 people.

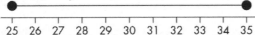

- Now ask students to think of other quantities that are discrete data, e.g. money, number of letters in the post or shoe size.
- Ask a question about money, such as: I have £5 to the nearest pound. What is the most I could have? (£5.49)

Continuous data

- Ask students how far it is to a nearby town. Pick out an answer, for example 8 miles, and ask if it this is the exact amount. Tell students to assume that the distance is measured to the nearest mile, and to suggest the minimum distance and maximum distance it could be.
- Show the information on a number line. Discuss the open (excluding) and closed (including) circles.

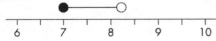

A mathematical peculiarity

- Use the example above to explain how the upper bound would actually round to the next value (in this case 9 miles). Point out that they do not always have to use recurring decimals, although these are correct (in this case $8.4\dot{9}$ miles). (This peculiarity has already been discussed in Part 3 of Section 16.1.)
- Work through Examples 11, 12 and 13.
- **Students can now do Exercise 16H from the Student Book. Less able** could work in pairs from question 2.

N 1–3, 6, 7	Calculator n/a	CM n/a	MR 9	PS 4, 8	EV 5

Part 3

- Prepare students for the next lesson by introducing the idea of multiple items (see Question 7 of Exercise 16H). Discuss what would really happen with the marbles. (Some would weigh more than 65 g and some would weigh less than 65 g.)
- Ask what the biggest possible difference between the masses of any two of the marbles could be. (65.5 g – 64.5 g = 1 g)

Learning objectives

- Combine limits of two or more variables to solve problems

Resources and homework

- Student Book 16.5: pages 455–459
- Practice Book 16.5: pages 150–151

Making mathematical connections

- Rounding
- Percentages
- Area, surface area and volume

Making cross-curricular connections

- **Business** – cost effectiveness/efficiency
- **Relevance** – applications to manufacturing and project management

Prior learning

- Students should be able to write down upper and lower bounds for values to any given degree of accuracy.
- They should know and be able to use basic area and volume formulae, e.g. square, cube.
- Students should also know the formula for calculating percentage error.

Working mathematically

- Students should always work out both the lower bounds and the upper bounds of the given values so that the actual values needed in the calculation can be clearly identified. As students gain confidence and accuracy with these questions, they could begin to identify the required values without doing this.

Common misconceptions and remediation

- Students sometimes use a maximum rather than a minimum value (or vice versa) in subtraction, multiplication or division probems. If students are unsure which bounds to use, encourage them to work out the answers to all combinations and select the correct answer.
- Ask students to copy this table into their books to help them to remember the bounds.

Operation	Minimum	Maximum
Addition ($a + b$)	$a_{min} + b_{min}$	$a_{max} + b_{max}$
Subtraction ($a - b$)	$a_{min} - b_{max}$	$a_{max} - b_{min}$
Multiplication ($a \times b$)	$a_{min} \times b_{min}$	$a_{max} \times b_{max}$
Division ($a \div b$)	$a_{min} \div b_{max}$	$a_{max} \div b_{min}$

- **Less able** students may have difficulty coping with all four rules or even two of the rules, so break down the exercise into smaller, more manageable parts.
- Rather than dealing with the rules straight away, ask students to work out and write down the upper and lower bounds of the values in each questions. (Completing this step will gain credit in examination questions.) You could do this orally instead of Part 1 of this section.

Probing questions

- In question 13 of Exercise 16I, two values are given as being exact and two measurements are given to the nearest 0.1 cm. How can these two values be given exactly?
- Why is it not possible for the other two also to be given exactly?

Literacy focus

- Key terms: There are no new key terms in this section.
- Ask students to describe, with examples, why lower bounds and upper bounds are combined in the eight ways shown in the table. Focus on combinations for division and multiplication.

Part 1

- Tell students: A square tile has a side length of 15 cm to the nearest cm.
  Ask: What are the limits of accuracy? (14.5 cm ≤ length < 15.5 cm)
  Ask: What are the lower and upper bounds? (14.5 cm and 15.5 cm)
- Tell students: Ten of these tiles are in a row.
  Ask: What is the longest possible length? (155 cm)
  Ask: What is the shortest possible length? (145 cm)
- Tell students: I need to make sure I have enough tiles.
  Ask: If the length to be tiled is 3 m, how many tiles do I need for one row? (21)
  Ask: If the length to be tiled is 12 m, how many tiles do I need for one row? (83)
- Ask students why the answer for 12 m is *not* four times the answer for 3 m.
  (300 ÷ 14.5 = 20.7 → 21 tiles, 1200 ÷ 14.5 = 82.8 → 83 tiles)

Part 2

Addition and subtraction

- Show two books or similar objects. Tell the class that each book has a mass of 1700 g to the nearest 100 g. Ask: What is the greatest possible total mass of the books? (3500 g)
  Now ask: What is the greatest difference between the masses? (100 g)
- Work through this section in the Student Book.

Multiplication and division

- Now say that you have a pile of books; there are 30 books (to the nearest 10).
- Ask students how to calculate the maximum possible mass of these books. (34 × 1750 g)
- Repeat for the minimum possible mass of these books. (25 × 1650 g)
- Now say that you are going to work the question backwards. A pile of books has a total mass of 34 kg to the nearest kilogram. Each book weighs 1700 g to the nearest 100 g.
  Ask for the calculation needed to work out the least possible number of books in the pile.
  (33 500 ÷ 1750)
  Ask them to work this out and round appropriately. (19.14, so 20)
- Discuss why it is: minimum mass of pile ÷ maximum mass of each book. If students are not convinced, ask them to use calculators to work out all other possible answers, using upper and lower bounds.
- Repeat for the calculation for the greatest possible number of books in the pile.
  (34 500 ÷ 1650 = 20.91, so 20)
- Repeat for a pile of books with mass 50 kg to show that answers can vary.
  (minimum = 49.5 ÷ 1.75 = 28.3 → 29 books, maximum = 50.5 ÷ 1.65 = 30.6 → 30 books)
- Work through Examples 14 and 15.
- **Students can now do Exercise 16I from the Student Book.**

N 1, 2, 5–8, 11–18	Calculator 5–17, 19	CM n/a	MR 3, 9	PS 4, 10, 19	EV n/a

Part 3

- Write these amounts on the board: 3000 g, 4000 g and 5000 g. Say that each amount is accurate to the nearest 100 g. Ask which of the following are possible total amounts for all three items: 11 500 g 12 050 g   12 500 g   12 600 g   13 000 g (12 050 g)
- Now say that the amounts are accurate to 1 sf. Ask students which of them are possible total amounts for all three items. (All)
- Show **less able** students the calculations to demonstrate the limits of accuracy each time.

Section 16.7 Choices and outcomes

Learning objectives
- Work out the number of choices, arrangements or outcomes when choosing from lists or sets

Resources and homework
- Student Book 16.5: pages 459–466
- Practice Book 16.5: page 152

Making mathematical connections
- Probability

Making cross-curricular connections
- **Sports** – fixture schedules
- **Relevance** – applications to manufacturing and project management, developing logical thinking

Prior learning
- Students should appreciate, from working with probability, that there are a differing number of outcomes depending on circumstances and constraints. The same logic applies here.

Working mathematically
- Encourage students to articulate the reasons for the choices they make; vocalising a solution helps to screen the good ideas from the flawed ideas.

Common misconceptions and remediation
- Students often fail to recognise that the solution has constraints that need to be fulfilled with both product rule counting and systematic counting. Encourage students to think (very quickly) of possible solutions. This should draw attention to any constraints that are built into the question. Highlight this as you work through Example 19.

Probing questions
- The sports department at your school is running a 'Round Robin' tennis competition in which every player has to play every other player. How would you work out how many matches are required to complete the competition?
- What if there were multiple tables for different levels or standards of play?

Literacy focus
- Key terms: combination, factorial, permutation, product rule for counting, systematic counting
- Ask students to create a grid showing all the possible ways of picking out two cards from a choice of five possible cards. (M, A, T, H, S, page 459 of the Student Book; 20 combinations)

Part 1
- Write the numbers 1, 2, 3, 4 on the board. Ask students, in turn, to give you a 3-digit combination made from these numbers. How many combinations can you create? (24) Challenge students to find them all.

Part 2

Permutations; Permutation with repetition; Permutation without repetition

- Work through the text in the Student Book under these headings.
- Make sure students can use the 'factorial' button on their calculators.
- Ask students to find the factorial of a variety of random integers.
- Ask: What is the largest factorial that can be displayed on the calculator display as an ordinary number (as opposed to standard form)? (13 → 6227020800)
- Ensure that students are comfortable (if not confident) with the difference between the two scenarios – allowing an element to be repeated or not.
- Demonstrate how to use the formulae given in the Student Book for permutation with and without repetition by working through an example, such as having a 4-digit numerical code on their tablet (digits 0–9). If all the digits had to be different, there would be

  ($\frac{10!}{(10-4)!}$ = 5040 possible code combinations.

  If digits could be repeated there would be 10^4 = 10 000 possible combinations.
- Ask students to copy the formulae and write their own example for each one to illustrate the difference.
- Help students to locate the **nPr** button on their calculators and check the answers to their own examples using this button.
- Work carefully though Examples 16 and 17 from the Student Book, responding to any queries that the students have.
- Use another example, such as the opening letters and number combinations of UK post codes, which are 1 or 2 letters followed by 1 or 2 numbers (no leading zeros). How many combinations could there be? (66 925 – a terrific number of possibilities, but in reality not all combinations are assigned to a geographical locality)

Combinations

- Work carefully through the text under this heading.
- Introduce and demonstrate the formula for the number of ways of picking items when order does not matter by working through an example, such as: A restaurant has 10 different speciality main course meals in its recipe bank but only five are ever on the menu at one time. If the menu changes every day, how many days will it take before the menu must be repeated? (250days)
- Ask students to copy the formula and write their own example to illustrate.
- Work through Examples 18 and 19 from the Student Book.
- Use as additional example, if required: You have a four-digit code to unlock your smartphone, but you have only a vague memory of what it is. You know that the first digit is 3; the last digit is an even number (not zero); the two middle digits are both different. How many possible combinations might you need to enter to unlock your smartphone? (360)
- Work carefully through Example 20.
- Use this additional example, if required: You have forgotten the password to your tablet. The password is a rearrangement of the letters of your pet tortoise's name, HANNIBAL. How many different combinations of these eight letters are there? (10 080)
- **Students can now do Exercise 16J from the Student Book.**

| N 3, 6–9, 12–17 | Calculator 3 | CM 10, 18 | MR 2, 4, 5 | PS 1, 11, 17b | EV 9d, 16b |

Part 3

- Ask students to work in pairs to devise some of their own problems and solutions.
- Students circulate their problems for other students to solve.

Chapter 17 Algebra: Quadratic equations

Overview

17.1 Plotting quadratic graphs

17.2 Solving quadratic equations by factorisation

17.3 Solving a quadratic equation by using the quadratic formula

17.4 Solving quadratic equations by completing the square

17.5 The significant points of a quadratic curve

17.6 Solving one linear and one non-linear equation using graphs

17.7 Solving quadratic equations by the method of intersection

17.8 Solving linear and non-linear simultaneous equations algebraically

17.9 Quadratic inequalities

Prior learning

Know how to substitute into simple algebraic functions.
Know how to plot a graph from a given table of values.
Know how to draw linear graphs.
Know how to find the equation of a graph.
Know how to collect together like terms.
Know how to multiply together two algebraic expressions.
Know how to solve simple linear equations and inequalities.

Learning objectives

Ensure that students can: draw quadratic graphs; solve quadratic equations by factorisation, the quadratic formula and completing the square; solve problems involving quadratic equations; recognise and find the significant points of a quadratic graph; use graphs to solve a pair of simultaneous equations, one linear and one non-linear; use the method of intersection to solve one quadratic equation, using the graph of another quadratic equation and an appropriate straight line; solve quadratic inequalities.

In the examination, students will be expected to:
- draw and read values from quadratic graphs
- solve a quadratic equation by factorisation
- rearrange a quadratic equation so that it can be factorised
- solve a quadratic equation by using the quadratic formula
- recognise why some quadratic equations cannot be solved
- solve a quadratic equation by completing the square
- identify the significant points of a quadratic function graphically
- identify the roots of a quadratic function by solving a quadratic equation
- identify the turning point of a quadratic function by using symmetry or completing the square
- use graphs to solve a pair of simultaneous equations where one is linear and one is non-linear
- solve equations by the method of intersecting graphs
- solve simultaneous equations where one equation is linear and the other is non-linear
- solve quadratic inequalities.

Extension

Explore the intersection of quadratic graphs with other non-linear graphs such as those involving cubic or reciprocal terms. Solve graphically 2 quadratic simultaneous equations.

Curriculum references

Section	GCSE specification
17.1	A 8, 12
17.2	A 4, 18
17.3	A 18
17.4	A 11, 18
17.5	A 11

Section	GCSE specification
17.6	A 16
17.7	A 18
17.8	A 19
17.9	A 22

Route mapping

Exercise	Accessible	Intermediate	Challenging	AO1	AO2 MR CM	AO3 PS EV	Key questions
17A	1–5	6		1–3, 5	4, 6		3, 6
17B	1	2–5	6–8	1, 2, 4,	8	3, 5–7	2, 6
17C		1–4	5–7	1, 2, 6	3, 5	4, 7	2, 7
17D		1–4	5–7	1, 5	3, 4, 7	2, 6	1, 6
17E			1–5	1	2–4	5	1, 3
17F		1	2–9	1, 3, 4	5–7	2, 8, 9	1, 6
17G			1	1			1a
17H		1–3	4–14	1–6, 9, 10	11, 12	7, 8, 13, 14	1, 11
17I		1	2–5	1	2–4	5	2, 5
17J			1–8	1–4	5–7	8	1, 7
17K		1, 2	3–14	1–5, 8	6, 7, 9, 11	10, 12–14	2, 12
17L		1	2–12	1–6	7, 9, 11, 12	8, 10	3, 10

Key questions are those that demonstrate mastery of the concept, or which require a step-up in understanding or application. Key questions could be used to identify questions that students must tackle to support differentiation, or those that should be teacher-marked rather than student-marked.

About this chapter

Making connections: The chapter brings together a number of concepts and skills, all relating to quadratic equations: plotting, interpreting, solving, combining and solving with other equations. These graphical methods are accompanied by corresponding algebraic methods, to ensure that students revise and practise factorising and algebraic manipulation.

Relevance: There are applications in engineering, architecture, manufacturing, project management and many other areas: STEM careers are a strong focus.

Working mathematically: When working with graphs, can students sketch the graph identifying intercept and turning point, with the approximate location of the roots of the curve *before* actually plotting it? This is an extremely useful skill to have.

Assessment: In each section of this chapter, ensure that students have a good grasp of the key questions in each exercise before moving on. (Refer to the 'Route mapping' table above.) Encourage students to read and think about the 'Ready to progress?' statements on page 504 of the Student Book. Check students' understanding at the end of the chapter, formatively, using peer assessment. Students could do a mini test in the form of the 'Review questions' on pages 504–505 of the Student Book. Follow up the test with an individual target-getting session, based on any areas for development that a student may have.

Worked exemplars from the Student Book– suggestions for use
• Present students with the same question but using different numbers. Students should use the exemplar to mirror the working, in full or only the notes.

Answers to the Student Book questions are available on the CD-ROM provided.

Section 17.1 Plotting quadratic graphs

Learning objectives
- Draw and read values from quadratic graphs

Resources and homework
- Student Book 17.1: pages 471–474
- Practice Book 17.1: page 153

Making mathematical connections
- Working with coordinates in four quadrants
- Substituting into algebraic expressions

Making cross-curricular connections
- **Science** – using formulae
- **Relevance** – developing logical thinking

Prior learning
- Students must be able to substitute into algebraic functions to create a table of values.
- They should also be able to read and plot coordinates, including coordinates from tables of values.

Working mathematically
- Encourage students to create tables of values that have a row for each term in the equation. This enables students to see clearly the components that combine to make y and makes it easier to trace errors when they see that the curve does not have the correct shape.
- In the examination, students will usually be presented with just a row of x-values and a blank row to determine corresponding values for y, but they may add new rows for themselves.

Common misconceptions and remediation
- Students often produce poorly plotted/drawn curves. Remind them that in the GCSE all points should be within small squares on the graph paper, and the curve should also pass within a small square. The curve should be one clear continuous line, with no gaps.
- Students often plot points incorrectly because they have not interpreted the scales on the axes – especially the y-axis – accurately. Encourage students to examine the scale presented and work out the width of one small square before plotting any points.

Probing questions
- What is wrong with connecting the lowest two marked points with a straight line? Why does the equation need space to *turn round*?
- What value for y would you get if you worked out a coordinate using the midpoint value of x between those two points? What does this represent?

Literacy focus
- Key terms: parabola, quadratic
- Ask students to explain how to create a table of values.
- Ask students to describe how to plot a quadratic graph to find the roots of the equation.

Part 1
NB: This section may take more than 1 hour.

- Ask students to draw a set of axes numbered –5 to +5 on the x-axis and 0 to 30 on the y-axis and plot these points:

x	–5	–4	–3	–2	–1	0	1	2	3	4	5
y	25	16	9	4	1	0	1	4	9	16	25

- Ask them to join the points with a smooth curve. Walk around and check students' graphs, pointing out ways to improve them.
- Explain that this is the graph of $y = x^2$, which they should learn to recognise.
- Draw attention to the fact that the curve is a parabola and that it is symmetrical. These facts are true for any quadratic equation.

Part 2

- Explain that a quadratic equation is an equation containing a term in x^2.
- All quadratic graphs have the same basic shape (parabola) and are based on the graph of $y = x^2$ that they drew in Part 1.
- Work through the opening text and Example 1 from the Student Book. Ensure that students are clear about where all the rows in the tables come from and that they are confident about completing them accurately, using a calculator to work out values.
- Make sure students can use the graph to find a y-value for the equivalent x-value, and to find the two equivalent x-values for a y-value.
- Tell students that in examinations:
  - they will be given axes and a range of values for x.
  - they will usually be given a table with the x-values included and a row for the y-values.
  - most values will be filled in so they will probably only need to calculate two or three.

Drawing accurate graphs
- This section covers the common errors or difficulties made or faced by students.
- Read and discuss the information about the four errors and relate it to the errors that students may have made in Part 1. Discuss the suggestion to avoid these errors and generate a smooth, thin, single curve.
- Remind students that they should always label the graph.
- **Students can now do Exercise 17A from the Student Book.**

| A 1–3, 5 | Calculator n/a | CM 6 | MR 4 | PS n/a | EV n/a |

Part 3
- Compare the graphs of $y = x^2$, $y = 0.5x^2$ and $y = -x^2$
- What is the significance of the '+2' for the graphs of $y = x^2$ and $y = x^2 + 2$?
- Can you describe the position of $y = x^2 - 3$?

Section 17.2 Solving quadratic equations by factorisation

Learning objectives
- Solve a quadratic equation by factorisation
- Rearrange a quadratic equation so that it can be factorised

Resources and homework
- Student Book 17.2: pages 474–479
- Practice Book 17.2: pages 154–155

Making mathematical connections
- Rearranging simple formulae
- Solving equations
- Factorising quadratics

Making cross-curricular connections
- **Science** – using formulae
- **Computing** – application of logic
- **Relevance** – application to business, manufacturing and engineering problems

Prior learning
- Students need to be able to factorise a range of quadratic expressions. (*See Exercises 8J–L.*)

Working mathematically
- Encourage students to continue with the systematic methods they started to develop in sections 8.6 and 8.7 for finding the possible combinations of factors and the process of eliminating them.

Common misconceptions and remediation
- Remind students to check that the equation ends in '= 0' and is cancelled as far as possible before they start to factorise.
- Students often give positive solutions as negative, and vice versa. Encourage students to write out the options before writing down the final solution, e.g. for $(x + 2)(x - 3) = 0$, write $x + 2 = 0$ or $x - 3 = 0$ and then write $x = -2$ or $x = 3$.
- Students often get the signs wrong when solving linear equations. Go through more worked examples if this persists.

Probing questions
- How might you solve $x^4 - x^2 - 6 = 0$? Look to solve this by factorising: $(x^2 \ldots)(x^2 \ldots) = 0$. Then solve for x.
- Solve $4x^4 + 14x^2 + 12 = 0$.

Literacy focus
- Key terms: There are no new key terms in this section.
- Ask students to describe and then record the process of: factorising a quadratic into two brackets that are equal to zero and using this to find values for x.

Part 1
- Write on the board: $a \times b = 0$. Ask students for pairs of values of a and b that make it true. List these as coordinate pairs, e.g. (0, 7), (–6, 0), (0, 0), (2.3, 0).
- Now write on the board: $x(x - 1) = 0$. Ask for values of x that make it true.
- The students may feel that a coordinate pair of answers is necessary, but in fact there are only two possible answers: 0 and 1.

- Demonstrate this if necessary: $0 \times (0 - 1) = 0 \times -1 = 0$, or $1 \times (1 - 1) = 1 \times 0 = 0$
- Now ask what values make $(x + 3)(x - 2) = 0$ true. (– 3 or 2)
- Repeat with similar examples if necessary, emphasising that one of the brackets must equal 0 for the result to be 0.

Part 2

Solving the quadratic equation $x^2 + ax + b = 0$

- If students have mastered factorisation, then solving quadratics is a straightforward step up.
- Work through Examples 2, 3 and 4 from the Student Book, drawing attention to the fact that, in certain contexts such as length or mass, a negative result can be rejected.
- Highlight the need to set up the equations in Example 4.
- **Students can now do Exercise 17B from the Student Book.**

| A 1, 2, 4 | Calculator n/a | CM n/a | MR 8 | PS 3, 6, 7 | EV 5 |

Solving the general quadratic equation by factorisation

- Again, this is not a big step providing students can factorise expressions. The main errors occur when solving equations with negative signs, so pay special attention to this as you work through the examples.
- Work through Example 5 and Example 6, noting the simplifying tactic in Example 5, part b.

Special cases

- Remind students that not all equations that have a term ax^2 will need to be solved by factorising into two pairs of brackets. They should look carefully at the terms that are in the equation. If either b or c is zero (or null or missing), they can solve by rearranging or factorising using only one pair of brackets.
- Remind them that if a is zero, the equation is linear and not quadratic.
- Work carefully through Example 7 from the Student Book.
- **Students can now do Exercise 17C from the Student Book.**

| A 1, 2, 6 | Calculator n/a | CM n/a | MR 3, 5 | PS 4, 7 | EV n/a |

Part 3

- Ask students to solve the equation $(x + 2)^2 - 9 = 0$ and work through the process:
  $(x + 2)^2 - 9 = 0$
  $(x + 2)^2 = 9$
  $x + 2 = 3$ or $x + 2 = -3$
  $x = 1$ or $x = -5$
- Now ask students to solve: $x^2 + 4x - 5 = 0$
  $(x - 1)(x + 5) = 0$
  $x = 1$ or -5
- Write on the board: $(x + 2)^2 - 9 = x^2 + 4x - 5$
- Ask students if $(2x + 3)^2 + 4 = 0$ and $4x^2 + 12x = 5$ can be similarly equated. (no)
- Remind students to justify their answers by showing their working.

Section 17.3 Solving a quadratic equation by using the quadratic formula

Learning objectives

- Solve a quadratic equation by using the quadratic formula
- Recognise why some quadratic equations cannot be solved

Resources and homework

- Student Book 17.3: pages 480–483
- Practice Book 17.3: pages 155–156

Making mathematical connections

- Rearranging simple formulae
- Solving equations

Making cross-curricular connections

- **Science** – using formulae
- **Relevance** – application to business, manufacturing and engineering problems

Prior learning

- Students must be able to substitute into formulae, understand the implications of the ± sign, and have good calculator skills.

Working mathematically

- Encourage students to work methodically through these calculations, writing down each stage. This should remove the temptation to enter the whole calculation into the calculator at once. This is, essentially, a problem involving substitution, so it is important that students substitute the three values of a, b and c into the formula before they start to simplify.

Common misconceptions and remediation

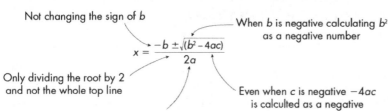

- Provide students with plenty of practice, pointing out errors as they occur.
- Encourage working in stages or using brackets. Entering the whole calculation into a calculator is the source of many errors.

Probing questions

- Describe what a *discriminant* is. What does it do, or tell you? What does its value tell you?

Literacy focus

- Key terms: quadratic formula, soluble, discriminant
- Ask students to create a chart similar to one above Example 10 on page 482 of the Student Book (three equation types and an explanation of relevance of the discriminant value).

Part 1

- Ask students to use their calculators to work out these problems in turn. If students write down answers, ask for at least 4 dp. Check the answers at each stage.

$$\frac{-3 + 2.5}{4} \ (-0.125) \qquad \frac{-3 - 2.5}{4} \ (-1.375) \qquad \frac{-3 + \sqrt{65}}{4} \ (1.2655...) \qquad \frac{-3 - \sqrt{65}}{4} \ (-2.7655...)$$

- Revise brackets until all students can calculate the above correctly. There are many types of calculators, so it may help to pair students with the same calculators to work together. **Less able** students can work with **more able** students.

Part 2

- Show students the diagram above ('Common misconceptions and remediation') and explain that it shows common causes of errors. Suggest they copy into their books (or photocopy it for them to stick in) and use it to identify where they went wrong if they make an error.
- Remind students that if they show the stages of working they can still gain some method marks, even when they make an error.
- Work through Examples 8 and 9. Make sure that all students set up the equations correctly, arrive at the correct answers and can use their calculators correctly.
- Demonstrate the solution of $x^2 + 5x + 6 = 0$ using the quadratic formula.
  Identify: $a = 1$, $b = 5$ and $c = 6$
  Substitute these values into the formula using brackets around each term:
  $$x = \frac{-(5) \pm \sqrt{(5)^2 - 4(1)(6)}}{2(1)}$$
  (This will give them a method mark in the examination.)
  Work out the square root and tidy up the terms and brackets:
  $$x = \frac{-(5) \pm \sqrt{1}}{2}$$
  Evaluate both answers, ensuring that students understand there are two solutions:
  $$x = -2 \text{ or } -3$$
- Compare this to the answer obtained by factorising: $x^2 + 5x + 6 = 0$
  $$(x + 2)(x + 3) = 0$$
  $$x = -2 \text{ or } -3$$

  Say that you would usually solve this equation by factorising rather than using the formula.
- Demonstrate the solution of $2x^2 - 7x - 3 = 0$ using the quadratic formula:
  $a = 2$, $b = -7$ and $c = -3$; $x = \dfrac{-(-7) \pm \sqrt{(-7)^2 - 4(2)(-3)}}{2(2)}$; $x = \dfrac{7 \pm \sqrt{73}}{4}$; $x = 3.89$ or -0.39

- Tell students that the denominator divides the whole top line and not just the square root.
- You may wish to explain to **more able** students that modern calculators will evaluate this without the intermediate step. Encourage **less able** students to do the calculation in steps and to be careful with minus signs.
- **Students can now do Exercise 17D from the Student Book.**

| A 1, 5 | Calculator all | CM 4 | MR 3, 7 | PS 2, 6 | EV n/a |

Quadratic equations with no solution
- Look at the three diagrams in the Student Book and read the accompanying descriptions.
- Explain that having a solution means having a value for x when $y = 0$.
- The equation shown in the graph on the right will not have a solution because the parabola does not cross the x-axis. Explain that this would also be true if the coefficient of a was negative, because the maximum point of the curve would then be under the x-axis.
- Discuss Examples 10 and 11 to remind students how to calculate the *discriminant*.
- **Students can now do Exercise 17E from the Student Book.**

| A 1 | Calculator all | CM n/a | MR 2–4 | PS n/a | EV 5 |

Part 3

- Solve $x^2 + 2x + 1 = 0$ using the quadratic formula ($x = -1$).
- Ask students if they can explain why there is only one solution.
- Look at the factorisation: $(x + 1)^2 = 0$.
- Ask students to create a quadratic equation that has no solution.

Section 17.4 Solving quadratic equations by completing the square

Learning objectives

- solve a quadratic equation by completing the square

Resources and homework

- Student Book 17.4: pages 483–486
- Practice Book 17.4: page 156

Making mathematical connections

- Rearranging simple formulae
- Solving equations
- Working with surds, square roots

Making cross-curricular connections

- **Science** – using formulae
- **Relevance** – application to business, manufacturing and engineering problems

Prior learning

- Students should be able to factorise quadratic expressions.
- They should also be able to recognise and use the difference of two squares.

Working mathematically

- Encourage students to work towards a solution systematically, following the required steps.

Common misconceptions and remediation

- Students may forget to subtract a^2 or forget to take the negative square root. Practice and more worked examples should help to reduce these problems.

Probing questions

- Give an example of a quadratic equation best solved by: factorising; using the quadratic formula; completing the square. Why is this method most suitable?

Literacy focus

- Key term: completing the square
- In pairs: One student describes the process of solving $x^2 - 4x = 3$, the other follows the instructions. Do the instructions result in the correct solution? (−0.65, 4.65)

Part 1

- Ask students to:
  - Factorise: $x^2 - 4$ $[(x - 2)(x + 2)]$
  - Expand: $(x - 2)^2$ $[x^2 - 4x + 4]$
  - Expand and simplify: $(x + 2)^2 - 2^2$ $[x^2 + 4x]$
  - Expand and simplify: $(x + 3)^2 - 3^2$ $[x^2 + 6x]$
  - Guess: $(x + 5)^2 - 5^2$ $[x^2 + 10x]$

Part 2

- The main problem is getting students to link the x^2 and x terms with the $(x + a)^2 - b$.
- Explore this in depth with **less able** students as this is the starting point of the process.
  $(x + a)^2 = x^2 + 2ax + a^2$
  Therefore, $x^2 + 2ax = (x + a)^2 - a^2$
  If necessary, work through multiple examples of the type $x^2 + 6x = \ldots$
- Work through Example 12 from the Student Book.
- It may be helpful to work though question 1 with **less able** students at this point.

- The next step is to add a constant term: $x^2 + 2ax - b = (x + a)^2 - a^2 - b$
- Demonstrate this by working through Example 13, emphasising the steps that are being taken to complete the process.
- Work through additional examples until students are confident with the steps in the process.
- Work through Example 14. Ensure that students are confident about leaving an answer in surd form rather than evaluating to a particular degree of accuracy.
- **Students can now do Exercise 17F from the Student Book.**

| A 1, 3, 4 | Calculator all | CM 5, 7 | MR 6 | PS 2, 9 | EV 8 |

Part 3

- Review the steps involved in solving a quadratic equation by completing the square.
- Complete the activity outlined in 'Literary focus' or a similar activity with a different equation if the students have already done this.

Section 17.5 The significant points of a quadratic curve

Learning objectives

- Identify the significant points of a quadratic function graphically
- Identify the roots of a quadratic function by solving a quadratic equation
- Identify the turning point of a quadratic function by using symmetry or completing the square

Resources and homework

- Student Book 17.5: pages 487–491
- Practice Book 17.5: pages 157–158

Making mathematical connections

- Solving equations
- Symmetry
- Working with coordinates in four quadrants

Making cross-curricular connections

- **Science** – using formulae
- **Relevance** – application to business, manufacturing and engineering problems

Prior learning

- Students should know how to solve a quadratic equation by completing the square.
- They should also be familiar with line symmetry and be able to draw quadratic graphs.

Working mathematically

- Building on the skills used in Section 17.1, encourage students to look for symmetry in quadratic graphs. They should check their table of values when symmetry is not evident.
- Encourage students to sketch the parabola and mark significant points before they plot accurately.

Common misconceptions and remediation

- Reinforce the importance of using a ruler to draw axes and a sharp pencil for all mathematical drawing.
- Students frequently misread y-values. Remind them to look vertically (up the graph) to read the value. Conversely, remind them that to look horizontally (along the graph) to read the x-value.
- To distinguish between the two axes, encourage students to think of x as a cross, so you look across to get the value.

Probing questions

- Is it possible to tell from the turning point of a quadratic equation whether the equation has a solution? How can you decide this? How would you describe this to someone?

Literacy focus

- Key terms: maximum, minimum, roots, turning point
  Ask students to write one- or two-sentence definitions of each of the points A, B, C and D shown in the two graphs immediately above Exercise 17H.

Part 1

- Sketch a linear graph on the board, as shown.
- Ask for a possible equation for this line, e.g. $y = 2x + 1$.
- Ask what points we might be interested in as mathematicians (the two points where the line crosses the axes).
- Discuss how to find these points for the equation provided and then work them out. [For $y = 2x + 1$ these are $(0, 1)$ and $(-0.5, 0)$] The intersection of the y-axis is the constant term.
- The intersection on the x-axis occurs when y (in this case $2x + 1$) = 0.

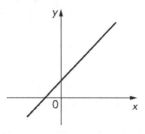

Part 2

Do not allow students to open their textbooks for the start of this work.
- Draw a quadratic curve on the board, as shown, and ask what points would be of interest to mathematicians.
- Students will suggest the points where the graph crosses the axes. If they do not suggest the 'vertex', encourage them by saying there is another point.
- **Work through part i ($y = x^2 - 4x - 5$) of question 1, Exercise 17G.**
- Ensure that students can complete all parts: plot the graph accurately and find the y- intercept, the roots and the turning point and make interpretive comments.
- **Students can now complete Exercise 17G from the Student Book.**

A 1	Calculator n/a	CM n/a	MR n/a	PS n/a	EV n/a

The roots; The y-intercept; The turning point
- Work through Examples 15 and 16 from the Student Book, highlighting the methods used to solve the equations.
- **Students can now do Exercise 17H from the Student Book.** Support **less able** students with questions 3–6 by suggesting they refer back to Examples 15 and 16. For questions 7 onwards, these students could work in pairs.

A 1–6, 9, 10	Calculator n/a	CM n/a	MR 11, 12	PS 8, 13, 14	EV 7

Part 3

- Display a range of quadratic equations. For each equation ask individual students questions such as:
  - Is the parabola inverted?
  - What is the y-intercept?
  - What are the roots?
  - Does the equation have a solution?
  - What is the coordinate of the turning point?
  - What is its line of symmetry?

Section 17.6 Solving one linear and one non-linear equation using graphs

Learning objectives

- Solve a pair of simultaneous equations where one is linear and one is non-linear, using graphs

Resources and homework

- Student Book 17.5: pages 492–494
- Practice Book 17.5: page 158

Making mathematical connections

- Plotting quadratic equations
- Plotting linear equations
- Solving simultaneous equations by graph

Making cross-curricular connections

- **Science** – using formulae
- **Relevance** – application to business, manufacturing and engineering problems

Prior learning

- Students should be able to draw linear and quadratic graphs.

Working mathematically

- Students make the connection between the point(s) where a linear and quadratic graph cross and the solutions to the pair of simultaneous equations.
- Students recognise that, in most cases, there will be two solutions and check their working carefully when this is not the result.

Common misconceptions and remediation

- Students often miscalculate values and/or plot points incorrectly.
- In many cases they give only the x-values as opposed to both the x- and y-values.
- Work through lots of examples in which these errors frequently occur.

Probing questions

- In what situations will there be only one solution?
- In what situations will there be no solutions?

Literacy focus

- Key terms: linear, non-linear
- Ask students to write a bulleted list of the main steps that should be followed to find solutions to questions 1g and h of Exercise 17I.
-

Part 1

- Write the equations $x^2 + y^2 = 25$ and $y = x + 7$ on the board and ask students to recall the methods for solving them.
- Work through the steps:
  - Substitute the linear equation into the non-linear equation: $x^2 + (x + 7)^2 = 25$
  - Expand the bracket: $x^2 + x^2 + 14x + 49 = 25$
  - Rearrange into the standard quadratic: $2x^2 + 14x + 24 = 0$
  - Cancel by a factor of 2: $x^2 + 7x + 12 = 0$
  - Factorise: $(x + 3)(x + 4) = 0$
  - Solve: $x = -3$ or -4
  - Substitute to find y: when $x = -3$, $y = 4$ and when $x = -4$, $x = 3$
  - Hence the solutions are $(-3, 4)$ or $(-4, 3)$.

Part 2

- Say that this lesson is about solving problems like the one in Part 1 by graphical as opposed to algebraic means.
- Work through the text and Example 17.
- Work through the graphical solution of the two equations in Part 1 ($x^2 + y^2 = 25$ and $y = x + 7$).
- Most students will be able to plot the graphs and read the points of intersection.
- All students, in particular **less able** students, will benefit from having pre-prepared grids.
- **Students can now do Exercise 17I from the Student Book.**

A 1	Calculator n/a	CM 2–4	MR n/a	PS 5	EV n/a

Part 3

- Recall the use of the discriminant ($b^2 - 4ac$) in the latter questions of the exercise. This still provides information about the solution to the combined equations.
- What does using the discriminant in this way tell us about the intersections of the graphs?

Section 17.7 Solving quadratic equations by the method of intersection

Learning objectives
- Solve equations by the method of intersecting graphs

Resources and homework
- Student Book 17.5: pages 494–498
- Practice Book 17.5: pages 159–160

Making mathematical connections
- Plotting quadratic equations
- Plotting linear equations
- Solving simultaneous equations by graph

Making cross-curricular connections
- **Science** – using formulae
- **Relevance** – application to business, manufacturing and engineering problems

Prior learning
- Students should be able to draw linear graphs and quadratic graphs.
- Students should be confident subtracting with negative numbers.

Working mathematically
- Ensure that students are comfortable with plotting quadratic and linear equations.
- Students should also be able to subtract equations, in the same way they would to solve simultaneous equations by elimination.

Common misconceptions and remediation
- Students often make errors with signs because they do not show their method of subtraction clearly. Students also make errors with directed numbers when subtracting equations. Provide plenty of practice with this.

Probing questions
- Ask students to produce a 'proof' of the solution for question 4, Exercise 17J. Prompt them to follow the logic demonstrated on pages 493–494 of the Student Book.

Literacy focus
- Key terms: There are no new key terms in this section.
- Ask students to take one part of question 5, Exercise 17J and describe to a partner how they arrived at their solution.

Part 1
- Ask a variety of directed number subtraction problems, for example:
  $5 - 8 (-3)$ $6 - -2 (8)$ $1 - -3 (4)$ $-2 - 1 (-3)$
- Continue until students are competent with this type of simple subtraction problem.

Part 2
- Tell students that this lesson is about solving a quadratic equation by using the graph of another quadratic equation and a straight line.
- Work through the opening text as far as Example 18. This can be a difficult concept, especially for **less able** students, so encourage students to solve the quadratic equation ($x^2 + 3x - 2 = 0$), to prove that the method works.
- Work through Example 18. Again, solve the quadratic equation, if necessary, to prove the method.

- Access to graphing software is useful to support this topic.
- Repetition of the process will gradually make the concept clearer, so let students practise multiple questions similar to question 6, Exercise 17J.
- There is mutual benefit to pairing **less able** and **more able** students in this topic, as more able students will benefit from explaining the process.
- **Students can now do Exercise 17J from the Student Book.**

A 1–4	Calculator n/a	CM n/a	MR 5–7	PS n/a	EV 8

Part 3

- Ask students, in pairs, to create a problem similar to that of question 4 in Exercise 17J, and to present the solution to the class.

Section 17.8 Solving linear and non-linear simultaneous equations algebraically

Learning objectives

- Solve simultaneous equations where one equation is linear and the other is non-linear

Resources and homework

- Student Book 17.5: pages 498–500
- Practice Book 17.5: pages 160–161

Making mathematical connections

- Solving simultaneous equations by substitution
- Rearranging equations

Making cross-curricular connections

- **Science** – using formulae
- **Relevance** – application to business, manufacturing and engineering problems

Prior learning

- Students should be able to solve linear simultaneous equations by substitution.
- They should also be confident in algebraic manipulation.

Working mathematically

- Students should annotate the equations that they are working with so that they (and others) can easily follow their method.

Common misconceptions and remediation

- Errors may occur in any of the steps outlined.
- Mistakes are commonly made when expanding brackets, collecting like terms or factorising the equation.
- Students sometimes fail to finish a solution as soon as two values for one of the variables has been found, confusing these for the x- and y-values of the solution, rather than going on to find the other half for each.
- Remind students frequently that because one equation is non-linear (parabola or circle), they need to supply two (x, y) solutions.

Probing questions

- Do the equations $y^2 + x^2 = 9$ and $y = x + 5$ intersect? How can you tell?
- Can you extend the skills learnt to find the points of intersection of $y^2 + x^2 = 9$ and $y^2 + (x - 2)^2 = 9$? ($x = 1, y = 2.8$ and $x = 1, y = -2.8$)

Literacy focus

- Key terms: There are no new key terms in this section.
- Ask students to choose one of the pairs of equations (one linear, one non-linear) that they used to solve any part of question 2, Exercise 17J and fully explain the solution algebraically. Refer them to the solution of $x^2 + y^2 = 5$ and $x + y = 3$ shown at the start of this section in the Student Book.

Part 1

- Ask students to solve the simultaneous equations $2x + 3y = 7$ and $y = 6x - 6$.
- If necessary, remind them of the substitution method.
  $2x + 3(6x - 6) = 7$; $2x + 18x - 18 = 7$; $20x = 25$; $x = 1.25, y = 1.5$
- Make sure that students are confident with the algebraic skills required (substitution, expansion, solving linear equations).

Part 2

- Remind students that they have already learned how to solve a pair of linear simultaneous equations. Say that this lesson will show them how to solve a pair of simultaneous equations where one is linear and the other is non-linear.
- Remind students that a linear equation represents a straight line and that a non-linear equation represents a curve.
- Students will need to be confident with substitution (see Part 1) as this is the first part of the method.
- **Less able** students may find this high-level topic difficult. Good algebra skills are required to accurately solve these simultaneous equations.
- Encourage **less able** students to practise the three steps (listed below) in isolation.
  - **Step 1:** Substitute the linear equation into the non-linear equation. Expand squared bracketed terms accurately.
  - **Step 2:** Rearrange the expanded expression into a general quadratic form.
  - **Step 3:** Solve the equations and find the equivalent x- or y-values to give a pair (x, y) of solutions.

  Ultimately, however, what makes this a high-level topic is that they need to put the three steps together to work out a complete solution.
- Work carefully through the solution of $x^2 + y^2 = 5$ and $x + y = 3$ shown in the Student Book. Make sure that students can identify these three steps as the solution gradually emerges.
- In examination questions on this topic, the curve will be a standard parabola (a general quadratic equation) or a circle centred on the origin.
- **Students can now do Exercise 17K from the Student Book.**

| A 1–5, 8 | Calculator all | CM 6, 7 | MR 9, 11 | PS 10, 12–14 | EV n/a |

Part 3

- On the board, write $y - 3x = 5$, $x^2 + y^2 = 5$.
- Talk through the process required to solve this pair of simultaneous equations.
  - Rearrange the linear equation to get $y = 5 + 3x$.
  - Substitute into the non-linear equation to get $10x^2 + 30x + 20 = 0$.
  - Cancel by 10 to get $x^2 + 3x + 2 = 0$.
  - Factorise and solve to get $x = -1$ and $x = -2$.
  - Substitute back to get y. $(-1, 2)$ and $(-2, -1)$

Section 17.9 Quadratic inequalities

Learning objectives
- Solve quadratic inequalities

Resources and homework
- Student Book 17.5: pages 501–503
- Practice Book 17.5: pages 161

Making mathematical connections
- Linear inequalities
- Roots of a quadratic equation
- Set notation

Making cross-curricular connections
- **Business** – optimisation of resources
- **Relevance** – applications to manufacturing and project management

Prior learning
- Students should understand the notation used to represent linear inequalities on a number line.
- Students should also be able to solve quadratic equations to find their roots confidently.

Working mathematically
- Encourage students to think of *critical values*, that is the roots of the quadratic equation and the key to answering these kinds of questions.
- Students need to practise the skill of sketching a quadratic graph using the roots – they do not need the other significant points (intercept and turning point).

Common misconceptions and remediation
- Students often do not recognise that the solution to the problem is two sets of data and not just one. This might be because they assume the roots are the lower and upper limits of the solution set. Encourage students to sketch the graph and then reread the question – referring to the sketch they have drawn – in order to establish what part(s) of the *x*-axis fulfils the criteria given.

Probing questions
- A quadratic equation could have, as its root, a value of zero. What inequality might result in this equation not having a solution set?

Literacy focus
- Key terms: critical values, quadratic inequality
- Ask students to describe how a quadratic inequality differs from a linear inequality.

Part 1
- Write these on the board: $2 < 3x - 1 \leq 14$ and $16 \leq 3x + 4 < 22$
- Ask students to write down all the integer values for x in each case {2, 3, 4, 5} and {3, 4, 5}.
- Which values appear in both lists? {3, 4, 5}
- Ask students to draw both these solution sets on a single number line. This will give them a visual indication of the overlap.

Part 2
- Work through Example 19 from the Student Book. Students will already be familiar with tables of values and so the challenge here is interpretation. Explain the answers to **ii** and **iii** so that all students understand them.

- Work through Example 20. This is a good visual illustration of quadratic inequalities.
- **Students can do questions 1 to 6 of Exercise 17L.**
- Work through Example 21 from the Student Book, paying particular attention to how to set up the inequalities.
- Emphasise, as in Example 19, the importance of being able to sketch a graph from minimal information. The number line at the end of the solution acts as a checking mechanism and demonstrates how useful the sketching techniques revised in Part 1 are.
- **Students can now complete Exercise 17L from the Student Book.**

| A 1–6 | Calculator all | CM n/a | MR 7, 9, 11, 12 | PS 8, 10 | EV n/a |

Part 3

- Have some extra questions similar to those in question 3 of Exercise 17L written on cards.
- On another set of cards, write the solution sets for these quadratic equations.
- Ask students to link each solution set with its quadratic equation.

Chapter 18 Statistics: Sampling and more complex diagrams

Overview

18.1 Sampling data	**18.4** Box plots
18.2 Frequency polygons	**18.5** Histograms
18.3 Cumulative frequency graphs	

Prior learning

Know how to work out the mean, the median, the mode and the range from given data.
Know how to calculate an estimate for the mean from a grouped frequency table.
Know how to extract information from statistical diagrams.
Know the meaning of the terms *discrete data* and *continuous data*.

Learning objectives

Ensure that students can: collect data to obtain an unbiased sample; draw and interpret frequency polygons; draw and interpret cumulative frequency graphs; draw and interpret box plots; draw and interpret histograms.

In the examination, students will be expected to:
- show that they understand different methods of sampling
- explain how to collect unbiased reliable data for a sample
- draw and interpret frequency polygons
- draw and interpret cumulative frequency graphs
- draw and interpret box plots
- draw and interpret histograms where the bars are of equal width
- draw and interpret histograms where the bars are of unequal width
- calculate the median, quartiles and interquartile range from a histogram.

Extension

Ask students to create: a frequency polygon, a cumulative frequency graph, and a histogram from a frequency table that contains grouped continuous data with unequal class intervals. Students could use the cumulative frequency graph and the frequency table to provide values for drawing a box plot.

Curriculum references

Section	GCSE specification
18.1	S 1, 4
18.2	S 3
18.3	S 3, 4
18.4	S 4
18.5	S 3

Route mapping

Exercise	Accessible	Intermediate	Challenging	AO1	AO2 MR CM	AO3 PS EV	Key questions
18A	1, 2	3–7		1	2–4	5–7	3, 7
18B	1–7			1, 3	7	2, 4–6	2, 7
18C		1–6	7, 8	1, 3, 5	2, 4, 6	7, 8	5, 8
18D		1–7	8	5	6, 7	1–4, 8	3, 5
18E		1–3	4–9	1, 2, 5, 6, 8	4, 7	3, 9	2c, 7

Key questions are those that demonstrate mastery of the concept, or which require a step-up in understanding or application. Key questions could be used to identify the questions that students must tackle, to support differentiation, or to identify the questions that should be teacher-marked rather than student-marked.

About this chapter

Making connections: This chapter extends the work on creating charts started in Chapter 3. It underpins this work by looking at the process of collecting and analysing data, in addition to presenting it, starting with how to decide on a source of data.

Relevance: Creating informative, visual summaries and analysing and interpreting data are useful across many areas including the Humanities, Sciences, Engineering, Business Studies and Social Studies.

Working mathematically: Students should recall the work on statistical measures from Chapter 3, particularly estimating the mean and the median. Students should be able to decide how to test a hypothesis and draw conclusions from the data. They should be able to produce frequency polygons, cumulative frequency graphs and histograms from frequency tables and read and use the significant data values from a cumulative frequency graph to produce a plot box. Students should be able to make interpretive statements and comparisons from any of these graphical representations of data.

Assessment: In each section of this chapter, ensure that students have a good grasp of the key questions in the exercises before moving on. (Refer to the 'Route mapping' table above.) Encourage students to read and think about the 'Ready to progress?' statements on page 535 of the Student Book. Check students' understanding at the end of the chapter, formatively, using peer assessment. Students could do a mini test in the form of the 'Review questions' on pages 535–537 of the Student Book. Follow up the test with an individual target-getting session, based on any areas for development that a student may have.

Worked exemplars from the Student Book – suggestions for use
- Present students with the same question but using different numbers. Students should use the exemplar to mirror the working, in full or only using the notes.
- Copy and cut the exemplar into cards. Students should match the working with the notes. (You may need to remove the words 'first, second', and so on.)
- Ask students to write their own exemplar questions based on those in the Student Book.

Answers to the Student Book questions are available on the CD-ROM provided.

Section 18.1 Sampling data

Learning objectives
- Understand different methods of sampling
- Collect unbiased reliable data for a sample

Resources and homework
- Student Book 18.1: pages 509–513
- Practice Book 18.1: pages 162–163

Making mathematical connections
- Percentages
- Two-way tables
- Ratio

Making cross-curricular connections
- **Geography, Sciences, Business Studies** – developing the skills required for investigative statistical analysis in a wide variety of subjects
- **Relevance** – many applications in science, humanities and business

Prior learning
- Students should be familiar with the process of carrying out surveys and the nature of using, if not designing, questionnaires. However, they are unlikely to have thought about bias in relation to designing questions or collecting data.

Working mathematically
- Encourage students to see the cross-curricular nature of this topic and its application in other aspects of their studies such as in Geography, Physical Education or English.
- A statistician's tasks encompass identifying the population and sample size for data collection as well as summarising and analysing the data collected to convey meaningful information.

Common misconceptions and remediation
- Students can sometimes confuse *population* with, literally, the whole population of their home country, rather than the whole set of the subjects of the investigation. Make sure they understand key statistical terms.
- Students often get confused when working with the stratified sampling and their proportions. Encourage students to use a table of all the groups for clear and accurate results.

Probing questions
- Investigate systematic sampling. How does this differ from stratified sampling?
- What areas of investigation might lend itself to this method?

Literacy focus
- Key terms: bias, hypothesis, population, primary data, random sample, sample, sample size, secondary data, unbiased
- Ask students to list and define each of the key terms.
- Ask students to list and/or describe the stages needed to carry out a successful investigation and draw appropriate and meaningful conclusions.

Part 1
- Tell students you are going to conduct a quick survey on their television-watching habits.
- Choose five students at random. Ask silly questions about what was on television last night.

- After asking the questions, ask: What was wrong with my sample?
  Students may say that it was not completely random, but you can argue otherwise.
- Ask: How could I choose a more representative sample? (Prompt, if necessary: Should the sample be exactly half boys and half girls? Should I ask the five oldest students?)
- Age (across a certain range) and gender often influence viewing habits.

Part 2

Data collection

- Discuss this hypothesis: *Boys get more pocket money than girls.* Choose another way to divide into two groups if the students are all male/female.
- Say that you want to test this, and ask the nearest boy and girl to say how much pocket money they receive. Then ask: Is the hypothesis true?
- Ask: Can I improve the investigation of this hypothesis? Elicit the response that the investigation can be improved by asking more students.
- Ask students to work in two groups (girls and boys) to calculate their average pocket money. Collate and display the results.
- Discuss whether or not the hypothesis is true. You could ask if the investigation could be further improved. Suggestions include asking people of different ages or from different classes, schools or geographical areas.
- Work through the text describing the data-handling cycle in the Student Book. Explain how the process begins with a given problem, often a hypothesis. The next step is to make a plan about how to test this. Next, gather the data and analyse it to see whether or not it proves the hypothesis. Finally, return to the beginning to decide if the plan should be modified.
- Work through Example 1, highlighting the four parts that correspond to the four parts of the data-handling cycle. Question students about this scenario, pointing out the key terms introduced so far and how they apply to this example.

Sampling methods

- Discuss the two sampling methods: random sampling and stratified sampling.
- Explain that choosing a random sample may not give representative results. A stratified sample takes into consideration the subgroups (or strata) of the population. It has the same make-up, proportionally, as the whole population. Tell students that most polls currently aim for stratified sampling.
- Demonstrate how to find the number of people in each category of a stratified sample by working through Example 2.
- Explain how to round values at the end. Tell **more able** students that although this rounding can lead to a slight difference in sample size from the one specified, the difference will be so small that it will not have a significant effect on their results. Demonstrate by experimenting with some figures, if students need convincing.

Sample size

- Talk about the practical and financial restrictions on surveying a whole population.
- Discuss sample size – the larger the sample, the more accurate the results will be.
- Work through Example 3. This should stimulate discussion and encourage students to explore the idea of sampling.
- **Students can now do Exercise 18A from the Student Book.**

| S 1 | Calculator n/a | CM 2, 3, 6, 7 | MR 4 | PS 5, 8 | EV n/a |

Part 3

- Test students' understanding of the key terms and concepts through the use of scenarios for testing hypotheses or choosing representative samples.

Section 18.2 Frequency polygons

Learning objectives
- Draw and interpret frequency polygons

Resources and homework
- Student Book 18.2: pages 513–516
- Practice Book 18.2: pages 163–164

Making mathematical connections
- Working with grouped data
- Estimating the mean

Making cross-curricular connections
- **Geography, Sciences, Business Studies** – presentation of data analysis
- **Relevance** – many applications in science, humanities and business

Prior learning
- Students should be familiar with the concept of estimating the mean from grouped data.
- They should also be able to plot line graphs.

Working mathematically
- Frequency polygons resemble line graphs but are used to show the distribution of data rather than to compare trends. Remind students that in frequency polygons, the *y*-axis represents frequency.

Common misconceptions and remediation
- Students often incorrectly connect the left-most plotted point to the intersection of the *x*- and *y*-axes. This can be corrected by practice and regularly asking students to interpret the graph they have drawn.

Probing questions
- Why is it important to connect the plotted points with straight lines?
- Why are frequencies plotted at the mid-class value?

Literacy focus
- Key terms: frequency polygon, grouped data, mid-class value
- Ask students to explain the differences between a line graph and a frequency polygon.

Part 1
- Show students a bar chart and a line graph. Ask: What are the defining characteristics of a line graph? (e.g. the gap between the bars, display discrete data) What are the defining characteristics of a line graph? (e.g. showing a trend over time, plotted points do not have to connect to the axes)
- Show students a frequency polygon. Ask: What are the similarities between a frequency polygon and a line graph / bar chart? (bar chart – frequency on *y*-axis; line graph – plotted points do not connect to axes, points joined by straight line…).
- Explain that a frequency polygon, like a bar chart, represents a distribution. Establish that it uses straight lines to connect points like a line graph, but unlike a line graph it cannot be used to predict a value midway between plotted points.

Part 2

- Check that students can define the terms *discrete data* and *continuous data*.
- As you work through Example 3 and Example 4 from the Student Book, emphasise these points:
  - Frequency is always plotted on the *y*-axis
  - Points are plotted at the mid-class value: (lower limit + upper limit) ÷ 2
  - The left-most point is not connected to the axes, since there is nothing known about the data below that point.
- Illustrate how to draw a frequency polygon from discrete data by working through Example 3.
- Illustrate how to draw a frequency polygon from continuous data by working through Example 4.
- Ask what is different about a frequency polygon drawn from continuous data and one drawn from discrete data. (For discrete data, the points are plotted at the specific *x*-axis value; for continuous data, points are plotted at the mid-class value.) Remind students that they should use a mid-class value to estimate the mean.
- Revise calculating an estimated mean from grouped data using $\frac{\Sigma fx}{\Sigma f}$, where *x* is the mid-class value.
- **Students can now do Exercise 18B from the Student Book.**

S 1, 3	Calculator n/a	CM n/a	MR 7	PS 5, 6	EV 2, 4

Part 3

- Prepare some frequency tables and their corresponding frequency polygons on separate sheets of paper, introducing some errors into the frequency polygons.
- Ask students to match each polygon with the correct frequency table, and use it to identify the errors in the polygons.

Section 18.3 Cumulative frequency graphs

Learning objectives
- Draw and interpret cumulative frequency graphs

Resources and homework
- Student Book 18.3: pages 517–522
- Practice Book 18.3: pages 165–166

Making mathematical connections
- Working with grouped data
- Estimating the mean

Making cross-curricular connections
- **Geography, Sciences, Business Studies** – presentation of data analysis
- **Relevance** – many applications in science, humanities and business

Prior learning
- Students should be able to estimating the mean from grouped data. They should understand the distinction between lower and upper class boundaries and mid-interval values.
- Students should also be familiar with the term 'median'.

Working mathematically
- Students recognise that in cumulative frequency diagrams (unlike bar charts and frequency polygons), the y-axis does not represent frequency.
- Students should use visual clues to identify (quickly) the type of chart required by a question – frequency table with a cumulative frequency column, graph space with cumulative frequency as a title/scale on the y-axis.

Common misconceptions and remediation
- **Less able** students may write the median as $\frac{n}{2}$ rather than the $\frac{n}{2}$ th value and therefore do not read the value from the cumulative frequency curve.
- Students may get confused with their working on estimating the mean and plot mid-class intervals rather than upper class boundaries along the x-axis.
- To target these errors, work through several examples with students, emphasising how to plot and read from the cumulative frequency curve.

Probing questions
- What is the benefit of concentrating on the middle 50% of the data – the interquartile range?
- What problems do the outlying lower 25% and upper 25% pose?
- What is meant by 'a measure of dispersion'?

Literacy focus
- Key terms: cumulative frequency, cumulative frequency graph, cumulative frequency curve, dispersion, interquartile range, lower quartile, quartile, upper quartile
- Ask students to provide definitions and examples for each key term to support their learning.

Part 1
- Tell students that this lesson focuses on grouped continuous data.
- Write various class intervals on the board, e.g. $0 \le h < 10$, $10 \le h < 20$ and ask students to identify the lower class boundary, the midpoint of the interval and the upper class boundary.
- Demonstrate how to estimate the mean from a grouped distribution by using the frequency table in Example 4 from the previous section.

- Emphasise that to estimate the mean from grouped data, students must plot the mid-interval values. In contrast, they should use upper class boundaries to estimate the median from grouped data.

Part 2

- Using the text in the Student Book, or otherwise, explain to students how to calculate cumulative frequencies and plot a cumulative frequency graph.
- Tell students that it does not matter whether the points are connected by a series of straight lines or one continuous smooth curve.

The median
- Students should be familiar with the term *median* from Section 3.2. If necessary, remind them that the median value is located in the middle of the data set.
- Tell students that they can estimate the median from a cumulative frequency graph. It is only an estimate because the line(s) connecting the plotted points assume that frequencies in the class intervals are evenly spread across the interval.
- Say that the frequency scale is treated as continuous.

The interquartile range
- Introduce the terms *lower quartile* and *upper quartile*. You could point out the link to quarters to help students remember the terms.
- The concept should not cause problems, but tell students to be accurate when they calculate the relevant values and careful when reading the corresponding values from the *y*-axis.
- Explain that the interquartile range excludes the less typical, unusual or extreme values that a data set contains.
- Work through Example 5 from the Student Book. This draws together all the elements introduced in this section and provides an excellent illustration of how to answer this type of question.
- Remind students to leave the lines drawn to find the LQ, M and UQ on their graphs. These provide evidence of working.
- **Students can now do Exercise 18C from the Student Book.**

| S 1, 3, 5 | Calculator n/a | CM n/a | MR 2, 4, 6 | PS 7, 8 | EV n/a |

Part 3

- Ask: Which is better, a high interquartile range or a low interquartile range?
- Discuss students' own views.
- Ask students to suggest practical examples where it would be preferable to obtain:
  - a low interquartile range
  - a high interquartile range.

Section 18.4 Box plots

Learning objectives
- Draw and interpret box plots

Resources and homework
- Student Book 18.4: pages 523–526
- Practice Book 18.4: pages 166–168

Making mathematical connections
- Cumulative frequency graphs

Making cross-curricular connections
- **Geography, Sciences, Business Studies** – presentation of data analysis
- **Relevance** – many applications in science, humanities and business

Prior learning
- Students should be able to find the lower quartile, median and upper quartile of a set of continuous grouped data from a cumulative frequency diagram.

Working mathematically
- Students often find box plots odd because they are only plotted against one axis. Remind students that the elements in this chart are a visual representation of significant values.
- The diagrams require no working; they are purely about interpreting the original data.

Common misconceptions and remediation
- If class intervals are described in terms of inequalities, then students sometimes take the least and greatest values – the ends of the whiskers – to be the midpoints of the first and last class intervals respectively. Point out this error to help students avoid making it.

Probing questions
- The ends of the whiskers represent the range of the data set. Is the least value always zero? Why?/Why not?
- Is the line that represents the median always in the middle of the box? Why?/Why not?

Literacy focus
- Key terms: box-and-whisker plot, box plot
- Ask students to describe and then write down the connection between the five significant points of a plot box.

Part 1
- Ask students to recall what they can find out from a cumulative frequency curve (the lower quartile, median and upper quartile).
- Ask for suggestions to define precisely: the lower quartile, the median, upper quartile.

Part 2
- Introduce the term *box-and-whisker plot* and tell students it is a way of representing data when the range and quartiles are known.
- Draw or display a box-and-whisker plot on the board so that students can see where the name comes from. Say that it is often simply called a *box plot*.
- Describe the five points of reference: lowest value, lower quartile, median, upper quartile and highest value.

- Display a cumulative frequency graph with space *below* the x-axis (to plot the corresponding box plot).

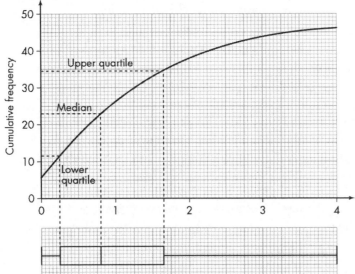

- Locate the LQ, M and UQ on the cumulative frequency graph and then extend the lines below the x-axis. Use these lines to construct the plot box.
- This gives a definite visual connection between the placing of the plot box on the scale and the graph that the LQ, M and UQ have been derived from.
- You could challenge **more able** students by introducing the concept of skewed distributions – this is beyond the GCSE syllabus.
- Work through Example 6 from the Student Book. This shows how to draw a box-and-whisker plot diagram and how to compare two distributions.
- **Students can now do Exercise 18D from the Student Book.**

S 5	Calculator n/a	CM n/a	MR 6, 7	PS 8	EV 1–4

Part 3

- Discuss the advantages or disadvantages of a box plot compared with a cumulative frequency diagram.

Section 18.5 Histograms

Learning objectives

- Draw and interpret histograms where the bars are of equal width
- Draw and interpret histograms where the bars are of unequal width
- Calculate the median, quartiles and interquartile range from a histogram

Resources and homework

- Student Book 18.5: pages 526–532
- Practice Book 18.5: pages 168–170

Making mathematical connections

- Grouped continuous data
- Calculating the mean and interquartile range
- Locating the lower and upper quartiles, the median

Making cross-curricular connections

- **Geography, sciences, business** – presentation of data analysis
- **Relevance** – many applications in science, humanities and business

Prior learning

- Students should know how to estimate the mean from a grouped frequency table.
- Students should also be familiar with a scale that represents continuous data and be able to calculate the area of a rectangle.

Working mathematically

- Students are often challenged by the concept of frequency density and that the area rather than the height of a column represents the frequency in a histogram.
- Encourage students to read the graph and its accompanying frequency table very carefully to avoid serious errors.

Common misconceptions and remediation

- Students mix up the calculation: frequency density = frequency ÷ class interval
- Students often make mistakes in finding the quartiles because of the difficulties involved in finding their position in the class and then estimating their values. Encourage practice and careful thought to help students understand and remember this routine.

Probing questions

- Investigate the measure *frequency density*.
- Why is frequency density used in a histogram? What difference would it make if the *y*-axis were simply 'frequency'?
- Redraw the histogram in Example 8 using frequency rather than frequency density. Compare this graph with the one in Example 8.
- What is the modal group in each graph? Should it be the same?

Literacy focus

- Key terms: class interval, frequency density, histogram
- Ask students to describe the process of: calculating the frequency density from a frequency table; calculating the frequency of a class interval from a histogram.

Part 1

- Draw a normal distribution (bell-shaped) curve on the board. Explain that the frequencies are greatest for the middle values and smallest at the extremes and this is quite normal in many real-life situations, such as people's height – hence 'normal distributions'.
- Recap with students that quartiles divide a population into four equal parts: first quarter point gives the lower quartile; second point gives the median (second quartile); top quarter point gives the upper quartile. Show these on the normal distribution curve and point out that the area under the curve at each division is one-quarter of the whole frequency.

Part 2

Histograms with equal class intervals

- Work through the text in the Student Book, making sure that students fully understand the four key differences between a histogram and a bar chart.
- Check that students can identify the times it takes people to walk to work in both the frequency table and histogram.
- Focus particularly on the width of the class intervals and the calculation of frequency density, making sure students see the connection between the column area and its width and height.

Histograms with unequal class widths

- Display the table of data from Example 7 and ask students what they notice about the class intervals (different sizes). This may be the first time students have met unequal class widths.
- Ask students to copy the table but to draw it vertically, adding two columns for class width and frequency density.
- Show students how to work out and record the class widths (the differences between the upper and lower class boundaries) and then use these values to calculate the frequency density for interval. Note that the maximum frequency density is 47, so mark the scale to 50.
- Ask students to draw the histogram using the values in their tables and check that students' histograms are the same as the one that appears in the Student Book. (They will need this in the next part of the lesson.)

Calculating the median, quartiles and mean from a histogram

- Work carefully through Example 8, demonstrating how to: work out the frequencies from a histogram by multiplying the class intervals by the column heights / frequency density; calculate the median, quartiles and mean.
- **More able** students may challenge this and suggest that the median should be at the mean of the 199th and the 200th daffodils rather than the 200th daffodil. Explain briefly that the median is only an estimate and, in practice, after rounding, they will generally get the same value unless the frequency is very small.
- Once all students understand the processes involved in calculating the median and quartiles, return to the table that students drew from Example 7. Ask them to add another column to the right of frequency density and calculate the cumulative frequency.
- Now calculate an estimate for the median (154.51), the IQR (3.74) and the mean (154.87).
- **Students can now do Exercise 18E from the Student Book.**

| S 1, 2, 5, 6, 8 | Calculator n/a | CM n/a | MR 4, 7 | PS 3, 9 | EV n/a |

Part 3

- Ask which of the two ways of displaying continuous grouped data with unequal class intervals – the frequency polygon and the histogram – students think is more useful. Does the 'usefulness' depend on the type of data being analysed?

Chapter 19 Probability: Combined events

Overview

19.1 Addition rules for outcomes of events	**19.4** Independent events
19.2 Combined events	**19.5** Conditional probability
19.3 Tree diagrams	

Prior learning

Know how to work out the probability of an outcome.
Know how to use a two-way table to work out probability.

Learning objectives

Ensure that students can: work out the probability of two events; draw and use tree diagrams; use probability for independent events; use conditional probability.

In the examination, students will be expected to:
- work out the probability of different outcomes of combined events
- work out the probability of two outcomes or events occurring at the same time
- use tree diagrams to work out the probability of combined events
- use the connectors 'and' and 'or' to work out the probabilities for combined events
- work out the probability of combined events when the probabilities change after each event.

Extension

Provide examples to enable **more able** students to practise more advanced use of the 'and' and 'or' rules. Provide students with questions about conditional probability. Explore more complicated probabilities involving combinations and permutations.

Curriculum references

Section	GCSE specification
19.1	P 9
19.2	P 9
19.3	P 9
19.4	P 9
19.5	P 9

Route mapping

Exercise	Accessible	Intermediate	Challenging	AO1	AO2 MR CM	AO3 PS EV	Key questions
19A	1–6	7–10		1–5, 9	6, 8	7, 10	7, 8, 10
19B	1–12			1–4, 6, 7	5, 9, 12	8, 10, 11	7, 8, 11
19C		1–8	9–11	1–7	10, 11	8, 9	1, 7, 9, 11
19D		1–3	4–12	1–3, 5, 6, 8	7, 9, 12	4, 10, 11	3, 9, 10
19E		1	2–10	1–4	5–8	9, 10	4, 7, 10

Key questions are those that demonstrate mastery of the concept or which require a step-up in understanding or application. Key questions could be used to identify the questions that students must tackle, to support differentiation, or to identify the questions that should be teacher-marked rather than student-marked.

About this chapter

Making connections: The chapter brings together tree diagrams, the 'and' and 'or' rules and conditional probability. Encourage students to look for a question asking for one thing AND another, one thing OR another and whether or not an object is replaced. For much of the chapter, the next step is A Level content.

Relevance: Making judgements, predictions and looking for trends.

Working mathematically: Students will need to be able to multiply and add fractions, decimals and percentages with confidence. Students should explain how they would then use the information they are given or have worked out to make judgements and predictions.

Assessment: In each section of this chapter, ensure that students have a good grasp of the key questions in the exercises before moving on. (Refer to the 'Route mapping' table above.) Encourage students to read and think about the 'Ready to progress' statements on page 556 of the Student Book. Check students' understanding at the end of the chapter, formatively, using peer assessment. Students could do a mini test in the form of the 'Review questions' on pages 556–557 of the Student Book. Follow up the test with an individual target-getting session, based on any areas for development that a student may have.

Worked exemplars from the Student Book – suggestions for use

- Present students with the same question but using different numbers. Students should use the exemplar to mirror the working, in full or only the notes.
- Copy and cut the exemplar into cards. Students should match the working with the notes. (You may need to remove the words 'first, second' and so on.)
- Copy and cut the working into cards, splitting the label/description from the working. Students should put the working in order, then match it with the descriptions.

Answers to the Student Book questions are available on the CD-ROM provided.

Section 19.1 Addition rules for outcomes of events

Learning objectives
- Work out the probability of different outcomes of combined events

Resources and homework
- Student Book 19.1: pages 539–541
- Practice Book 19.1: pages 171–172

Making mathematical connections
- Equivalent fractions
- Adding and subtracting fractions, decimals and percentages
- Multiplying and dividing fractions, decimals and percentages

Making cross-curricular connections
- **Engineering** – probability of failure
- **Relevance** – developing logical thinking

Prior learning
- Students should know how to find the probability of an event. They should also know how to express one number as a fraction of another, and how to simplify, add and subtract fractions.

Working mathematically
- Encourage students to explain and discuss their methods for numerical fractions (equivalence including cancelling; addition and subtraction; multiplication and division) and then to apply these to probability.
- Structure tasks so students can work out the methods for themselves, either by increasing the difficulty incrementally or through one straightforward and one complex example.

Common misconceptions and remediation
- Students may be familiar with playing cards and have worked with them in section 13.2. However, it may be a good idea to remind them by showing them a real pack of cards and recap related terminology, such as *suits*.
- Students often make numerical errors when calculating probabilities. Recap decimal subtraction with the class, e.g. $1 - 0.45 = 0.55$.
- Students may not always understand when it is appropriate to add probability fractions and when it is not.

Probing questions
- Tell students to discuss reasons for their explanations, to ensure their arguments are clear.
- Students should remember to multiply the probabilities for independent events and add the probabilities for exclusive events.

Literacy focus
- Key terms: There are no new key terms in this section.
- Ensure that students understand the terms *mutually exclusive*, *addition rule* and *expected outcome*.
- Ask students to be explicit about the language of equivalence. They should avoid 'cross-multiplication'.

Part 1

Review calculating with numerical fractions

- Display five proper fractions.
- Ask individual students to choose a pair of fractions to add.
- Then ask a student to choose any three fractions to add, then any four, and finally to add all five.
- Discuss answers with the class and ask them to share any observations.

Part 2

- Work through Example 1 from the Student Book. The scenario is:

  A bag contains twelve red balls, eight green balls, five blue balls and fifteen black balls. A ball is drawn at random.

- Ask students: How many balls there are in total? What is the probability of picking a red ball? Establish P(red) = $\frac{12}{40}$ = $\frac{3}{10}$

- Ask students: What is the probability of picking a black ball? Establish P(black) = $\frac{15}{40}$ = $\frac{3}{8}$

- Ask students what we could do to work out the probability of picking one ball or another ball, for example picking a red ball or a black ball.

- Explain that to calculate 'or', we add together the probabilities of the events:

  P(red or black) = P(red) + P(black) = $\frac{12}{40}$ + $\frac{15}{40}$ = $\frac{27}{40}$

- Ask students how we could work out the probability of not picking a ball of a certain colour.
- Take suggestions and establish that we subtract the probability of picking that colour from 1:

  P(not green) = 1 – $\frac{8}{40}$ = $\frac{32}{40}$ = $\frac{4}{5}$

- Now ask them how they could work out the probability of picking a ball that is neither green nor blue. Prompt them, if necessary, to look at the probabilities of the remaining outcomes,

  i.e. red or black: P(neither green nor blue) = P(red or black) = $\frac{3}{12}$ + $\frac{15}{40}$ = $\frac{27}{40}$

- **Less able** students are likely to need support working out probabilities of one thing or another.
- Encourage students to check their answers and simplify their fractions. Remind **more able** students to use subtraction when working out the probability of an outcome not happening.
- **Students can now do Exercise 19A from the Student Book.**

| P 1–5, 9 | Calculator n/a | CM 8 | MR 6 | PS 7, 10 | EV n/a |

Part 3

- Display a target board with whole numbers on it.
- Ask for probabilities of events such as:
  - picking a multiple of 4 or 6
  - picking a prime number or a factor of 100
  - picking a number that is a factor of 40 and 60.
- The choice of questions will depend on the numbers displayed.

Section 19.2 Combined events

Learning objectives
- Work out the probability of two outcomes or events occurring at the same time

Resources and homework
- Student Book 19.2: pages 541–544
- Practice Book 19.2: pages 172–174

Making mathematical connections
- Adding and subtracting fractions
- Multiplying and dividing fractions
- Equivalent fraction, decimal and percentages

Making cross-curricular connections
- **Science** – planning an experiment
- **Computing** – application of logic
- **Relevance** – programming languages

Prior learning
- Students should know how to work out the probability of an event.

Working mathematically
- Encourage students to visualise the outcome(s) of an experiment.
- This activity lends itself to sorting the steps into order, finding the probability of one event and then another event.
- As an extension, ask students what to do if more than two events are being trialled.

Common misconceptions and remediation
- Students may make errors because they do not read the question carefully. Encourage them to reread the question to check that their answer makes sense.
- Make sure that students understand that each cell of a sample space diagram can be used to show two separate results or the outcome of both results as required, e.g. the total scores on two dice or the difference between the scores on two dice. Students should make their own decisions about what to record.

Probing questions
- Can you always use a sample space diagram? If not, what else could you use?

Literacy focus
- Key terms: combined event, sample space diagram, theoretical probability space diagram
- Ask students to describe the scenario and place emphasis on what is happening in the trial: a coin AND a spinner; a chocolate OR a toffee.

Part 1
- Give each pair of students two dice.
- Ask each pair to throw the dice and record the total score on the two dice after each throw. They should do this for 2 minutes.
- Collate the results from each pair on a tally chart on the board.
- Ask students to work out the relative frequencies, or experimental probabilities, of each score.

Part 2

Throwing two dice; Coins and dice

- Following on from the activity in Part 1, ask each pair which total score they got most often. Answers may vary, but expect 7 to come up most frequently.
- Ask why some total scores seem to occur more than others. For example, the totals 2 and 12 are unlikely to occur often because there is only one way to get a 12 (6, 6) and one way to get a 2 (2, 2). The total 1 is impossible and there are only two ways to get 11 (5, 6 and 6, 5). There are several ways of getting some of the other totals.
- Ask the class: How many ways are there are of getting each total score? How could we find out? Discuss this and then, on the board, show the class a sample space diagram for two dice. Show that, for example, there are six ways to get a total of 7, but only two ways to get 11 as a total, so they can expect to get more 7s than 11s.
- Discuss the two examples in the text in the Student Book and the different ways in which to draw sample spaces: making a list of possibilities for tossing two coins; drawing a grid for the coin and the dice.
- Show **less able** students that each point represents one equally likely outcome, so the diagram gives the total number of possibilities and the number of the required outcomes.
- Ask students to draw a simple sample space diagram to illustrate the results of throwing two coins.
- Discuss the results with students. Ask if H, T is the same as T, H in this example.
- Ask students to draw a simple sample space diagram to illustrate the results of throwing a coin and a dice.
- Discuss the results with students. Ask them how to work out the probability of (H, even number).
- **Students can now do Exercise 19B from the Student Book.**
- **Less able** students can complete questions 1–5 and move on to 6–12 if they feel confident. Offer help, as needed, or let them work with a partner.

| P 1–4, 6, 7 | Calculator n/a | CM 5 | MR 9, 12 | PS 8, 10, 11 | EV n/a |

Part 3

- Ask students if they notice any differences between the theoretical probabilities found in question 1 of Exercise 19B and the experimental probabilities they found in Part 1. Should they expect any differences?
- Remind students that the more trials of an event they do, the closer the experimental probabilities will be to the theoretical probabilities.

Section 19.3 Tree diagrams

Learning objectives
- Use tree diagrams to work out the probability of combined events

Resources and homework
- Student Book 19.3: pages 544–548
- Practice Book 19.3: pages 174–176

Making mathematical connections
- Multiplying and dividing fractions, decimals and percentages
- Adding and subtracting fractions, decimals and percentages

Making cross-curricular connections
- **Science** – survival rates
- **Relevance** – developing logical thinking

Prior learning
- Students should be able to use sample space diagrams to support calculating the probability of two events happening at the same time.
- They should also be confident in adding and multiplying simple fractions and decimals.

Working mathematically
- Encourage students to visualise the outcome(s) of an experiment.
- This activity lends itself to ordering the steps, finding the probability of one event and then another event diagrammatically.
- Extend by asking students what to do if more than two events are being trialled. What might happen if one is not replaced?

Common misconceptions and remediation
- Some students add rather than multiply probabilities along the branches. Tell students to always check that a probability is ≤ 1.
- Encourage students to draw a tree diagram (of a reasonable size) and label each branch with its corresponding probability, irrespective of what the question requires.

Probing questions
- How would you calculate the probability of one event AND another event?
- How would you calculate the probability of one event OR another event?

Literacy focus
- Key term: tree diagram
- Ask students to describe how to work out the probability of: one event AND another event; one event OR another event.
-

Part 1
- Ask students to calculate the sum and product of various fractions. They need to be confident with this in order to focus on the new material covered in the lesson.

Part 2

- Display on the board the six shape cards and the sample space diagram shown on page 544 of the Student Book. Discuss whether this diagram is easy to construct. (no)
- Ask students to use the sample space diagram to answer simple questions, e.g. What is the probability of choosing two cards and getting a square and a triangle in any order? $\left(\dfrac{12}{36}\right)$
- Work through Example 2 from the Student Book.
- Explain that a tree diagram can be a simpler way to represent the same scenario.
- On the board, draw the first part of the tree diagram showing the three branches of square, triangle and circle. Write the probabilities on the branches as fractions with a denominator of 6. **More able** students can cancel these, but **less able** students will find the calculations easier if they are not simplified.
- Draw the next set of branches for the second card at the end of each first branch, and again write the probabilities on the branches.
- Illustrate, using the bottom branches, that P($\bullet$,$\bullet$) can be seen as one-sixth of one-sixth, so is found by multiplying the two probabilities.
- Explain that this means that to find the combined probability of event A and then event B happening, you multiply the two probabilities.
- Do this for the other branches so at the end of each branch there is a probability fraction with a denominator of 36.
- Reinforce the rule for multiplying by showing that these probabilities are exactly the same as those obtained from the sample space diagram.
- You could talk through question 1 in Exercise 19C to help **less able** students.
- Work through Example 3 to reinforce the multiplication rule.
- **Students can now do Exercise 19C from the Student Book. Less able** students could work with a partner for questions 9–11.

P 1–7	Calculator n/a	CM n/a	MR 10, 11	PS 8, 9	EV n/a

Part 3

- Compare tree diagrams with sample space diagrams.
- Ask students what advantages or disadvantages one might have over the other, e.g. sample space diagrams give good visual presentations.
- Ask students to suggest scenarios where it is clearly preferable to use tree diagrams and vice versa.

Section 19.4 Independent events

Learning objectives

Use the connectors 'and' and 'or' to work out the probabilities for combined events

Resources and homework

- Student Book 19.4: pages 549–551
- Practice Book 19.4: pages 176–178

Making mathematical connections

- Use of Venn Diagrams to visualise independent events
- Multiplying and dividing fractions, decimals and percentages
- Adding and subtracting fraction, decimals and percentages

Making cross-curricular connections

- **Computing** – using logic gates
- **Relevance** – developing logical thinking

Prior learning

- Students should be familiar with tree diagrams. They should know how to find the probability of combined events using sample space diagrams and tree diagrams.
- They should also be familiar with mutually exclusive events, and know that if A and B are two such events, then P(A or B) = P(A) + P(B).

Working mathematically

- Encourage students to visualise the outcome(s) of an experiment.
- This activity lends itself to ordering the steps, finding the probability of one event and then of another event diagrammatically.
- Extend by asking students what to do if more than two events are being trialled. What might happen if one is not replaced?

Common misconceptions and remediation

- When considering outcomes of compound events, students often consider one but not all possibilities, e.g. when a coin is tossed twice, they consider only one way of getting a head and a tail. Encourage students to think of all the possibilities before the probabilities. Encourage them to write P(head and tail) = P(H, T) + P(T, H).

Probing questions

- If you throw three coins, what is the probability of getting the same side three times in a row? (Prompt HHH or TTT)

Literacy focus

- Key term: independent events
- Ask students to verbalise what a tree diagram shows and to place emphasis on event A **AND** event C also event A **AND** C **OR** event C **AND** A.

Part 1

- Ask students how they would work out the probability of throwing two dice and getting two numbers the same.
- Discuss which type of diagram (sample space or probability tree) is better to represent this. (A sample space diagram gives the information much more simply.)
- Ask students how they would work out the probability of throwing two dice and not getting a total of 11 or 12.

- Suggest a tree diagram, if necessary. Ask students which branches they would use and what probabilities should be put on the branches.

Part 2

- Work through Example 4, encouraging students to think carefully about what is required. Suggest that they write down, in full, what they need to do.
  Hitting the target both times means hit AND hit. This means you multiply.
  Hitting the target once means hit AND miss OR miss AND hit.
- Note the connections between the word 'AND' and the operation 'multiply', and the word 'OR' and the operation 'add'.

'At least problems'

- Work through Example 5, which requires students to read the question and extract the required information. Students need to work out the total number of balls in the bag and note that the ball is replaced each time.
- Encourage **more able** students to explore what would happen if Anton did not replace the ball.

More advanced use of 'and' and 'or'

- Ask students: How could you work out the probability of cutting a pack of cards twice and getting two Aces or two Kings or two Queens or two Jacks.
- Discuss that it would be difficult to draw a sample space diagram or a tree diagram for this as there would be too many options / branches.
- Ask: Is it necessary to draw the full tree diagram or could you draw only the relevant branches?
- On the board, draw the four pairs of branches for Ace then Ace, King then King, Queen then Queen and Jack then Jack. Write on the probabilities as fractions in their simplest terms. (The denominators will get too large if you do not use simplified fractions.) Multiply the probabilities along each of the four pairs of branches.
- Ask how to find the probability of any one of these happening. (Add them together.)
- Work through Example 6, again pointing out that they can imagine rather than draw the tree diagram.
- **Students can now do Exercise 19D from the Student Book. Less able** students may need support to complete questions 7–11.

| P 1–3, 5, 6, 8 | Calculator n/a | CM 9, 12 | MR 7 | PS 4, 10, 11 | EV n/a |

Part 3

- Ask students to define *mutually exclusive events* and *independent events*.
- Ask:
  o If two events, A and B, are mutually exclusive, what can you say about P(A or B)?
  o If two events A and B are independent, what can you say about P(A and B)?
- Ask students to suggest two events that are mutually exclusive and two that are not.
- Ask students to suggest two events that are independent, and two that are not.

Section 19.5 Conditional probability

Learning objectives
- Work out the probability of combined events when the probabilities change after each event

Resources and homework
- Student Book 19.5: pages 552–554
- Practice Book 19.5: pages 178–179

Making mathematical connections
- Using Venn Diagrams to visualise independent events
- Multiplying and dividing fractions, decimals and percentages
- Adding and subtracting fraction, decimals and percentages

Making cross-curricular connections
- **Relevance** – applications to manufacturing and project management

Prior learning
- Students should be confident in calculating probabilities of compound events, with and without tree diagrams.

Working mathematically
- Encourage students to visualise the outcome(s) of an experiment.
- This activity lends itself to ordering the steps, finding the probability of one event and then another event diagrammatically.
- Extend by asking students what to do if more than two events are being trialled. What might happen if one is not replaced?

Common misconceptions and remediation
- Students often forget to change the second probability as a consequence of the first event. Practice will help to reduce this error.

Probing questions
- In a box of ten chocolates, there are seven that you like. You pick out two chocolates at random. The first chocolate is one that you like. What is the probability that you like the second chocolate?

Literacy focus
- Key term: conditional probability
- Ask students to verbalise what a tree diagram is showing, and to place emphasis on event A **AND** event C; also event A **AND** C **OR** event C **AND** A.

Part 1
- Ask students how to work out the probability of throwing three dice and not getting the same number each time.
- If necessary, lead them to suggest first finding the probability of getting the same number, i.e. 1, 1, 1 or 2, 2, 2, and so on. Ask them to work this out. $\left[6 \times \left(\dfrac{1}{6} \times \dfrac{1}{6} \times \dfrac{1}{6} \right) = \dfrac{1}{36} \right]$
- Now ask for the probability of not getting the same number each time. $\left(1 - \dfrac{1}{36} = \dfrac{35}{36} \right)$

Part 2

- Ask: What is the probability of being dealt two cards from a normal pack of cards and getting two hearts?

- Ask for an explanation of any answers offered. Students may say $\frac{1}{16}$, as the probability of getting a heart is $\frac{1}{4}$ and $\frac{1}{4} \times \frac{1}{4} = \frac{1}{16}$. Discuss why this is wrong.

- Help students see that once the first card has been dealt, there are only 51 cards in the pack, so the probability of getting any card changes.

- Draw on the board the two branches of a tree diagram: heart followed by heart. Ask the class for the chance of the first card being a heart. $\left(\frac{1}{4} \text{ or } \frac{13}{52} \right)$

- Now ask for the chance of the second card being a heart, if the first card is a heart. Allow a good discussion but lead the class to realise that now there are only 12 hearts left in the pack and only 51 cards in all, so the probability has changed to $\frac{12}{51} \left(= \frac{4}{17} \right)$.

- Encourage **more able** students to cancel where possible as this will result in smaller numbers.

- Now ask students to work out the probability of getting two hearts in a row. $\left(\frac{1}{4} \times \frac{4}{17} = \frac{1}{17} \right)$

- Now ask: What is the chance of getting at least one heart?
- Guide students to see that they can find this using $1 - P(\text{no hearts})$.

  $P(\text{no hearts}) = \left(\frac{3}{4} \times \frac{38}{51} = \frac{19}{34} \right)$

  $P(\text{at least one heart}) \left(1 - \frac{19}{34} = \frac{15}{34} \right)$

- This is not an easy concept so **less able** students will probably need extra help.
- Work through Example 7.
- **Students can now do Exercise 19E from the Student Book.**

| P 1–4 | Calculator n/a | CM 5, 8 | MR 6, 7 | PS 9, 10 | EV n/a |

Part 3

- Ask the class: How could you find the probability that there will be a question on conditional probability in your GCSE examination?
- Encourage discussion and lead them to suggest using historical evidence. Discuss whether, if they knew this probability, it would affect the revision for their own GCSE examination.

Chapter 20 Geometry and measures: Properties of circles

Overview

20.1 Circle theorems	**20.3** Tangents and chords
20.2 Cyclic quadrilaterals	**20.4** Alternate segment theorem

Prior learning

Know that the three interior angles of a triangle add up to 180°.
Know that the four interior angles of a quadrilateral add up to 360°.
Know the properties of angles formed by a straight line (transversal) across parallel lines.
Know the correct terms for different parts of a circle.

Learning objectives

Ensure that students can: prove and use circle theorems to work out angles; work out angles in cyclic quadrilaterals; use tangents, chords and alternate segment theorem to work out angles in circles.

In the examination, students will be expected to:
* prove and use circle theorems to work out angles created in a circle from points on the circumference
* find the sizes of angles in cyclic quadrilaterals
* use tangents and chords to find the sizes of angles in circles
* use the alternate segment theorem to find the sizes of angles in circles.

Extension

Explore the proofs of circle theorems and be able to show why they work. Use algebra in explanations of proofs.

Curriculum references

Section	GCSE specification
20.1	G 10
20.2	G 10
20.3	G 10
20.4	G 10

Route mapping

Exercise	Accessible	Intermediate	Challenging	AO1	AO2 MR CM	AO3 PS EV	Key questions
20A		1–3			1–3		3
20B		1–11		1–4	5–9, 11	10	2, 6, 11
20C		1–8	9–11	1, 2, 4–6	8–11	3, 7	4, 5, 8, 10
20D		1–6	7–9	1–4	6, 7	5, 8, 9	4, 7, 8
20E		1–3		1	2, 3		1, 2, 3
20F		1–6	7, 8	1–4	7, 8	5, 6	4, 6, 7, 8

Key questions are those that demonstrate mastery of the concept or which require a step-up in understanding or application. Key questions could be used to identify the questions that students must tackle, to support differentiation, or to identify the questions that should be teacher-marked rather than student-marked.

About this chapter

Making connections: The chapter brings together interior and exterior angles, angles in triangles, angles in quadrilaterals, properties of angles formed on straight lines and within parallel lines and the correct use of the terminology of parts of a circle. For much of the chapter, the next step is A Level content.

Relevance: There is an emphasis on the use of logic, proof and thinking in steps. There are applications in engineering, architecture, manufacturing, project management and many more areas, with STEM careers being a strong focus.

Working mathematically: In addition to showing how they derived their answers, students also need to use proofs. Weaker students are likely to struggle with the proof aspect; however stronger students and those with good algebra should flourish here.

Assessment: In each section of this chapter, ensure that students have a good grasp of the key questions in the exercises before moving on. (Refer to the 'Route mapping' table above.) Encourage students to read and think about the 'Ready to progress?' statements on page 578 of the Student Book. Check students' understanding at the end of the chapter, formatively, using peer assessment. Students could do a mini test in the form of the 'Review questions' on pages 578–579 of the Student Book. Follow up the test with an individual target-getting session, based on any areas for development that a student may have.

Worked exemplars from the Student Book – suggestions for use
- Present students with the same question but using different numbers. Students should use the exemplar to mirror the working, in full or only the notes.
- Copy and cut up the exemplar into cards. Students should match the working with the notes. (You may need to remove the words 'first, second' and so on.)
- Copy and cut the working into cards, splitting the label/description from the working. Students put the working in order, and then match them with the descriptions.

Answers to the Student Book questions are available on the CD-ROM provided.

Section 20.1 Circle theorems

Learning objectives

- Prove and use circle theorems to work out angles created in a circle from points on the circumference

Resources and homework

- Student Book 20.1: pages 559–565
- Practice Book 20.1: pages 180–181

Making mathematical connections

- Parts of a circle
- Using names in correct context
- Properties of angles on straight lines and interior and exterior angles.

Making cross-curricular connections

- **Sport** – using angles
- **Science** – using formulae
- **Relevance** – developing logical thinking

Prior learning

- Students should know that the sum of the interior angles of a triangle is 180° and the sum of the interior angles in a quadrilateral is 360°. They should also be familiar with the angle properties of isosceles triangles.
- Students should understand and be able to use circle terms such as *centre, chord, segment, circumference, diameter, radius* and *arc.*

Working mathematically

- Encourage students to articulate their methods for calculating missing angles and then to apply these to proofs.
- Structure tasks so students can work out the methods for themselves, either by increasing the difficulty incrementally or through one straightforward and one complex example.

Common misconceptions and remediation

- Students may find it difficult to solve problems about angles in circles in which they have to find more than one angle. Advise them to mark, on their diagram, all the angles they know before proceeding with the question.

Probing questions

- What is the same about all semi-circles? Why?
- Which theorem shows the angle at the centre and the angle at the circumference?
- What is special about angles subtended from the same arc?

Literacy focus

- Key terms: prove, theorem
- Give students blank circles and ask them to explain, using words and diagrams, each theorem and what is shows.

Part 1

NB: This section may take more than 1 hour.

Revise circle terms

- Draw one or more circle diagrams on the board and ask individual students to name each part.
- Extend by asking another student to define the term precisely, e.g. draw a chord on a circle and ask students to identify and then define a chord.

Part 2

- Go through the text at the beginning of this section with the class.
- **Students can now do Exercise 20A from the Student Book.**

P n/a	Calculator n/a	CM n/a	MR 1–3	PS n/a	EV n/a

- Review the work from Exercise 20A and formalise the circle theorems.
- Display the diagram and measure ∠ACB and ∠AOB. The angle made at the centre (∠AOB) is twice the angle made at the circumference (∠ACB). Explain that this is always true when the angles are subtended by the same arc.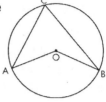
- You may need to spend some time explaining to students what *subtends* means. Showing lots of examples will help.
- Formalise **circle theorem 1**: The angle at the centre of a circle is twice the angle at the circumference when they are both subtended by the same arc.
  This is usually abbreviated to: angle at the centre is twice the angle at the circumference.
- Display the diagram on the right and measure ∠ACB (90°). AB is a diameter of the circle. Explain that this is always true and show some other examples.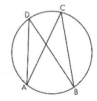
- Formalise **circle theorem 2**: Every angle subtended at the circumference of a semicircle by the diameter is a right angle.
  This is usually abbreviated to: angle in a semicircle is 90°.
- Show students how to give reasons in brackets: ∠ACB = 90° (angle in a semicircle)
- Now display this diagram and measure ∠ACB and ∠ADB (both angles are the same). Explain that this is always true.
- Formalise **circle theorem 3**: Angles subtended at the circumference in the same segment of a circle are equal. Explain that the segment is the part of the circle above the chord AB. This is usually abbreviated to: angles in the same segment are equal.
- Direct the **more able** students to the proof of theorem 1 or show it to them in Part 3.
- Work through Examples 1, 2 and 3. Focus on showing working and writing reasons at each stage of working.
- Example 1 involves: angles in the same segment are equal, base angles and side lengths of an isosceles triangle are equal and the angle at the centre is twice the angle at the circumference.
- Example 2 involves: angles on a straight line, angles around a point and angle at the centre is twice the angle at the circumference.
- Example 3 requires students to use a lot of angles facts and circle theorems. Highlight the step-by-step methodology.
- **Students can now do Exercise 20B from the Student Book.**

G&M 1–4	Calculator all	CM 5, 6, 8, 9	MR 7, 11	PS 10	EV n/a

Part 3

- Use the properties of an isosceles triangle to prove circle theorems 1, 2 and 3.
- Demonstrate all three proofs, or prove theorem 1 and ask students to prove theorems 2 and 3.

Section 20.2 Cyclic quadrilaterals

Learning objectives
- Find the sizes of angles in cyclic quadrilaterals

Resources and homework
- Student Book 20.2: pages 566–568
- Practice Book 20.2: pages 181–182

Making mathematical connections
- Parts of a circle and using names in the correct context
- Properties of angles on straight lines and interior and exterior angles

Making cross-curricular connections
- **Sport** – using angles
- **Science** – using formulae
- **Relevance** – developing logical thinking

Prior learning
- Students should be able to find angles in circles using the theorems introduced in the previous section.

Working mathematically
- Encourage students to articulate their methods for calculating missing angles and then to apply these to proofs.
- Structure tasks so students can work out the methods for themselves, either by increasing the difficulty incrementally or through one straightforward and one complex example.

Common misconceptions and remediation
- Students may find it difficult to solve problems about angles in circles in which they have to find more than one angle. Advise them to mark, on their diagram, all the angles they know before proceeding with the question.

Probing questions
- How do you find the missing angles in a cyclic quadrilateral? Show me why. Prove it.
- Are all quadrilaterals in a circle cyclic? Why/why not?

Literacy focus
- Key term: cyclic quadrilateral
- Ask students to describe the steps in finding missing angles in cyclic quadrilaterals.
- Ask them to articulate what is meant by 'cyclic quadrilateral'.

Part 1
- Ask students to summarise the three circle theorems they have covered so far.
- Ask **more able** students to prove the first three circle theorems algebraically.

Part 2
- Tell students that they will be learning another circle theorem.
- Ask them to draw the diagram, with O as the centre of the circle.
- Explain that the quadrilateral ABCD, with all its vertices on the circumference of a circle, is a *cyclic quadrilateral*.
- Ask students to measure the four interior angles of the quadrilateral and write down anything they notice.
They should find that opposite angles add up to 180°.

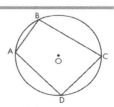

- Explain that this is always true for cyclic quadrilaterals and leads to another circle theorem.
- Formalise **circle theorem 4**: The sum of the opposite angles of a cyclic quadrilateral is 180°. $a + c = 180°$ and $b + d = 180°$. This is usually abbreviated to: angles in a cyclic quadrilateral.

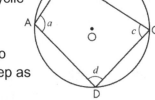

- Work though Example 4 in the Student Book. Encourage students to write down each stage of their working, giving a reason for every step as shown in this example.
- Direct **more able** students to the proof of theorem 4 in the exercise or show it in Part 3.
- **Students can now do Exercise 20C from the Student Book.**
- Go through the earlier questions with **less able** students before they tackle questions 9–11. They could work in pairs for these questions.

G&M 1, 2, 4–6	Calculator all	CM 8–11	MR n/a	PS 3, 7	EV n/a

Part 3

- Ask students: Are all quadrilaterals are cyclic?
- After discussion, explain that a quadrilateral is cyclic only if one pair of opposite angles adds up to 180°.
- Show **more able** students the proof to circle theorem 4.
  From circle theorem 2, $y = 2x$.
  Therefore the reflex angle at the centre of the circle is:
  $360° - y = 360° - 2x$.
- Using circle theorem 2 again, with regard to this reflex angle,
  $360° - 2x = 2z$.
  So $z = 180° - x$ and $x + z = 180°$.

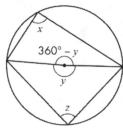

Section 20.3 Tangents and chords

Learning objectives

- Use tangents and chords to find the sizes of angles in circles

Resources and homework

- Student Book 20.3: pages 569–572
- Practice Book 20.3: pages 183–184

Making mathematical connections

- Parts of a circle and using names in the correct context
- Properties of angles on straight lines and interior and exterior angles.

Making cross-curricular connections

- **Sport** – using angles
- **Science** – using formulae
- **Relevance** – developing logical thinking

Prior learning

- Students should be able to calculate angles in circles using the theorems introduced in the previous two sections.
- Students should be familiar with Pythagoras' theorem and trigonometric ratios.

Working mathematically

- Encourage students to articulate their methods for calculating missing angles and then to apply these to proofs.
- Structure tasks so students can work out the methods for themselves, either by increasing the difficulty incrementally or through one straightforward and one complex example.

Common misconceptions and remediation

- Students may find it difficult to solve problems about angles in circles in which they have to find more than one angle. Advise them to mark, on their diagram, all the angles they know before proceeding with the question.

Probing questions

- How could you use Pythagoras' Theorem or trigonometry alongside circle theorems?
- How can you create a right-angled triangle inside or outside of a circle? What would the lines be called and what is special about their properties?

Literacy focus

- Key term: point of contact
- Ask students to explain Pythagoras' Theorem and trigonometric ratios.
- Show a circle with a radius and tangent making a triangle. Ask students to articulate what they see and suggest questions that they might be asked.

Part 1

- Ask students to summarise the four circle theorems they have learned so far.

Part 2

- Revise the terms *tangent* and *chord*. A tangent is a line that touches a circle at a point, known as the point of contact. A chord is a line that joins any two points on the circumference of a circle.
- Ask students to draw the diagram shown, with O as the centre of the circle. OA and OB are radii of the circle and XZ and YZ are tangents that touch the circle at A and B.
- Ask them to measure ∠OAZ and ∠OBZ and write down anything they notice. They should find that both angles are 90°.
- Tell students that this is always true and formalise **circle theorem 5**: A tangent to a circle is perpendicular to the radius drawn to the point of contact. This is usually abbreviated to: the tangent is perpendicular to the radius.
- Ask students to measure the length of AZ and BZ and write down anything they notice. They should find that they are both the same length.
- Tell students that this is always true and formalize **circle theorem 6**: Tangents to a circle from an external point to the points of contact are equal in length. This is usually abbreviated to: tangents from a point are equal.
- Ask students to measure ∠OZA and ∠OZB and write down anything they notice. They should find that the angles are both the same size.
- Tell students that this is always true and formalise **circle theorem 7**: The line joining an external point to the centre of a circle bisects the angle between the tangents. This is usually abbreviated to: a line from the centre bisects the angle between the tangents.
- Ask students to draw the diagram on the right, with O as the centre of the circle. OA is a radius that meets the chord BC at X at 90°.
- Ask students to measure the lengths of BX and CX and write down anything they notice. They should find that the lengths are the same.
- Explain that this is always true and formalise **circle theorem 8**: A radius bisects a chord at 90°. This is usually abbreviated to: the radius–chord property.
- Direct **more able** students to the proofs of theorems 6 and 7.
- Work through Example 5 in the Student Book. This demonstrates how students can use Pythagoras' Theorem alongside circle theorem 5.
- **Students can now do Exercise 20D from the Student Book.**
- Go through the earlier questions with **less able** students before they tackle 7–9.

G&M 1–4	Calculator all	CM 6, 7	MR n/a	PS 5, 9	EV 8

Part 3

- Draw the diagram shown on the board.
- Ask individual students to explain the four circle theorems involving tangents and chords.

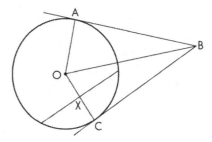

Section 20.4 Alternate segment theorem

Learning objectives
- How to use the alternate segment theorem to find the sizes of angles in circles

Resources and homework
- Student Book 20.4: pages 573–575
- Practice Book 20.4: pages 184–185

Making mathematical connections
- Parts of a circle and using names in the correct context
- Properties of angles on straight lines and interior and exterior angles

Making cross-curricular connections
- **Sport** – using angles
- **Science** – using formulae
- **Relevance** – developing logical thinking

Prior learning
- Students should be able to calculate angles in circles using the eight circle theorems introduced in the previous three sections.

Working mathematically
- Encourage students to articulate their methods for calculating missing angles and then to apply these to proofs.
- Structure tasks so students can work out the methods for themselves, either by increasing the difficulty incrementally or through one straightforward and one complex example.

Common misconceptions and remediation
- Students may find it difficult to solve problems about angles in circles in which they have to find more than one angle. Advise them to mark, on their diagram, all the angles they know before proceeding with the question.

Probing questions
- What are alternate angles? What is a segment? What is meant by the alternate segment.
- Why does the tangent not make a right angle with the triangle?

Literacy focus
- Key term: alternate segment
- Write all the key terms from sections 20A to 20E on the board. Ask students, in pairs, to describe each key term to each other in context.

Part 1

- Revise the eight circle theorems covered so far.
- Students could work in pairs or small groups to see who can be first to summarise them all accurately.

Part 2

- Explain that the angle in the *alternate segment* is the angle subtended from the chord to the circumference on the opposite side of the chord.
- Tell students they will now discover the ninth and final circle theorem.
- Students may find this a difficult theorem to remember, so **less able** students could omit it.
- **Students can now do Exercise 20E from the Student Book.**

| G&M 1 | Calculator n/a | CM n/a | MR 2, 3 | PS n/a | EV n/a |

- Review students work on Exercise 20E.
- Display the diagram, with O as the centre of the circle and XY a tangent to the circle at C.
- Measure ∠BAC and ∠BCY (the angles are the same). Explain that this is always true and this leads to the final circle theorem.
- **Circle theorem 9**: Refer students to the Student Book and tell them that the angle between a tangent and a chord through the point of contact is equal to the angle in the alternate segment. This is usually abbreviated to: alternate segment theorem.
- Show **more able** students that the theorem still holds for obtuse angles.
- Direct **more able** students to the proof of theorem 9 or discuss it in Part 3.
- Work through Example 6.
- **Students can now do Exercise 20F from the Student Book.**

| G&M 1–4 | Calculator all | CM 7, 8 | MR n/a | PS 6 | EV 5 |

Part 3

- Split the class into nine groups of similar ability and ask each group to design a small poster to explain each of the nine circle theorems covered.
- You could use the posters as a classroom display.

Chapter 21 Ratio, proportion and rates of change: Variation

Overview

21.1 Direct proportion	21.2 Inverse proportion

Prior learning

Know squares, square roots, cubes and cube roots of integers.
Know how to substitute values into algebraic expressions.
Know how to solve simple algebraic equations.

Learning objectives

Ensure that students can: solve problems where two variables are connected by a relationship in which they vary in direct proportion; solve problems where two variables are connected by a relationship in which they vary in indirect proportion; recognise graphs that illustrate direct and inverse proportion.

In the examination, students will be expected to:
- solve problems where two variables have a directly proportional relationship (direct variation)
- recognise graphs that show direct variation
- solve problems in which two variables have an inversely proportional relationship (inverse variation)
- work out the constant of proportionality.

Extension

Explore real-life examples of proportion such as exchange rates, interest charges or depreciation of cars. Try to make a model for these situations.
Discuss with students how the scale factor for length, area and volume is in proportion.
Ask **more able** students to research the cross-product.

Curriculum references

Section	GCSE specification
21.1	R 13
21.2	R 13

Route mapping

Exercise	Accessible	Intermediate	Challenging	AO1	AO2 MR CM	AO3 PS EV	Key questions
21A		1–8	9, 10	1–6	7	8–10	5, 8, 10
21B			1–16	1–13	14, 15	16	9, 14, 15
21C		1, 2	3–15	1–10	11, 12	13–15	4, 14, 15

Key questions are those that demonstrate mastery of the concept or which require a step-up in understanding or application. Key questions could be used to identify the questions that students must tackle, to support differentiation, or to identify the questions that should be teacher-marked rather than student-marked.

About this chapter

Making connections: This chapter brings together algebraic manipulation, solving equations and rearranging formulae. The work on iteration builds on students' understanding of sequences, and graphical representation of sequences is a clear way of demonstrating convergence/divergence. For much of the chapter, the next step is A Level content.

Relevance: There is an emphasis on the use of logic and thinking in steps. There are applications in engineering, architecture, manufacturing, project management and many more areas, with STEM careers being a strong focus.

Working mathematically: Rearranging equations; using inverse operations and finding the value of a constant, k.

Assessment: In each section of this chapter, ensure that students have a good grasp of the key questions in each exercise before moving on. (Refer to the 'Route mapping' table above.) Encourage students to read and think about the 'Ready to progress?' statements on page 594 of the Student Book. Check students' understanding at the end of the chapter, formatively, using peer assessment. Students could do a mini test in the form of the 'Review questions' on pages 594–595 of the Student Book. Follow up the test up with an individual target-getting session based on any areas for development that a student may have.

Worked exemplars from the Student Book – suggestions for use

- Present students with the same question but using different numbers. Students should use the exemplar to mirror the working, in full or only the notes.
- Copy and cut the exemplar into cards. Students should match the working with the notes. (You may need to remove the words 'first, second', and so on.)
- Copy and cut the working into cards, splitting the label/description from the working. Students put the working in order, and then match these with the descriptions.

Answers to the Student Book questions are available on the CD-ROM provided.

Section 21.1 Direct proportion

Learning objectives
- Solve problems where two variables have a directly proportional relationship (direct variation)
- Work out the constant of proportionality
- Recognise graphs that show direct variation

Resources and homework
- Student Book 21.1: pages 581–587
- Practice Book 21.1: pages 186–188

Making mathematical connections
- Equivalent fractions
- Rearranging equations and substitution

Making cross-curricular connections
- **Science** – using formulae
- **Relevance** – developing logical thinking

Prior learning
- Students should know squares, square roots, cubes and cube roots of integers. This will speed up their working for many of the questions.
- Students should be able to substitute values into algebraic expressions and solve simple algebraic equations.

Working mathematically
- Encourage students to articulate their methods for numerical fractions and then to apply these to algebraic fractions.
- Structure tasks so students can work out the methods for themselves, either by increasing the difficulty incrementally, or through one straightforward and one complex example.

Common misconceptions and remediation
- Some students find the constant k and then do not complete the question. Encourage students to reread the question and check that their answer makes sense.
- Students often assume that all relationships are linear. Encourage students to highlight or underline words such as 'square', 'cube', 'square root' and 'cube root', so that they remember to take account of them in their equations.

Probing questions
- In a spring, the tension (T newtons) is directly proportional to its extension (x cm). When the tension is 150 newtons, the extension is 6 cm.
- How would you find a formula for T in terms of x?
- How would you calculate the tension, in newtons, when the extension is 15 cm?

Literacy focus
- Key terms: constant of proportionality, direct variation
- Be explicit about the language of equivalence and avoid talking about 'cross-multiplication'.
- Ask students to explain why a constant of proportionality is needed.

Part 1
NB: This section may take more than 1 hour.

- Use quickfire questions to test students' recall of squares, square roots, cubes and cube roots (GCSE requirements are to know the square numbers of 1–15 and the cube numbers of 1–5 and 10 and their corresponding roots.)
- Make a table showing squares and ask students to tell you the answers. Repeat for cubes.

Part 2

- Display this table and ask students for the connections between y and x ($y = 2x$). Show students how to obtain the equation if they cannot spot it.

x	1	2	3	4	5
y	2	4	6	8	10

- Ask for the value of y when $x = 150$ (300). Explain that as x increases, y increases at a constant rate. Since the graph of $y = 2x$ also passes through the origin, we can say that the quantities are directly proportional.
- Write: y is directly proportional to x. Show students how to write this using symbols: $y \propto x$.
- Explain that this means y is a constant multiple of x so,
    $y = kx$, where k is called the constant of proportionality.
- Explain that as they know some values for x and y they can find k.
  For example, using $x = 1$ and $y = 2$ gives $2 = k \times 1$, so $k = 2$ and $y = 2x$.
- Repeat for other tables of values.
- Demonstrate the four steps of the formal method by working through Example 1.
- Repeat with other examples, using different letters for the variables, e.g.
  C is directly proportional to t. When $C = 36$, $t = 9$. Work out the value of C when $t = 7$. (28)
- **Students can now do Exercise 21A from the Student Book. Less able** students could work with a partner for later questions.

R 1–6	Calculator 4–7	CM n/a	MR 7	PS 9, 10	EV 8

Direct proportions involving squares, cubes, square roots and cube roots

- Demonstrate pouring a cup of water slowly onto a piece of paper.
- Ask students what happens to the surface area as more water is poured and the radius of the circle increases. (increases)
- Explain that the relationship shows direct proportion but the connection is between the area and the square of the radius.
- Write $A \propto r^2$ so $A = kr^2$ and ask students to work out the value of k.
- Work through Example 2 with the students.
- You may want to tells students that in the GCSE examination, the relationships are restricted to squares, cubes, square roots and cube roots.
- Show **less able** students an example using cube roots, e.g. y is directly proportional to the cube root of x. When $x = 1000$, $y = 5$. Work out the value of y when $x = 8$. (1)

Recognising graphs showing direct proportion

- Show students graphs for $y = kx^2$, $y = kx^3$, $y = k\sqrt{x}$ and $y = k\sqrt[3]{x}$.
- Working through Example 3, making sure students can recognise and read value for direct proportion from graphs.
- **Students can now do Exercise 21B from the Student Book. Less able** students can work in pairs if necessary.

R 1–13	Calculator 1–13, 16	CM n/a	MR 14, 15	PS n/a	EV 16

Part 3

- Prepare students for the next section on inverse variation by asking them to think of variables where as one increases, the other decreases, e.g. number of people building a wall and time taken.

Section 21.2 Inverse proportion

Learning objectives
- Solve problems in which two variables have an inversely proportional relationship (inverse variation)
- Work out the constant of proportionality

Resources and homework
- Student Book 21.2: pages 587–591
- Practice Book 21.2: pages 188–189

Making mathematical connections
- Rearranging simple formulae
- Solving equations
- Using reciprocal

Making cross-curricular connections
- **Science** – using formulae
- **Computing** – application of logic
- **Relevance** – programming languages; business use of flow diagrams

Prior learning
- Students should know squares, square roots, cubes and cube roots of integers. This will speed up their working for many of the questions.
- Students should be able to substitute values into algebraic expressions and solve simple algebraic equations.

Working mathematically
- Encourage students to be able to move forwards and backwards within a rearrangement and to be able to articulate how they are 'balancing' at each step.
- Give students numbers and fractions and ask for their reciprocals.
- Extend by asking students to create formulae from a proportionality statement that includes more complicated elements such as powers and roots.

Common misconceptions and remediation
- Students may ignore the inverse part and treat as direct proportion.
- They frequently make errors when, following substitution, they rearrange a formula to find the value of the required variable.
- Point out these errors as students make them and provide extra examples for practice.
- Students often assume that all relationships are linear. Encourage them to highlight or underline words such as 'square', 'cube', 'square root' and 'cube root', so that they remember to take account of them in their equations.

Probing questions
- What is meant by direct proportion?
- What is meant by inverse proportion?
- How do you go from a statement of proportionality to writing an equation?

Literacy focus
- Key terms: inverse proportion, inverse variation
- Ask students to describe the steps required from setting up a proportion statement to writing a complete equation.

Part 1
- Tell students: Tom (or pick a student) hired a taxi to take him ice-skating. It cost him £30.
- Ask: If Tom and a friend shared a taxi, how much would it cost them each?

If Tom and two friends shared a taxi, how much would it cost them each?
If Tom and three friends shared a taxi, how much would it cost them each?
Record the information in a table.

People in taxi	1	2	3	4	5
Cost per person	£30	£15	£10	£7.50	£6

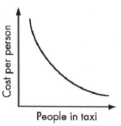

- Generalise: the more people who share the taxi, the less it costs each of them. This is an example of inverse proportion.
- Sketch the graph to show inverse proportion and explain to students that it is a reciprocal graph.

Part 2

- Work through Example 4, showing how to set up the equation to find the constant from the statement of proportionality and how to substitute values into the equation.

Indirect proportions involving squares, square roots and cubes

- Explain that the only difference between direct and indirect variation is that indirect variation uses reciprocals.
- Illustrate this using the tables below. Ask students to complete for square and cube roots.
- Show students an inversely proportional relationship between two variables, such as speed and travel time. (e.g. Speed is inversely proportional to travel time. When I walk at 2 mph, the journey to my nan's takes 20 minutes.)
- Discuss setting up the equation from the statement of proportionality and then how to find the constant.
- Show students the indirect variation graphs shown in the Student Book.
- Work through Example 5 in the Student Book.

Direct variation		Indirect variation	
$y \propto x$	$y = kx$	$y \propto \dfrac{1}{x}$	$y = \dfrac{k}{x}$
$y \propto x^2$	$y = kx^2$	$y \propto \dfrac{1}{x^2}$	$y = \dfrac{k}{x^2}$
$y \propto x^3$	$y = kx^3$	$y \propto \dfrac{1}{x^3}$	$y = \dfrac{k}{x^3}$

- **Students can now do Exercise 21C from the Student Book. Less able** students can work in pairs. Provide support as needed.

R 1–10	Calculator 1–7, 9–11, 14, 15	CM n/a	MR 11, 12	PS 13–15	EV n/a

Part 3

- Students may not understand why inverse proportion graphs all have similar shapes when the functions are different. Demonstrate the differences by asking students to plot the graphs for each of these tables on the same grid. Use scales from 0 to 6 for both axes.

x	1	2	3	4	5	6
$y = \dfrac{6}{x}$	6	3	2	0.5	1.2	1

x	1	2	3	4	5	6
$y = \dfrac{6}{\sqrt{x}}$	6	4.2	3.5	3	2.7	2.4

x	1	2	3	4	5	6
$y = \dfrac{6}{x^2}$	6	1.5	0.7	0.4	0.2	0.2

Chapter 22 Geometry and measures: Triangles

Overview

22.1 Further 2D problems	**22.4** Solving any triangle
22.2 Further 3D problems	**22.5** Using sine to calculate the area of a triangle
22.3 Trigonometric ratios of angles between 0° and 360°	

Prior learning

Know how to use Pythagoras' theorem to work out the sides of right-angled triangles.
Know how to use sine, cosine and tangent to work out angles and sides of right-angled triangles.
Know how to use bearings and calculate angles of elevation and depression.
Know how to use circle theorems.

Learning objectives

Ensure that students can: use trigonometric ratios to solve more complex 2D problems and 3D problems; calculate the sine, cosine and tangent of any angle from 0° to 360°; use the sine and cosine rules to solve problems involving non right-angled triangles; use the formula $A = \frac{1}{2} ab \sin C$ to calculate the area of a triangle.

In the examination, students will be expected to:
- use trigonometric ratios and Pythagoras' theorem to solve more complex two-dimensional problems
- use trigonometric ratios and Pythagoras' theorem to solve more complex three-dimensional problems
- calculate the sine, cosine and tangent of any angle from 0° to 360°
- use the sine rule and the cosine rule to work out sides and angles in any triangle
- work out the area of a triangle if you know two sides and the included angle.

Extension

Consider this problem. Look at the following diagram and prove that $a + b = c$.

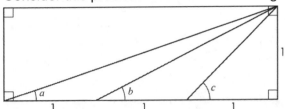

Curriculum references

Section	GCSE specification
22.1	G 20
22.2	G 20
22.3	G 20; A 12
22.4	G 22
22.5	G 22, 23

Route mapping

Exercise	Accessible	Intermediate	Challenging	AO1	AO2 MR CM	AO3 PS EV	Key questions
22A			1–9	3, 8	6	1, 2, 4, 5, 7, 9	4, 9
22B			1–7	1–3	6	4, 5, 7	3, 6, 7
22C		1, 2			1, 2		1, 2
22D		1, 2			1, 2		1, 2
22E			1–8	1, 5	2, 3, 6, 7	4, 8	2, 4, 8
22F			1–11	1–3, 6	4, 5	7–11	5, 11
22G		1–4			1–4		4
22H			1–5	2	3, 4	1, 5	3, 5
22I		1, 2	3–15	1, 2, 14	3, 5, 11, 13, 15	4, 6–10, 12	1, 2, 15
22J		1–5	6–13	1, 3, 6	9, 12	2, 4, 5, 7, 8, 10, 11, 13	1, 2, 11, 12
22K		1, 2	3–7	1	6	2–5, 7	1, 5, 6
22L		1–3	4–12	1–3, 5	8	4, 6, 7, 9–12	8, 9, 12

Key questions are those that demonstrate mastery of the concept or which require a step-up in understanding or application. Key questions could be used to identify the questions that students must tackle, to support differentiation, or to identify the questions that should be teacher-marked rather than student-marked.

About this chapter

Making connections: The chapter brings together the work on circle theorems, angles and lengths of triangles, area of triangles and trigonometry.

Relevance: There is an emphasis on the use of logic and thinking in steps. There are applications in engineering, architecture, manufacturing, project management and many more areas, with STEM careers being a strong focus.

Working mathematically: Students will need to know trigonometric ratios (sine, cosine and tangent) between 0° and 360°. Students must be able to calculate lengths and areas for all triangles, and know which rule to use. They will also have to find the area of any triangle.

Assessment: In every section of this chapter, ensure that students have a good grasp of the key questions in each exercise before moving on. (Refer to the 'Route mapping' table above.) Encourage students to read and think about the 'Ready to progress?' statements on page 626 of the Student Book. Check students' understanding at the end of the chapter, formatively, using peer assessment. Students could do a mini test in the form of the 'Review questions' on pages 626–627 of the Student Book. Follow up the test with an individual target-getting session, based on any areas for development that a student may have. You could also give students a list of angles and ask them for the trigonometric ratio for each function.

Worked exemplars from the Student Book – suggestions for use
- Present students with the same question but using different numbers. Students should use the exemplar to mirror the working, in full or only the notes.
- Copy and cut the exemplar into cards. Students should match the working with the notes. (You may need to remove the words 'first, second', and so on.)
- Copy and cut the working into cards, splitting the label/description from the working. Students should put the working in order, and then match it to the descriptions.

Answers to the Student Book questions are available on the CD-ROM provided.

Section 22.1 Further 2D problems

Learning objectives
- Use trigonometric ratios and Pythagoras' theorem to solve more complex two-dimensional problems

Resources and homework
- Student Book 22.1: pages 597–600
- Practice Book 22.1: pages 190–191

Making mathematical connections
- Use Pythagoras' theorem in 2D
- Use trigonometry in 2D

Making cross-curricular connections
- **Sport** – using lengths and areas
- **Science** – using formulae
- **Relevance** – developing logical thinking

Prior learning
- Students should know how to use Pythagoras' theorem to find the sides of right-angled triangles. They should also be able to use the sine, cosine and tangent ratios to find missing angles and sides of right-angled triangles.

Working mathematically
- Encourage students to articulate their methods and show each stage in their calculation clearly: they should mark the known information and the information they want to identify on their diagrams, to support identification of the correct ratio; they should write out the formula and show their substitutions.
- Structure tasks so students can work out the methods for themselves, either by increasing the difficulty incrementally or through one straightforward and one complex example.

Common misconceptions and remediation
- Students often lose marks by rounding too early in a calculation. Remind students to round only their final answers, not intermediate working.
- Students may not always identify the correct ratio to use. Using a clearly labelled diagram should help eradicate this error.

Probing questions
- When should you use: tan? cosine? sine?
- Talk me through how you got this answer.

Literacy focus
- Key terms: There are no new key terms in this section.
- Encourage students to be explicit about the language of the names of the sides, the formulae they are using and describing the stages in their workings.

Part 1
NB: This section may take more than 1 hour.

Revise circle theorems
- Draw the relevant diagrams and ask students to explain each theorem.
  - o Angles in the same segment are equal.
  - o A radius bisects a chord at right angles.
  - o Tangents from a point are equal in length.
  - o The angle at the centre is twice the angle at the circumference.
  - o A radius is perpendicular to a tangent.

Part 2

- Explain that this section is about using trigonometry in more complex 2D problems.
- Recap Pythagoras' theorem and the three trigonometric ratios for right-angled triangles.
- Using the triangle on the right:

Pythagoras' theorem states: $H^2 = O^2 + A^2$

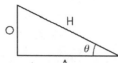

$$\sin \theta = \frac{O}{H} \qquad \cos \theta = \frac{A}{H} \qquad \tan \theta = \frac{O}{A}$$

- Display the diagram shown below and tell students you are going to calculate the length of CD.
- Work through this example, showing students how to set out the solution to a problem.

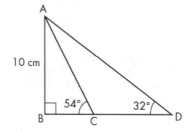

Calculate the length BD: $\qquad \tan 32° = \dfrac{10}{BD}$

$$BD = \frac{10}{\tan 32°} = 16.00\ldots$$

Calculate the length BC:

$$\tan 54° = \frac{10}{BC}; BC = \frac{10}{\tan 54°} = 7.265\ldots$$

Subtract: $\qquad CD = 16.00 - 7.265 = 8.74$ cm (3 sf)

- Tell students to give final answers to 3 sf, unless the question states otherwise. Any intermediate values should be given to at least 4 sf, but should ideally be stored in the calculator memory unrounded. Remind **less able** students how to do this.
- Tell **more able** students that they should still write down their working even if they work out the answer by entering directly into their calculators.
- Work through Examples 1 to 4. These provide useful revision and consolidation of previous work on trigonometry, areas of triangles, Pythagoras' theorem and circle theorems.
- **Students can now do Exercise 22A from the Student Book.**

G&M 3, 8	Calculator all	CM n/a	MR 6	PS 1, 2, 4, 5, 7	EV 9

Part 3

- Use this section to consolidate students' knowledge.
- Go through some questions in class, so that as many students as possible understand the different types of approaches used to solve basic trigonometric problems.
- Ask students to list all the topics they have used in this section.

Section 22.2 Further 3D problems

Learning objectives
- Use trigonometric ratios and Pythagoras' theorem to solve more complex three-dimensional problems

Resources and homework
- Student Book 22.2: pages 600–603
- Practice Book 22.2: pages 191–192

Making mathematical connections
- Use Pythagoras' theorem in 2D
- Use trigonometry in 2D

Making cross-curricular connections
- **Science** – using formulae
- **Computing** – application of logic
- **Relevance** – programming languages; business use of flow diagrams

Prior learning
- Students should be confident using trigonometric ratios and Pythagoras' theorem to solve problems in two dimensions.

Working mathematically
- Encourage students to move forwards and backwards applying trigonometry and Pythagoras' theorem. This activity lends itself to putting the steps in order. Students will need to work logically and break down a task into sections.
- Help students by asking them to articulate each step of their working; encourage drawing of each step so they can visualise a flat, 2D representation of the 3D task.

Common misconceptions and remediation
- Students often lose marks by rounding too early in a calculation. Remind students to round only their final answers, not intermediate working.

Probing question
- How can you construct a 2D representation of a 3D problem?
- How do you find angles using trigonometry?

Literacy focus
- Key terms: There are no new key terms in this section.
- Ask students to describe and then follow the steps needed to construct a 2D representation of a 3D shape.

Part 1
- Introduce visually the concept of the angle between a line and a plane to the class.
- Ask students to define this angle. It is crucial that their definition includes a line that is perpendicular to the plane. Only **more able** students are likely to formalise their ideas in this way.

Part 2
- Explain that this section is about using trigonometry in more complex 3D problems.
- Not all students will be able to recognise right-angled triangles in a 3D diagram. It is useful for them to have a model of a cuboid to refer to. Alternatively, turn a table upside down and join the bottom of one table leg with the top of the diagonally opposite one with string.

- Work through this example, carefully explaining each stage in the working and noting the importance of drawing clearly labelled diagrams.
  ABCDEFGH is a cuboid.
  Calculate the length of the diagonal BH.

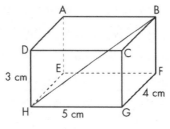

Look for a right-angled triangle with BH as one of its sides and label the known side and the two unknown sides.

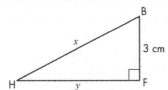

Look for a right-angled triangle with HF (y) as one of its sides.
Use Pythagoras' theorem to find y.
$y^2 = 5^2 + 4^2$, so $y = \sqrt{41}$
Use this value of y to calculate x.
$x^2 = y^2 + 3^2 = 41 + 9 = 50$, so $x = \sqrt{50}$
BH = 7.07 cm (3 sf)

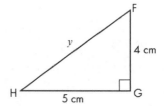

- Extend this asking: Calculate the angle between BH and the base EFGH.
  Draw a diagram showing this angle and label all the known information.
  Use any of the trigonometric ratios to find θ as all three sides are known.

$$\sin \theta = \frac{3}{x} = \frac{3}{\sqrt{50}} = 0.4243\ldots$$

$\theta = 25.1°$ (3 sf)

- Work through Examples 5 and 6 in the Student Book, again focusing on the importance of drawing 2D representations of the 3D problem and showing all stages of working.
- **Students can now do Exercise 22B from the Student Book.**

| G&M 1–3 | Calculator all | CM 6 | MR n/a | PS 4, 5 | EV 7 |

Part 3

- Go through the exercise with the class. Pay particular attention to question 4, as many students will find it difficult to identify the angle between a line and a plane.

Learning objectives

- Calculate the sine, cosine and tangent of any angle from 0° to 360°

Resources and homework

- Student Book 22.3: pages 604–611
- Practice Book 22.3: pages 193–194

Making mathematical connections

- Trigonometry
- Plotting and drawing graphs

Making cross-curricular connections

- **Science** – using formulae, drawing graphs, periods of graphs and waves
- **Computing** – logic gates; formulae in spreadsheets; flow diagrams
- **Relevance** – developing logical thinking

Prior learning

- Students should be confident applying sine, cosine and tangent to problems in right-angled triangles.

Working mathematically

- Research: Find the exact values of the trigonometric functions.
- Display the graphs of sin x, cos x and tan x and ask students how they have been plotted, their symmetrical properties repeating periods.

Common misconceptions and remediation

- Students often confuse the graphs of sine and cosine. Wall displays showing examples may help students increase familiarity.

Probing questions

- What are the key features of the sine, cosine and tangent graphs?

Literacy focus

- Key term: periodic
- Ask students to work in pairs and verbalise the key features of a graph. The partner should work out what graph is being described from its key features.

Part 1

- Ask students to produce accurately plotted graphs for $y = \sin x$, $y = \cos x$ and $y = \tan x$ for $0° \leq x \leq 360°$, each filling, as far as possible, a sheet of A4 graph paper in landscape mode. They can use these graphs as a reference for work in this section.
- When plotting $y = \tan x$, students may ask why tan 90° and tan 270° give error messages on their calculators. Suggest that they leave out these values and plot the graph first.
- Discuss the idea of an asymptote later.

Part 2

The sine curve; The cosine curve

- Tell students that they need to learn the shapes and characteristics (including range) of the graphs $y = \sin x$ and $y = \cos x$ for $0° \leq x \leq 360°$.
- Discuss the characteristics of $y = \tan x$, including asymptotes for the graph of, alongside the sine and cosine curves.

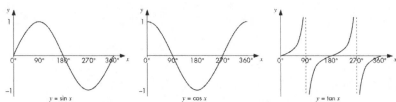

$y = \sin x$ $y = \cos x$ $y = \tan x$

- Emphasise the difference between sketch graphs (draw some as examples) and accurately plotted graphs. They need to be able to produce sketch graphs; they are also extremely useful tools in solving simple trigonometric equations using symmetries of the graphs.
- Work through Examples 7–10.
- The activities suggested lead students towards formalising the trigonometric ratios for any angle in terms of the ratio of the respective acute angle. So, for:
  - ○ $90° < x < 180°$, sin x = sin(180 − x), cos x = −cos(180 − x), tan x = −tan(180 − x)
  - ○ $180° < x < 270°$, sin x = −sin(x − 180), cos x = −cos(x − 180), tan x = tan(x − 180)
  - ○ $270° < x < 360°$; sin x = −sin(360 − x), cos x = cos (360 − x), tan x = −tan(360 − x)
- Students do not need to memorise these. Demonstrate their use as a point of reference by providing one or two specific examples such as sin 30° = sin 150.
- **Students can now do Exercise 22C from the Student Book. Less able** students may need support to be able to complete some questions.

G&M n/a	Calculator all	CM n/a	MR 1, 2	PS n/a	EV n/a

- Examples 7 and 8 show the need for knowing some exact values of the sine ratios and how to use a calculator to find angles.
- **Students can now do Exercise 22D from the Student Book.**

G&M n/a	Calculator all	CM n/a	MR 1, 2	PS n/a	EV n/a

- Examples 9 and 10 show the need for knowing some exact values of the cosine ratios and how to use a calculator to find angles.
- **Students can now do Exercise 22E from the Student Book.**

G&M 1, 5	Calculator all	CM n/a	MR 2, 3, 6, 7	PS 4	EV 8

- **Students can now do Exercise 22F from the Student Book.**

G&M 1–3, 6	Calculator all except 5	CM n/a	MR 4, 5	PS 8–10	EV 7, 11

The tangent curve

- The tangent curve is also periodic and students will need to know how to interpret and plot it in the same way as the sine and cosine curve.
- **Students can now do Exercises 22G and 22H from the Student Book.**

G&M n/a	Calculator all	CM n/a	MR 1–4	PS n/a	EV n/a

G&M 2	Calculator all	CM n/a	MR 3, 4	PS 1	EV 5

Part 3

- Ask students for suggestions as to what happens to trigonometric ratios of angles larger than 360°. By drawing a sketch graph, ask them to solve the equation: cos x = $\frac{1}{2}$ for $0° \leq x \leq 720°$
- Can they predict any further solutions?
- If they know one solution, for example: $x = 60°$, can they suggest a formula for the solution of: cos x = $\frac{1}{2}$? Guide students towards the expression $360n \pm 60$ (perhaps verbally at first).

Section 22.4 Solving any triangle

Learning objectives
- Use the sine rule and the cosine rule to work out sides and angles in any triangle

Resources and homework
- Student Book 22.4: pages 611–621
- Practice Book 22.4: pages 194–197

Making mathematical connections
- Trigonometry
- Substitution

Making cross-curricular connections
- **Sport** – using angles and lengths
- **Science** – using formulae
- **Computing** – logic gates; formulae in spreadsheets; flow diagrams
- **Relevance** – developing logical thinking

Prior learning
- Students should know how to use sine, cosine, tangent and Pythagoras' theorem to calculate the angles and sides of right-angled triangles.

Working mathematically
- Give students a blank triangle and label the sides a, b, c and opposite angles A, B, C.
- Show students the sine rule and the cosine rule and ask: When might you use each formulae? Are there any generalisations? How could you rearrange the cosine formula?

Common misconceptions and remediation
- Students often lose marks by rounding too early in a calculation. Remind students to round only their final answers, not intermediate working.

Probing questions
- When would you use the sine rule? When would you use the cosine rule?
- How could you rearrange the formulae to find the sides or angles?

Literacy focus
- Key terms: cosine rule, included angle, sine rule
- Ask students to discuss what the formulae are actually doing, and any generalisations. For example, the cosine rule can only be used if you have, or are finding, an included angle.

Part 1
- Draw a copy of the triangle, as shown, on the board.
- Ask: How can you find the length of side b?
  Why can't we use the trigonometric ratios?
- Draw a perpendicular from vertex C.
- Ask: Can you see how we might find the length of line AC?

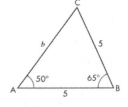

- This should lead to $b \sin 50° = 5 \sin 65°$ and in turn to $\dfrac{b}{\sin 65°} = \dfrac{5}{\sin 50°}$.

- Point out that the equal ratios are the lengths of the sides divided by the sines of the opposite angles. Ask: Is this always true?
- Draw 'the general triangle' on the board and show how the sides and angles are labelled: uppercase letters for vertices or angles and lowercase letters for sides.
- Derive the sine rule from the general triangle.

Part 2

The sine rule; The ambiguous case

- Explain that the sine rule is needed to solve problems involving non right-angled triangles. Such problems occur in many areas from navigation to engineering.
- The sine rule can be used to calculate unknown measures as long as three values in the triangle, including at least one side and one angle, are known.
- Introduce the sine rule: $\dfrac{a}{\sin A} = \dfrac{b}{\sin B} = \dfrac{c}{\sin C}$ or $\dfrac{\sin A}{a} = \dfrac{\sin B}{b} = \dfrac{\sin C}{c}$. They should use sides on top to calculate a side and sines on top to calculate an angle.
- Show students how to apply the sine rule by calculating the size of angle A.

  Use the inverted form of the sine rule with sines on top: $\dfrac{\sin A}{a} = \dfrac{\sin B}{b}$

  Substitute the known values into the formula: $\dfrac{\sin A}{10} = \dfrac{\sin 50°}{8}$

  Rearrange: $\sin A = \dfrac{10 \sin 50°}{8}$, so A = 73.2° (3 sf)

- Work through Examples 11 and 12, reminding students not to round intermediate values.
- **More able** students can work through the ambiguous case in Example 13.
- **Students can now do Exercise 22I from the Student Book. Less able** students could work in pairs to complete later questions in the exercise.

G&M 1, 2, 14	Calculator all	CM 15	MR 3, 5, 11, 13	PS 6–9, 12	EV 4, 10

The cosine rule

- Draw the triangle on the board and introduce the cosine rule:
  $$a^2 = b^2 + c^2 - 2bc \cos A$$
- This can be rearranged to give: $b^2 = a^2 + c^2 - 2ac \cos B$
  $$c^2 = a^2 + b^2 - 2ab \cos C$$
- This is used to find an unknown side if the other two sides and the included angle are known.
- The formula can be rearranged to find an unknown angle, e.g. $\cos A = \dfrac{b^2 + c^2 - a^2}{2bc}$
- Show students how to apply the cosine rule by calculating the length AC.
  Let AC = b $AC^2 = a^2 + c^2 - 2ac \cos B$
  Substitute the known values into the formula:
  $$b^2 = 10^2 + 8^2 - 2 \times 10 \times 8 \times \cos 50° = 61.15...$$
  $$AC = \sqrt{61.15...} = 7.82 \text{ cm (3 sf)}$$
- Tell students that both the sine rule and the cosine rule are given in GCSE examinations.
- Work through Examples 14, 15 and 16.
- **Students can now do Exercise 22J from the Student Book.**

G&M 1, 3, 6	Calculator all	CM 12	MR 9	PS 4, 5, 7, 8, 10, 11, 13	EV 2

Choosing the correct rule

- Discuss the conditions for using the various rules shown in the Student Book.
- **Students can now do Exercise 22K from the Student Book.**

G&M 1	Calculator all	CM 6	MR n/a	PS 2–5	EV 7

Part 3

- Students of a similar ability can work in pairs to make up a question that uses either the sine rule or cosine rule. They should swap and work out the other person's question. Allow time to check their answers.

Section 22.5 Using sine to calculate the area of a triangle

Learning objectives
- Work out the area of a triangle if you know two sides and the included angle

Making mathematical connections
- Sine rule
- Area of a triangle
- Trigonometry

Resources and homework
- Student Book 22.5: pages 621–623
- Practice Book 22.5: page 198

Making cross-curricular connections
- **Sport** – using angles and lengths
- **Science** – using formulae
- **Computing** – logic gates; formulae in spreadsheets; flow diagrams
- **Relevance** – developing logical thinking

Prior learning
- Students should be able to use the sine and cosine rules to work out the value of missing sides and angles in any triangle.

Working mathematically
- Give students a right-angled triangle and ask them to find the area using $\frac{1}{2}bh$.
- Now give students a triangle with two sides and an included angle marked, but nor perpendicular height. Ask students how they could find the area.
- In groups, ask students to describe how to find the height of a triangle using trigonometry and how to apply this to the area of triangle. Can they create the formula themselves?

Common misconceptions and remediation
- Students often lose marks by rounding too early in a calculation. Remind students to round only their final answers. Intermediate working should be to at least 4 sf, but ideally unrounded values.

Probing questions
- Why would we need to use trigonometry to find the area of a triangle? How can we write a general formula if we can find the height using trigonometry and the area using $\frac{1}{2}bh$?

Literacy focus
- Key terms: area rule
- Ask students to work in small groups to devise a resource to explain trigonometry, Pythagoras' theorem, the sine rule and the cosine rule.

Part 1
- Illustrate a specific example of the formula for finding the area of a triangle, using two sides and the included angle, by working from first principles.
- Draw this triangle on the board.
- The area of the triangle is given by: Area $= \frac{1}{2} \times 15 \times h$

$$\sin 50° = \frac{h}{8} \rightarrow h = 8 \sin 50°$$

So area $= \frac{1}{2} \times 15 \times 8 \times \sin 50° = 46.0 \text{ cm}^2$

Part 2

- Tell students that there is a formula for finding the area of a triangle that is not right-angled.
- Go through the proof, which is quite straightforward. (**Less able** students could omit this.)
  Draw the general triangle on the board and label the perpendicular height as h.
  Show that $h = b \sin C$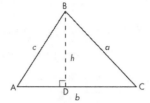
  To find the area of the general triangle ABC, use the formula:

  Area $= \frac{1}{2}$ base $\times$ height

  $\qquad = \frac{1}{2} \times a \times b \sin C$

  $\qquad = \frac{1}{2} ab \sin C$

- Explain that this is the general formula to find the area of a triangle if two sides and the included angle are known. Using different perpendicular heights for the general triangle, the formula can also be written as: Area $= \frac{1}{2} ac \sin B$ or area $= \frac{1}{2} bc \sin A$

  Tell students that the formula is given in GCSE examinations.

- Demonstrate how to apply the formula by working out the area of triangle XYZ.
  Two sides and an included angle are given, so substitute the values
  directly into the formula:

  Area $= \frac{1}{2} \times 7 \times 6 \times \sin 72°$

  $\qquad = 20.0 \text{ cm}^2 \text{ (3 sf)}$

- Work through Example 17.
- Tell students that, in examination questions, they may need to apply the sine rule or cosine rule first.
- Demonstrate using an example for **more able** students.
  Work out the area of triangle ABC.
  Three sides are given, so first find an angle. (It doesn't matter
  which one.)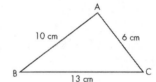

  $\cos B = \dfrac{13^2 + 10^2 - 6^2}{2 \times 13 \times 10}$

  $\quad B = 26.34°$ (Leave the exact value on the calculator display.)
  Use the area formula: Area $= \frac{1}{2} \times 13 \times 10 \times \sin B$

  $\qquad = 28.8 \text{ cm}^2 \text{ (3 sf)}.$

- Work through Example 18 to consolidate the method for two-step questions.
- **Students can now do Exercise 22L from the Student Book.**

G&M 1–3, 5	Calculator all	CM 8	MR n/a	PS 4, 6, 7, 9–11	EV 12

Part 3

- Draw 'the general triangle' on the board.
- Ask students to summarise the three trigonometric formulae they have met.

Chapter 23 Algebra: Graphs

Overview

23.1 Distance–time graphs	**23.5** Equation of a circle
23.2 Velocity–time graphs	**23.6** Other graphs
23.3 Estimating the area under a curve	**23.7** Transformations of the graph $y = \mathrm{f}(x)$
23.4 Rates of change	

Prior learning

Know how speed, distance and time are related.
Know how to draw linear graphs and quadratic graphs.
Know how to find the gradient of a line.
Know how to find the equation of a graph using the gradient-intercept method.
Know how to find the equation of a perpendicular line.
Know that a tangent to a circle and a radius that meet at a point are perpendicular.
Know how to transform a shape by a translation (with a column vector) and a reflection (in a mirror line).

Learning objectives

Ensure that students can: work out speed from a distance–time graph; interpret the gradients of straight lines on a velocity–time graph; calculate and interpret the area under a velocity–time graph consisting of straight lines; draw a graph of the depth of liquid as a container is filled; estimate and interpret the area under a curve; work out and interpret a gradient at a point on a curve; find the equation of a tangent to a circle; recognise and draw cubic, reciprocal and exponential graphs; transform a graph.

In the examination, students will be expected to:
*   interpret distance–time graphs
*   draw a graph of the depth of liquid as a container is filled
*   read information from a velocity–time graph
*   work out the distance travelled from a velocity–time graph
*   work out the acceleration from a velocity–time graph
*   use areas of rectangles, triangles and trapeziums to estimate the area under a curve
*   interpret the meaning of the area under a curve
*   draw a tangent at a point on a curve and use it to work out the gradient at a point on a curve
*   interpret the gradient at a point on a curve
*   find the equation of a tangent to a circle
*   recognise and plot cubic, exponential and reciprocal graphs
*   transform a graph.

Extension

Investigate what the trapezium rule is. Ask students to research what integration is and how this relates to the trapezium rule.
Explore more complex algebraic fractions, for example partial fractions. Use a wider range of mathematics in functions including trigonometric functions.
Explore iteration in coding, in particular the generation of fractals.

Curriculum references

Section	GCSE specification
23.1	A 15
23.2	A 15
23.3	A 15
23.4	A 15

Section	GCSE specification
23.5	A 16
23.6	A 12, 14
23.7	A 7, 13

Route mapping

Exercise	Accessible	Intermediate	Challenging	AO1	AO2 MR CM	AO3 PS EV	Key questions
23A	1–8			1, 3, 4	2, 5, 6, 8	7	3, 7, 8
23B	1, 2	3			1–3		1–3
23C	1–6			1, 2	3, 6	4, 5	1, 4, 5
23D		1, 2	3	1, 2		3	1–3
23E			1–5	1, 2	4	3, 5	1, 3
23F			1–4	1, 4	2, 3		2, 3, 4
23G		1–4	5–10	1, 2, 5, 7	4, 6, 8, 9	3, 10	1, 3, 7, 10
23H		1–8	9–12	1–5, 7, 8	6, 11	9, 10, 12	2, 6–8
23I	1, 2			1, 2			1, 2
23J			1–9	1, 2, 4, 6	3, 8	5, 7, 9	2, 3, 4, 9
23K			1–3	1, 2	3		1–3

Key questions are those that demonstrate mastery of the concept or which require a step-up in understanding or application. Key questions could be used to identify the questions that students must tackle, to support differentiation, or to identify the questions that should be teacher-marked rather than student-marked.

About this chapter

Making connections: This chapter brings together plotting and interpreting graphs, gradients of lines, parts of circles and transformations. For much of this chapter, the next step is A Level content.

Relevance: Finding speed, velocity, distance or time; working out rates of change on a distance–time graph to find velocity; drawing, interpreting and transforming all graphs.

Working mathematically: Working out speed, distance or time, plotting and interpreting distance–time graphs and using this to work towards velocity–time graphs.

Assessment: In each section of this chapter, ensure that students have a good grasp of the key questions in the exercises before moving on. (Refer to the 'Route mapping' table above.) Encourage students to read and think about the 'Ready to progress' statements on page 663 of the Student Book. Check students' understanding at the end of the chapter, formatively, using peer assessment. Students could do a mini test in the form of the 'Review questions' on pages 663–665 of the Student Book. Follow up the test with an individual target-getting session based on any areas for development that a student may have.

Worked exemplars from the Student Book – suggestions for use
- Present students with the same question but using different numbers. Students should use the exemplar to mirror the working, in full or only the notes.
- Copy and cut the exemplar and working into cards. Students should match the working with the notes.

Answers to the Student Book questions are available on the CD-ROM provided.

Section 23.1 Distance–time graphs

Learning objectives
- Interpret distance–time graphs
- Draw a graph of the depth of liquid as a container is filled

Resources and homework
- Student Book 23.1: pages 629–634
- Practice Book 23.1: pages 199–201

Making mathematical connections
- Substitution
- Interpreting graphs

Making cross-curricular connections
- **Science** – using compound measures and formulae
- **Relevance** – developing logical thinking

Prior learning
- Students should know that speed, distance and time are related by the formula:
  speed = distance ÷ time.
- Students should be confident plotting points on coordinate axes and reading scales on axes.

Working mathematically
- Students should know that:
  - Time is always plotted as the horizontal axis.
  - The gradient of a distance–time graph represents the speed.
  - A straight line represents a steady average speed. However, in reality, speed varies due to traffic conditions.

Common misconceptions and remediation
- Students often mistake the minutes for a decimal, e.g. entering 2 hours 30 minutes as 2.3 on a calculator instead of 2.5. Work through some common conversions as a class.
- Students often make mistakes as a result of misreading scales. Remind them to pay attention to this and, if necessary, give them extra practice in reading different scales.

Probing questions
- What is half an hour as a decimal?
- What is one hour and 15 minutes as a decimal?
- How would you write 6 minutes as a decimal value of an hour?
- How would you write $\frac{1}{3}$ of an hour in minutes?

Literacy focus
- Key term: distance–time graph

Part 1
- Ask students to convert the following times to:
  - hours and minutes: 230 min (3h 50 min), 165 min (2h 45 min), 84 min (1h 24 min)
  - minutes: 1h 55 min (115 min), 2h 15 min (135 min), 3h 16 min (196 min)
  - hours: 1h 30 min (1.5 h), 2h 45 min (2.75 h), 3h 20 min (3.3333… h)
  - hours and minutes: 2.666… (2h 40 min), 3.25 (3h 15 min), 1.1 (1h 6 min)
- Make sure students know the decimal equivalents of 15 minutes, 30 minutes, and so on.
- Ask students to draw a set of axes, label them 'distance' and 'time' and draw a graph of their journey to school this morning. On post-it notes, ask classmates to describe the journey and any key features.

Part 2

- Sketch a graph as shown on the right.
- Discuss the differences between this graph and the one they drew in Part 1. (It returns to the original point.)
- Discuss the slopes of the lines. Ask: Which part shows the fastest part of the journey? Make sure students understand that the steeper the line, the higher the speed.

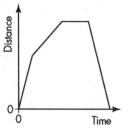

- Ask: Which is the second-fastest part of the graph? This may cause confusion, as the return journey is the second fastest. Make it clear that the direction of the slope is not relevant.
- Ask students to recall the connection between speed, distance and time. Then draw the speed–distance–time triangle.
- Make sure **less able** students understand how to calculate average speed: divide total distance travelled by total time taken.
- Explain that the ratio method is often more straightforward than using the formula. For example, if you travel 15 km in 20 minutes, multiply both parts by three to find the distance travelled in an hour. (45 km in an hour, speed 45 km/h)
- Work through Example 1 from the Student Book, encouraging students to look at the time taken and distance travelled to make their conclusions.
- Remind students:
  - o to use integer grid lines when drawing a triangle to measure the gradient
  - o to divide the change in the vertical direction (distance) by the change in the horizontal direction (time)
  - o that lines that slope from top left to bottom right have a negative gradient. On a distance–time graph, this means that the person or vehicle is on the way back.
- The gradient, whether positive or negative, is the speed. **More able** students should understand the concept of velocity. (It is a vector, so has a value and a direction.)
- **Students can now do Exercise 23A from the Student Book.**

A 1, 3, 4	Calculator n/a	CM 6	MR 2, 5, 8	PS 7	EV n/a

Filling containers

- If possible, show filling different containers as a practical experiment and then draw the corresponding graphs. Students should correlate a straight line in a graph (constant rate) with straight sides and a curved line with tapered sides.
- Work through Example 2.
- **Students can now do Exercise 23B from the Student Book.**

A n/a	Calculator n/a	CM n/a	MR 1–3	PS n/a	EV n/a

Part 3

- Ask some quickfire questions about calculating speed. How fast would you be travelling if you covered:
  - o 60 miles in two hours? (30 mph)
  - o 3 kilometres in 30 minutes? (6 km/h)
  - o 10 kilometres in 15 minutes? (40 km/h)
  - o 210 miles in three hours? (70 mph)
- Ensure that students can convert to distance per hour.

Section 23.2 Velocity–time graphs

Learning objectives
- Read information from a velocity–time graph
- Work out the distance travelled from a velocity–time graph
- Work out the acceleration from a velocity–time graph

Resources and homework
- Student Book 23.2: pages 635–639
- Practice Book 23.2: pages 201–203

Making mathematical connections
- Speed, distance and time
- Substitution
- Area of a trapezium

Making cross-curricular connections
- **Science** – using formulae
- **Computing** – application of logic
- **Relevance** – programming languages; business use of flow diagrams

Prior learning
- Students should know and be able to use the relationships between speed, distance and time and be able to interpret a distance–time graph.
- Students should know and be able to use the formulae for the area of triangle and a trapezium.

Working mathematically
- Students need to substitute values into the formula for the area of a trapezium to calculate the distance travelled in journey shown on a velocity–time graph.
- They can use the total distance travelled to work out the average speed and use this information to make judgements and predictions.

Common misconceptions and remediation
- Students often make errors with average speed. Remind students that to calculate average speed for a whole journey, they first need to work out the total distance travelled by finding the area under the graph.
- Students often mistake the minutes for a decimal, e.g. entering 2 hours 30 minutes as 2.3 on a calculator instead of 2.5. Work through some common conversions as a class.

Probing questions
- What are the key differences between a distance–time graph and a velocity–time graph?
- What is the difference between velocity and speed?

Literacy focus
- Key terms: acceleration, deceleration, velocity–time graph, zero gradient
- Ask students to think of a rollercoaster ride. In pairs, ask them to describe a roller coaster ride and represent it on a velocity–time graph.

Part 1

- A car travels at 20 m/s for 30 seconds; it then increases its speed at a steady rate over 30 seconds to reach a top speed of 30 m/s. It travels at this velocity for 30 seconds and then decreases its speed at a steady rate, reaching a stop after 60 seconds.
- Sketch the velocity–time graph for this journey.
- Point out areas of 'acceleration', 'deceleration' and 'constant velocity'.

Part 2

- Work through Example 3 from the Student Book. Display the velocity–time graph on the board, noting the clearly labelled axes. Discuss what is meant by velocity and establish that a straight-horizontal line means the car is travelling at a constant or steady velocity.
- Tell students that the distance travelled is equal to the area underneath the graph and ask them to work out this distance.
- Work through Example 4 from the Student Book. Discuss the train journey that it represents. The journey starts from a station, so the train starts from a zero velocity, increases speed at a steady rate, travels at a constant speed and then decreases speed at a steady rate to stop at the next station.
- Show students how to calculate the total distance travelled by splitting the area underneath the graph into a rectangle and a triangle and in one step by calculating the area of a trapezium. (Both give the same answer.)
- Ask: Which is more efficient?
- Ask students to calculate the average speed between stations.
- **Students can now do Exercise 23C from the Student Book.**

A 1, 2	Calculator all	CM n/a	MR 3, 6	PS 4, 5	EV n/a

Acceleration

- Tell students that the gradient of a velocity–time graph gives the rate at which the velocity is increasing or decreasing in a given time. If the gradient is positive, the object is accelerating; if the gradient is negative, the object is decelerating.
- Discuss with students that acceleration or deceleration = change in velocity ÷ time taken for the change. Show how the units for acceleration or deceleration are derived.
- Work through Example 5 from the Student Book, encouraging students to choose a suitable start and end-point on the line and then divide the change in vertical distance (velocity) by the change in horizontal distance (time).
- **Students can now do Exercise 23D from the Student Book.**

A 1, 2	Calculator all	CM n/a	MR n/a	PS 3	EV n/a

Part 3

- Give students five minutes to solve this problem, in pairs.
  A boat is travelling in a straight line down a river. On one particular stretch of the river the boat is moving with constant acceleration; its velocity increases from 10 m/s to 20 m/s in 4 seconds.
  - How far does the boat travels on this stretch?
  - Calculate the acceleration of the boat.

Section 23.3 Estimating the area under a curve

Learning objectives

- Use areas of rectangles, triangles and trapeziums to estimate the area under a curve
- Interpret the meaning of the area under a curve

Resources and homework

- Student Book 23.3: pages 640–643
- Practice Book 23.3: pages 204–205

Making mathematical connections

- Area of rectangles, triangles and trapeziums
- Distance–time graphs
- Velocity–time graphs

Making cross-curricular connections

- **Science** – using formulae
- **Computing** – logic gates; formulae in spreadsheets; flow diagrams
- **Relevance** – developing logical thinking

Prior learning

- Students must be able to calculate areas of rectangles, triangles and trapeziums.

Working mathematically

- Students visualise breaking up a curve into familiar shapes in order to estimate the area under a curve.
- Students need to substitute values into formulae for the area of triangles, trapeziums and rectangles to estimate the distance travelled in a journey shown on a velocity–time graph.
- They can use the total distance travelled to work out the average speed and use this information to make judgements and predictions.

Common misconceptions and remediation

- Students often make errors with average speed. Remind students that to calculate average speed for a whole journey, they first need to work out the total distance travelled by finding the area under the graph.
- Students often mistake the minutes for a decimal, e.g. entering 2 hours 30 minutes as 2.3 on a calculator instead of 2.5. Work through some common conversions as a class.

Probing questions

- How can you tell if your estimate of area is an over-estimate or an under-estimate?
- How could you increase the accuracy of your estimate?

Literacy focus

- Key terms: There are no new key terms in this section.
- Talk about the most efficient way to break up a compound shape. Describe areas of rectangles, triangles and trapeziums using words that relate it to the shape they can make underneath the curve.

Part 1

- Draw five or six triangles, rectangles and trapeziums on the board and ask students to find the area of each. Increase the challenge by mixing up the units.
- Draw two or three compound shapes on the board and ask students to work out the area of each by splitting them into simpler shapes. Again, mix up the units.

Part 2

- Look at the graph in Example 6 in the Student Book. Remind students that this is a velocity–time graph and that the area underneath the curve represents the total distance travelled.
- Work through Example 6, splitting the area under the curve into triangles and trapeziums. Label each shape so that they can work out each area separately without confusion.
- Ask students to work out the area of each shape and add them together to find an estimate of the total distance travelled.
- If the shapes are underneath the curve it will be an under-estimation and if the shapes are above the curve it will be an over-estimation. Discuss why they need to know this.
- Work through Example 7, making sure that students understand why the distance calculated is an over-estimation.
- **Students can now do Exercise 23E from the Student Book.**

| A 1, 2 | Calculator all | CM 4 | MR n/a | PS n/a | EV 3, 5 |

Part 3

- Display a graph similar to the one shown on the right.
- Tell students that the graph gives information about the velocity of an electric hybrid car during the first 40 seconds of motion.
  Ask them to:
  Calculate an estimate for the distance travelled during the first 40 seconds.
  State, with a reason, whether your answer is an over-estimate or under-estimate of the true distance travelled.

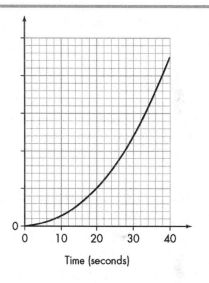

Time (seconds)

Section 23.4 Rates of change

Learning objectives

- Draw a tangent at a point on a curve and use it to work out the gradient at a point on a curve
- Interpret the gradient at a point on a curve

Resources and homework

- Student Book 23.4: pages 643–645
- Practice Book 23.4: pages 205–206

Making mathematical connections

- Finding the gradient of a straight line
- Understanding what is meant by a tangent and a chord

Making cross-curricular connections

- **Science** – using formulae
- **Computing** – formulae in spreadsheets
- **Relevance** – developing logical thinking

Prior learning

- Students should be familiar with distance–time and velocity–time graphs and be able to calculate gradients of straight lines.
- They should also be able to calculate the distance travelled and average journey speed from a velocity–time graph.

Working mathematically

- Draw a tangent to the curve and encourage students to think of it as a right-angled triangle. The change in velocity is the vertical (or rise) distance and the change in time (or run) will be the horizontal distance.
- Students substitute their values into gradient = change in y ÷ change in x.

Common misconceptions and remediation

- Students often make errors with average speed. Remind students that to calculate average speed for a whole journey, they first need to work out the total distance travelled by finding the area under the graph.
- Students often mistake the minutes for a decimal, e.g. entering 2 hours 30 minutes as 2.3 on a calculator instead of 2.5. Work through some common conversions as a class.
- Students sometimes draw the tangent incorrectly. Point this out to students when it occurs.

Probing questions

- How would you find the rate of change if the object was decelerating?

Literacy focus

- Key term: tangent
- Give students a list of terms such as *velocity*, *acceleration*, *speed*, *gradient*, and so on. Ask students to write a description of each term and form a card-sort matching activity or write additional descriptions and produce a multiple choice quiz.

Part 1

- Display several straight-line graphs on the board (or on a worksheet) and ask students to work out the gradient of each graph.
- Remind students that gradient = change in y ÷ change in x.
- An easier way to remember this may be rise ÷ run.

Part 2

- Ask, or remind, students what a tangent is.
- Explain that, if you draw a tangent to a curved graph, you can use it to work out the gradient of the graph at that point.

Distance–time graphs

- Remind students that the gradient of a distance–time graph represents the speed of the object.
- Show the students how to find the rate of change of a curved distance–time graph by working through the steps in the Student Book.

Velocity–time graphs

- Remind students that the gradient of a velocity–time graph represents the acceleration of the object.
- Work through Example 8 from the Student Book. Show students how to draw a tangent, making sure that it only has one point of contact with the curve; mark a right-angled triangle between two integer points on the tangent and label the base and height. Remind students that they can find the gradient by dividing the height by the base (rise ÷ run). Discuss how to find the units for acceleration.
- **Students can now do Exercise 23F from the Student Book.**

A 1, 4	Calculator all	CM 3	MR 2	PS n/a	EV n/a

Part 3

- Show various unusual graphs to the students such as the ones below.

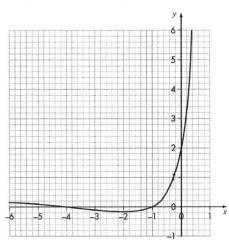
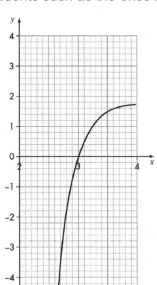
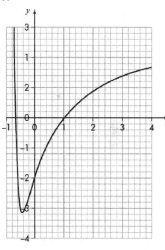
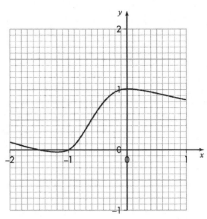

- Give each pair a specific *x* value and ask them to find the *y*-coordinate at that position.

Section 23.5 Equation of a circle

Learning objectives
- Find the equation of a tangent to a circle

Resources and homework
- Student Book 23.5: pages 646–648
- Practice Book 23.5: pages 206–207

Making mathematical connections
- Equations of straight lines
- Equations of quadratics
- Graphs of straight-lines and quadratics

Making cross-curricular connections
- **Science** – interpreting graphs
- **Relevance** – logical thinking

Prior learning
- Students should be able to match graphs with the real-life situation they represent.
- They should also be able to sketch a graph of a particular situation.

Working mathematically
- Students substitute x and y coordinates into the formula for the area of a circle and simplify surds.
- Students know and use the property that the product of two perpendicular gradients is 1.

Common misconceptions and remediation
- Students often forget to square root to find the final value of x, y or r.
- They may not read a question properly and so use the measurement for the diameter as the radius.
- Encourage students to show each stage of their working clearly and re-read the question to make sure their answer makes sense.
- Remind them regularly that a tangent is perpendicular to a radius at the point of contact.

Probing questions
- What is the gradient of a radius if the gradient of the tangent where it meets the radius is $\frac{5}{3}$?
- What is the radius of a circle with the equation $x^2 + y^2 = 36$? Why?

Literacy focus
- Key terms: There are no new key terms in this section.
- On the board, draw a circle with centre (0, 0). Draw a tangent to the circle. Ask students to describe key features of the diagram.

Part 1
- Tell students that the equation for a circle with its centre at the origin and radius r is:
    $$x^2 + y^2 = r^2$$
- Ask students to draw a circle with the equation: $x^2 + y^2 = 5^2$
- Ask: Is the point (4, 3) on the circumference of the circle? Why?
  (Yes, because $4^2 + 3^2 = 5^2$)

Part 2

- Demonstrate the method for working out the equation of a tangent to a circle at a given point by working through Example 9 from the Student Book.
- Remind students that the formula for a circle is $x^2 + y^2 = r^2$, so the radius is $\sqrt{52}$. Work through the simplification of the surd: $\sqrt{52} = \sqrt{4} \times \sqrt{13} = 2\sqrt{13}$ and then double to find the length of the diameter.
- The coordinates of two ends of the radius are given, so use change in y ÷ change in x to work out the gradient.
- Remind students that a tangent is perpendicular to a radius at the point of contact. This means that the product of their gradients will be –1.
- Students can then substitute the values of m, x and y into $y = mx + c$ and work out the value of c to give the equation of the tangent.
- Make sure they can show that this is equivalent to the equation given.
- Work through Example 10, highlighting the steps that students need to take to work out the equations of the tangents: work out the gradient of the diameter; the equation of the diameter; the point of contact the tangents.
- **Students can now do Exercise 23G from the Student Book.**

| A 1, 2, 5, 7 | Calculator n/a | CM 6 | MR 4, 8, 9 | PS 3, 10 | EV n/a |

Part 3

- Give students a circle already drawn on axes such as the one on the right.
- Ask them to design a question based around the circle and the associated mark scheme.

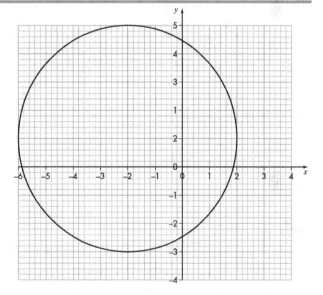

Learning objectives

- Recognise and plot cubic, exponential and reciprocal graphs

Resources and homework

- Student Book 23.5: pages 649–654
- Practice Book 23.5: pages 207–208

Making mathematical connections

- Equations of straight lines
- Equations of quadratics
- Graphs of straight-lines and quadratics

Making cross-curricular connections

- **Science** – interpreting graphs
- **Relevance** – logical thinking

Prior learning

- Students need good calculator skills to complete tables of values.
- Students should be able to draw clear quadratic graphs – these graphs require the same skills to draw one smooth curve passing through all plotted points.
- Students should also be able to use the power button on their calculators.

Working mathematically

- Students use graphing software to explore cubic, reciprocal and exponential graphs.
- Students work in small groups to describe key features of each type of graph using terms such as *turning point*, *minimum point*, *maximum point* and *asymptote*.

Common misconceptions and remediation

- Students frequently miscalculate powers. More practice and worked examples should help to reduce the frequency of these errors.

Probing questions

- What is the same/different about quadratic and cubic graphs?
- What would a graph of x^4 or x^5 look like?
- What would an exponential graph/reciprocal graph look like?
- What is meant by an *asymptote*?

Literacy focus

- Key terms: asymptote, cubic, exponential function, reciprocal
- Ask students to describe and then write down what is meant by these terms: intersect; asymptote; minimum vertex; maximum vertex.

Part 1

- Ask students to use their calculators to work out a range of calculations involving powers, e.g. $2 \times (3^4 - 2^8) - 9$ (−359); $4^{0.5}$ (2); $(3 + 8)^5$ (16 1051);$3^{0.6}$ (1.933...)
- Continue until you are confident that students can use the power button on their calculators correctly.
- Ask questions about exponential growth and ask students to spot the rule, e.g.
  Bacteria double in number every 20 minutes. If you start with one bacterium, how many will there be after: one hour? (8) six hours? (262 144) 12 hours? (6.87 × 10^{10})
  How many will there be after x hours? (2^{3x})

Part 2

Cubic graphs

- Tell students that they should use the same techniques to plot and draw cubic graphs as they use for linear and quadratic graphs.
- Work through Example 11, highlighting the first step of drawing and completing a table of values. Emphasise that when a negative number is cubed, the result will be negative.
- Remind students of the relevant graph terminology.
  - The *roots* of a graph are the values of x when $y = 0$, that is where the graph crosses the x-axis. A quadratic can have up to two roots, a cubic up to three roots, and so on.
  - The minimum vertex is the lowest turning point of the curve.
  - The maximum vertex is the highest turning point of the curve.
- **Less able** students could do questions 1–4 of Exercise 23H before continuing with the lesson.

Reciprocal graphs

- A reciprocal function has the form $y = \dfrac{a}{x}$. All reciprocal graphs have a similar shape and some have symmetrical properties.
- Remind students that an *asymptote* is a line that gets closer and closer to the axes, but never actually touches them.
- Again, encourage students to draw and complete a table of values before plotting the graph.
- **Less able** students could do questions 5 and 6 of Exercise 23H before continuing with the lesson.

Exponential graphs

- An exponential function has an equation in the form $y = k^x$.
- Demonstrate how to calculate the points and draw an exponential graph by working through Example 12. Make sure students can use their calculators to find the required y-values.
- Discuss the key features of an exponential graph.
- **Students can now do or complete Exercise 23H from the Student Book.**

| A 1–5, 7, 8 | Calculator n/a | CM 6 | MR 11 | PS 9, 10, 12 | EV n/a |

Part 3

- Make sure students can use their calculators to work out sine and cosine values.
- Ask students to use their calculators to work out sin 60° (0.866…) and cos 80° (0.1736…).

Section 23.7 Transformations of the graph $y = f(x)$

Learning objectives
- Transform a graph

Resources and homework
- Student Book 23.5: pages 655–660
- Practice Book 23.5: pages 208–210

Making mathematical connections
- Substitution
- Plotting graphs
- Trigonometric graphs

Making cross-curricular connections
- **Science** – plotting graphs
- **Relevance** – applications to manufacturing and project management

Prior learning
- Students should know how to transform a shape by a translation (as a vector), reflection, and enlargement.
- They should to be able to sketch the graphs of: $y = x$, $y = x^2$, $y = x^3$, $y = \sin x$, $y = \cos x$, and $y = \tan x$.

Working mathematically
- Students use graphing software to plot functions of x and explore what happens for: $f(x) + a$, $f(x - a)$, $-f(x)$ and $f(-x)$
- Students work in small groups and each transform a different function of x, recording the result of each transformation.
- Students look at the effect of transformations on turning points.

Common misconceptions and remediation
- When transforming $f(x)$ to $f(x + a)$, students translate by $\begin{pmatrix} a \\ 0 \end{pmatrix}$ rather than $\begin{pmatrix} -a \\ 0 \end{pmatrix}$. Revise frequently and point out errors when they occur.

Probing questions
- Which rule transforms, for example, $y = x^2$ to $y = x^2 - 5$?
- Ask similar questions to cover all four rules.

Literacy focus
- Key terms: function, transform

Part 1
- Ask students to sketch the graphs of $y = x$, $y = x^2$, $y = x^3$, $y = \sin x$, $y = \cos x$, and $y = \tan x$.
- Remind them of what happens when we move a point using a column vector such as:

$$\begin{pmatrix} 2 \\ 0 \end{pmatrix}, \begin{pmatrix} 3 \\ 0 \end{pmatrix}, \begin{pmatrix} -2 \\ 0 \end{pmatrix}, \begin{pmatrix} 0 \\ -3 \end{pmatrix}$$

Part 2

- Students need to be familiar with a range of transformations. An investigative approach is often the most successful.
- **Students start by exploring transformations in Exercise 23I from the Student Book.**

| A 1, 2 | Calculator n/a | CM n/a | MR n/a | PS n/a | EV n/a |

- Revise function notation and discuss the four rules of transformations with students: $f(x) + a$, $f(x - a)$, $-f(x)$ and $f(-x)$. Use graph-drawing software to show the results of the transformations, if possible.
- Although this is an A* topic, **less able** students will find the functions $f(x) + a$ and also $-f(x)$. accessible. Pay particular attention to $f(x + a) / f(x - a)$ as this is not what most students will expect.
- Work through Example 13 from the Student Book. The process of sketching and then describing encourages students to visualise and then articulate the changes.
- Work through Example 14, highlighting that the transformations are the same for the sine curve, but noting the effect of the scale on the x-axis (degrees).
- If needed, break down the exercise. The questions 'investigate' each rule, so to help **less able** students to build their knowledge base, pick out only the questions that cover one rule.
- **Students can now do Exercise 23J from the Student Book.**

| A 1, 2, 4, 6 | Calculator n/a | CM n/a | MR 3, 8 | PS 5, 9 | EV 7 |

Completing the square
- Work through the text in the Student Book, which shows how to describe a transformation from a completed square equation.
- **Students can now do Exercise 23K from the Student Book.**

| A 1, 2 | Calculator n/a | CM n/a | MR 3 | PS n/a | EV n/a |

Part 3

- Sketch the graph of any function on the board. For example:

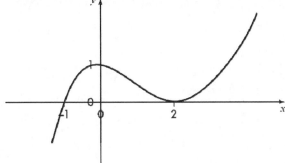

- Ask what would happen to the graph after the following transformations:
  $y = f(x - 2)$, $y = f(x + 1)$, $y = f(x) + 1$, $y = -f(x)$
- Make sure students are aware of any invariant points under each transformation.

Chapter 24 Algebra: Algebraic fractions and functions

Overview

24.1 Algebraic fractions	**24.4** Composite functions
24.2 Changing the subject of a formula	**24.5** Iteration
24.3 Functions	

Prior learning
Know how to substitute numbers into an algebraic expression.
Know how to factorise linear and quadratic expressions.
Know how to expand a pair of linear brackets to form a quadratic expression.

Learning objectives
Ensure that students can: combine fractions algebraically and solve equations with algebraic fractions; rearrange and change the subject of a formula where the subject appears twice, or as a power; find the inverse function and the composite of two functions; find an approximate solution for an equation using the process of iteration.

In the examination, students will be expected to:
- simplify algebraic fractions
- solve equations containing algebraic fractions
- change the subject of a formula where the subject occurs more than once
- find the output of a function
- find the inverse function
- find the composite of two functions
- find an approximate solution for an equation using the process of iteration.

Extension
Write some algebraic fraction questions that are quadratic and give the answer 4.
Explore more complex algebraic fractions, for example, partial fractions.
Use a wider range of mathematics in functions including trigonometric functions.
Explore iteration in coding, in particular the generation of fractals.

Curriculum references

Section	GCSE specification
24.1	N 8, A 4
24.2	A 4
24.3	A 4
24.4	A 7, 20
24.5	A 7, 20

Route mapping

Exercise	Accessible	Intermediate	Challenging	AO1	AO2 MR CM	AO3 PS EV	Key questions
24A		1–7	8–19	1–6, 8–10, 13, 14, 18	7, 12, 15, 17	11, 16, 19	3, 6, 13, 18
24B		1–6	7–11	1–6, 9		7, 8, 10, 11	3, 10, 11
24C	1–4	5–7		1–3, 5, 6	4, 7		5–7
24D		1, 2	3	1, 2	3		1–3
24E		1, 2	3, 4	1, 2	3	4	1, 2, 4
24F		1–7	8–11	1–4	5, 6, 8	7, 9–11	2, 8, 11

Key questions are those that demonstrate mastery of the concept or which require a step-up in understanding or application. Key questions could be used to identify the questions that students must tackle, to support differentiation, or to identify the questions that should be teacher-marked rather than student-marked.

About this chapter

Making connections: The chapter brings together substitution into algebraic expressions, factorising linear and quadratic expressions and expanding brackets. Students will need to know how to rearrange formulae and use inverse operations.

Relevance: To use a spreadsheet competently, students will need to understand how functions work.

Working mathematically: Expanding and factorising expressions, adding, subtracting, multiplying and dividing fractions, rearranging equations and iterations.

Assessment: In each section of this chapter, ensure that students have a good grasp of the key questions in the exercises before moving on. (Refer to the 'Route mapping' table above.) Encourage students to read and think about the 'Ready to progress?' statements on page 684 of the Student Book. Check students' understanding at the end of the chapter, formatively, using peer assessment. Students could do a mini test in the form of the 'Review questions' on pages 684–685 of the Student Book. Follow up the test with an individual target-getting session, based on any areas for development that a student may have.

Worked exemplars from the Student Book – suggestions for use
- Present students with the same question but using different numbers. Students should use the exemplar to mirror the working, in full or only using the notes.
- Copy and cut the exemplar into cards. Students should match the working with the notes. (You may need to remove the words 'first, second', and so on.)
- Ask students to write their own exemplar questions based on those in the Student Book.

Answers to the Student Book questions are available on the CD-ROM provided.

Section 24.1 Algebraic fractions

Learning objectives
- Simplify algebraic fractions
- Solve equations containing algebraic fractions

Resources and homework
- Student Book 24.1: pages 667–672
- Practice Book 24.1: pages 211

Making mathematical connections
- Adding, subtracting, multiplying and dividing fractions
- Simplifying linear and quadratic expressions
- Expanding and factorising

Making cross-curricular connections
- **Science** – using compound measures and formulae
- **Relevance** – developing logical thinking

Prior learning
- Students should be able to of add, subtract, multiply and divide numerical fractions.
- They should also be able to factorise, multiply and simplify algebraic expressions confidently.

Working mathematically
- Encourage students to articulate their methods for numerical fractions (equivalence, including cancelling, addition and subtraction, multiplication and division) and then to apply these to algebraic fractions.
- Structure tasks so students can work out the methods for themselves, either by increasing the difficulty incrementally or through one straightforward and one complex example.

Common misconceptions and remediation
- Students often fail to cancel common factors, and make errors when multiplying two negative values. Remind students to look for these things when checking their work.

Probing questions
- Describe how cancelling common factors in an algebraic fraction can make calculating the answer more straightforward.

Literacy focus
- Key term: algebraic fraction
- In pairs, give students an algebraic fraction. Ask them to describe the steps used to solve it. Students can produce a sort-card activity where they break down each step to the final answer on separate bits of paper and then sort each other's cards out in the correct order.

Part 1
- Ask students to use their calculators to work out: $\frac{1}{3} + \frac{2}{5}$; $\frac{3}{5} - \frac{1}{8}$; $\frac{3}{4} \times \frac{1}{5}$; $\frac{3}{5} \div \frac{2}{3}$
- They should write their answers in full, for example: $\frac{1}{3} + \frac{2}{5} = \frac{5}{15} + \frac{6}{15} = \frac{11}{15}$

Part 2

- Introduce the four rules of fractions outlined on page 665 of the Student Book.
- Explain that these rules work for any pair of fractions.
- Explain that a, b, c and d can be any values, numbers or expressions.
- Revisit the four calculations from Part 1 and ask individuals to come to the board and use the rules to work out the answers to the fraction calculations. $\left(\frac{11}{15}, \frac{19}{40}, \frac{3}{20}, \frac{9}{10}\right)$
- Ask half the class to do the calculations below on their calculators and the other half to use the rules: $\frac{5}{8} + \frac{1}{6}$ $\frac{3}{4} - \frac{3}{10}$
- Swap over the calculator group with the other group and repeat using these calculations: $\frac{5}{9} \times \frac{3}{10}$ $\frac{8}{9} \div \frac{2}{3}$
- Compare answers. Explain that the rules always work, but may not give the answer in its simplest form.
- Write the expression $x^2 - 9$ on the board and ask students what they can tell you about it. Prompt, if necessary, that it is a difference of two squares and remind students that this can be factorised to $(x - 3)(x + 3)$.
- Repeat with $4a^2 - 25$ and other examples until students are confident with the method.
- Work through Examples 1 to 8 from the Student Book. **More able** and **less able** students will benefit from working through these as the algebraic skills required gradually increase.
- Before working through Example 3, remind students that the denominator must be the same before they can add or subtract, so they will need to cross-multiply.
- **Students can now do Exercise 24A from the Student Book.**

| A 1–6, 8–10, 13, 14, 18 | Calculator n/a | CM 7, 15, 17 | MR 12 | PS 19 | EV 11, 16 |

Part 3

- Ask students to expand $x^2 + (x + 2)^2 = 16$ and then rearrange this into the general quadratic form of $ax^2 + bx + c = 0$ ($2x^2 + 4x - 12 = 0$).
- Tell students that this is not fully simplified and urge them to cancel the common factor of 2.
- Repeat with $x^2 + (2x + 5)^2 = 40$ which finally cancels to $x^2 + 2x - 3 = 0$. Ask students to solve this equation ($x = -3$ and $x = 1$).

Section 24.2 Changing the subject of a formula

Learning objectives
- Change the subject of a formula where the subject occurs more than once

Resources and homework
- Student Book 24.2: pages 672–674
- Practice Book 24.2: pages 211–212

Making mathematical connections
- Rearranging equations using inverse operations
- Factorisation

Making cross-curricular connections
- **Science** – using formulae
- **Computing** – using formulae
- **Relevance** – programming languages; business use of flow diagrams

Prior learning
- Students should be able to factorise and manipulate algebraic fractions. This lesson will help develop their algebraic skills.

Working mathematically
- Encourage students to articulate their methods for rearrangement, and to be explicit in their intention to 'change sides change signs'.
- Students factorise and eliminate common factors.
- Structure tasks so students can work out the methods for themselves, either by increasing the difficulty incrementally or through one straightforward and one complex example.

Common misconceptions and remediation
- Students make errors due to inadequate algebraic skills or careless errors, for example they rearrange $a + b = c$ as $a = c + b$, forgetting to change the sign.
- Students may forget to use brackets or apply inverse operations in the incorrect order, for example they incorrectly rewrite $2a + b = c$ as $a = c - b \div 2$ instead of $a = (c - b) \div 2$, or $a = \dfrac{c - b}{2}$.
- Extra practice and worked examples should help students to reduce these errors.

Probing questions
- What is meant by factorising x out of the left-hand side?

Literacy focus
- Key terms: There are no new key terms in this section.
- Working in small groups, ask students to describe the steps involved in simplifying algebraic fractions in the work they did in the previous section.

Part 1
What is my rule?
- Say that you have a simple rule in your head and it, for example, involves adding a number to a starting number. You will give a final number and they must guess the starting number. For example, if the rule is $y = x + 6$:
  - Say: My final number is 13. What number did I start with?
  - Once a student guesses the correct answer (7), record it and say:
    Now my final number is 20. What number did I start with? (14)

- o After several examples, some students will realise the rule. Ask them to give the rule, or continue until more students spot it.
- If students do not spot the rule, make it easier. Start with the result for 1 (7), then 2 (8).
- If answers are sequential, students will spot the rule more easily.
- Make the rules less or more complex depending on students' ability.
- Straightforward rules include $x - 3$, $2x$ and $x \div 5$.
- Challenge **more able** students with more complex rules such as $2x + 1$, $3x - 2$ and even $\frac{x}{2} + 1$, $\frac{x + 1}{5}$ or $x^2 + 3$, if appropriate.

Part 2

- Students will have met rearranging equations before, but remind them of the process.
- Demonstrate or prompt students to rearrange $y = 3x + 5$ to make x the subject.

$$y = 3x + 5$$
$$y - 5 = 3x \qquad \text{(Subtract 5 from both sides)}$$
$$x = \frac{y - 5}{3} \qquad \text{(Divide by 3)}$$

- Now write $y + 2x = x + 4$ on the board. Ask students why this is different from previous examples. (The subject appears twice.)
- Again, they should have met this before. Work through to get:

$$y + 2x = x + 4$$
$$y + x = 4 \qquad \text{(Subtract } x \text{ from both sides)}$$
$$x = 4 - y \qquad \text{(Subtract } y)$$

- When rearranging a formula where the subject appears twice, such as $ax + b = d - cx$, the subject term must be taken out of at least two terms as a common factor. Remind students that the first step is to rearrange the formula, so that all the terms containing the subject are on the same side and all terms that don't contain the subject are on the other side, i.e. $ax + cx = d - b$. They should then factorise the expression: $x(a + c) = d - b$. The final stage is to divide both sides by $a + c$, so $x = \frac{d - b}{a + c}$.
- Work through Examples 9 and 10 from the Student Book. In Example 9, **less able** students may struggle to factorise the variable out of the left-hand side, so be prepared to provide more practice.
- Students may be let down by poor algebraic skills so, before these students try this topic, give them some practice in basic algebra (expanding brackets, collecting terms, factorising).
- **Students can now do Exercise 24B from the Student Book.**

| A 1–6, 9 | Calculator all | CM n/a | MR n/a | PS n/a | EV 7, 8, 10, 11 |

Part 3

- Recall the method for adding and subtracting fractions, such as: $\frac{2}{3} + \frac{1}{4}$, $\frac{4}{5} - \frac{1}{3}$.

Learning objectives

- Find the output of a function
- Find the inverse function

Resources and homework

- Student Book 24.3: pages 674–677
- Practice Book 24.3: pages 212–213

Making mathematical connections

- Function machines
- Inverse operations
- Substitution

Making cross-curricular connections

- **Science** – use of formulae
- **Computing** – logic gates; formulae in spreadsheets; flow diagrams
- **Relevance** – developing logical thinking

Prior learning

- Students will have some understanding of using function machines and inverse operations.
- Students should be able to factorise, use brackets and manipulate algebraic fractions. This lesson will help develop their algebraic skills.

Working mathematically

- Encourage students to use a function machine to visualise an equation in steps. This will clearly show the order of the operations and inverse operations.
- Introduce $f(x)$ to mean a function of x, reminding students that x is a variable and can take on any numerical value.
- Introduce $f^{-1}(x)$ to mean the inverse of a function. This means how to find the input from the output. Remind students that they should replace y with x.
- Structure tasks so students can work out the methods for themselves, either by increasing the difficulty incrementally or through one straightforward and one complex example.

Common misconceptions and remediation

- Students make errors due to inadequate algebraic skills or careless errors, for example they rearrange $a + b = c$ as $a = c + b$, forgetting to change the sign.
- Students may forget to use brackets or apply inverse operations in the incorrect order, for example they incorrectly rewrite $2a + b = c$ as $a = c - b \div 2$ instead of $a = (c - b) \div 2$, or $a = \dfrac{c - b}{2}$.
- Extra practice and worked examples should help students to reduce these errors.

Probing questions

- What is meant by the *inverse of an operation* or *inverse of a function*?
- What are the inverse operations, including inverses of powers and roots?

Literacy focus

- Key terms: inverse, inverse function
- In pairs, encourage students to play a 'winner stays on' style inverse operations game. One player states an operation, e.g. x^2, and the partner states the inverse. Partners swap roles when an error is made.
- You could get a competition going to find the best pair.

Part 1

- Explain to students that a function is an operation, or series of operations, that transforms one set of numbers into a different set of numbers.
- Introduce, or recap, the notation for 'a function of x', $f(x)$.
- Using an example, such as $f(x) = (4(x + 5) - 1) \div 2$, unpick the set of operations that must be performed on an input and the order in which they are carried out. (add 5, multiply by 4, subtract 1, divide by 2)
- Ask the students to work out the value of, e.g. $f(2)$, $f(-3)$, and display their answers on mini whiteboards.

Part 2

- Demonstrate the method by working through some examples of function questions.
- $f(x) = 2x^2 - 6x$ Calculate the value of $f(-1)$.
  $f(x)$ tells us what function to use and $f(-1)$ tells us what to replace the x with.
  The first step is to replace 'x' with '-1'
  $f(x) = 2x^2 - 6x$
  $f(-1) = 2(-1)^2 - 6(-1)$
  Encourage students to enter the calculation into the calculator taking care to use brackets correctly.
  $f(-1) = 8$
- $f(x) = 8x - 7$ Calculate the value of x for which $f(x) = 9$.
  We need to find the value of x that makes the function equal to 9.
  The first step is to replace '$f(x)$' with '9'.
  $f(x) = 8x - 7$
  $9\ \ = 8x - 7$
  $16 = 8x$
  $x\ \ = 2$
- Work through Examples 11 and 12 from the Student Book. **Students can now do Exercise 24C from the Student Book. Less able** students may need support with questions 5–7.

A 1–3, 5, 6	Calculator all	CM n/a	MR 4, 7	PS n/a	EV n/a

Inverse functions

- Introduce the notation for the inverse function $f^{-1}(x)$.
- Work through Example 13 with the class.
- **Students can now do Exercise 24D from the Student Book.**

A 1, 2	Calculator all	CM n/a	MR 3	PS n/a	EV n/a

Part 3

- Ask students to find the value of x if: $f(x) = \dfrac{1}{4x + 1}$, $g(x) = \dfrac{3}{2x - 7}$ and $f(x) = g(x)$.

- Prompt if necessary. As $f(x) = g(x)$, the two different functions give the same value, so set them equal to each other!
- Ask them to check by substitution that their answer is correct.

Section 24.4 Composite functions

Learning objectives

- Find the composite of two functions

Resources and homework

- Student Book 24.4: pages 677–678
- Practice Book 24.4: pages 213–214

Making mathematical connections

- Equations, expressions identities and functions
- Function machines and inverse operations

Making cross-curricular connections

- **Science** – using formulae
- **Computing** – logic gates; formulae in spreadsheets; flow diagrams
- **Relevance** – developing logical thinking

Prior learning

- Students should know how to substitute values into expressions.
- They should be able to calculate the inputs and outputs of function machines and understand the notation for f(x).

Working mathematically

- Give students a function f(x) and a function g(x) and show how we can combine functions to get fg(x) or ff(x), get values from their inputs.
- This can easily be differentiated: Support – provide a set of g(x) functions to choose from. Challenge – only give fg(x) and a set of functions, so students must identify f(x) and g(x).

Common misconceptions and remediation

- Students may be let down by poor algebraic skills. Practise basic algebra skills (expanding brackets, collecting terms, factorising) before starting this section.

Probing questions

- Which method is best for finding composite functions in simple cases?
- Does the best method change if: one function has more operations? the second (last) function has more than one x?

Literacy focus

- Key term: composite
- Ask the class to describe how to find the inverse of a function, the notation for functions and the key words that they have met so far in this section.

Part 1

- Give students problems such as: Find y when $y = 2 + 3 \times 6$.
  Students use BIDMAS/BODMAS to calculate the value of the expression.
- How would they work for problems like: Find y when $3 = 2 + y \times 6$?
  They need to work backwards (SAMDIB/SAMDOB), which is the process for changing the subject.
- The process is similar to solving an equation, but gives an algebraic rather than numerical answer.
- Increase the level of difficulty to include multistep, fractions, powers and roots.

Part 2

- Revise substitution into a function f(*x*) or g(*x*).
- Work through Example 14 with students, showing students the two steps to find the output of a composite function. Make sure they understand the order in which the functions are applied.
- Demonstrate the process of substituting one function into another by working through Example 15. Again, show the order in which the functions are applied.
- Work through more examples as **less able** students may be uncomfortable with the concept of an expression rather than a numerical answer.
- **Students can now do Exercise 24E from the Student Book.**

A 1, 2	Calculator n/a	CM 3	MR n/a	PS 4	EV n/a

Part 3

- Give students two multistep function machines.
- Ask them to write the functions algebraically, work out the inverse functions and substitute various values into their function to ensure they get the expected input and output values.
- Tell them to call one f(*x*) and one g(*x*).
- Ask them to use their values to find fg(*x*) and gf(*x*).
- Ask them to find the algebraic function for fg(*x*) and gf(*x*).

Section 24.5 Iteration

Learning objectives

- Find an approximate solution for an equation using the process of iteration

Making mathematical connections

- Substitution
- Simplify algebraic fractions
- Changing the subject of a formula
- Composite functions
- Trial and improvement

Resources and homework

- Student Book 24.5: pages 678–681
- Practice Book 24.5: page 214

Making cross-curricular connections

- **Computing** – efficient coding using 'repeat' or loops
- **Relevance** – logical thinking

Prior learning

- Students should know how to use function machines to find input and output values and be able to work out inverse functions.
- Students should be able to factorise, use brackets and manipulate algebraic fractions. This lesson will help develop their algebraic skills.
- Students should have a good working knowledge of sequences and the nth term.

Working mathematically

- Students should use graphing software to identify where the roots of an equation lie: to the nearest whole number, to one decimal place, and so on. They should be able to describe how this helps with both trial and improvement and iteration.
- Students use graphing software to generate, for example, $y = x^4 - 10x - 14$ and $y = \sqrt[4]{10x + 14}$ to ensure understanding of equivalence.
- Students work in groups of four, one pair using iteration and one pair using trial and improvement, to solve an equation.
- They should identify the most efficient calculator method and then compare methods.
  - Which is easiest?
  - Which is quickest?
  - Which is more efficient when the equation is longer?

Common misconceptions and remediation

- Students may be let down by poor algebraic skills. Practise basic algebra skills (expanding brackets, collecting terms, factorising) before starting this section.

Probing questions

- Compare 'trial and improvement' and 'iteration'.
- Give me an example of a convergent sequence … and another one … and a more general one… [prompt towards an algebraic form].

Literacy focus

- Key term: iteration
- Ask students to describe in their own words what is meant by iteration.

Part 1

- Show students how they can use their calculator to speed up the process of iteration.
- With the class rearrange, for example, $x^2 - 4x - 12 = 0$ to give the iterative formula $x_{n+1} = \sqrt{4x_n + 12}$ and explain the notation.
- Let $x_1 = 4$. Show students how to input this into their calculators. (Try to circulate around students with different calculators to make sure they can do this on their own device.)
- Show students how to find further iterations on their calculators.

Part 2

- Work through Example 17, reminding students how to input the initial value into their calculators.
- The iterative formula is given. Show them how to obtain the solution to a given number of decimal places. Remind them to keep note of each iteration and its corresponding x value.
- Work through Example 18, asking students to input the iteration into their calculator and record the results of each iteration.
- Work through Example 19, showing students how this sequence cycles around. What patterns can they see? (Every sixth value (multiple of 6) gives the same number.) They should use the pattern to find the closest estimate to x_{200}, in this case $x_2 = -\frac{3}{2}$.
- **Students can now do Exercise 24F from the Student Book.**

A 1–4	Calculator all	CM 5, 6, 8	MR n/a	PS 10	EV 7, 9, 11

Part 3

- Ask students to work in small groups to solve this problem.
  A square has sides of $(3x - 1)$ cm and $(2x + 2)$ cm.
  - Show that $6x^2 + 4x - 2 = 0$.
  - Use the iterative formula $x_{n+1} = \sqrt{\dfrac{2 - 4x_n}{6}}$ and an initial input of $x_1 = 3$ to find the area of the square, correct to the nearest integer.
  - How reliable is your answer for the area of the square?

Chapter 25 Geometry and measures: Vector geometry

Overview

25.1 Properties of vectors	**25.2** Vectors in geometry

Prior learning

Know that vectors are used to describe translations.

Learning objectives

Ensure that students can: add and subtract vectors; understand the properties of vectors; use vectors to solve geometrical problems; prove geometric results.

In the examination, students will be expected to:
* add and subtract vectors
* use vectors to solve geometrical problems.

Extension

Explore what a vector is and what a scalar is. Solve vector equations.

Curriculum references

Section	GCSE specification
25.1	G 25
25.2	G 25

Route mapping

Exercise	Accessible	Intermediate	Challenging	AO1	AO2 MR CM	AO3 PS EV	Key questions
25A		1–12	13–16	1, 2, 5, 7	3, 4, 6, 8, 9, 15, 16	10–14	11, 15, 16
25B			1–12		1, 2, 5, 7, 8, 11, 12	3, 4, 6, 9, 10	2, 8, 12

Key questions are those that demonstrate mastery of the concept or which require a step-up in understanding or application. Key questions could be used to identify the questions that students must tackle, to support differentiation, or to identify the questions that should be teacher-marked rather than student-marked.

About this chapter

Making connections: This section brings together the vector notation used in translations with other areas of geometry such as Pythagoras' theorem, ratio and properties of shapes to find distances, gradients and midpoints and develop geometric proofs. For much of the chapter, the next step is A Level content.

Relevance: Making judgements, predictions and looking for trends.

Working mathematically: Finding distances between points using geometric reasoning, gradients, ratio and midpoints, applying Pythagoras' theorem to find the distance between two points on a right-angled triangle.

Assessment: In each section of this chapter, ensure that students have a good grasp of the key questions in the exercises before moving on. (Refer to the 'Route mapping' table above.) Encourage students to read and think about the 'Ready to progress?' statements on page 700 of the Student Book. Check students' understanding at the end of the chapter, formatively, using peer assessment. Students could do a mini test in the form of the 'Review questions' on pages 700–701 of the Student Book. Follow up the test up with an individual target-getting session, based on any areas for development that a student may have.

Worked exemplars from the Student Book – suggestions for use
- Present students with the same question but using different numbers. Students should use the exemplar to mirror the working, in full or only using the notes.
- Copy and cut the exemplar into cards. Students should match the working with the notes. (You may need to remove the words 'first, second', and so on.)
- Ask students to write their own exemplar questions based on those in the Student Book.

Answers to the Student Book questions are available on the CD-ROM provided.

Section 25.1 Properties of vectors

Learning objectives

- Add and subtract vectors

Resources and homework

- Student Book 25.1: pages 687–692
- Practice Book 25.1: pages 215–217

Making mathematical connections

- Writing a vector and understanding what it describes
- Pythagoras' theorem
- Geometric proofs
- Ratio
- Midpoints

Making cross-curricular connections

- **Science** – magnitudes and resultant forces
- **Relevance** – developing logical thinking

Prior learning

- Students should be able to use column vectors to describe translations.
- Students should be able to find distances between points of a right-angled triangle using Pythagoras' theorem.

Working mathematically

- Encourage students to think of a vector as a journey or a movement.
- Structure tasks so students can work out the methods for themselves, either by increasing the difficulty incrementally or through one straightforward and one complex example.

Common misconceptions and remediation

- Students often use the incorrect vector notation. Remind students to write **a** or a̲, as these represent a journey or movement, rather than *a*, as this is an algebraic variable that represents a number. Similarly $\overrightarrow{AB}$ since AB represents the length of a line from A to B.
- Students often falter when asked to identify a shape based on vector information. Remind students about properties of shapes.

Probing questions

- What can you say about the gradients of two parallel lines?

Literacy focus

- Key terms: direction, magnitude, position vector, resultant vector, scalar, vector
- Discuss in pairs how you would use vectors to translate yourself into various different positions in the classroom from the centre, e.g. negative 2 left and positive 5 forwards.

Part 1

- Draw the points A to E, as shown, on a square grid.
- Ask students to give the column vectors for: $\overrightarrow{AB}$, $\overrightarrow{BA}$, $\overrightarrow{CE}$, $\overrightarrow{EC}$ …
- Show, on the grid, that one unit across = **a** and one unit up = **b**.
- Ask students to express the column vectors for $\overrightarrow{AB}$, $\overrightarrow{BA}$, $\overrightarrow{CE}$, $\overrightarrow{EC}$ … in terms of **a** and **b**.

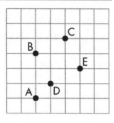

E.g. $\overrightarrow{AB} = \begin{pmatrix} 0 \\ 3 \end{pmatrix} = 3\mathbf{b}$, $\overrightarrow{BA} = \begin{pmatrix} 0 \\ -3 \end{pmatrix} = -3\mathbf{b}$, $\overrightarrow{CE} = \begin{pmatrix} 1 \\ -2 \end{pmatrix} = \mathbf{a} - 2\mathbf{b}$…

Part 2

Addition and subtraction of vectors

- Discuss the properties of vectors – magnitude and direction – and encourage students to think of vectors in terms of journeys.
- Use the text in the Student Book and Example 1 to demonstrate how to add and subtract vectors. For example, for two vectors **a** and **b**, **a** + **b** is defined as the translation of **a** followed by the translation of **b**.
- Suggest that students think of this vector addition as a journey from A to B followed by a journey from B to C. $\overrightarrow{AB} + \overrightarrow{BC} = \overrightarrow{AC}$

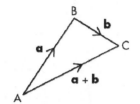 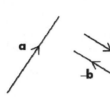 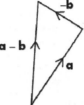

- Similarly, for two vectors **a** and **b**, **a** − **b** is defined as the translation of **a** followed by the translation of −**b**.
- Draw this grid on the board.
  $\overrightarrow{OA}$ = **a** and $\overrightarrow{OB}$ = **b**
- Show students how to find the vectors $\overrightarrow{OC}$, $\overrightarrow{BF}$, $\overrightarrow{CE}$, $\overrightarrow{FA}$ and $\overrightarrow{DE}$. Ensure that they use the correct notation. ($\overrightarrow{OC}$ = **a** + 2**b**, $\overrightarrow{BF}$ = 4**a** + 2**b**, $\overrightarrow{CE}$ = 2**a** − **b**, $\overrightarrow{FA}$ = −4**a** − 3**b**, $\overrightarrow{DE}$ = **a** − **b**)

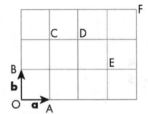

- Work through Example 2, showing students how to use their knowledge of Pythagoras' theorem and similar triangles in conjunction with vectors. Check that they use the correct notation.
- **Students can now do Exercise 25A from the Student Book.** Questions 15 and 16 are suited to **more able** students.

| G&M 1, 2, 5, 7 | Calculator n/a | CM 6, 8, 9, 15, 16 | MR 3, 4 | PS 10–12 | EV 13, 14 |

Part 3

- On a grid on the board, draw a vector $\overrightarrow{AB}$. Ask someone to give the column vector for $\overrightarrow{AB}$.
- Now add point C, drawing the vectors $\overrightarrow{AC}$ and $\overrightarrow{CB}$. Ask what $\overrightarrow{AC} + \overrightarrow{BC}$ equals, and why.
- Returning to the original vector diagram $\overrightarrow{AB}$, add new points C, D, E, F and G. Again, ask for the sum of all the individual vectors $\overrightarrow{AC}, \overrightarrow{CD}, \overrightarrow{DE}, \overrightarrow{EF}, \overrightarrow{FG}, \overrightarrow{GB}$.

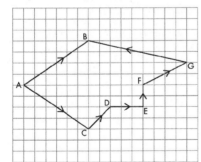 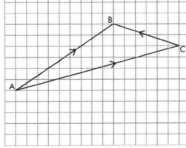 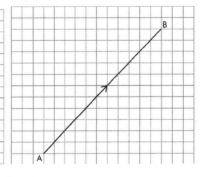

Section 25.2 Vectors in geometry

Learning objectives

- Use vectors to solve geometrical problems

Resources and homework

- Student Book 25.2: pages 692–697
- Practice Book 25.2: pages 217–219

Making mathematical connections

- Geometric proofs
- Properties of shapes

Making cross-curricular connections

- **Science** – position vectors, resultants
- **Relevance** – using logic

Prior learning

- Students should be confident with finding and using vectors such as:
  $\frac{3}{2}\mathbf{a} - \frac{3}{2}\mathbf{b}$ and $2(2\mathbf{a} - \mathbf{b}) - 3(\mathbf{a} - \mathbf{b})$

Working mathematically

- Wherever possible student write algebraic expressions so that they start with a positive variable, so $3y - 2x$ rather than $-2x + 3y$. The same is true of vectors, so $3\mathbf{b} - 2\mathbf{a}$ rather than $-2\mathbf{a} + 3\mathbf{b}$. Also, as in algebra, $3(\mathbf{a} + \mathbf{b}) = 3\mathbf{a} + 3\mathbf{b}$.
- Encourage students to break down the problem into smaller tasks and to break the 'journey' into smaller steps.

Common misconceptions and remediation

- Students often make errors when asked to write down vectors from a line segment given in a ratio form. Work through this example:
  B is a point on AC such that AB : BC = 2 : 1.
  If $\overrightarrow{AC} = \mathbf{c}$, then $\overrightarrow{AB} = \frac{2}{3}\mathbf{c}$ and $\overrightarrow{BC} = \frac{1}{3}\mathbf{c}$

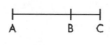

Probing questions

- If you know the distance AB, how would you find the midpoint?
- How would you show that two things are: parallel? perpendicular?

Literacy focus

- Key term: collinear
- Ask students to design a report, in groups, describing the distance of CD. (CD could be the diagonal of a square, rhombus or other quadrilateral, where the side lengths of the quadrilateral are given as a vector.) They can be creative here and make a map. Encourage the use of key words and have requirements such as 'there must be negative or collinear points'.

Part 1

- Draw the parallelogram PQRS. Ask students to express $\overrightarrow{PS}, \overrightarrow{PQ}, \overrightarrow{PR}$ and $\overrightarrow{QS}$ in terms of **a** and **b**.
  ($\overrightarrow{PS} = \mathbf{a}$, $\overrightarrow{PQ} = \mathbf{b}$, $\overrightarrow{PR} = \mathbf{a} + \mathbf{b}$, $\overrightarrow{QS} = \mathbf{a} - \mathbf{b}$)

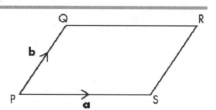

- Draw the triangle PQS.
- Ask: What is $\overrightarrow{QS}$ in terms of **a** and **b**?
  (To get from Q to S, go from Q to P, then P to S, so
  $\overrightarrow{QS}$ = −**b** + **a** or **a** − **b**.)

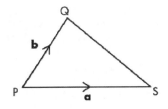

Part 2

- The aim of this lesson is to enable **more able** students to use vectors to show and prove results in a geometric context.
- Ensure that students have understood the two examples in Part 1.
- Work through the following example, promoting the idea of vectors as journeys and emphasising the importance of correct notation.
  OAB is a triangle.
  M is the midpoint of OB.
  C and D are points on AB such that AC = CD = DB.

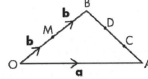

  $\overrightarrow{OA}$ = **a** and $\overrightarrow{OB}$ = 2**b**.

- Explain how to find the three vectors $\overrightarrow{BA}$, $\overrightarrow{MD}$ and $\overrightarrow{OC}$ in terms of **a** and **b**, giving answers in their simplest form.

  $\overrightarrow{BA} = \overrightarrow{BO} + \overrightarrow{OA} = -2\mathbf{b} + \mathbf{a} = \mathbf{a} - 2\mathbf{b}$

  $\overrightarrow{MD} = \overrightarrow{MB} + \overrightarrow{BD} = \overrightarrow{MB} + \frac{1}{3}\overrightarrow{BA} = \mathbf{b} + \frac{1}{3}\mathbf{a} - \frac{2}{3}\mathbf{b} = \frac{1}{3}\mathbf{a} + \frac{1}{3}\mathbf{b}$

  $\overrightarrow{OC} = \overrightarrow{OA} + \overrightarrow{AC} = \overrightarrow{OA} + \frac{1}{3}\overrightarrow{AB} = \overrightarrow{OA} - \frac{1}{3}\overrightarrow{BA} = \mathbf{a} - \frac{1}{3}\mathbf{a} + \frac{2}{3}\mathbf{b} = \frac{2}{3}\mathbf{a} + \frac{2}{3}\mathbf{b}$

- Ask students to look at quadrilateral OMDC and decide what type of quadrilateral it is.
- Remind students that $\overrightarrow{MD} = \frac{1}{3}\mathbf{a} + \frac{1}{3}\mathbf{b}$ and $\overrightarrow{OC} = \frac{2}{3}\mathbf{a} + \frac{2}{3}\mathbf{b}$.

  Since $\overrightarrow{OC} = 2\overrightarrow{MD}$, OC is parallel to MD (and twice as long).
  OMDC must be a trapezium.
- Work through Examples 3 and 4. Discuss how the problem is broken down into smaller, logical steps and explanations are given when necessary.
- **Students can now do Exercise 25B from the Student Book.**

G&M n/a	Calculator n/a	CM 1, 11, 12	MR 2, 5, 7, 8	PS 3, 6, 10	EV 4, 9

Part 3

- Draw this diagram on the board.
- ABCDEF is a regular hexagon and M is the midpoint of DE.
- Talk through how to find the vector $\overrightarrow{AM}$.

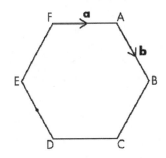

William Collins' dream of knowledge for all began with the publication of his first book in 1819. A self-educated mill worker, he not only enriched millions of lives, but also founded a flourishing publishing house. Today, staying true to this spirit, Collins books are packed with inspiration, innovation and practical expertise. They place you at the centre of a world of possibility and give you exactly what you need to explore it.

Collins. Freedom to teach

Published by Collins
An imprint of HarperCollins*Publishers*
News Building
1 London Bridge Street
London SE1 9GF

Browse the complete Collins catalogue at
www.collins.co.uk

© HarperCollins*Publishers* Limited 2015

10 9 8 7 6 5 4 3 2 1

ISBN 978-0-00-811393-3

A Catalogue record for this publication is available from the British Library

Rob Ellis, Kath Hipkiss and Colin Stobart assert their moral rights to be identified as the authors of this work.

Commissioned by Lucy Rowland and Katie Sergeant
Project managed by Elektra Media and Hart McLeod Ltd
Project edited by Jennifer Yong
Development edited by Gudrun Kaiser
CD-ROM additional content authored by Kath Hipkiss
With thanks to Christine Watson
Copyedited by Marie Taylor
Proofread by Helen Atkinson
Illustrations by Ann Paganuzzi
Typeset by Jouve India Private Limited
Designed by Ken Vail Graphic Design
Cover design by We Are Laura
Cover photographs by Procy/Shutterstock (top) and joingate/Shutterstock (bottom)
Production by Rachel Weaver
Printed and bound by Martins the Printer, Berwick upon Tweed

Acknowledgements

The publishers gratefully acknowledge the permissions granted to reproduce copyright material in this book. Every effort has been made to contact the holders of copyright material, but if any have been inadvertently overlooked, the publisher will be pleased to make the necessary arrangements at the first opportunity.